AUTHORITY, POWER AND LEADERSHIP IN THE JEWISH POLITY:
CASES AND ISSUES

THE MILKEN LIBRARY OF JEWISH PUBLIC AFFAIRS

The "Unseen" Israelis: The Jews from Turkey in Israel (1988)

Economic and Social Policy in Israel: The First Generation (1989)

Morality and Power: Contemporary Jewish Views (1989)

Maintaining Consensus: The Canadian Jewish Polity in the Postwar World (1990)

Israel's Odd Couple: The 1984 Elections and the National Unity Government (1990)

Authority, Power and Leadership in the Jewish Polity: Cases and Issues (1990)

Forthcoming:

Major Knesset Debates (1948-1981), Vols. 1-3

Made possible by a gift from the
Milken Family Foundation

Authority, Power and Leadership in the Jewish Polity

Cases and Issues

Edited by
Daniel J. Elazar

Assisted by
Stuart A. Cohen
Jane Gerber
Robert Freedman

Lanham • New York • London

Copyright © 1991 by
The Jerusalem Center for Public Affairs
University Press of America®, Inc.
4720 Boston Way
Lanham, Maryland 20706

3 Henrietta Street
London WC2E 8LU England

Co-published by arrangement with
The Jerusalem Center for Public Affairs

Managing Editor: Mark Ami-El
Typesetting: Custom Graphics and Publishing, Ltd., Jerusalem

"The Political Dynamics of the Medieval German Jewish
Community" copyright © 1991 by Ivan G. Marcus

"The Ethics of National Power: Government and War from the
Sources of Judaism" copyright © 1991 by Reuven Kimelman

Library of Congress Cataloging-in-Publication Data

Authority, power, and leadership in the Jewish polity : cases
and issues / editor Daniel J. Elazar ; assisted by Stuart A.
Cohen, Jane Gerber, Robert Freedman.
p. cm.
1. Jews—Politics and government.   2. Judaism and state.
3. Judaism and politics.   4. Leadership—Religious
aspects—Judaism.   5. Jewish leadership.
I. Elazar, Daniel Judah.
DS140.A98   1991
323.1' 1924—dc20   90-29105 CIP

ISBN 0-8191-8128-5 (hardcover, alk. paper)
ISBN 0-8191-8129-3 (pbk., alk. paper)

This book is dedicated to
Moshe Davis
Mentor and friend

ACKNOWLEDGEMENTS

We would like to acknowledge the role of the International Center for University Teaching of Jewish Civilization in making this book possible. Special acknowledgement is due to Moshe Davis, Academic Chairman of the International Center, Natan Lerner, its former director, and Matelle Godfrey, Workshops Coordinator. The staff of the Jerusalem Center for Public Affairs, especially Tzipporah Stein and Chaya Herskovic, coordinators of the JCPA's Program in Jewish Political Studies and of the Workshop on the Study and Teaching of the Jewish Political Tradition, conducted jointly by the Jerusalem Center and the International Center, the secretariat, and Mark Ami-El, Coordinator of Publications, all played vital roles. We also wish to thank the participants in the Workshop on the Study and Teaching of the Jewish Political Tradition, where most of these chapters were first presented and discussed.

CONTENTS

INTRODUCTION

Daniel J. Elazar

Jewish Political Studies as a Field

Jewish political studies is one of the most recent fields to be separately articulated within the framework of the social scientific study of the Jews. It should be noted at the very beginning that one of the characteristics of Jewish political studies is that, while there is a very strong contemporary and empirical dimension to it, it is historical and textual as well. To study the political phenomenon of the Jewish people — at any time, at any place, under any circumstances — requires a combination of empirical research and reference to historical documentation and the classic texts of the Jewish tradition.[1]

This is not the place for a review of the development of the field, even though its intellectual history is interesting in its own right. As with most intellectual phenomena, the academic discipline owes a substantial debt to events in the development of its own self-articulation. Just as sociology grew out of attempts to systematize and analyze events of the nineteenth century, so Jewish political studies in great measure stands in debt to Zionism, to the reestablishment of the State of Israel, to the conscious decision on the part of Jews to restore their own polity.

The work that has been done in the field to date demonstrates that the Jews continued to exist as a polity throughout the years of exile and dispersion. Nevertheless, in terms of conscious perceptions of matters political, the field emerged because of the decision on the part of large numbers of Jews to become political as Jews, and not just as individuals, in their respective societies. The Zionist revolution, the establishment of the State of Israel and the carry-over in the diaspora, particularly the United States, some fifteen or twenty years after the establishment of the State of Israel, gave all this an additional impetus.

Indeed, we see this reflected in Jewish historiography. The work of the Zionist historians such as Yitzhak Baer and Ben-Zion Dinur was part of the prologue to this perception.[2] They turned the study of Jewish history in a Zionist direction by focusing on the ways in which Jews functioned in communities and maintained them as polities under the various conditions of exile and dispersion, thereby reinforcing Zionist aspirations from their respective points of view.

The systematic and comprehensive study of the Jewish experience from a political science perspective began in the late 1950s. A group of interested political scientists was formed in 1968 and organized together into what ultimately became the Center for Jewish Community Studies in 1972. The first course in the field was a graduate seminar that Gerald Blidstein and this writer offered at Temple University in 1970. Charles Liebman, Eliezer Don-Yehiya, and this writer began the development of a substantial program at Bar-Ilan University shortly thereafter, offering the first advanced degrees in the field including the Ph.D. Subsequently, course offerings spread to over twenty universities on three continents.

There followed two other intellectual turning points. One was the convening of a seminar at Kibbutz Lavi in Israel in 1975 under the auspices of the Institute for Judaism and Contemporary Thought and with the cooperation of the Center for Jewish Community Studies, which examined the Jewish political tradition and its contemporary manifestations. That seminar produced a volume entitled *Kinship and Consent: The Jewish Political Tradition and its Contemporary Uses*, the first to attempt to delineate the field.[3] It was followed by a second seminar a year later, under the same auspices, exploring Israel as a Jewish state.

In the summer of 1981 the Center for Jewish Community Studies, by then part of the Jerusalem Center for Public Affairs, inaugurated the Workshop in the Study and Teaching of the Jewish Political Tradition. It led to the writing and publication of *The Jewish Polity* and to the introduction of new courses in the field.[4] In 1983, the Workshop became an annual event under the auspices of the International Center for the University Teaching of Jewish Civilization, in cooperation with the Jerusalem Center for Public Affairs.

One other factor of importance is that at the beginning of this decade Jewish political studies as a discipline found a profession with which to relate and interact, the emergent profession of Jewish communal service, particularly but not exclusively in the United States. While Jewish political studies was being articulated as a separate discipline in Jewish studies, the social workers in the communal agencies of the United States who staffed the

Jewish community federations, rather than, say, the Jewish community centers or Jewish family service agencies, began to detach themselves from their social work colleagues, at least to the extent of defining themselves as a sub-field of Jewish communal service. They created a professional association, the Association of Jewish Communal Organization Professionals (AJCOP), and several professional schools to provide training for people planning to enter the field, some of which were tied closely to social work, but others of which sought a new direction. In the process of doing this, Jewish communal organization became a profession which increasingly found that it was drawing intellectually upon the resources of Jewish political studies. That offered another set of opportunities for teaching, one which required the development of professional school courses.[5]

The Theoretical Framework of This Book

Jewish political studies as a field of inquiry has developed a theoretical framework of its own within which to operate. That theoretical framework gives teaching and research in the field a coherence of its own, not as some kind of "party line," but in the way that proper theory does, by creating a dialogue among people who are concerned with the problem of system and coherence in a particular intellectual activity.

An outline of that theoretical framework will be of help to the reader of this book since the chapters in it are built on that framework or in reference to it. First of all, we can define the field in the simplest way as that sub-field of political science, on the one hand, and of Jewish studies, on the other hand, which deals with the Jewish people as a corporate entity functioning as a body politic in any place where Jews are organized for public purposes, even for limited ones, and in some places, as in the State of Israel, where they are organized in a comprehensive way. It is not only concerned with contemporary Jewry, but with the phenomenon of the Jewish collectivity at any time and in any place.

This approach to the field rests upon certain assumptions. The first is that the Jewish people is a corporate entity, hence by definition it must find some way to function as a polity under different circumstances in order for it to pursue its normative aspirations, whether these be defined as survivalism, as seems to be the case for much of contemporary Jewry, or whether they be defined in the traditional terms of Jewish religion as the pursuit of *malkhut shamayim* (the Kingdom of Heaven), or anything in between.[6] Jews sooner or later — usually sooner rather than later — come to the conclusion that the Jewish people must function as a polity in order to pursue their normative ends. Therefore, the Jewish people will always seek ways to function as a polity.

Central to the Jewish political tradition is the idea of covenant (*brit* in Hebrew) and its application to the world of action. The constitution of the Jewish people as a whole reflects a mixture of kinship and consent. In other words, people born into a particular set of tribes consented through covenant to function as a community. One can read the Sinai Covenant from a political point of view as the establishment of Israel as both *am* (people) and *edah* (congregation or assembled community). In Jewish political terminology harking back to the Bible, an *am* is a nation (*goy*) with a God-given vocation. For Jews, that vocation was established by covenant. The *am* becomes the kin consenting while the *edah* is the organized product of that consent — the polity.[7]

The second assumption is that exploration of the Jewish polity can be undertaken with the tools of political science. We are not merely reviewing Jewish history, philosophy, or sociology under another "hat," however much we draw upon these sister disciplines. Rather, we are bringing our own tools and perspectives, and therefore, adding another dimension to understanding Jewish phenomena.

The third assumption is that Jews have continued to function as a polity throughout their history. One of the most intellectually interesting aspects of the discipline is the study of the adaptation of what is, after all, the oldest extant polity in the Western world to a great variety of circumstances. Its closest rival in longevity is the Catholic Church, some 1500 years younger at least. Interestingly, these two oldest polities of the Western world operate on diametrically different principles of organization with regard to the allocation of authority and the organization of power. The Catholic Church is hierarchical; the Jewish people, covenantal or federal (based on the Latin *foedus*=covenant). The intellectual opportunities for exploring the adaptation of two long-lasting political frameworks operating on such diametrically opposed principles is in itself a contribution to the study of political science.

Working, then, with those definitions and assumptions, we have developed certain propositions for research and teaching in the field. One is that the Jewish people is organized in several arenas. The people as a whole constitutes itself as an *edah* — in principle the assembly of all citizens of the polity — the entire population for constitutional matters — which, of course, had to be adapted once the Jews were no longer in the desert, to something other than the literal assembly of the entire citizenry. In classic political language, *edah* is the Hebrew equivalent of the democratic republic because it is based on the consent of its citizens. The way in which Jews have periodically reconstituted themselves as an *edah* in response to changing circumstances is a major issue for both study and teaching, one that is addressed in this volume over the entire range of Jewish history and in the present.

Within the framework of the *edah* there is an intermediate arena of organization. Initially it was composed of the tribes (*shevatim* in Hebrew) and subsequently, territorial jurisdictions (*medinot* – jurisdictions, or *aratzot* – lands). All three of these terms are used in Jewish political language.

The local arena is the smallest arena of Jewish political organization. At one time, prior to permanent settlement, it was the extended family (*bet av*). After settlement in Eretz Israel it became the township (*ir*) and, in the diaspora, the community (*kehillah*).

These three arenas are constants in Jewish political organization. There is never a time when there is not an effort to organize simultaneously in all three arenas, though the character of the organization has varied tremendously from the time when the *edah* was a concentrated population in a state in *Eretz Israel* to the situation, at certain times during the Middle Ages, in which the *edah* was no more than a communications network of *posekim* (rabbinic decisors). Some of the chapters in this volume address themselves to the *edah* as a whole while others focus on the intermediate and smaller arenas.

The second proposition is that the Jews organize or constitute themselves in their respective political frameworks through covenants or covenant-like arrangements, whether they are called *britot,* as they are a good part of the time, *amanot* (compacts), or *haskamot* (articles of agreement), following the same principle. This is not merely a terminological matter, but often involves an actual covenanting when a constitutional change takes place.

The third proposition is that the polity is one of separated but shared powers. It can be said that it is so built that power is never concentrated in a single human authority.[8] Because the Jewish polity embraces a complete civilization including its religious dimension, even prior to the classic separation of powers into executive, legislative, and judicial, the *edah* separated spheres of authority, known classically in Hebrew as the three *ketarim* (literally: crowns). The clearest expression of that separation is in *Pirkei Avot* (Sayings of the Fathers), Chapter 4, which mentions *keter torah* (the Crown of Torah), *keter kehunah* (the Crown of Priesthood), and *keter malkhut* (the Crown of Kingship or civil rule), and then goes on to claim that *keter shem tov* (the crown of a good name) is greater than all three. That verse assumes that Jews in the time of the Second Commonwealth understood that authority and power in their polity were divided among these three *ketarim*.[9] The division can be represented as in Figure 1.

Figure 1

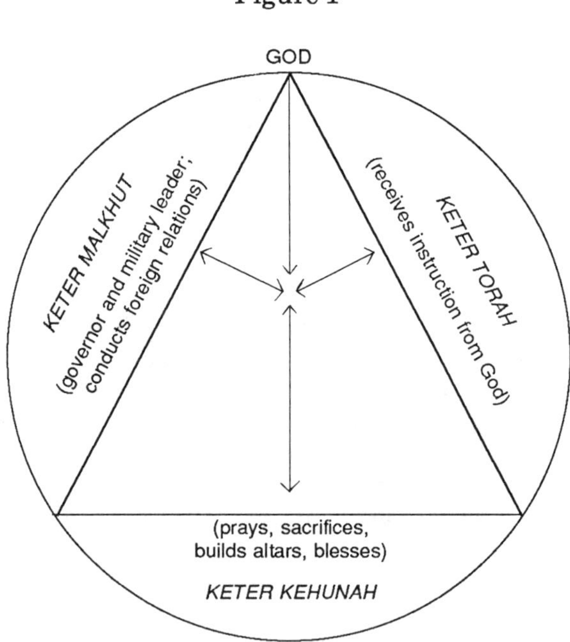

The *keter torah* is responsible for the communication of God's will to the *edah*. *Torah* was communicated to the *edah* first through the *Eved Adonai* (God's Chief Minister, a title bestowed only on Moses and Joshua), then through the *ro'eh* (seer) and the *neviim*

(prophets — singular, *navi*), and ultimately through the *hakhamim* (sages) and *rabbanim* (rabbis).

Understood from a political perspective, the *keter kehunah* is responsible for enabling the *edah* to communicate with God, whether through sacrifices, prayer, or whatever. This domain is explicitly separated from the *keter torah* by a separate covenant. The *keter torah* was transmitted through Moses; the *keter kehunah* was transmitted through Aaron. After the destruction of the Temple and the disappearance of the *kohanim* (priests) as an active political force, the *keter* ceased to have institutional embodiment for the *edah* as a whole, but new institutions were developed in the *kehillot*, such as the *hazan* (originally the governor of the synagogue, now the reader or cantor) and the modern congregational rabbi, to carry out those purposes and to exercise authority in that domain.

Finally, there is the *keter malkhut*, which deals with the civil dimension of the *edah* and which is responsible for the tasks of normal governance. Its first separately articulated representatives were the *zekenim* (elders), an institution that dates back at least to the Egyptian bondage, and their principal officers, the *nesiei haedah* (the magistrates), and continues through the *shofetim* (judges), *melakhim* (kings), *nesiim* (patriarchs), and *parnasim* (officers) down to the present time. Each of these offices is recognized in the Bible and the separate legitimacy of *keter* as a whole is manifested in God's covenant with David (though there is a controversy in Jewish political thought regarding kingship itself). Thus each of these *ketarim* is independent of the others, drawing its authority directly from Divine mandate, though in practice the bearers of each *keter* must work with the others in order to govern the *edah*.

The fourth proposition is that the *edah* has undergone periodic reconstitutions because of changing circumstances. Those reconstitutions have recurred at regular intervals which can be mapped out. Consequently, Jewish history can be studied as political history, indeed as constitutional history, through a number of epochs. We have identified fourteen epochs of Jewish history, each of which involves a constitution or reconstitution which brought with it reorganization in all three arenas, within each *keter*, and in the power relationships among the *ketarim*. Each of these epochs follows a reasonably regular pattern of political and constitutional development.[10] Table 1 lists the epochs and their principal characteristics.

Table 1

THE CONSTITUTIONAL PERIODIZATION OF JEWISH HISTORY

	Epoch	Dates	Constitution	Founding Events	Climactic Events	Culminating Events
1.	HA-AVOT (The Forefathers)	BCE c.1780–1500	Abraham's Covenant	Abraham leaves Haran	Jacob becomes Israel	Descent to Egypt
2.	AVDUT MIZRAYIM (Egyptian Bondage)	c.1500–1280	Patriarchal covenant as reaffirmed	Settlement in Goshen	Egyptian slavery	Exodus
3.	ADAT BNEI YISRAEL (The Congregation of Israelites)	c.1280–1004	Mosaic Torah	Sinai	Gideon rejects kingship	David accepted as king
4.	BRIT HAMELUKHAH (The Covenant of Kingship)	1004–721	Covenants of Kingship	David's kingship	Division of kingdom	Destruction of Israel
5.	MALKHUT YEHUDA (The Kingdom of Judah)	721–440	Deuteronomy	Judean rule consolidated	Josianic reform	Abortive restoration of monarchy
6.	KNESSET HAGEDOLAH (The Great Assembly)	440–145	Ezra/Nehemiah Covenant	Ezra restoration	Shift to Hellenistic world	Hasmonean revolt
7.	HEVER HAYEHUDIM (The Jewish Commonwealth)	145 BCE– 140 CE	Oral Tradition (Torah)	Hasmonean kingship	Destruction of Temple	Bar Kochba Rebellion

8

8. SANHEDRIN VE-NESI'UT (The Sanhedrin and Patriarchate)	CE 140–429	Mishnah	Organization of Mishnah/Renewal of Exilarchate	Christian ascendancy established anti-Jewish policy	End of Patriarchate
9. YESHIVOT VE-RASHEI HAGOLAH (The Yeshivot & Exilarch)	429–748	Gemara	Completion of Gemara	Jews come under Islam	Reunification of Jews under Islamic rule
10. YESHIVOT VE-GEONIM (The Yeshivot & the Geonim)	749–1038	Talmud & Codes	Geonim and first codes	Last Israel-Babylonian controversy	End of Gaonate
11. HAKEHILLOT (The Communities)	1038–1348	Constitutional Responsa	Passage of hegemony to Europe	Kabbalah in Spain. Reestablishment of Jewish settlement in Jerusalem	Black Death massacres
12. VAADEI KEHILLOT (Community Federations)	1348–1648	Arba'ah Turim	Polish Jewry's charters. Council of Aragonese community	Spanish expulsion and aftermath	Sabbatean movement
13. HITAGDUYOT (Voluntary Associations)	1648–1948	Shulhan Arukh	Rise of Modernism	Emancipation	The Holocaust
14. MEDINAH VE-AM (State and People)	1948–	?	Establishment of Israel	?	?

A fifth proposition is that there is a Jewish political tradition that has emerged out of all this, with a language of politics and a way of thinking and acting politically that has shown great persistence and continuity and continues to inform Jewish public life. In a sense, the identification of this political tradition, the language of politics, the modes of thought and the modes of action, constitute the substance of the field. That tradition, despite its continuities, is not monolithic. It is like a river full of currents and eddies. That is why we talk about a "tradition" and not an ideology or doctrine. We need not look for uniformity past a certain point to be able to identify the tradition, its implications and manifestations. What holds the tradition together are shared questions, issues, and concerns.

The Reassertion of Jewish Political Expression Today

In our time the expression of the Jewish political tradition, whether consciously or not, is growing because the mode of Jewish collective expression today is becoming increasingly political. The mode of Jewish expression in pre-modern times was comprehensive in the sense that Jews expressed themselves as Jews in every facet of their lives. They had a complete civilization. Modernity tried to transform that mode of expression into religious expression alone because those were the terms for entering Western society. The end of modernity came with the revival of the search for political expression in Zionism and, a little later, in renewed expressions of Jewish ethnicity in the West.

Outside of Israel, most Jews no longer live within a comprehensive Jewish environment, and even those who live in Israel are subject to the pervasive influences of contemporary culture. At the same time, most Jews do not find a sufficient basis for full expression of their Jewishness through what was defined as "religion" in the modern epoch. Indeed, many Jews are finding that they express themselves Jewishly through political means, if at all, whether that entails support of Israel or other causes which then become "Jewish" causes, or through working within the political and communal organizations of the Jewish people, which increasingly are perceived for what they are, namely, means of organizing power.

Israelis have always understood this since Zionism was avowedly political from the first. By the late 1960s, diaspora

Jewish leaders began to perceive that their Jewish activities were not simply philanthropy. By the early 1980s, the most perceptive of them understood that what they were doing was a form of governing. The result was a reversal of the modernist dictum of Y.L. Gordon, the great poet of the Eastern European Hebrew Enlightenment, that one should be a Jew in his tent and a man outside. People who do not know how to be Jews in their tents anymore want to be Jews outside — in the political arena. Thus the study of the Jews as a body politic takes on an added contemporary importance. Moreover, the traditional foundations of the Jewish polity remain the bases for Jewish political and communal organization.

Issues of Leadership, Domain and Representation in the Contemporary Jewish Polity

The most accurate and intrinsically most Jewish way to understand the divisions in Jewish public life today remains the division into the three *ketarim*. This classic model tells us more about Jewish public affairs than any other model we might choose, just as understanding the Jewish community as an *edah* and its leaders as *nesi'ei ha-edah* is a more useful way of conceptualizing the Jewish polity than any other.[11] Once we understand that authority and power in the community are shared among the representatives of these three *ketarim*, the discussion shifts from the conventional question of who is entitled to do what in the Jewish community — rabbis or laymen, professionals or volunteers, synagogues or community federations — to one of how each of these institutions is to be understood and what its role and functions are to be in the overall scheme of things.[12]

The leaders in the communal-welfare, Israel-overseas, and external relations spheres of contemporary Jewish life, both voluntary and professional, have assumed the mantle of *keter malkhut*. This is not to say that there are not other actors in the community who play some role, but it is essentially a residual one. In the United States, for example, the federations gained this mantle in the post-World War II generation after turning back a challenge by synagogues. In France, the *Consistoire* had more or less absorbed the functions of that *keter* in the nineteenth century, but lost to the FSJU and the CRIF during that same generation. In Britain, on the other hand, the *keter* has been firmly in the hands of the Board of Deputies since the eighteenth century, while in Israel it is unquestionably vested in the state institutions.

What are the issues that have developed for this domain? Most have to do with intra-*ketaric* competitions, such as the conflict between the federations and the community relations organizations in various diaspora communities. Some echoes of such earlier contests remain but only in relation to specific functions, not overall role. No doubt there will continue to be controversies of this kind between these various spheres, and there will never be a time without controversy, but there is a difference — it is not now a struggle for the *keter malkhut* as such.

Today, the *keter kehunah* is mostly in the hands of rabbis and *hazanim*. Indeed, the major change that has taken place in the rabbinate as a result of the modern epoch was to give rabbis responsibility for the functions of the priesthood, the sacerdotal functions of the *edah*, especially the rites of passage, functions previously performed by *baalei-batim*, while rabbis functioned within the *keter torah* as *dayanim* and *posekim*, (*halakhic* jurists). Indeed, although there are some authoritative personalities in other spheres of Jewish life who play something of a sacerdotal role on the symbolic level for the *edah* as a whole, this function is basically a local one in rabbinic hands, assisted by the *hazanim*.

The question of who is a rabbi has reemerged within the last decade as a major issue around the questions of ordination of women and Orthodox recognition of non-Orthodox rabbis, both schismatic issues in the public life of the Jewish community. A similar issue confronted Western Jewry one hundred years ago and more when non-Orthodox movements emerged that required rabbis who functioned in other than the traditional pattern and were trained accordingly. The result at that time was that the *edah* (although not all its parts) recognized non-Orthodox rabbis but, in the process, shifted the rabbinate as a whole from the *keter torah* to the *keter kehunah*, *de facto* if not *de jure*.

An even more important question is whether rabbis' functions are a matter of private right or are they public responsibilities? This is an issue that is perhaps most strongly manifested in the Reform movement, where every rabbi is entitled to personally decide whether or not to perform a marriage between a Jew and a non-Jew and under what conditions. The movement has expressed a negative view of such an act (and others of similar import, such as the question of patrilineal descent), but sees it as a private decision in which every rabbi is sovereign. Yet the question is not as easily disposed of. Is every rabbi authorized to decide who is a Jew without being responsible to any system? Are these public responsibilities? Is this part of the privatization of Jewish life, and is it going to have a great effect on the definition of citizenship within the Jewish polity? In its essentials, this is a question of citizenship, of who is eligible to be part of the Jewish people. The notion that any person may privately decide who is eligible to be part of the Jewish people is a very problematic one from the perspective of the polity no less than from a traditional religious perspective.

One of the major contemporary issues which has emerged with regard to the *keter torah* grows out of the question of who represents this *keter*. There is a certain contest between the various claimants for prime roles as its representatives. Rabbis, for example, have not easily conceded the function. The studies indicate that congregational rabbis continue to define themselves first and foremost as teachers, but that their congregants do not because they expect ritual, pastoral, or counseling services from their rabbis first and foremost.

Today, authoritative scholarly personalities, most but not all of whom hold rabbinical ordination (*semikha*: literally, a grant of authority), are the principal bearers of *keter torah*. Few, if any, hold pulpits. Most are Torah scholars at *yeshivot*, seminaries, or universities, who possess the personal ability to reach out. It is not the fact that they are rabbis that makes them authoritative. The title may add to their status, but it does not define it. A few are professors whose scholarly attainments are less traditional in character but who play a similar role. Finally, there are the rebbes and "gurus" who, for their own personal followers, are seen as bearing the *keter torah*.

The second issue is more critical than ever before, and that is the question of what constitutes "Torah"? Between the time of the Karaite schism in the eighth century of the common era and the nineteenth century, common traditional understanding of Torah prevailed. Even those who rejected Judaism shared in that common understanding. Since the rise of Reform, that understanding has faced one challenge after another. Today we are seeing even greater competition for the definition of what Torah is, including some very strange definitions. In one sense, this is a tribute to the strong hold that the principle of Torah retains on Jews of all kinds, so much so that every ideological claim on Jews as Jews must find its link with Torah. On the other hand, some of the claims attack the very foundations of reasonable understanding of what is expressed in the Torah and its tradition.

A third issue, growing out of the second, is how do Jews see themselves bound by Torah. For both the *am* and the *edah*, Torah is constitutional. However much room there may be for interpretation and choice within the tradition, it is not merely a nice set of ideas and traditions to be taken or left as one pleases. Contemporary Jewry has recognized the truth of this in at least one modest way, by introducing certain standards of Jewish observance such as *kashrut, motzi,* and *birkat hamazon,* or *kiddush* and *havdalah* where appropriate in Jewish public institutions (including those of the State of Israel) and at public functions. On a private level, the issue is nowhere nearly as resolved. Moreover, Jewish public institutions have not really grappled with the constitutional character of Torah outside of the ritual sphere, all too often reducing its role to questions of ritual observance.

All of these are issues which will continue to confront the institutions of the Jewish polity since there are practical decisions to be made in the community with regard to each. Sooner or later every one of these institutions confronts the necessity to make such decisions, must decide who will participate in them, and will be called to account for them by one constituency or another.

In a sense, these institutions have addressed themselves to these issues in two ways. One is by providing funds to help educate the next generation, including the future bearers of the *keter torah*. Beyond that, the institutions of the *keter malkhut*, to a great extent, have been the legitimizers of the new authoritative personalities who have challenged the congregational rabbis for more major roles within the *keter torah*. This is a reflection of how, in the postmodern epoch, the *keter malkhut* has become a major source of authoritative recognition for most Jews. This is true not only in the case of the professors who are featured at their functions from time to time, only a few of whom are brought to teach Torah. To a certain extent, even major figures in the traditional rabbinate have acquired authority beyond their immediate circles because of recognition by the *keter malkhut* and its leadership, whether by election as chief rabbis in Israel and those diaspora communities which maintain that institution and place it within the jurisdiction of the *keter malkhut*, or by common consent.

Note, for example, the role which that leadership has played in the rise to universal prominence of the Lubavitcher Rebbe (who certainly does not see their recognition as in any way authoritative) and his Habad movement and the expansion of its influence in contemporary Jewish life — through their contributions as private individuals, through opening doors to community institutions, and simply by lending Habad their prestige. The same thing occurred in connection with the Rav (Rabbi Joseph) Soleveichik, in a more subtle way. Jewish institutions began to seek his counsel. No board or executive meeting decided that he was the new authoritative personality. Rather, it happened within the informal dimensions of the *keter malkhut.*

What this suggests is that in the perennial competition among the three *ketarim*, today the *keter malkhut* has the upper hand, marking the end of a period of one thousand years or more in which the *keter torah* had the upper hand. The breakdown of the traditional community, the secularization of Jewish life, and the reestablishment of the Jewish state, have all led in that direction, but it is only in this generation that Jews are beginning to feel its consequences.

In no small measure, the increasingly dominant role of the *keter malkhut* comes from its function as the only domain where Jewish unity can be maintained under current conditions. Thus the Orthodox camp refuses to sit together with representatives of non-Orthodox movements within the framework of the *keter torah* since that would mean recognition of the legitimacy of those movements within that *keter.* (In truth, the ultra-Orthodox will not sit with the mainstream Orthodox either.) Much the same is true for the *keter kehunah*, although there the record is mixed in certain diaspora communities, especially in the United States. Yet all camps and their subdivisions will sit together within the institutions of the *keter malkhut,* whether the World Zionist Organization, the World Jewish Congress, the Knesset and government of Israel, countrywide boards of deputies, or local federations, since it is only in the other domains that the Orthodox camp insists on maintaining its monopoly. That strengthens the role of the *keter malkhut* immeasurably.

Another issue with regard to *keter malkhut* is the role of Israeli leadership. In the course of the first postmodern generation, the Israeli leadership was given a major role in the *keter malkhut* by virtue of Israel's status as the Jewish state. It will continue to play a major role but it will not necessarily be accepted in as uncritical a manner as was true in the first generation because of the changes which have taken place in Israel and in Israel-diaspora relations in the past decade. During that decade, a new intimacy was established between Israel and the diaspora and, as is always the case where intimacy is involved, familiarity removes pedestals. To the extent that Israeli leaders gained status because of those pedestals, their standing has been altered. While this had a temporary deflating effect, in the long run it should create a new and stronger basis upon which Israelis can play a leadership role, rooted in mutual acquaintance and understanding.

Finally, the 1970s witnessed the emergence of a world Jewish leadership. The catalyst for this division was the reconstitution of the Jewish Agency in 1970. The reconstituted Agency offered a forum for leaders of the diaspora communities to become involved in Israel and world Jewish affairs in other than philanthropic ways. Once tasted, this became a very attractive opportunity indeed. Moreover, as a forum, it brought together Jewish leaders from various parts of the world and from various modes of Jewish involvement, creating bonds among them whose implications are just beginning to be manifested.

In sum, when we look at the classic Jewish model of the three *ketarim*, we see that the issues of Jewish leadership have been conceptualized incorrectly for many years. That question was all too often phrased as "Who will lead the Jewish community?" — as if there were to be one leader, one institution, or one narrow group that was to do so. But the Jewish community classically is governed through the kind of mixed system of checks and balances represented by the division of authority and power among the three *ketarim*.

The problem of the contemporary Jewish polity is no longer one of addressing that old question, but rather that of addressing the new issues that are derived from the new balance of power among the *ketarim*. One of the issues is the question of how new issues are raised and placed on the Jewish agenda. In a polity based on trusteeship, it is not possible to rely upon the trustees to look for all the new issues. All that can be expected from the trustees is that they will be willing to respond to issues raised elsewhere. The trustees are busy dealing with existing issues and maintaining consensus, such as it is.

When the new issues which well up are major ones, of critical import, they are most likely to gain recognition through at least a modicum of confrontation. That is part of the natural history of such things and it is not a bad thing. Not every confrontation need lead to change. What can be expected is that the trustees will be brought to respond in some appropriate way because of the values which they and their colleagues share. What is bad is when there is polarization which cannot be bridged.

Generally speaking, contemporary Jewry has not done badly in that regard. As a result there is general consent, at worse grudgingly given, to the present system, even on the part of its declared critics. In the last analysis, however, it is necessary to make a constant effort to keep the *edah* from simply becoming a new kind of oligarchy, either of the interested volunteers or the professionals. The Jewish civil service must be encouraged to regulate themselves (and one of the virtues of professionals is that they emphasize self-regulation; they do set standards for themselves and their members). That is necessary but not sufficient, because no person or group can be the judge of his or its own cause. Hence all segments of the polity must work together to create the appropriate relationship between the bearers of the three *ketarim* and between the various leadership circles and the Jewish public such as it is, as appropriate manifestations of the continuing yet reconstituted *edah*.

The *keter malkhut* itself has developed more elaborate and intricate governance structures as it has increased in power within the Jewish polity. What is important to note, however, is the degree to which those structures resemble each other, whether in Israel or the diaspora, and within the various community structures that exist.

This common governance structure can be described as congressional in character (as distinct from parliamentary, presidential, or separation-of-powers, or any nonrepublican system), in the sense that it is based on assemblies, congresses, trustees, or delegates who come together to constitute a common body without surrendering their responsibilities as trustees or delegates; i.e., do not become collective bodies with a sense of collective responsibility. The structure includes two or three planes, serving the *edah*, its *medinah* and *artzot*, and their *kehillot*. Governance in each plane begins with a large forum designated as the principal decision-making body, in which all the elements federated together to form the entity are represented. This large body will meet relatively infrequently, either annually or only every several years if it serves the *edah* as a whole or some major segment of it; quarterly or annually for countrywide communities; and monthly or quarterly if it serves a local *kehillah*. It elects a smaller board to handle continuing policy-making responsibilities on a regular basis, which meets more frequently, usually once a month or more. Either the assembly or the board chooses an executive committee which handles the daily business of governance. The executive committee usually functions on the basis of community and collective agreement (without a sense of collective responsibility), although the chairman or president may have some special status as its convener and spokesman.[13]

The congressional principle of representation of the federated bodies usually continues to be of some importance in both the board and executive committee as well as the assembly, although the smaller the body, the more the element of collective responsibility is present. At the same time, while in theory the larger bodies are superior to the smaller, in fact, as in parliamentary systems, the smaller tend to direct the larger. At best, the larger exercise veto powers over policy proposals generated by the smaller ones or, where there are three planes, perhaps the largest two have something of a check and balance relationship with one another.

Representative Government Within the *Edah*

From the first, three principal strands have shaped the *edah*. It is federal in the fundamental sense of being grounded in covenant as well as in its structure. It is republican in the fundamental sense of being a *res public*, belonging to its public and the private preserve of no one. It is theocratic in the fundamental sense that it strives for the holy commonwealth on earth (*theos*=God, *cratos*=rule). The combination of these strands means that within the framework of its constitution, its government must be participatory and representative of its people and their communities.

Representative government within the *edah* subsequent to the period of the Exodus and conquest of the land is, in many respects, a continuing effort to maintain ancient forms of participation in new guises, forms which have disappeared in other modern polities and which are only now beginning to change for the *edah* as a whole.[14] At least formally, the basis of governance in the original *edah* (ca 1280-1000 BCE) was the assembly of all its citizens for covenanting and other fundamental constitutional questions, all adult males for deciding basic policy questions (e.g., declarations of constitutionally permitted wars), and the tribally selected *nesi'im* on an *ad hoc* basis for special tasks and a permanent basis for continuing ones. Governance in the periods between the increasingly less fragmented *edah*-wide assemblies was in the hands of notables, apparently designated by some form of consensus, based upon the recognition of certain families as leading ones.

By the time of the institution of kingship (1000-722 BCE), it was already apparent that the *edah* no longer attempted to assemble as a whole, although there were still assemblies of notables drawn from all of the functioning tribes to play the role of the assembly of the whole. This system may have persisted in Judah after the fall of the northern kingdom (ca. 721-440 BCE) — evidence is scanty — with assemblies of the *Am Ha-aretz*, consisting of local notables, replacing assemblies of tribal leaders.

When Ezra and Nehemiah reconstituted the Jewish polity (ca. 440 BCE), a majority of world Jewry continued to live outside of Eretz Israel, hence assembly of the entire *edah* was impossible even in theory. It was then that a system of virtual representation was formally introduced through the establishment of the *Anshei Knesset HaGedolah*, which assembled in Jerusalem. This new body was made up of 120 members symbolically representing a *minyan* (quorum of ten men) from each of the twelve tribes and, hence, the *edah* as a whole, a sign that virtual representation was the intent behind its establishment. In fact, it was composed of people who lived in Judah plus one or two *olim* from the various communities of the exile who came to settle in Judah and could be added to the body, who spoke, at least nominally, for the whole diaspora. The nature of the transportation technology at the time made any other system impossible.

This system of virtual representation continued through the next nine hundred years of Jewish history, even after the diaspora Jewish communities developed fully articulated governing institutions of their own. The only changes were that in certain periods there was regularized representation from the diaspora in the *edah's* sitting decision-making body located in Jerusalem until 70 CE and subsequently in other parts of Eretz Israel. It came to an end only with the abolition of the *Nesiut* (Patriarchate) by the Romans, ca. 429 CE.

The *yeshivot* in Babylonia continued this pattern when power passed to them. They became the virtual representatives of the *edah* in its rule-making and adjudication functions, paralleling the *Rosh HaGolah* (Exilarch), who was the *edah's* chief magistrate. The *yeshivot* continued the tradition of bringing in people from around the Jewish world to the extent possible on a voluntary, personal choice basis, consisting of those who decided to come, study, and stay. This arrangement persisted for six hundred years, until the system was disrupted by the abolition of the office of *Rosh HaGolah* in 1042 CE.

After that, the *edah* was unable to sustain equivalent common institutions, surviving as a communications network for *halakhic* decision-making through correspondence rather than an assembly. Political organization was confined to local, country-wide, or, in rare cases, multicountry regions. Hence, the system of virtual representation existed in principle rather than practice as the structure of the *edah* changed over the next nine hundred years, being expressed through a handful of notable *halakhic* figures whose decisions gained *edah*-wide acceptance or a handful of *shtadlanim* whose influential services were recognized *edah*-wide.

The problems of transportation and communication encountered by Ezra and Nehemiah in the fifth century BCE remained unchanged until well into the nineteenth century CE. Indeed, at times, deterioration of conditions made them even greater. It was not until the development of the steamboat, railroad and telegraph that a new technology made continental and intercontinental links feasible.

The World Zionist Congress, convened in 1897, was the first effort made to establish a body representative of the *edah* in modern terms, namely, through constituency elections of delegates to a worldwide congress in which all communities were potentially, if not actually, to be represented. Since that time, there has been a striving to establish such institutions. The WZO was and is a membership organization. It did become worldwide in scope but never embraced a majority of the *edah* as members. The World Jewish Congress, established in 1936, tried to overcome that problem by being based on country affiliates, the major representative bodies from each countrywide Jewish community, but its strength was and is concentrated in Europe and Latin America, with no real presence in the world's largest Jewish communities — the U.S.A., Israel, the USSR, and France.

Framing organizations were established in the local and countrywide arenas by the end of the modern epoch or during the first generation of the postmodern epoch as a culmination of the modernization process. They were accompanied by a general revolution in transportation and communications based on air travel and the airwaves. Jews are now engaged in the reestablishment of effective, continuing, *edah*-wide framing institutions, principally through the reconstitution of the Jewish Agency and the WZO. Since transportation and communication technologies now permit this, it is likely that something serious will come out of the effort. Nevertheless, this will not be the whole story since there are structural limitations to the degree to which formal representatives of all segments of the *edah* can assemble on a regular basis. Thus, we are returning to the situation of ancient Israel, only on a worldwide scale, when leading figures representing the various elements of the *edah* come together at regular intervals, are involved in consultations in between, but the day-to-day business is still conducted by virtual representatives, including people co-opted into the governing circles who might not be formally chosen through the standard processes because of their proximity or their wealth.

It should be noted that the effort to reconstitute the Jewish Agency for Israel (JAFI) as an *edah*-wide instrument was not initiated without a struggle. Initially, the reestablished State of Israel was viewed by many, especially Israelis, as the sole institutional embodiment of the *edah*, hence, the Israeli Knesset was established with 120 members in imitation of *Anshei Knesset HaGedolah* and with the clear intention of being the virtual representative of all of world Jewry because of its constituent position as the center of authority in the Jewish state. This did not happen because the diaspora would not — indeed, could not — accept the Israeli legislative body as its spokesman, hence the need to go back to the WZO/Jewish Agency to develop a more broadly representative body, albeit one in which Israel would play the leading role.

This pattern is carried over to the other arenas as well. The growth of Jewish population and its concentration in larger metropolitan centers means that, except in the smallest communities, even the local arena cannot function on the basis of the assembly of all citizens. The congressional model, then, serves as a substitute similar to that of the limited town meeting in New England. The advantage is that in the local arenas, there can be real representation of different constituencies, not only virtual representation. The governance structure that has emerged reflects this pattern.

The other dimension of representation in the Jewish polity is that Jewish leaders tend to wear many different hats, hence both the representatives and the represented appear simultaneously in many forms and either represent or need to be represented in many different forms. Not only are there so many different bodies, but Jews, if active at all, tend to be members and even active in many overlapping organizations and institutions. It is well to remember how many Jews belong to more than one synagogue, not to speak of membership in a number of different Zionist organizations or Zionist and other organizations, in addition to contributing to the *Magbit* or paying taxes to the Israeli government or whatever.

This is not simply a contemporary phenomenon; it was always true to a greater or lesser extent. Even in the small medieval community, Jews who were members of a common *kahal* were also members of different *hevrot*. They sought to express themselves through the *kahal* as a whole and through the special interests of the *hevrot*.

Given the somewhat amorphous nature of the community's boundaries and the inability to decide on one comprehensive set of institutions or instruments of governance, this weaving of many nets serves to strengthen Jewish unity and make more intensive use of Jewish talent. Hence it is accepted as inevitable and necessary, in Israel as well as in the diaspora. There is every reason to believe that, like the congressional system, it is part and parcel of Jewish political culture.

Both of these dimensions reflect the way in which the Jewish polity is one of those which is built from the ground up, that is to say, from the smallest arena to the largest rather than vice-versa. In this respect it is like the Swiss and American polities, whose origins were simultaneously to be found in the *Landesgemeinde* and the town meeting, respectively, as well as in larger arenas. The result of this ground-up construction is that political life begins with all citizens expecting to participate as equals in some respect, an expectation which they retain even after larger arenas have been established, and which they seek to transfer to these larger arenas in some appropriate, if lessened, way. Like the Americans and the Swiss, the Jewish polity has had to maintain some kind of primary citizen involvement through appropriate mechanisms applied to its very different and unusual situation. The vulnerability of these systems to large scale public reactions, whether in the form of demonstrations, as in the State of Israel, or in some other way, is a constant reminder of where the locus of power lies.

All this stands in sharp contrast to polities organized from the top down in which citizens do not expect to participate on a continuous basis, merely to be consulted, or to ratify, or to choose which elites will govern them — all of which leads to a very different approach to representation. This is the difference between the parliamentary and the congressional systems, despite their external structural similarities. Parliaments developed within hierarchical polities to modify the control exercised by those on the top (usually monarchs), by requiring them to secure the approval of representatives of the people or the various estates of the realm before pursuing their policy ends, whereas congressional systems developed from the bottom up or, more accurately, from smaller to larger arenas. A full examination of the representative institutions of the Jewish polity as examples of congressional government has yet to be undertaken.

The Focus and Contents of This Book

This book is divided into three parts. The first deals with the historical polity. It begins with a chapter by Daniel J. Elazar on "The Polity in Biblical Israel." In it, this writer delineates the political organization of ancient Israel in biblical times utilizing the models outlined above. In addition to describing the various political regimes of biblical Israel, the chapter shows how the main institutions and relationships of the Jewish polity were established in the biblical period and serve as a paradigm for what comes later, this despite the changes in the specifics of regime, office and locale.

In the second chapter, Stuart A. Cohen focuses on "Continuities and Convulsions: The Three *Ketarim* During the Second Jewish Commonwealth." In it he provides a comprehensive treatment of the functioning of the threefold division of political authority in the critical epochs of the formation of rabbinic Judaism. He reveals the political dimension of the struggle of the Pharisees for control of the *edah*.

Chaim Milikowsky continues this discussion in "Authority and Conflict in Post-Destruction Roman Judea: The Patriarchate, the Rabbis, the People, and the Romans." Milikowsky traces out the history of the conflict over authority in the centuries following the destruction of the Second Commonwealth, showing how the principles of politics established in the biblical period were adapted to a new set of relationships between rulers and ruled.

These three chapters, which cover a period of nearly 1800 years, are followed by one by Ivan G. Marcus on "The Political

Dynamics of the Medieval German Jewish Community" that focuses on the medieval Jewish community in Ashkenaz (France and Germany of today). The period that he treats is known as the classic age of the *kehillah*, when circumstances fragmented the Jewish polity among myriad separate local communities. While Dr. Marcus does not use the terminology of Jewish political studies in his analysis, his article should be read with that terminology in mind since it demonstrates the continuity of the original biblical model in a very different setting.

In Part II, we confront the contemporary polity after the Jewish people lost both its autonomy in the diaspora and its homogeneity as a faith community and, with one exception, after the Holocaust and the reestablishment of the State of Israel. While the focus of Part II is on the diaspora, Israel and the diaspora are part of the same continuing political tradition in which the elements identified at its very beginning emerged after another readaptation to shape and direct Jewish affairs.

One of the classic models of modern Jewish communal organization is the Board of Deputies of British Jews, whose origins go back to 1760 and hence is the oldest continuing governing institution of any functioning diaspora community today. While the Board of Deputies is structured as an institution of the *keter malkhut*, it is organized so as to maintain an established relationship with the *keter torah* as well. David Cesarani examines the workings of the Board in the early twentieth century in "The Politics of Anglo-Jewry Between the Wars." Cesarani's chapter focuses on the struggle between Zionists, non-Zionists and anti-Zionists for control of the *keter malkhut* from the Balfour Declaration to the Holocaust. While Cesarani does not use the political models and terminology upon which this volume is anchored, it is relatively easy to apply both as one reads his case study.

In Chapter Six, Jonathan S. Woocher looks at "The Democratization of the American Jewish Polity." He traces the emergence of a structured American Jewish community after World War II and how the governance of that community moved from the hands of a group of self-selected notables to a broader set of constituencies which more or less represent all the segments of American Jewry. Woocher sees the American Jewish community as solidly within the Jewish political tradition, even though it represents such a radical departure from premodern Jewish tradition in so many other respects. Hence he examines community organization within the framework of the model posited here.

French Jewry is usually hailed as the first formally emancipated community, but, in fact, the population of French Jewry has been transformed at least twice since the revolution. The French Jewish community today, with its majority of Sephardim from North Africa, is a far different community from the one of the interwar period or the Jewish community of nineteenth century France. In Chapter Seven, Ilan Grielsammer examines "The Democratization of a Community: The Case of French Jewry." Grielsammer's article parallels Woocher's, since he looks at the process of movement from control by a handful of notables to a more popular model, a process which has not gone as far in France as it has in the United States. In "The Dynamics of the Three *Ketarim* in the Political Transformation of Contemporary French Jewry," Shmuel Trigano examines the patterns of power in the contemporary French Jewish community in terms of the classical model.

In Part III, four distinguished scholars examine four of the continuing issues that have confronted the Jewish polity since its beginning and which continue to do so. In "Leadership in the Jewish Polity: Early Rabbinic Views," Stuart A. Cohen examines the overall question of leadership within the context of the models and terminology presented here. Reuven Kimmelman focuses on "The Ethics of National Power: Government and War in the Jewish Tradition," with an eye to the problems confronting the renewed independent Jewish state in Eretz Israel. Gerald J. Blidstein probes a minor but real note in the Jewish political tradition in his chapter "On Political Revolution in the Jewish Tradition," in which he examines the biblical and *halakhic* treatment of the problem of resisting illegal or unjust authority. Finally, Morton Weinfeld and Phyllis Zelkowitz examine the most important continuing task of any Jewish community, but particularly the diaspora Jewish communities of today, namely, the education of the next generation, in "Reflections on the Jewish Polity and Jewish Education," using the Canadian experience as a case study of the problematics of universal Jewish education under contemporary conditions.

Needless to say, a collection of this kind cannot be comprehensive. At most, it dips into a rich history and tradition at certain critical points and in relation to some important topics. In doing so, it serves students of the subject in the way in which geological mapping does the oil industry — a generalized map is prepared on the basis of a series of test bores. This volume concentrates on the empirical dynamics of the Jewish polity. As such, it is a companion volume to *Kinship and Consent: The Jewish Political Tradition and its Contemporary Manifestations,* which provides an outline of the theory of the Jewish political tradition, and *The Jewish Polity: Jewish Political Organization from Biblical Times to the Present,* which outlines the constitutional and institutional structure of the Jewish polity.

Notes

1. For an overview of the field, see Daniel J. Elazar and Stuart A. Cohen, "A Framework and Model for Studying and Teaching the Jewish Political Tradition," *Jewish Political Studies Review* 1:3-4 (Fall 1989).

2. Yitzchak Baer, *A History of the Jews in Christian Spain* (Philadelphia: Jewish Publication Society of America, 1961); Ben Zion Dinur, *The Historical Foundations of the Rebirth of Israel* (New York: Harper and Row, 1955) and *Jewish History; Its Uniqueness and Continuity* (Neuchatel: Editions de la Baconniere, 1968).

3. Daniel J. Elazar, ed., *Kinship and Consent: The Jewish Political Tradition and Its Contemporary Uses* (Ramat Gan: Turtledove, 1981).

4. Daniel J. Elazar and Stuart A. Cohen, eds., *The Jewish Polity: Jewish Political Organization from Biblical Times to the Present* (Bloomington: Indiana University Press, 1985).

5. Cf. Daniel J. Elazar, *Participation and Accountability in the Jewish Community* (New York: Council of Jewish Federations, 1981).

6. Cf. Jonathan Woocher, *Sacred Survival* (Bloomington, Ind.: Indiana University Press, 1986); and Ella Belfer, "The Jewish People and the Kingdom of Heaven: A Study of Jewish Theocracy," *Jewish Political Studies Review* 1:1-2 (Spring 1989).

7. Cf. Daniel J. Elazar, "Covenant as the Basis of the Jewish Political Tradition," in *Kinship and Consent.*

8. Obviously, from a traditional point of view, there is a single Divine authority. Indeed, the first mention in the literature of what later became the classic Montesquieuian formulation of the three branches of government is in Isaiah, Chapter 33, verse 22, which reads: *"Adonai shofteinu, Adonai mechokikeinu, Adonai malkeinu; Hu oshi'ainu"* (God is our judge, God is our legislator,

God is our king; He will save us). It both acknowledges the reality of the three branches of government and their ultimate concentration in Divine hands.

9. Cf. Stuart A. Cohen, "The Concept of the Three *Ketarim*: Its Place in Jewish Political Thought and Its Implications for a Study of Jewish Constitutional History," *AJS Review* IX:1 (Spring 1984).

10. Cf. Daniel J. Elazar and Stuart A. Cohen, *The Jewish Polity*.

11. Stuart A. Cohen, "The Concept of the Three *Ketarim*."

12. Cf. Daniel J. Elazar and Stuart A. Cohen, *The Jewish Polity*, Epoch 14.

13. For the definition of congress, see the *Oxford English Dictionary*. On forms of representative government, see Edmund Burke, *A Letter to the Sherriffs of Bristol* (Cambridge: Cambridge University Press, 1936); Alfred de Grazia, *Public and Republic: Political Representation in America* (New York: Knopf, 1951) and *Apportionment and Representative Government* (New York: Praeger, 1963); John Stuart Mill, *Considerations on Representative Government* (New York: Liberal Arts Press, 1958); Carl J. Friedrich, *Man and His Government: An Empirical Theory of Politics* (New York: McGraw-Hill, 1963); Lewis Anthony Dexter, "The Representative and His District," *Human Organization*, no. 16, pp. 2-13; and "Representation," in David Sillo, ed., *International Encyclopedia of the Social Sciences*, 18 vols. (New York: Macmillan, 1968-1979), pp. 461-479.

14. Cf. Elazar and Cohen, *The Jewish Polity*.

PART I –

THE HISTORIC POLITY

Chapter 1

THE POLITY IN BIBLICAL ISRAEL

Daniel J. Elazar

The political experience of ancient Israel as recounted in the Bible laid the foundations of the Jewish political tradition in all its aspects. The Bible's concern with teaching humans, particularly Jews, the right way to live in this world gives its political dimension particular importance. The highly social character of biblical concern with achieving the good life leads to its emphasis on the good commonwealth. The biblical account of the history of the Israelites can be seen in that light.[1]

At the same time, the biblical discussion of the government of ancient Israel stands at the very beginning of Western political life and thought. The record of that experience represents the oldest stratum in Western political thought and, since the record is derived very directly from the Israelites' experience, the latter is in itself an important factor in the development of Western political institutions.[2] If this is more difficult to perceive today than it was in Spinoza's time, it is because the study of the political experience of ancient Israel has been generally neglected since the Reformed Protestant theologians and state-builders and the political philosophers of the sixteenth and seventeenth centuries paid serious attention to it in shaping the political views of the moderns who were to reject Scripture.[3]

The political experience of ancient Israel remains the foundation of the Jewish political world view, particularly as it pertains to the organization and government of the Jewish people. In traditional terms, Judaism itself is essentially a theopolitical phenomenon, a means of seeking salvation by constructing God's polity, the proverbial "city upon a hill," through which the covenantal community described in the Bible takes on meaning and fulfills its purpose in the scheme of things. The biblical account of the origins of the Jewish people reflects a blend of kinship and consent that generates a special political culture and a variety of institutions at home in it. A family of tribes becomes a nation by consenting to a common covenant with God and with each other, out of which flow the principles and practices of religious life and political organization that have animated the Jews as a corporate entity ever since.[4]

Methods and Procedures

Biblical political ideas are expressed through the description of the institutions, events, and prophesies connected with the government of ancient Israel. Less formally articulated than Greek political thought, the biblical political teaching must be discovered in the same manner that all biblical knowledge must emerge, by careful examination and analysis of the text with careful attention to recurring patterns and the reconciliation of apparent contradictions.

Understanding the method necessary to approach the subject, it is indeed possible to learn much about the theory and practice of government in ancient Israel both in terms of the way in which the Israelites governed themselves and in terms of their response to the great questions of politics which they confronted in their unique way, as every people must.

As in the case with other biblical teachings, the Bible does not offer us a philosophically systematic presentation of its political theory or of the workings of particular political institutions. Rather, the theory must be derived inductively from the biblical discussion of the political history and hopes of the Israelites and from biblical critiques of institutions not fully described. Contemporary understanding of biblical political ideas and institutions rests in great measure on our expanded understanding of the political institutions in the ancient Near East as a whole, particularly those of the civilizations of the Fertile Crescent. Advances in the study of the history and life of the ancient Near East made during the past two generations have enabled us to better understand the Bible in its political dimension as well as in so many others.[5]

Constitutional Epochs and Their Characteristics

The political life and thought of ancient Israel can best be understood in light of the constitutional epochs through which the Israelites passed (see Table 1 in Introduction).[6] Four constitutional epochs can be identified from the time of nation-building connected with the Exodus from Egypt to the completion of the biblical canon. Two others preceded the Exodus. Each was marked by an initial constitutional development that significantly changed the governmental structure, institutions, and functions of the nation, a later modification of that constitutional change in an effort to perfect it, and a final governmental crisis leading to a substantial reconstitution involving more radical changes in structure, institutions, and functions. Each constitutional period lasted approximately three hundred years or nine generations, with a new founding coming in the tenth generation — a pattern presented in the Bible itself.[7]

If the present theories are correct, the period of Jewish history prior to the Exodus from Egypt encompassed between five hundred and seven hundred years, or approximately a span of two constitutional epochs. Indeed, the biblical accounts suggest that it can be divided into the epoch of the patriarchs and the epoch of the Egyptian sojourn. During both, the Jewish people had a pre- or protonational existence. During the first epoch the patriarch was the sole repository of governmental powers. He was governor and military leader and he conducted foreign relations. He also received instructions from God and made the covenants with Him which constituted the constitutional framework for the emergent Jewish people. In that context he prayed, sacrificed, built altars and monuments, and offered blessings.[8]

At the beginning of the second epoch of Jewish history, the families of the twelve sons of Jacob were well-ensconced in Egypt, living under a foreign rule which sooner or later reduced them to slavery. There were no more patriarchs. In their place were *zekenim* (elders) and *shotrim* (maintainers of the peace), officials who administered the customary law of the tribes, perhaps recalling in a latent way the patriarchal covenants.[9]

The first constitutional epoch after the Exodus stretches from the founding of the Israelite tribal confederacy to the establishment of the monarchy. The founding of the tribal confederacy immediately after the Exodus from Egypt comes simultaneously with the founding of the nation, or the transformation of the Hebrew tribes into a national entity. Since ancient times, Moses has been recognized as the founder of the nation and its constitution-maker.[10]

The Mosaic constitution laid the foundations for the first Israelite polity, which was organized federally around a loose union of tribes, traditionally twelve in number. This union, perhaps the first true federal system in history, was bound together by a common constitution and law, but maintained relatively rudimentary national institutions grafted onto more fully articulated tribal ones whose origins may have antedated the Exodus. This situation prevailed, in great part, because the constitution specified that God Himself was to be considered the direct governor of the nation as a whole, assisted by a "servant" or Prime Minister (Hebrew: *Eved Adonai*) who would be His representative and who, in turn, would maintain a core of judges and civil servants to handle the transmission of his or, more correctly, God's instructions to the tribal and familial authorities. Depending on the importance of the issue in constitutional terms, the Prime Minister also interacted with the assembly of the children of Israel congregated as a whole — men, women, and children — the assembly of all men of military age, a national council representing the tribes, or ad hoc assemblies of tribal elders (*zekenim*) or delegates (*nesi'im*) for purposes of policy-making.

During for first two generations of the tribal confederacy, a single *Eved Adonai*, who was granted God's charisma, exercised authority over all the tribes, according to the biblical account. Moses and Joshua were the two figures to bear that title and exercise such authority. To the extent that the *Eved Adonai's* principal function was to serve as God's messenger, as was particularly true in the case of Moses, we already have the embryonic division of powers which was to become classic in the Jewish polity and which a thousand years later was to be defined in terms of three *ketarim* (literally, crowns or investitures of authority). Under this system the principal task of the *Eved Adonai* was to bring God's word to the people. This later became the task of the prophets and the *soferim* ("Scribes") who developed the *ketaric* terminology.[11]

The *Eved Adonai* also shared power with the priests, particularly Aaron and his sons, who had their own covenant with God establishing them as a hereditary priesthood with certain constitutional functions, principally judicial in character, as well as cultic ones.

The principal function of the priests was to provide a channel of communication from the people to God. They continued this function throughout the biblical period, through what was later termed the *keter kehunah*.

The *nesi'im* (literally, those raised up, best translated as magistrates) and *zekenim* (elders) were responsible for the day-to-day governance of the people, a function which was later defined as the *keter malkhut* (literally, crown of kingship, understood more generally as the domain of civil rule). They had a dual function in that they headed the individual tribes and also participated in the governance of the nation as a whole.[12] An additional republican guarantee of this system was the fact that the Israelites had no standing army but relied for protection on the tribal militias consisting of every male aged twenty or over.

The entire body politic was known as *Adat B'nai Yisrael* from the time of the Exodus onward. *Edah* means congregation or assembly and reflects the popular and republican basis of the Israelite polity. Thus, from Sinai onward, constitutional decisions were taken by the entire *Edah*: men, women, and children, assembled together to give their consent, while major policy decisions such as declarations of war were made by the *Edah* in its more limited form of men of military age. Day-to-day governance was in the hands of the institutions mentioned above, who represented the *Edah*. It was the *Edah* which God led directly and to which He spoke through the *Eved Adonai*. Within the limits of God's constitution the *Edah* acted autonomously.[13]

Once the nation had been formed by Moses and settled in the land by Joshua, no single national leaders of this kind emerged until the very end of the first constitutional epoch. Instead, regional *shoftim* (judges) — also charismatic leaders — appeared from time to time, according to the biblical account, at least one in each generation, to act as proto-national leaders, under God's direct sovereignty, primarily, though not exclusively, in the military realm. The term "judge," introduced in English Bibles as the translation of the Hebrew term, carries roughly the same meaning as the term originally did in Anglo-American political life, that is to say, an executive office whose duties may include the settling of disputes, but are essentially directed toward the authoritative execution of the law, as in the case of the traditional county judge who actually serves as the chief executive officer of the county.[14]

If the terminology used in the Pentateuch and the Book of Joshua is accurate, the use of the term "judges" to describe the post-Joshua leadership of the nation accurately reflects the less than nationwide scope of the judges' authority. The Ministers of the Lord had in their governmental structures judges and officers, lesser figures responsible to them whose authority may have been parallel to that of the later judges, though limited by the existence of a national leader. Only after their departure did the judges acquire a leading role of their own.

The first constitutional epoch came to an end with the advent of the monarchy, which was instituted with some reluctance to cope with the Philistine threat to the very existence of Israel. The epoch's last stage was dominated by Samuel, the last of the judges and the first of the prophets, who brought the period to a close with his efforts to revive national unity in the traditional manner through a single nationwide leader with limited authority, primarily in the military field. His grant of such limited authority to Saul, whom he designated as "governor" (*nagid*), represented an effort to restore the kind of national institutions needed to promote energetic national unity that had existed in the days of Moses and Joshua.[15]

For Samuel, the Israelite constitution demanded that energetic government be limited government under God's continuing sovereignty. He emphasized the idea of dividing authority between the governor (*keter malkhut*) and the prophet (*keter torah*), with the former holding executive powers limited by the latter's mediation of God's word. Samuel failed for a number of reasons, not the least of which was the fact that the successful implementation of such a political arrangement was not to occur for many centuries. In the end, he himself took the decisive steps necessary to create a more conventional monarchy, though one limited by the traditional constitution.

The establishment of the kingship opened a new constitutional epoch in Israelite history, one marked by the institutionalization of a limited monarchy and the struggle over the means to insure its limitation. David can be considered the first true king of Israel, with Saul a transitional figure who was really part of the older federal republican tradition. At the same time, the struggle between Samuel and Saul did set the stage for the character of the political struggle in the monarchic period. As Saul was endowed with increasingly monarchic powers, Samuel transformed his own role from that of judge to that of *navi*, or prophet, whose main task was to keep the monarch within the limits of the constitution in the largest. To that end, he introduced the *mishpat hamelukhah* (the law of the kingdom) as the framework for the limited kingship. This tension between king and prophet was to be the primary constitutional feature of the second constitutional epoch. During most of that period, the prophets functioned to direct and restrict kingly action and powers.[16]

David was the first to formally assume the mantle of kingship. Like Saul, he did so through a combination of divine designation (anointment by a prophet) and popular consent (covenants with the elders of Judah and Israel). He established most of the fundamental powers of the king during his long reign, including the power of hereditary succession within his "house." He did so by grafting the kingship and institutions designed to support it upon the governing base of the old tribal federation, preserving most of the institutions of the federation otherwise intact but increasingly subordinate to the king and court. David accomplished this by utilizing military necessity as the basis for creation of a ruling class and a standing army whose powers came from their military role rather than from traditional sources and who were consequently tied to the king first and foremost.

Brilliantly, he captured Jerusalem and made it his city, the functional equivalent of a federal district in our time, outside of the jurisdiction of any individual tribe, and then proceeded to build his court there. He further strengthened the *keter malkhut* by developing a royal bureaucracy and a small professional army. Through the transfer of the Ark of the Covenant and the designation of the Zadokites as the priestly guardians of the Ark, David both strengthened the *keter kehunah* and gained control over it. He showed similar wisdom in dealing with the *keter torah* as represented by the prophets, encouraging the leading prophets to take up residence at his court by giving them free rein to criticize him without penalty, but by the same token subtly tying them to the king as their protector. In sum, rather than seek to exert control by destroying the traditional institutions of the Israelite polity, he co-opted them.

Solomon intensified this trend by transforming the ruling class from a military elite to a more complex military-bureaucratic-religious one, introducing bureaucratic administrative forms as vehicles for centralizing power in the country. Both did what they did, however, within the purview and under the gaze of prophetic counterparts who were able to maintain some constitutional limitations on the exercise of kingly power if not on the increase in its scope. Indeed, there is good reason to believe that the prophets were not initially opposed to the centralization of power under the first two Davidic monarchs, seeing the new centralization as a way to better implement God's law in the nation as a whole.[17]

However, when Rehoboam attempted to further extend and intensify the actions of his father and grandfather and impose burdens on the Israelite public that were not only taxing but visibly arbitrary as well, the major prophetic leadership deserted him and fostered a revolution which led to the division of the kingdom into two.[18] While this division brought about an important regime change on one level, on another it did not mark a full constitutional revolution because even under David and Solomon the northern tribes and Judah (which had virtually absorbed the tribe of Simeon by that time) had been separate groupings that accepted the rule of David and his son in separate actions. The refusal of the northern tribes to accept Rehoboam, then, was an act fully consonant with the Israelite constitution as they understood it.

What the division did inaugurate was the development of two different ways of integrating the monarchy into the constitutional framework of Israel.[19] In the southern kingdom, where the Davidic dynasty continued to rule, the tension between the kings and prophets was usually resolved in favor of the king, even to the point where specific monarchs temporarily suppressed the prophetic schools, though at no point was the tension eliminated. The maintenance of the dynastic principle insured this result in a way that was not possible in the northern kingdom, where the succession itself was founded upon an opposition to dynastic rule and a desire to restore the tradition of charismatic leadership.

In the north, the prophets were sufficiently strong to prevent the entrenchment of any particular dynasty and, indeed, the prophetic role became one of supporting or rejecting particular candidates for the kingship (by extending or refusing them God's charisma) and thereby encouraging dynastic changes. Consequently, kingship in the northern tribes meant, in no small degree, a restoration of the principles and practices of the tribal federation, with the kings far more limited in power than their southern counterparts and the older institutions of the tribal federation stronger in their governing role. At the same time, a national ruling elite did emerge that was tied to the monarchy, even if its composition changed with the dynastic changes that took place in the north.

The active role of the prophets is attested to in the biblical account which reveals far more prophetic activity in the northern kingdom than in the southern, whether the activity of such political leaders as Elijah or the more limited kind of protest prophecy of Amos and Hosea. It is characteristic of the situation that the leading prophet in this constitutional epoch to appear in the southern kingdom was Isaiah, a relative of the king and a member of the ruling elite, whose background stands in great contrast to that of Amos and Hosea, not to mention Elijah himself.[20]

With the destruction of the northern kingdom in 722 BCE, the second constitutional epoch came to an end and the third began. The southern kingdom stood alone as the single politically independent entity of the Jewish people and, indeed, extended its sway over part of the north and many of its people. It is fair to say that the real meaning of the destruction of the northern kingdom was not the dispersion of the people as recorded in the legends of the "ten lost tribes" so much as the destruction of the ten tribes as political entities.[21] Subsequent Jewish tradition, which sees the restoration of the tribes as a major element in the coming of the messianic age, confirms this.[22]

The architects of the extended kingdom of Judah were King Hezekiah and the prophet Isaiah. Hezekiah was the most important king between Solomon and Josiah, principally because he had the opportunity to reunite the Jewish people and did so, reinstituting the Passover pilgrimage to Jerusalem and extending Judean control over territories of the northern kingdom. In doing all this he was supported by Isaiah, who raised prophecy to a new level in Judah.[23]

Still, elimination of the northern kingdom had the consequence of greatly weakening the role of the prophets as defenders of the traditional constitution in the south, a tendency that was further strengthened by the elimination of the federal institutions that had survived in the north as additional constitutional bulwarks. In the south, where the tribes had already merged into the single polity of Judah, the old federal traditions were preserved only in the local arena. Consequently, the century between the destruction of the northern kingdom and the ascension of King Josiah was marked by the greatest violations of the traditional constitution ever to occur in the biblical period. These violations led to a major constitutional reform under Josiah, whereby the limitations on the monarchy which the prophets had tried to sustain were, in effect, brought together in the form of a more clearly written constitution (the Book of Deuteronomy) that successfully changed the power of relationships in the country, at least partly because the kingship itself ceased to be a reality shortly thereafter.[24]

The Josianic reform centered on the introduction of the Book of Deuteronomy as the basic constitutional document of a reconstituted and more limited kingship. The king was further limited by the loss of Israelite independence shortly after Josiah's death. The reduction of the Davidic ruler to vassal status in the Babylonian empire at the beginning of the sixth century BCE led, ultimately, to the disappearance of the throne itself in a restored Judea early in the fifth century. By the end of the third constitutional epoch, the monarchy had disappeared as a viable institution, though hope for its restoration became part of Israel's messianic dream. The mysterious disturbances surrounding the last scion of the House of David in the period immediately following the restoration under Cyrus marked the closing of the monarchic chapter in biblical history (and, except for the Hasmonean interlude, in Jewish history as a whole).[25]

The necessity to develop new modes of group survival in exile enhanced the importance of the Torah as written constitution as a source of authority in Israel. Consequently, in this third epoch, the Torah became the ascendant political authority in the Israelite polity, with the heirs of the prophets turning their attention to expounding its principles and elucidating its promises for future political success rather than being solely responsible for the maintenance of the constitution.

The removal of the last of the Davidides from the political scene ended the third constitutional epoch and led to the inauguration of a second historical period, known as the Second Commonwealth, and a fourth constitutional epoch, which brought with it the restoration of fully republican government. At the beginning of the epoch, the Jewish people was divided among three concentrations: the Persian province of Yahud, or Judea — a small territory around Jerusalem in Eretz Israel; a major concentration in the Persian Empire from Mesopotamia eastward into Iran; and in Egypt's Nile Valley. Biblical history concentrates on the Judean community as the continuation of Jewish independence, although, in fact, as the Bible itself indicates, Yahud was only an autonomous Persian province.[26] While there are only a few sources on the subject, it appears that the Jewish communities in the diaspora also had substantial autonomy.[27]

Significantly, the biblical account of the inauguration of this fourth constitutional epoch features the promulgation by Ezra and Nehemiah of the Torah as Israel's constitution by popular demand in a special ceremony at which public consent to the Torah was reaffirmed. Thus the Bible presents the covenantal process as having come full circle. At Sinai, God initiated the covenant which, among other things, launched the first constitutional period in Jewish history. After three epochs, that period came to an end and a new period was inaugurated by the Jewish people in Jerusalem, initiating a renewal of the covenant with God.[28]

Characteristic of this fourth constitutional epoch was rule by the *Anshei Knesset HaGedolah*, a council which shared power with the high priest and the *soferim* (scribes). Thus the separation of powers system inaugurated in the previous constitutional period was maintained. The *Anshei Knesset HaGedolah* represented the *keter malkhut*. The term *knesset* itself was a Hebrew adaptation of the Aramaic *kenishtah*, which means *edah*. The High Priest continued to represent the *keter kehunah* and the *soferim* inherited the mantle of the *keter torah*. Indeed, the three *ketarim* become known as such during this epoch.[29]

What happened within this separation of powers system was a shift in power, with first the *soferim* and then the High Priest becoming the principal leaders of the people. While the biblical canon was not yet completed in this epoch, after the Bible recounts the history of the reconstitution under Ezra and Nehemiah, the period itself drops out of the Bible's purview except for the two accounts of events in the diaspora in the Scroll of Esther and the Book of Daniel.

Forms of Political Organization

By and large, our knowledge of the forms of Israelite political organization is limited. The Bible offers the only available account of the subject, although it can be supplemented by limited archaeological evidence and documents from other West Asian polities of the biblical era. We are assisted by the biblical discussion of political institutions in the context of its larger purposes and our increased understanding of the political institutions of the ancient Near East in general.

Three arenas of political organization are to be noted: local, tribal, and national, each of which underwent transformation through the various constitutional epochs. Local institutions had their origins in the familial structure developed before the first national constitution when the Israelites were semi-nomads. The various *mishpahot* (clans) formed by the combination of households (*bet ab*) formed the tribal substructure in those times. After Israelite settlement of Canaan during the first constitutional period, the clans settled down in discrete villages or townships (a more accurate term) and the relationship among those households was transformed into one that was linked with the particular locality of their settlement.

The clans were governed by elders (*zekenim*), no doubt consisting of the heads of their several households. After the conquest, these became local councils known as *Shaarei Ha'ir* (the Gates of the City), referring to the location within the Israelite township at which they met to conduct their business. These local councils seem to have persisted throughout the biblical period and, with some changes, into the post-biblical period as well. We must assume that these local councils handled whatever governmental functions were conducted locally, combining within them such legislative, executive, and judicial functions as were exercised at the various periods of their existence. It is possible that the judicial functions were shared with locally based priests from time to time. These local councils adjudicated disputes, regulated markets, spoke in the name of the township on local affairs and in conjunction with tribal and national bodies. While they were apparently selected by consensus, they were responsible to the township assembly, known in the Bible as *yotzei ha'ir* (those who go out from the city), consisting variously of all local inhabitants on constitutional matters or the military age males constituting the local militia on others.

Tribal political institutions also grew out of the familial structures of the presettlement period. During the first constitutional epoch, the tribes were entrusted with the major governmental responsibilities of the nation, with the linkages among them being essentially confederal. Tribal government was apparently vested in a council of elders representing the various families and clans within each tribe. Specific members of the council of elders or others co-opted for the purpose were given special responsibilities of an executive character, while policy-making and adjudicating functions remained in the hands of the tribal council. It is unclear whether tribes were led by *nesi'im* (singular, *nasi*, erroneously translated as "prince" in many English versions of the Bible, and actually meaning "he who is raised up" or selected to represent; a reasonable English equivalent is "magistrate"), or whether such *nesi'im* were simply selected to represent the tribes in national activities. During this first period, reference is also made to *sarim* (singular, *sar* or officer) and *alufim* (singular, *aluf*, leader of a thousand), both military titles used to describe commanders of tribal levies.

During this period, the tribes also took on a territorial basis so that in the course of a few generations, the very term *shevet* acquired strong territorial connotations. The land as divided into tribal segments was further subdivided into private and tribal parcels, with cultivated lands passing into family ownership and pasture lands remaining the common property of the tribe.

During the second constitutional epoch, the governmental role of the tribes was substantially reduced as the role of national authorities was strengthened. In the southern kingdom, the virtual merger of the tribes led to the emergence of a single council of elders which became, in effect, the popular organ of the state, which shared power with the king in ways not quite clear from the information we have on hand. In the northern kingdom, where central authority remained weak, the tribal councils apparently continued to function and exercise substantial control over tribal affairs. Constitutionally, their powers remained relatively uncircumscribed by the fact of kingship, though particular kings exercised great power over them by virtue of their power position in the kingdom as a whole. These tribal councils disappeared with the fall of the northern kingdom.[30]

The elimination of separate tribal governments with the fall of the northern kingdom ended the federal structure of the biblical polity, though it did not eliminate the use of federal principles in the organization of power in that polity. In the third constitutional epoch, tribal institutions as such were no longer in evidence though the tribal council survived as the popular body of the Kingdom of Judah, in the pattern which had already emerged during the previous constitutional epoch. The pattern was carried over into the fourth constitutional epoch when the council became the dominant political institution in the country as the *Anshei Knesset HaGedolah*.

The greatest changes in political forms in the biblical period took place on the national plane. These changes have already been described above. Examining them more directly, we find that in the first constitutional epoch national institutions were rudimentary, consisting primarily of leaders exercising authority nationwide or over several tribes with small entourages of assistants responsible to them, plus councils and commissions constituted for particular purposes. A rudimentary corps of officials existed in the form of the *shotrim*, who were responsible for implementation of the decisions of the national leadership. In addition to the charismatic leaders, the High Priest (and perhaps lesser priests in the period of the Judges) also exercised authority in certain fields, apparently sharing certain powers with the charismatic leadership, particularly where certain impartiality among the tribes was required.

It is unclear as to whether there was a continuing national assembly during the first constitutional epoch or whether ad hoc assemblies of tribal elders functioned in lieu of such a body when the occasion arose. Beyond that, the biblical account portrays the constitution of special commissions for special purposes on the basis of one representative per tribe, such as the commission of the twelve spies to scout out Canaan prior to its conquest, the commission which carried the Ark of the Covenant across the Jordan when the invasion commenced, and the commission established to work with Joshua and Elazar, the High Priest, to allocate the land among the tribes after the conquest was completed. Smaller commissions, comprising representatives of more than two but less than the full number of tribes, appear to have functioned during the period of the judges to assist them from time to time. Thus, national government, in the first constitutional epoch, emphasized joint action on the part of the tribes for very limited purposes.

During the second constitutional epoch, separate, autonomous, and continuing national institutions emerged, centered around the king. The first of these were military and related to the development of a military command structure. This command structure gradually gained civil responsibilities as well and was strengthened by the addition of strictly civil components based on the priesthood and non-Israelite elements.

During the reign of Solomon, a civil bureaucracy was created and the country was divided into administrative districts which were probably coordinated with the tribal governments over most of the country, but which in the south, at least, superseded them. While the thrust of this new national structure was primarily to undertake national executive and judicial functions in a political system where legislation in the modern sense was unknown, it essentially preempted the powers of authoritative decision-making to itself in all matters which the king deemed to be of national importance, except where he was constitutionally or politically restrained from doing so by effective local institutions or prophetic actions.

These national institutions reached the high point of their strength in the third constitutional epoch and then disappeared in the catastrophe that destroyed the First Commonwealth. Their reemergence in the fourth constitutional epoch was in a substantially different guise, since the kingship could no longer serve as their focal point. Apparently, the scribes staffed the reconstituted national administrative structure functioning within the boundaries of the Torah.

The Exercise of Political Functions

Very little is known about the exercise of political functions in the biblical period. Modern conceptions of limited or unlimited government are not easily applied to a period in which the role of the family was extraordinarily strong in fields later to become governmental responsibilities, and the connections between the political and the cultic aspects of life were inseparable. It is clear that Israelite government was not intended to be one that penetrated into all aspects of life. At the same time, the notion of government limited to the exercise of political powers also would have been foreign to the ancient Israelites. Political and cultic authority were so intertwined as to be inseparable even for analytic purposes. The community felt free to regulate the economy in numerous ways and the state undertook economic development tasks, but government-sponsored social services were essentially nonexistent.[31]

Israelite government pursued a limited but active role in the affairs of society, a role whose level depended upon the needs of the time. It is very likely that local authorities exercised some control over local economic conditions, if only to regulate competition. By the same token, after the rise of the kingship and the development of the commercial dimension of Israel's economy, the national government pursued clearly mercantilistic policies designed to promote commerce through joint governmental-private ventures which tended to favor the ruling elite.[32] It was during this period that the national government took responsibility for providing a proper infrastructure in the way of roads and security protection for the fostering of commerce. In the domain of religion, it seems that there was general agreement that government had a responsibility to foster proper observance of cultic forms. This was true regardless of whether the cultic forms were those of Israel's God or foreign gods, with the struggle being between parties that wished to direct government effort one way or another.

While the Bible makes provision for public activity in the realm of education and the social services, there is no particular indication that this public activity must be governmental in any way, and it is unclear as to whether there were any governmental roles played in this realm.[33]

Even less is known about the way in which political interests were articulated and aggregated in the biblical period. Was there voting? What does the Bible mean when it says the entire people would gather together to affirm or ratify particular decisions? How were elders chosen? How did one enter the ruling elite in the second and third constitutional epochs? These are questions which remain substantially unanswered.

The Bible does describe various covenant affirmation ceremonies in which the people or its representatives would reaffirm a covenantal relationship with God and a particular constitution or leader. These invariably occurred at points of constitutional crisis where it could not be assumed that a popular consensus persisted from the previous period. These covenantal acts are politically intriguing but their descriptions in the biblical accounts are not very revealing politically, so that we can only speculate regarding their relationship to the larger political system and processes of ancient Israel.

Fundamental Principles of Government and Politics

It may fairly be said that the fundamental principles animating government and politics in ancient Israel were theocratic, federal, and republican. The theocratic principle underlies all of Israel's political institutions. God is conceived to be directly involved in the governance of *Adat Bnai Yisrael*. During the first constitutional epoch, He is accepted as the great governor of the nation. Under the two constitutional periods in which the kingship existed, He was conceived to have, in effect, delegated that direct role to kings and, finally, in the fourth constitutional epoch, He was viewed as having resumed that role, though in ways which were at once better institutionalized and more obscure than in the first period.

This theocratic principle had two immediate consequences in shaping the Israelite conception of politics. In the first place, politics or the governance of the state was not an end in itself in the

Israelite scheme of things, but rather a useful way of serving divine purposes. This meant that the state did not exist as an end in itself. Indeed, Israelite political thought does not conceive of the state as a reified entity. There was no Israelite equivalent of the Greek *polis*, that is to say , the city whose value as a political entity exists independently of its inhabitants. There is no generic term for state in the Bible, only terms for different regimes, with *kahal* or *mamlakhah* coming closest to being used generically. *Medinah*, the contemporary Hebrew term, is used in Scripture to describe territories with juridical status and a measure of autonomy but without political independence. Even *Adat Bnai Yisrael*, important as it was in the fulfillment of God's plan, was conceived to be a kind of partnership of Israelites and not an entity that existed independently of its people. Political institutions were viewed not as serving the state but as serving this partnership which united the people with each other through their common linkage with God.

At the same time, politics was important because the establishment of the Holy Commonwealth, later to be called God's Kingdom of Earth in some quarters, was a primary goal of the Israelite nation, a goal mandated by God. Thus the character of Israelite political institutions was constantly judged in the Bible in terms of their success in fostering the development of the Holy Commonwealth. The very institution of the kingship became an issue because it involved the abandonment of God's direct rule over the people and thus was viewed by many as a departure from the path leading toward the Holy Commonwealth. Subsequent to the introduction of kingly rule, particular dynasties were judged in terms of their faithfulness to God's will in this connection. Thus the disappearance of the ten tribes as political entities is lamented as a break in the right order of things that must be mended if the Holy Commonwealth is to be achieved.

The biblical concern with political matters is so pervasive within its moral framework that references to such matters can be found in virtually every book and range from discussion of the origins of imperialism to the nature of statesmanship, aside from its major concern with the government of Israel. Thus, biblical thought is, on one hand, highly political and, on the other, very clear in its subordination of the political to higher goals. Political relationships in ancient Israel were based on the covenant or federal principle (the word federal is derived from the Latin *foedus* which means covenant). In fact, the Bible portrays the covenant principle as the basis for the relationships between God and man, between the nation of Israel and God, and among humans. Covenants in biblical thought are the means through which lasting relationships are forged, designed to preserve the respective integrities of the partners and to provide a basis for cooperation among them in order to achieve the common ends delineated in the compact. Thus the basis of all of Israelite society was federal down to its roots.

The first covenant between God and Israel according to the biblical account, the covenant with Abraham, is proto-political in character, involving as it does two promises — the establishment of the Jewish people and the allocation to them of the land of Canaan. The covenant at Sinai was the first great political covenant. It created the federal relationship between God and the Israelites. By doing so, it also constituted the Israelites as a nation, that is to say, as something more than a family or descendants of a putative common ancestor.

The Bible clearly relates the formation of the political institutions of Israel to the Sinai experience, whether in the form of the Book of the Covenant, which is the basis of the first constitution of the Israelite federation, or in connection with Moses' following the advice of his father-in-law to establish a national administrative and judicial structure, which is presented as taking place at the same time, though without the same divine character attached to it. The Bible is quite clear in indicating that no particular form of government is mandated by God, though some forms receive divine sanction and others do not.

The theopolitical aspects of this great covenant were reaffirmed at subsequent points in the history of the Israelites, invariably as times when constitutional change had taken place. Thus, the reaffirmation of the covenant under Joshua marked the point where the political institutions of Israel had to be adapted to permanent settlement in Eretz Israel. Similarly, David was made king by covenant, indeed, by two separate covenants: one with the elders of Judah, and the second with the elders of Judah and Israel. Covenant ceremonies were held at various times during the history of the kingship when the institution itself was in jeopardy. Finally, the institution of the Josianic reforms and the Deuteronomic constitution involved a major covenant renewal ceremony. The initiation of the fourth constitutional epoch involved another major covenant renewal ceremony with Ezra reading the Torah before the community at Sukkot to obtain their consent to it in the approved constitutional manner.

The covenant not only forms the basis for political organization in Israel but does even more than that. Israel becomes, in effect, a partnership held together by covenantal or federal ties which link the people to each other through their tribes and, through their tribes, also link them to God. These federal principles became so ingrained in Israelite political thought that, ever since, Jewish communities have been conceived as partnerships and have been organized through articles of agreement that are in themselves small covenants.

At first, these federal principles were translated into a federal system of government. Even when the Israelites abandoned the tribal confederacy as a form of government, they were careful to retain federal structural elements under the king and would have continued to do so by all accounts except for the conquest of the northern kingdom. Although this federal structure disappeared at the end of the second constitutional epoch because of objective conditions rather than for any internal reasons, the federal principles remained to animate the formally unitary structure that replaced it. At the same time, the federal structure of the earlier age was enshrined in the prophetic literature as a messianic goal. The various biblical descriptions of the ideal commonwealth all emphasize the federal structure as a major element within it.[34]

Republicanism is the third political principle of biblical Israel. Understood in its broadest sense, republicanism reflects the view that the political order is a public thing (*res publica*), that is to say, not the private preserve of any single king or ruling elite but the property of all of its citizens and that political power should be organized so as to reflect this fact. Republican government involves a limitation on the powers of those given authority and some provision for the representation of public concerns as a matter of right in the formulation and execution of public policy. All these conditions prevailed in biblical Israel except during periods when individual kings essentially usurped powers and were considered to be usurpers by the biblical account.

So republican was ancient Israel that even the institution of kingship, limited as it was, persisted for less than half of the biblical period (the precise length of time depending upon the way in which the biblical period is calculated). The Bible does not mandate kingship but makes its institution a matter of public choice and, in any case, clearly provides for constitutional limitations on the king, who is never the sovereign. The prophets, indeed, refrained from referring to kings as kings (*melakhim*), but rather referred to them as *negidim*, roughly translated as high commissioners; in other words, God's commissioners to lead His people or, in the case of Ezekiel, as *nesi'im*, God's elected ones.[35] This is a reflection of an antimonarchical tradition that persisted among the prophetic schools during the entire period of the kings, leading in the end to something of a dualism in Jewish political thought whereby the traditional role of Elijah became associated with a kind of prophetic republicanism, with or without a king as a national leader of a limited scope in the messianic age.[36]

Similarly, it seems that certain republican institutions were preserved through the period of kingship and emerged as more powerful institutions once that period had come to an end. These institutions embodied principles of shared power that were never relinquished.

Out of these three principles there emerges a picture of the ideal commonwealth as embodied in biblical political thought. Two principal descriptions of this ideal commonwealth have been canonized, with a third description that emphasizes political structure and organization less while portraying the kind of life and society that the commonwealth will create. The two descriptions are to be found in the Book of Joshua and in the prophecies of Ezekiel.

The Book of Joshua, an idealized version of the conquest and settlement of Canaan by the Israelites, can properly be viewed as an expression of what the ideal Israelite polity should be, describing as it does in some detail what the polity was conceived to have been at the time of Joshua, that is to say, at the time of its greatest achievements in Canaan. If this biblical utopia looks to a great past situation for its inspiration, Ezekiel's utopia looks to a great future situation; yet, the description that emerges is quite similar to that found in the Book of Joshua. Finally, Isaiah's messianic vision implicitly assumes conditions such as those described in Joshua and Ezekiel.[37]

Characteristic of these utopian accounts are the three principles described above and the separation of the three *ketarim*. In all three, the theocratic principle is fundamental. Politics becomes a means for achieving and maintaining the Holy Commonwealth. God is sovereign and exercises His sovereignty more or less directly, mediated only through His servants who act as national leaders and the traditional institutions of the people. Those institutions are federal and republican in character, with the federation of tribes at their base and the popular institutions growing out of that federation the major instrumentalities of governance alongside of God, His chief minister, and supporting staff.

This ideal biblical commonwealth, reflected in the idealization of the realities of political life in ancient Israel, became a major force in the political thought of the Western world, shaping the ideals and animating the visions of most Western thrusts toward republicanism. Echoes and expansion of that vision permeated Western political thought after the rise of Christianity, just as they continued to permeate Jewish political thought after the Bible itself was canonized and the biblical period came to its conclusion.

Notes

1. See, for example, Robert Gordis, "Democratic Origins in Ancient Israel — The Biblical Edah," in *The Alexander Marx Jubilee Volume* (New York, 1967); Martin Noth, *The History of Israel* (New York: Harper and Row, 1958); G.E. Mendenhall, "Ancient Oriental and Biblical Law," *Biblical Archeologist* 17 (2) (1954), pp. 26-46; C. Umhau Wolf, "Terminology of Israel's Tribal Organization," *Journal of Biblical Literature* 65 (1946); Norman Gottwald, *All the Kingdoms of the Earth* (New York: Harper and Row, 1964); N.H. Snaith, "The Covenant-Love of God," in *The Distinctive Ideas of the Old Testament* (New York, 1964), pp. 94-127.

2. For an overview of the contribution of the Israelite experience in the development of Western political institutions, see, *inter alia*, G.H. Dodge, *The Political Theory of the Huguenots of the Dispersion* (New York, 1947); Harold Fisch, *Jerusalem and Albion* (New York: Schocken, 1964); Christopher Hill, *Intellectual Origins of the English Revolution* (Oxford, 1965); Hans Kohn, *The Idea of Nationalism* (New York: Macmillan, 1961); Zacharas P. Thundyil, *Covenant in Anglo-Saxon Thought* (Madras: Macmillan of India, 1972); Eric Voegelin, *Israel and Revelation* (Baton Rouge: Louisiana State University Press, 1957); Michael Walzer, *Exodus and Revolution* (New York: Basic Books, 1985) and *The Revolution of the Saints* (Cambridge: Harvard University Press, 1965).

3. Johannes Althusius, *Politics*, trans. Frederick Carney (Boston: Beacon Press, 1964); Thomas Hobbes, *Leviathan* (Indianapolis: Bobbs-Merrill, 1958), p. 143; Benedict Spinoza, *Political-Theological Tractate* (Italian translation by C. Sarchi, 1875 [1670]); John Locke, *First and Second Treatises on Government*, ed. Peter Laslett (New York: Mentor, 1965); Daniel J. Elazar and John Kincaid, eds., *The Covenant Connection* (Grenshaw: Carolina Academic Press, 1990).

4. See Daniel J. Elazar, "Kinship and Consent in the Jewish Community: Patterns of Continuity in Jewish Communal Life," *Tradition*, Vol. 14, No. 4 (Fall 1974), pp. 63-79; "Covenant as the Basis of the Jewish Political Tradition," in *Kinship and Consent: The Jewish Political Tradition and its Contemporary Uses*, Daniel J. Elazar, ed. (Ramat Gan: Turtledove, 1981); and Daniel J. Elazar and Stuart A. Cohen, *The Jewish Polity: Jewish Political Organizations from Biblical Times to the Present* (Bloomington: Indiana University Press, 1985).

5. See, for example, Albrecht Alt, *Essays on Old Testament and*

Religion (Garden City, N.Y.: Doubleday, 1968), pp. 173-222; H. Tadmor, "'The People and the Kingship in Ancient Israel: The Role of Political Institutions in the Biblical Period," *Journal of World History* 11 (1968), pp. 46-68; Martin Noth, *History of Israel*; W.F. Albright, "Tribal Rule and Charismatic Leaders," in *The Biblical Period from Abraham to Ezra* (New York, 1968), pp. 35-52; Yehezkel Kaufmann, *The Biblical Account of the Conquest of Palestine* (Jerusalem: Magnes Press, 1953) and *The Book of Joshua: A Commentary* (Jerusalem: Kiryat Sepher, 1963).

6. Daniel J. Elazar, *The Constitutional Periodization of Jewish History* (Jerusalem: Center for Jewish Community Studies, 1980) and the files of the Jerusalem Center for Public Affairs, Jerusalem.

7. Elazar and Cohen, *The Jewish Polity*, Introduction and Epochs I-IV.

8. On the epoch of the patriarchs, see A. Malamat, "Origins and the Formative Period," in H.H. Ben Sasson, ed., *A History of the Jewish People* (Cambridge, Mass.: Harvard University Press, 1976), pp. 3-87; B. Mazar, ed., "The Patriarchs," *The World History of the Jewish People*, Vol. I (New Brunswick, 1970); E.A. Speiser, ed., "Genesis," *The Anchor Bible*, Vol. 1: *Social Institutions* (New York, 1965), pp. 3-15.

9. John Bright, *A History of Israel*, 3rd. ed. (Philadelphia: Westminster Press, 1982); G.E. Mendenhall, "Ancient Oriental and Biblical Law," *Biblical Archeologist* 17:2 (1954), pp. 26-46; M. Weinfeld, "Berit — Covenant vs. Obligation," *Biblica* 56:i (1975), pp. 109-128.

10. Aaron Wildavsky, *The Nursing Father: Moses as a Political Leader* (Tuscaloosa: University of Alabama Press, 1984); Leo Schwarz, *Great Ages and Ideas of the Jewish People* (New York: Holt, Rinehart and Winston, 1960), ch. 1; John Bright, "The Constitution and Faith of Early Israel," *A History of Israel*, Part II, Ch. 4; Moshe Weinfeld, "The Transition from Tribal Rule to Monarchy and Its Impact on History," *Kinship and Consent*; A. Malamat, "Origins and the Formative Period"; Daniel J. Elazar, "The Book of Joshua as a Political Classic," *Jewish Political Studies Review* I:1-2 (Spring 1989), pp. 93-150; Martin Noth, "Israel as the Confederation of the Twelve Tribes," Part I in *The History of Israel*; W.F. Albright, "Tribal Rule and Charismatic Leaders," *The Biblical Period from Abraham to Ezra* (New York, 1968), pp. 35-52; R.G. Bowling and G. Ernest Wright, eds., "Joshua," *The Anchor Bible*, Vol. 5 (New York, 1982); G.E. Mendenhall, *Law and Covenant in Israel and the Ancient Near East* (The Biblical Colloquium, 1955); *Studies in the Book of Joshua* (Jerusalem: Kiryat Sepher, 1960).

11.   M. Weinfeld, "Judge and Officer in Ancient Israel and in the Ancient Near East," *Israel Oriental Studies* 7 (1977), pp. 65-88; "Keter ve-Atarah," in *Encyclopedia Mikra'it*, Vol. 4 (Jerusalem, 1962), clmns. 405-408; Stuart A. Cohen, *The Concept of the Three Ketarim: Its Place in Jewish Political Thought and Its Implications for a Study of Jewish Constitutional History*, Working Paper No. 18 (Jerusalem: Center for Jewish Community Studies, 1982), pp. 1-40, and "Keter as a Jewish Political Symbol: Origins and Implications," in *Jewish Political Studies Review*, I:1-2 (Spring, 1989); C. Umhau Wolf, "Terminology of Israel's Tribal Organization," *Journal of Biblical Literature*.

12.   E.A. Speiser, "Background and Functions of the Biblical Nasi," *Catholic Biblical Quarterly* 25 (1965), pp. 111-117; M. Weinfeld, "Judge and Officer...".

13.   Moshe Weinfeld, "From God's Edah to the Chosen Dynasty"; R. Gordis, "Democratic Origins in Ancient Israel — The Biblical Edah," in *The Alexander Marx Jubilee Volume*.

14.   B. Lindars, "Gideon and the Kingship," *Journal of Theological Studies* 16 (1965), pp. 315-326; R.G. Bowling and G. Ernest Wright, "Judges," *The Anchor Bible*, Vol. 6 (New York, 1980); W.F. Albright, "Tribal Rule and Charismatic Leaders," *The Biblical Period from Abraham to Ezra and Samuel and the Beginnings of the Prophetic Movement in Israel* (Cincinnati: Hebrew Union College Press, 1961).

15.   A. Alt, "The Formation of the Israelite State," in *Essays on Old Testament History and Religion* (New York, 1966); Daniel J. Elazar, "Dealing with Fundamental Regime Change: The Biblical Paradigm of the Transition from Tribal Federation to the Federal Monarchy of David," in Jacob Neusner, Ernest S. Frerichs, and Nahum M. Sarna, eds. *From Ancient Israel to Modern Judaism* (Atlanta: Scholars Press, 1989), Vol. I, pp. 97-129; Moshe Weinfeld, "From God's Edah to the Chosen Dynasty: The Transition from the Tribal Federation to the Monarchy," in *Kinship and Consent*, pp. 151-166; J. Levenson, "The Davidic Covenant and Its Modern Interpreters," *Catholic Bible Quarterly* 41 (ii) (1979); W.A. Irwin, "Saul and the Rise of the Monarchy," *American Journal of Semitic Languages and Literature* 58 (1941), pp. 113-138.

16.   Benjamin Offenheimer, *Early Prophecy in Israel* (Jerusalem: Magnes Press, 1973); J. Muilenberg, "The 'Office' of the Prophet in Ancient Israel," in J.P. Hyatt, ed. *The Bible in Modern Scholarship* (1966), pp. 79-97; M. Galston, "Philosopher-King vs. Prophet," in *Israel Oriental Studies* 8 (1978), pp. 204-218; Roland de Vaux, *Jerusalem and the Prophets* (Cincinnati: Hebrew Union College Press, 1965); S. Talmon, "Kingship and Ideology of the

State," in *The World History of the Jewish People*, Vol. 4, Part II (Jerusalem, 1979), pp. 3-26.

17. A. Alt, "The Monarchy in the Kingdoms of Israel and Judah," in *Essays on Old Testament History and Religion* (1951), English translation (Oxford: Basil Blackwell and Mott, 1966), pp. 239-259; A. Malamat, "Organs of Statecraft in the Israelite Monarchy," *Biblical Archeologist* 28 (2) (1956), pp. 34-50; Roland de Vaux, "The Administration of the Kingdom," in *Ancient Israel* (New York, 1965), Vol. 1, pp. 133-142; B. Halpern, *The Constitution of the Monarchy in Israel* (Cambridge: Harvard Semitic Monographs, 1981), No. 25; Y. Kaufman, "The Monarchy," *The Religion of Israel* (Chicago, 1960), pp. 262-270.

18. B. Halpern, *Constitution of the Monarchy in Israel*; W.O.E. Oesterley and Theodore Henry Robinson, *History of Israel* (Oxford: Clarendon Press, 1932).

19. Daniel J. Elazar and Stuart A. Cohen, "Epoch IV: *Brit ha-Melukhah* (The Federal Monarchy)," in *The Jewish Polity*.

20. Norman K. Gottwald, *All the Kingdoms of the Earth* (New York: Harper and Row, 1964).

21. Bright, *A History of Israel*, Ch. 7, pp. 249-287; Albright, "Tribal Rule and Charismatic Leaders," *The Biblical Period from Abraham to Ezra*, Chapter 7, pp. 67-74; Noth, *The History of Israel*, Part III, Section I, pp. 253-299; Oesterley and Robinson, *History of Israel*.

22. Martin Cohen, "The Role of the Shilonite Priesthood in the United Monarchy of Ancient Israel," *Hebrew Union College Annual* Vol. 36 (Cinninnati: Hebrew Union College, 1965), pp. 59-98; B. Porten, *Archives from the Jews of Elephantine* (Berkeley, 1968).

23. John Bright, "The Monarchy: Crisis and Downfall," in *A History of Israel*.

24. E.W. Nicholson, *Deuteronomy and Tradition* (Oxford: Basil Blackwell and Mott, 1967); G. von Rad, *Studies in Deuteronomy*, English translation (London: SCM Press, 1953); H.H. Rowley, "The Early Prophecies of Jeremiah in their Setting," reprinted in *Men of God* (London: Thomas Nelson and Sons, 1963), pp. 133-168; Oesterley and Robinson, *History of Israel*.

25. John Bright, "Tragedy and Beyond: The Exilic and Postexilic Periods," in *The History of Israel*, pp. 76-94; Leo Schwarz, *Great Ages and Ideas*, pp. 341-401.

26. L. Falk, "The Temple Scroll and the Codification of Jewish Law," *Jewish Law Annual* 2 (1979), pp. 33-44; Leo Schwarz, *Great Ages and Ideas*; Elazar and Cohen, *The Jewish Polity*, Epoch VI; S.

Zeitlin, *The Rise and Fall of the Judean State*, Vol. 1 (Philadelphia, 1962).

27. *Ibid.*

28. E. Bickerman, *From Ezra to the Last of the Maccabees* (New York, 1962); J. Bright, "The Formative Period of Judaism," in *A History of Israel*; M. Snaith, "Nehemiah," in *Palestinian Parties and Politics that Shaped the Old Testament* (New York, 1971), pp. 126-147.

29. See Elazar and Cohen, *The Jewish Polity*, Epoch VI.

30. J. Bright, "The Monarchy: Crisis and Downfall," in *A History of Israel*.

31. Roland de Vaux, *Ancient Israel* (New York: McGraw Hill, 1965), 2 vols.

32. J. Bright, "Israel Under the Monarchy: The Period of Self-determination," in *A History of Israel*.

33. Roland de Vaux, *Ancient Israel*, especially Vol. 1, Social Institutions.

34. Daniel J. Elazar, *The Covenant Tradition in Politics*, Vol. I (forthcoming).

35. Moshe Greenberg, *Ezekiel 1-20. A new translation with introduction and commentary* (Garden City, N.Y.: Doubleday, 1983); Moshe Greenberg, "Ezekiel — XV," *The Anchor Bible*, V. 22, pp. 388; Moshe Greenberg and Charles Cutler Torrey, *Pseudo-Ezekiel and the Original Prophecy* (New York: Ktav, 1970); Yehezkel Kaufmann, *The Religion of Israel from its Beginnings to the Babylonian Exile*, translated and abridged by Moshe Greenberg (Chicago: University of Chicago Press, 1960), pp. 426-446.

36. Martin Cohen, *op. cit.*; William Lee Holladay, *Isaiah, Scroll of a Prophetic Heritage* (Grand Rapids, Mich.: W.B. Eermans, 1978); Yehezkel Kaufmann, *The Religion of Israel from its Beginnings to the Babylonian Exile*, Part III, Ch. 12, pp. 378-394 for Isaiah and Part III, Ch. 13, pp. 426-446 for Ezekiel; Robert H. Pfeiffer, *Introduction to the Old Testament* (New York: Harper, 1948), Part IV, "The Latter Prophets," I, The Book of Isaiah, pp. 415-481; Gil, III, pp. 518-565.

Chapter 2

CONTINUITIES AND CONVULSIONS: THE THREE *KETARIM* DURING THE SECOND JEWISH COMMONWEALTH

Stuart A. Cohen

The period of the Second Jewish Commonwealth (145 BCE-70 CE) illustrates three central features of the three *ketarim*: (i) the differing nature of their individual compositions; (ii) their separate capacity for internal adaptation to changing circumstances; (iii) their tendency towards conflict within the traditional parameters of Jewish political discourse. These facets are patently interdependent; indeed, to a large extent they nourished each other. Changes of institutional command and procedure within individual *ketarim* generated alternations in the overall balance of power between them. These, in turn, affected the composition and cohesion of the separate domains. From that point of view, the constitutional rhythm of the period was more cyclical than linear. Nevertheless, for the purposes of analysis, the three facets noted above will here be discussed *seriatim*.

1. Composition

Two circumstances facilitate a reconstruction of the composition of the individual *ketarim* during the Second Commonwealth period. One is the comparative abundance of available historical data. This is the earliest epoch of Jewish constitutional history for the study of which recourse can be had to a variety of literary sources, and whose chronicle is hence not preponderantly influenced by the tenor and bias of the biblical cannon. Gaps of course remain, some of which are crucial to our present concern. We are still ignorant, for instance, about the precise histories of some governmental institutions (notably the *Sanhedrin*) and the exact origin of some political parties (especially the Pharisees). Nevertheless, historians and archeologists have discovered materials of a variety sufficient to enable them to corroborate one account by reference to several others, and hence to compose synoptic studies of the period which reflect the multifaceted character of its constitutional and institutional development.[1]

The second circumstance is somewhat different in kind, and hinges upon the consideration that during the Second Commonwealth period the Jewish people manifestly possessed functioning authorities in all three *ketarim* which were both fully articulated and *edah*-wide. Indeed, it was during that period that something of an apotheosis in their development was attained, with the instruments of each *keter* being demarcated and delineated in a particularly decisive form. At one level, as much is indicated by the very introduction of the generic term *"keter"* into the contemporary political lexicon as a description of a governmental demesne.[2] At another, it is illustrated by the elaborate precautions taken — by representatives of all three *ketarim* — to ensure the identification and preservation of their separate privileges and procedures. Both circumstances appear to reflect a degree of self-consciousness previously unparalleled and subsequently unsurpassed.

1.1 The *Keter Kehunah*

Self-awareness was a particularly predominant trait of the membership of the *keter kehunah*. Principally, this was due to the centrality of the Jerusalem Temple and its service for all Jewish life. There did exist other sanctuaries, notably the "house of Onias" in Alexandria and the temple of the Elephantine community at Yev, but these were always regarded as inferior edifices of no more than limited and local attraction. *The* holy place of the entire Jewish people was the Temple at Jerusalem. That was the shrine to which regular pilgrimage was made; that was the structure to which regular taxes were paid and generous (often lavish) gifts were donated.[3] Those priests who ministered within its precincts were recognized to be *edah*-wide officers in the truest sense, and tended to comport themselves accordingly.

Membership of the *keter kehunah* was dependent entirely upon geneology. The priesthood of the time, as has been pointed out, constituted

> a community the boundaries of which were irrevocable since they were laid down forever by natural descent. No one not

belonging to the group would be admitted to it; and no one belonging to it through legitimate birth could be excluded from it.[4]

Essentially, of course, that had always been the case. Ever since its inception under Aaron, the priesthood had been officially restricted to his male descendants; despite possible occasional lapses during the early monarchical period, the tradition seems generally to have been observed. Nevertheless, the Second Commonwealth did witness distinct developments of the theme. For one thing, the emphasis on lineage seems to have become more pronounced. As early as the first Return from exile under Zerubavel, certain families had been expelled from the priestly order precisely because of their inability to provide satisfactory family geneologies (Ezra 2:61-63; Neh. 7:63-65). By the time of Josephus (who was himself proud of his own priestly origins), family registers seem to have been deposited in public archives (Josephus, *Vita*, 1:6). Furthermore, ancient provisions respecting the purity of the members of the *keter kehunah* were also elaborated and more strictly defined. In some cases, this involved little more than a tightening of existing regulations that priests refrain from contact with corpses (Lev. 21:1-4, 11-12; Ezek. 44:25-27). In others, however, it took the form of novel restrictions on the type of woman whom they might marry — a development which sometimes necessitated an intensive study of family trees in order to ascertain that a prospective wife did indeed satisfy the required (geneological) criteria.[5]

Notwithstanding such elaborate measures, or perhaps because of them, there seems to have been no shortage of priests. On the contrary, the sheer size of their number (estimated at several thousand in 70 CE) generated two further developments. One was the division of *kohanim* into twenty-four *mishmarot* and *ma'amadot* ("circuits"), which rotated Temple service; the other was the heightening of the distinction between priests proper and *levi'im* (Levites). The latter, too, formed a closed clan based on family descent, but they were now officially designated as "support staff" in a great variety of Temple duties and offices and in the administration of priestly dues and offices. Their subordination was regularized in their division into distinct courses of service, which corresponded to the *mishmarot* of the *kohanim*.[6]

To a large extent, the successful functioning of this intricate machinery depended upon its strict supervision by accredited *keter kehunah* institutions and officers. Some such framework had manifestly existed during earlier periods. Nevertheless, here too the Second Commonwealth seems to have witnessed a process of specification which greatly strengthened the bureaucratic underpinnings of the domain, and thereby endowed it with a unity of direction and form. At the same time this development further refined the hierarchical structure always inherent in the *keter*, whose institutional framework (at least, in its ideal state) very much resembled a pyramid.

At the base of the structure stood the twenty-four *mishmarot*, each of which was headed by a *rosh ha-mishmar* and several subordinate *rashei batei av* (perhaps collectively known as *ziknei kohanim* — Mishnah, *Yoma* 1:5). The cultic activities of these groupings were, in turn, supervised by a permanent corps of Temple civil servants, collectively known as *memunim*, whose administrative functions ranged over the preparation of the devotion, the division of the priestly work-load, and the arrangement of musical (usually vocal) accompaniment to the various offerings and services. To these must be added the standing body of treasury officials, entitled *amarkalim* (at least seven) and *gizbarim* (at least three) who were charged with the collection and supervision of Temple dues and offerings, and the immediate subordinates of the *segan ha-kohanim* (captain of the Temple) who was responsible for order in and around its precincts.[7]

At the apex of the entire *keter kehunah* stood the *kohen gadol* (High Priest). In possession of the exclusive right to perform certain activities of supreme cultic significance (notably, the offering of incense on the Day of Atonement), he was expected to be particularly strict in the preservation of his genealogical pedigree and personal purity. The former requirement, at least, would appear to have been generally observed, with the result that most of the high priests of the period were drawn from a limited range of families within which the office was often hereditary.[8] This is probably the self-contained and oligarchic caste referred to by both Josephus (*Wars* 6:114) and the Mishnah (*Ohalot* 17:5) as the "sons of the high priests." By the beginning of the common era, at the very latest, it had come to constitute a substantial 'pool' of senior *keter kehunah* office holders and seekers: high priests prospective; high priests emeritus (*kohen she'avar*); high priests *in locus* (*merubeh begadim*); and, of course, high priests incumbent.[9]

1.2 The *Keter Malkhut*

In more senses than one, the high priests of the Second Commonwealth had a foot in two camps. While their cultic distinction made them the linchpin of the *keter kehunah*, the very importance attached to their office by Jews both inside and outside the confines of Judea also invested them with considerable influence within the *keter malkhut. Kohanim gedolim*, accordingly, had always been princes as well as priests, with the Jewish policy as a whole thus approximating the "theocracy" of Josephus' description (*Against Apion*, 2:165). As early as the middle of the Persian period (c. 380 BCE), high priests had been considered responsible for the administration of an autonomous Judea; they had also been regarded as the people's representatives in their dealings with the foreign suzerain. This situation had persisted throughout the dominion over *Eretz Israel* of both the Ptolemies and the Seleucids. Those Hasmoneans who assumed the titles of king as well as high priests did no more, in this view, than take the inherent opportunities of the situation to its logical, albeit extreme, conclusion.[10]

To say that is not, however, to suggest a complete blurring of all differences between the *keter kehunah* and the *keter malkhut* during the Second Commonwealth. On the contrary, what needs to be noted and emphasized are the distinctions preserved between the two domains. At the personal level, these were underscored by the fact that for the majority of the period the principal officer of the *keter malkhut* did not also lay claim to the title of *kohen gadol*. He (or she, in the case of Queen Salome), occupied an entirely different office, variously referred to as *peḥah, ethnarch, melekh* or *nasi*. Furthermore, even when the principle of the separation of powers was breached in practice, it was nevertheless retained in theory. As much is indicated by such coins as have survived from the Hasmonean period. These refer to only a singly personality, but are careful to point out that he stood at the apex of two distinct agencies of government.[11]

Somewhat more problematic is the evidence relating to the separate infrastructure of the *keter malkhut*. The sources, all of which have been filtered through various traditions and literary forms, defy both generic analysis and conventional categorization. They do nevertheless appear to concur in the conclusion that at no point in its history was the civil government of the Second Commonwealth conducted solely through and in the Temple. There always existed, in one form or another, distinct and constitutionally separate bodies responsible for the management of political affairs. Locally, these took the form of urban councils;[12] nationally, they consisted of a series of political senates located in Jerusalem which were endowed with as much jurisdiction over the Jewish people as contemporary circumstances would allow. Even if priests, and especially high priests, did sit on such bodies (or even chair their meetings), they did not do so by virtue of the cultic importance of their *keter kehunah* office. The essential criteria for the membership of the *keter malkhut* agencies were temporal influence and material possessions.[13]

The practice whereby *keter malkhut* representatives met in council had, of course, a long history prior to the establishment of the Second Commonwealth. Arguably it can be traced back to the meetings of the heads of the twelve tribes in the wilderness.[14] Less ambiguous is the evidence relating to the period of Ezra and Nehemiah, when the direction of communal affairs was largely entrusted to groups of "elders," "nobles," and "dignitaries" (the *horim* and *seganim* of Neh. 2:16; 4:8,13; 5:7; 7:5), who probably met on an *ad hoc* basis. By the Seleucid period, however, such meetings seem to have become more regular and to have been conducted within the formal structure of an assembly occasionally referred to as the *"Gerousia."*[15] It was at some (possibly early) point during the Hasmonean period that both the functions and the numbers of this body were further expanded. It then became known as the *"Sanhedrin"* — an assembly possessing extensive (sometimes absolute) judicial, executive and representative powers — and one which also acted as the city council of the capital.[16] It was, in turn, this quantum growth in responsibilities which further necessitated a regularization of council proceedings and the establishment of a stratified network of subsidiary civil courts (variously known to us from Mishnaic sources as the "lesser *Sanhedrin*" and *"batei din."*[17]

The *Gerousia* and the *Sanhedrin* were aristocratic and elitist in character. Although both claimed to represent the people (referred to as *Hever ha-Yehudim*; lit. "The Community of Jews," i.e., the Jewish Commonwealth in its entirety),[18] neither ever did so in a democratic manner. Membership, which was conventionally restricted to seventy or seventy-one males of legitimate Jewish descent, was conferred by co-option rather than election. Moreover, prospective candidates were usually drawn from the wealthy or otherwise influential classes of the land — a category which obviously included the high priests and their immediate circle, but was not restricted to that group. Such criteria are inherently transient; and were especially so in the volatile world of late antiquity. Hence, the composition of Judea's state councils was rarely constant. Only during the lengthy period of priestly hegemony under the Ptolemies and Seleucids were sessions of the *Gerousia* principally attended by *kohanim*, and independently chaired by the *kohen gadol*. But the stability thus engendered did not long survive the Maccabean revolt. It was, in fact, completely undermined by the subsequent emergence of two separate and non-priestly power bases: the Hasmonean royal court and the Pharisaic party. Elements of both circles tended, albeit in varying degrees, to demand entry into the *Sanhedrin*, whose composition altered accordingly. Even if the high priests did continue to act as nominal presidents of the body until 66 CE (as is generally held to be the case),[19] their real influence over the management of its affairs was probably secondary to that of political forces beyond their immediate control.

The primary weakness of the *keter malkhut* as thus institutionalized lay in the *Sanhedrin's* tendency to become the arena of political conflicts. Its proceedings, especially during the second half of the period, seem to have been always tense, often turbulent, and sometimes terminal. (Herod, for instance, is said to have murdered forty-five of its members, if not all of them, on his accession; Josephus, *Antiquities*, XIV, 9:4 and XV, 1:2.) Therein, however, also lay an intrinsic virtue of the institution. It was because its membership tended to reflect the balance of forces within the polity that it retained its status as the fulcrum of political activity and development. Control of the *Sanhedrin* was a prize worth fighting for because it was a prize worth winning. A commanding voice in its affairs constituted a recognition of present status. It was also an indispensable prerequisite of future authority.

1.3 The *Keter Torah*

As much was certainly appreciated by spokesmen for the *keter torah*. They therefore became increasingly assiduous in their pursuit of power within the *Sanhedrin* and increasingly insistent on their right to dictate the tenor and direction of its affairs.[20] Nevertheless, the intensity and unity with which these ends were pursued must be neither antedated nor exaggerated, for in terms of composition the *keter torah* was the most heterogeneous of the three domains. Later rabbinic portraits, which describe the *keter* as a fairly monolithic body of largely anonymous "sages," must clearly be treated with care.[21] They are indeed often contradicted by the Mishnaic sources themselves, which emphasize that the distinction of this domain lay, *inter alia*, in its characteristic as an open society. Admittance to its ranks depended entirely on scholastic merit and spiritual avocation. In comparison to these criteria, those of genetic accident (the distinguishing mark of the *kohanim*) or material advantage (the ultimate test of the *malkhut*) were considered relatively inconsequential. This was a situation which certainly endowed the *keter torah*, at least as represented by the Pharisees, with a large measure of popular support.[22] At the same time, however, it also permitted and encouraged the entry into the *keter* of various types and personalities: priests and paupers, manual laborers and miracle workers, scribes and ascetics.[23] It thus tended to deprive the domain of a true sense of cohesion.

Nevertheless, the *keter torah* was not, during the Second Commonwealth, so entirely amorphous as to be virtually non-existent. The domain was undoubtedly an articulated entity, in possession of a focus and perspective which resonated strongly throughout the polity. Its importance was embedded in the entire community's covenantal commitment to the observance of the God-given Mosaic Torah (a commitment confirmed as recently as the period of Ezra and Nehemiah; Neh. 8:10). Its centrality was further ensured by the memory of the zeal and self-sacrifice with which that undertaking had been reaffirmed by the Maccabees.[24] Every subsequent generation of the period, without exception, witnessed efforts to attain the kingdom of heaven (*malkhut shamayim*)[25] through the study, observance and transmission of the Torah — fields of activity which were quite distinct from those of the Temple cult and the royal court.

The problem lay in the development of separate institutions and officers with the *edah*-wide authority to articulate that purpose. It was from that perspective that the *keter torah* was, in this period, most chronically deficient. It possessed no independent and universally-recognized institutions which could counterbalance the bureaucratic efficiency of either the Temple or the *Sanhedrin*. Schools (*batei midrash* and *batei va'ad*) were of course developed; within their walls sages (*talmidei ḥakhamim*) developed novel means of scriptural analysis and exegesis (*derash*);

these, in turn, supplied the base for an entirely new corpus of procedures and enactments (*takkanot*) collectively known as the *halakhah*.[26] But these activities, although of seminal importance for the later development of rabbinic Judaism, were neither organized nor uniform. During the Second Commonwealth, it is worth repeating, the *keter torah* simply did not yet possess a stratified machinery for the regulation of its affairs.[27] Rather, it was a domain of cherished individuality and internecine strife. Distinct parties competed for superiority in both the manner and the matter of scriptural interpretation, with the result that tension between the Pharisees, the Sadducees and the Essenes became endemic. Even differences within the various groupings could be frequent, and sometimes violent.[28]

2. Intra-*Keter* Development

Of the many conclusions to be derived from the above sketch of the internal composition of the three *ketarim*, perhaps the most important is that none of them remained static. On the contrary, all exhibited characteristics of adaptability and change that were themselves responses to and reflections of various transformations in the state of contemporary Jewish society. To an extent, as much was to be expected. The Second Commonwealth period was, after all, one of the most turbulent in all Jewish history. For one thing, it witnessed successive changes of regime. The independent Jewish state established by Simon the Maccabee in 134 BCE lasted less than eighty years; with the unopposed entry of Pompey's troops into Jerusalem in 63 BCE, Judea was transformed into a vassal polity; under Herod (who reigned from 37 to 4 BCE), it became a puppet kingdom. By the time of his death, Palestine (to use the Roman term) was for all intents and purposes already a subject province. The failure of the Great Rebellion of 66-70 CE merely confirmed the fact. Secondly, and throughout this chronicle of political turmoil, Jewish society also experienced severe socio-economic dislocation; to which must thirdly be added the prevalence of religious dissonance. The first circumstance fostered the emergence of distinct political parties, each of which advocated conflicting policies of accommodation with, or opposition to, the dominant foreign power. The second generated conflicts within and between rural and urban Jewish society, and fissures within its class structure. The third gave rise to the formation of distinct religious sects, each of which posited markedly different views of the Jewish condition — past, present, and future.[29]

Even singly, any one of these developments might have been expected to affect the internal texture of each of the three *ketarim*. What is significant about the period of the Second Jewish Commonwealth, however, is that they occurred jointly and in a highly irregular fashion. The changes which characterized the period were seismic rather than incremental; hence they cannot be described in terms of a linear development. Put another way, the march of events between 145 BCE and 70 CE did not permit the three *ketarim* to progress evenly from one stage of development to another. Instead, the vicissitudes of the period generated an entire series of crisis spasms, during the course of which the *ketarim* jerked along an uneven course replete with irregularities and uncertainties.

2.1 The *Keter Kehunah*

This situation did not affect each of the *ketarim* at the same juncture, nor indeed in equal measure. Their impact was least felt within the domain of the *keter kehunah*, which enjoyed the dual benefits of a caste-like insistence on the inviolability of its personnel and a strictly hierarchical organization. Such changes as did take place in this *keter* (at least until the hiatus of 70 CE) accordingly tended to consist of marginal realignments within the traditional framework rather than its fundamental rearrangement. At one level, they took the form of the development of a distinct pecking-order between the twenty-four *mishmarot*, and of ranks of distinction within individual courses. At another, they were expressed in frequent changes in the incumbency of the office of *kohen gadol*, appointments to which were increasingly apt to depend upon the blatant exercise of political muscle by the principal representatives of the *keter malkhut*.[30]

These developments, although limited in consequence, did have important repercussions. They contributed, for instance, to severe social and political conflicts within the priestly order — so much so that the priesthood was divided on the question of revolt in 66 CE (Josephus, *Wars*, ii 17:2-4). They also led to a severe decline in the popular prestige of the *keter*.[31] Nevertheless, they seem to have been brought about by the mundane pressures of contemporary economic forces and political circumstances; they did not reflect novel *keter kehunah* articulations of constitutional doctrine. Class conflicts within the order, for instance, can be attributed almost entirely to growing differentials in the incomes of the metropolitan-based and rural priesthood, most markedly expressed in the inequitable distribution of priestly dues and tithes.[32] Likewise, the intense interest of the ruling civil power in the incumbency of the high priesthood was a direct consequence of the political sensitivity of the latter office (and, it may be assumed, of the size of its emoluments). The Hasmonean response to this situation, as has been noted, was to combine the principal positions of both the *keter kehunah* and the *keter malkhut* in one sovereign body. Their successors — Herod, the Roman procurators, *and* the revolutionaries of 66 CE — merely adopted the alternative course of playing fast and loose with the principle of hereditary succession in order to ensure the appointment to the high priesthood of their own nominees.[33] This expedient may have broken the letter of the law,[34] but it did not indicate a fundamental desire to alter the classical structure of the *keter kehunah* in its entirety.

It is a testimony to the resilience of the domain that it was even able to survive the destruction of the Temple in 70 CE. Traumatic though that event undoubtedly was, its effects were not immediately debilitating. Some cultic rites might thereafter still have been performed on the Temple Mount; if so, a permanent priesthood on traditional lines would have been retained.[35] Far less ambiguous is the evidence which indicates that the reconstruction of the Temple in its original form remained a highly practical aspiration of all Jewish political activity — at least until 135 CE.[36] That is one reason why post-Destruction sages took such care to preserve the traditions relating to the privileges and structure of the *keter kehunah*, and even to discourage the emigration of priestly families from *Eretz Israel*.[37] That, too, explains the reappearance of a *kohen gadol* (one Elazar), during the ill-starred revolt led by Bar Kokhba.[38] Indeed, not until the fall of Betar in 135 CE were the aspirations thus articulated finally delegated to the realm of eschatological hopes, with the traditional *kohanim* reduced to the status of constitutional fossils deprived of all but honorific duties.[39]

2.2 The *Keter Malkhut*

Like the *keter kehunah*, the *keter malkhut* also possessed a lengthy tradition of institutional expression, with roots deeply embedded in Israel's biblical past. Nevertheless, it was not surrounded with quite the same aura of awe. In part, this was due to the thorny question of pedigree. An institutionalized monarchy had not been established until the time of Saul, and even then only as a grudging Divine concession. The concept of a dynastic succession was of an even later date.[40] More pertinent was the issue of status. From its inception, the rights and privileges of the monarchy had been carefully circumscribed (Deut. 17:14-20; I Sam. 10:25); even the title of the incumbent had been a matter of some doubt. Saul, after all, had been appointed *nasi*, not *melekh* (and the distinction was important), and it was the latter title which had been revived by such restoration prophets as Ezekiel and Zerubavel (e.g., Ezek. 34:23-24). Still more crucial was the contentious question of continuity. Even during the biblical periods, the principle that the *keter malkhut* was reserved solely for persons of Davidic descent had sometimes been violated. Indeed, Divine sanction had expressly been granted to the most successful secessionist of all — Jereboam ben Navat (I Kings 2: 29-39). By the time of the Return, the entire notion seems to have been put into cold storage, if not entirely abandoned.[41] Even if legitimate Davidic descendants did survive into the Second Commonwealth (a supposition on which Liver's researches have cast considerable doubt),[42] they were clearly too ineffectual to lay claim to the preeminent status which their illustrious forebears had enjoyed in the sphere of the *keter malkhut*. Principal offices in that domain had in any case gone elsewhere: to foreign appointees, such as Nehemiah; to high priests, such as Simon the Just; or to successful revolutionaries, such as the Maccabees. For all the individual distinction of these personalities, from an institutional perspective they constituted a motley collection. Even their official titles changed with disconcerting rapidity. Nehemiah was a *peḥah*; Simon the Maccabee, an *ethnarch* (in Hebrew, *nasi* — the title also assumed by Bar Kokhba); the official designation of the later Hasmoneans was *melekh* (although they rarely employed the Hebrew term).

There was more to these changes than mere distinctions of nomenclature. They also reflected alterations in the scope of individual franchises and the degree to which external (i.e., non-Jewish) influences periodically affected the style of government. Here, too, the comparison with the *keter kehunah* is instructive. Throughout the period, the latter could legitimately claim exclusive authority in cultic matters which remained indisputably Jewish. The boundaries of the *keter malkhut*, however, were far more fluid. Its political independence was, most obviously, for the majority of the period subject to varying degrees of foreign intervention and control. Equally important, if somewhat less blatant, were influences of a cultural nature. Although the Maccabees had risen to power as the leaders of a coalition opposed to the intrusion into Jewish life of Hellenism and all that it stood for, their successors did not uniformly retain that tradition.[43] Their style of government, their personal mores — even their language — in all essentials became increasingly Hellenistic. Agrippa I (41-44 CE), perhaps the only Hasmonean to attempt to reverse the trend,[44] is an exception who proves the rule. For most of the Second Commonwealth, the *keter malkhut* was the least intrinsically *Jewish* of all the three domains.

It would undoubtedly be too facile to attribute this development entirely to "assimilationist" tendencies within the ruling elites of the *keter malkhut*. Note must also be taken of two other contributory causes. One was the demographically cosmopolitan nature of the territories which were either conquered by the rulers of Judea (notably Hyrcanus I and Yannai) or given to them as gifts by their Roman protectors (as were the cities of Gaza, Samaria and Gadera to Herod by Augustus). Few of the inhabitants of these areas had any sympathy at all for Jewish traditions of government. The vast majority demanded to be treated as citizens of a Hellenistic *polis*.[45] To this must be added, secondly, the more general ambience of the times. Power in the fragmented, unstable and cruel world of the Second Jewish Commonwealth could not be won, nor kept, by the exercise of the conventional Hebraic virtues of tolerance, magnanimity and consensual compromise. These qualities, when manifested in the *keter malkhut*, undoubtedly marked out their possessor for complimentary historical regard (as manifested in later Mishnaic traditions concerning Agrippa; e.g., Mishnah, *Sotah* 7:8), but for little else. Those who wished to secure or augment their positions — and the list includes Yannai, Herod, and such leaders of the Sicarii as Menachem — seemed to require other attributes, principal among which was a temperamental affinity for ruthless despotism and a near-megalomaniac capacity for low intrigue. Not the least of the problems of the *keter malkhut* throughout the period lay in its inability to maintain an equilibrium between these two extremes. It was this failure which, to a large extent, deprived the domain as a whole of institutional and cultural continuity, and thus condemned it to a depressing cycle of internal convulsions.

2.3 The *Keter Torah*

Developments within the *keter torah*, although somewhat less tortuously dramatic, were certainly more influential; for it was during the period of the Second Commonwealth that normative rabbinic Judaism began to assume the form later to be consolidated in the Mishnah. There is hardly a chapter in that work which does not make explicit reference to decisions, opinions and traditions which it dates prior to 70 CE. Although the texts themselves are often anachronistic and occasionally inexact (sometimes both), the general thrust of their historical argument still remains valid. It was from this period that the *keter torah* inherited many of the procedures, premises and terminology which were subsequently to become its hallmarks. Later generations embellished, refined and universalized these traditions, but they did not invent them.[46]

Nevertheless, the antecedents of the mishnaic *keter torah* cannot be traced along a clearly defined continuum, stretching in an uninterrupted and magisterial line as far back as Moses. Patently inadmissible are such excursi as are to be found in Mishnah *Avot* 1:1 and *Eduyot* 8:7, which chart a linear progression from the written to the oral law. So, too, is the midrashic portrait of Moses, "our rabbi," as the embodiment of Pharisaic wisdom. Statements of that sort, although perhaps useful as political propaganda on behalf of the *keter torah*, constitute very inadequate history. They disregard the heterogeneity of this *keter*, to which reference has already been made. They also discount the corollary discontinuities in its development. In so doing, and no less tendentiously, they paper over the extent of dissension and dissonance which were characteristic of the *keter torah* prior to the emergence of rabbinic Judaism as its commanding force.

Any discussion of the geneology of the *keter torah* during the Second Commonwealth must begin by noting the generally felt absence of a strong tradition of prophecy throughout the period.[47] This marked a crucial break with the past. It deprived the *keter* of the means of expression which it had characteristically employed hitherto, and of its traditional exponents and instruments. These could not easily, or speedily, be replaced. The phenomenon of prophecy had, after all, been a pneumatic experience limited to the very few inspired and charismatic personalities granted sudden, and highly irregular, flashes of Divine revelation. If the phenomenon had now ceased, or at least had become less manifest, how was the Torah to be mediated and expounded? What was to prevent charlatans and fanatics from claiming legitimate succession to the prophets' mantle?

To a large extent, the history of the *keter torah* during the Second Commonwealth is the record of its attempt to wrestle with these dilemmas. Such was the number and variety of potential solutions that they defy generic analysis. However, through the thicket of conflicting claims, two broad alignments can be distinguished. One embraced the view that prophesy persisted: God continued to communicate with a select group of human worthies (the list includes Pharisees as well as early Christians),[48] all of whom loudly proclaimed His messages of dire warnings and messianic hope. This, however, was a minority attitude. The majoritarian position on the issue was that prophecy had indeed ceased, and that the *keter torah* had therefore necessarily passed into other hands. It could be argued that this had been apparent as early as the time of Ezra. By assuming the title of *sofer* (scribe), by appointing *dayyanim* (judges), and by taking it upon himself *lidrosh et ha-Torah* ("to expound the Torah," Ezra 7:10, 25), Ezra had established a complete framework of novel *keter torah* authorities. He had also forever severed that domain from its prophetic roots and origins.[49]

The latter position itself afforded an opportunity for the development of two further, subsidiary approaches. One posited the *keter kehunah* as the legitimate heir of the prophets' duties and functions. This was not altogether far-fetched. Ezra, after all, had himself been a priest (although he does not seem to have played upon the fact). What is more, a close — if also selective — reading of some of the biblical texts (e.g., Deut. 33:10) indicated that his predecessors among the *kohanim* had traditionally performed some teaching functions which were quite distinct from their activities as part of the process of constitutional adjudication. Added to this was the interest which their Temple offices gave them in the preservation of the pure text of the Holy Law. Even if priests were not themselves *soferim*, they were certainly in a position to supervise such scribal activities as the authentic reproduction of the sacred text. As such, they were ideally placed to become its masters.[50] Essentially, that seems to have been the position taken by Ben Sira. Himself probably a priest, he maintained that the Scriptures could only be interpreted through Aaronide eyes, and hence from the perspective of the *keter kehunah*.[51] With some modifications, the Sadducees put forward much the same argument. The latter, it has been pointed out, were not exclusively priests; neither were all priests (nor even all high priests) Sadducees. But the attitude of this camp as a whole towards the Torah can nevertheless be classified as priestly in its intrinsically conservative dismissal of any precept or teaching not explicitly found in the Holy Scriptures. In their view, it was the task of the *keter torah* to pronounce literal interpretations of the Law, not to cultivate either novel doctrines (such as the resurrection of the dead) or allusive scriptural interpretations.[52]

It was precisely the latter, however, which the Pharisees took for a compulsory *keter torah* function. They shared Sadducean reservations with regard to miracle-workers and charismatics, even those nominally members of their own party.[53] Where they differed was in their conception of the nature of biblical exegesis, the methods whereby it was to be carried out, and the persons authorized to do so. The Torah, they held, had to be nurtured by an intensive and scholarly search for new biblical nuances and inferences, and by the enrichment of a parallel corpus (unknown to the Scriptural cannon) which they termed the *torah she be'al peh* (Oral Law).[54] Neither process was simply the mechanistic consequence of the termination of prophecy. Rather, both had in a very specific way caused prophecy and prophets to become redundant. For its elucidation, the Torah need no longer depend on the occasional and irregular flash of prophetic inspiration granted to a few. Rather, recourse could be had to the intellectual attainments of the many, who achieved an understanding of Scripture's true meanings by virtue of their scholarly application and academic deliberations. The latter possessed a legitimacy of their own. Hence they were impervious to extraneous pressures, even if they took the form of interjections by a *bat kol* ("Heavenly voice").[55]

It must be emphasized that until 70 CE (at least) the Pharisees were, as their name suggests, a minority party. In all likelihood, they were originally a break-away faction from the grand Maccabean coalition of anti-Hellenizers, with a formal membership which probably hovered around 6,000 heads of families. Moreover, they tended to emphasize their exclusiveness by forming *havurot* (fraternities), whose members were enjoined to the strict observance of ritual purity.[56] Nevertheless, and unlike the Essenes, the Pharisees never became an inward-looking sect. On the contrary, they from the first wished to rule over all Israel in the spirit of the Oral Law. Thus, at an early stage in their history, they formulated a program which would enable them to do so ("Be moderate in judgement; set up many scholars/disciples; place a hedge around the Law" — Mishnah, *Avot* 1:1)[57] To the same end, they also established an embryonic hierarchy of ordained authorities[58] and a rudimentary framework of organizations and consultation (perhaps originally known as the *Anshei Kenesset Ha-Gedolah* — "Men of the Great Assembly" — later called a *Sanhedrin, Antiquities*, XIII, 10:5).[59] It was the fact that their popular success — to which Josephus attests — did not bring in its train the desired measure of executive power, which turned them into a politically militant party. As such, they not only persisted in their long-standing feud with the Sadducees and Essenes. They also, and with even greater force, threw themselves into a struggle for the defense of the *keter torah* (as they understood it) against the encroachments of the other two domains.

3. Inter-*Keter* Relations

Relations between the *ketarim* were decisively influenced by rivalries within them. The latter impelled spokesmen for each *keter* to sharpen their perception of their constitutional franchises, and thus to arrive at articulated conclusions regarding their place and function within the polity as a whole. In this way, they generated a series of debates between the *ketarim*, all of which appealed to competing interpretations of the proper form and structure of authority in the Jewish polity. Notwithstanding differences of tone, the theme of such disputes was remarkably uniform. Individually, each *keter* (through its representatives) posited its inherent and Divinely-sanctioned superiority to the others. Consequently, each also felt entitled to impinge upon spheres of activity which were not intrinsically its own, while at the same time jealously guarding its sovereignty within its own particular demesne. Thus perceived, the political gyrations of the period were essentially constitutional in focus and in thrust. Transcending the specifics of individual squabbles over the exercise of executive power lay a more fundamental struggle for its control. At issue, often implicitly but sometimes explicitly, was not the matter of government but the competence of its separate component agencies to wield jurisdictional authority in a variety of spheres. Not the least important aspect of the Second Commonwealth is the evidence which it provides for attempts to conclude this debate to the advantage of one *keter* or another.

The inter-*keter* struggles of the period were often ferocious. Nevertheless, they were generally conducted within parameters which were strictly circumscribed and, given the violence of the times, remarkably restricted. The weapons employed were those of usurpation rather than destruction. No accredited spokesman for any of the *ketarim* explicitly rejected the notion that the others possessed authority in constitutionally legitimated domains of government. Hence, at no point in the period was one *keter* ever eliminated by another (or by a combination of the other two). What can be observed, however, are various types of putative co-option. Principal instruments of one *keter* attempted (sometimes, and for limited periods, successfully so) to attain commanding authority within the polity by posing as the repositories of two domains. By thus amalgamating prerogatives and wearing, as it were, two crowns, they contrived to neutralize the constitutional influence of the third and to subject it to their own particular will.

At this level of analysis, the most critical issue of the epoch was the identification and maintenance of a proper equilibrium between the three *ketarim*. Something of the sort seemed to have been established at the genesis of the period, in 145 BCE, with the conclusion of a covenant between Simon the Maccabee and a great assembly of priests, people and *nesi'ei ha-am* (magistrates, lit. "princes of the people"; I Macc. 14:27-49). Under the arrangement thus constituted, the *keter malkhut* devolved upon Simon (whose heirs were to succeed him as *nasi* "until there should arise a true prophet"); the *keter torah* was entrusted to the *hasidim* who had inspired the original revolt against Seleucid Hellenism and its Jewish supporters; the *keter kehunah* remained the preserve of the priesthood. Each domain was thus separated from the others, with which it shared a position of equality.

3.1 The *Keter Malkhut* and *Keter Kehunah*

This situation was too delicate to last very long. Its balance was undermined within one generation when Simon's successors (now known as Hasmoneans) began to act as high priests.[60] It was utterly destroyed once they also assumed the title of king, a development which articulated and reflected the aggrandizement of the *keter malkhut* consequent to the establishment of a powerful state bureaucracy and the employment of an efficient mercenary army. Once thus set in motion, the process could not even be arrested by the physical demise of the original Maccabean line, for whom the Romans substituted Antipater and his descendants. Admittedly, the new appointments did restore the formal separation of the *keter kehunah* from the *keter malkhut*. Antipater's family, originally Idumean converts to Judaism, were manifestly not of priestly descent, but this circumstance did nothing to reinstate the original constitutional balance. The high priesthood remained firmly under *keter malkhut* aegis and incumbency of the office was a matter of Roman approval (if not appointment). Thus deprived of constitutional independence, the *keter kehunah* seemed to have become but an appendage to the *keter malkhut*.

Precisely what the *kohanim* made of this situation in its early stages will probably never be known. The existent sources are sketchy. They do, however, indicate at least some priestly dissatisfaction with a position of subjection to the Hasmonean royal court. An unfavorable response was probably to have been expected. As has been seen, the period immediately prior to the Maccabean revolt had been one of virtually unchallanged *keter kehunah* hegemony. Its claims to *edah*-wide supremacy had then been articulated in a particularly pungent form. That, indeed, had been the background against which Ben Sira had composed his idealistic portrait of Aaron, stressing not merely the independence of his office but also its scope:

> Moses ordained him, and anointed him with holy oil; it was an everlasting covenant for him and for his descendants all the days of heaven, to minister to the Lord and serve as priest and bless His people in His name...to make atonement for the people. In His commandments, He gave him authority in statutes and judgments, to teach Jacob the testimonies, and to enlighten Israel with His Law (Eccles. 45:15).

Hasmonean encroachments notwithstanding, these doctrines survived into the Second Commonwealth. One indication is provided by the petition presented to Pompey in 67 BCE. At a time when internecine strife had so weakened the Hasmonean royal house that a change in the structure of government seemed feasible, it was the specific request of the petitioners that they be allowed to return to their "ancient priestly rule" (Josephus, *Antiquities* XIV, 3:2).[61]

Far more persistent, if also more sectarian, was the attitude of the Essenes. Although initially part of Mattathias's anti-Hellenistic coalition, members of this group had very quickly been disillusioned by the Maccabean assumption of high priestly office. Thereafter, their opposition to the "wicked priest" and his successors remained a constant feature of the period.[62] There was more to their hatred than personal animosity. Also at issue was the independence of the *keter kehunah* in its pristine form. As much is indicated by the structure of communal government ordained for the community (*Yaḥad*) by its own Teacher of Righteousness in its place of eventual settlement at Qumran. Only in an eschatological situation did the true Law of the Covenant (as understood by the sect) provide for some communal affairs to be entrusted to a superior lay leader — a royal messiah referred to as the *nasi*.[63] Until such time, however, supreme authority was vested with the priests. It was the sons of Zadok (also referred to as the sons of Aaron) who possessed the final word on matters of doctrine, justice and purity (IQS 5:2; 9:7), and a priest-president-general (*ha-kohen asher yufkad al ha-rabim* — CD 14:6-12) who presided over the various courts, lay and clerical, which enforced the sect's strict code of purity and moral conduct.[64] The significance of this situation surely exceeds the implication that it represented "a significant and potentially subversive claim for the religious over the worldly arm."[65] The community code in fact constituted a microcosmic reflection of the Essene conception of proper Jewish government, within which the *keter kehunah* was to have the predominant voice.

The dramatic process whereby the Dead Sea Scrolls were discovered and deciphered has perhaps led to an exaggerated estimation of the strength of the Essenes. A more sober view suggests that they were always a minority, even within the ranks of the *keter kehunah*.[66] Most members of this domain were probably far less militant; some actively collaborated with the Hasmoneans, most were content to be fellow-travellers. Whatever the obvious material reasons for this choice, it could also be justified by an inverted perception of the history of the times. The Hasmonean period, it was possible to argue, had not witnessed the subjection of the *keter kehunah* to the *keter malkhut* but, rather, the incorporation of the *keter malkhut* into the *keter kehunah*. To defend the monarchy against the dual challenge of non-Jewish encroachment and Jewish dissent was, in this view, also to defend the independence of the Temple. Both institutions were vital to the defense of the state and its civil religion; representatives of both had therefore to adopt a policy of mutual support in the *Sanhedrin*. It was this outlook which lay behind the alliance of the lay and priestly aristocracy which became known as the Sadducean party.

It has already been pointed out that in matters of scriptural exegesis and religious doctrine the Sadducees claimed to speak from the domain of the *keter torah*. As a political grouping, however, they represented the interests of the *keter kehunah*; indeed, even the name of the party was derived from the priest Zadok who had been promised theocratic primacy in the book of Ezekiel (Ezek. 43-44). *Kohanim*, accordingly, constituted the most significant and vocal elements in Sadducean councils, and their importance increased once Herod had virtually wiped out the old Hasmonean nobility.[67] Thereafter, their weight within the government of Judea also steadily grew. *Sefer ha-Gezerot* ("The Book of Decrees," high priestly ordinances regulating punishments for those defying their ordinances) was rigorously enforced (Josephus, *Ant.* XVI, 1-5); and the independence of separate priestly courts was vigorously upheld.[68] The ground thus gained was not suddenly relinquished once the Romans established a system of direct rule. On the contrary, the evidence from Josephus has been interpreted to indicate that the *kohanim* reasserted their pre-Maccabean prerogatives throughout the period of the procurators, against whose deficiencies they were prepared to act by means of diplomacy, delegation, bribery and — at the very last — by defiance. Their ultimate eclipse by the extremist Zealots must not, therefore, be allowed to conceal their initial leadership of the provisional revolutionary government of 66 CE.[69] Even at that late date they remained committed to the notion that the government of the polity, in all its activities, had to remain the preserve of the *keter kehunah*.

3.2 The *Keter Torah*

Pharisaic opposition to the political pretensions of the *keter kehunah*, as thus expressed, took the form of an aggressive exposition of the constitutional claims of the *keter torah*. It is true that these were not formulated in a continuous or systematic manner. As Neusner (in particular) has insistently pointed out, care must be taken to distinguish between the various layers of Pharisaism and its diverse stages of development. Moreover, note must be taken of the provenance of the available texts. For the most part,

these date from a period later than 70 CE and constitute a version
of events undoubtedly colored by the triumph thereafter of a Pharisaic *keter torah*, which the sources were designed to justify and
extoll. Nevertheless, it can be argued that sufficient traces of earlier materials have remained to piece together a picture of the
principal themes of the Second Commonwealth period.[70] They
might also permit the extrapolation of consistencies in approach to
matters of constitutional import. From this point of view, the
Pharisees were perhaps less volatile than is sometimes claimed.
For no significant length of time did the majority of that party
adopt the passive stance of withdrawal, speaking exclusively to —
and for — the members of their own fraternity.[71] More commonly,
theirs was a message which was designed to embrace the entire
community and to affect its politics as well as its piety. Dividing
the Pharisees and Sadducees, therefore, was far more than the
dictates of either religious tenets or economic interests.[72] Portraits
of the Pharisees which depict their aims as essentially spiritual
and chiliastic (if not entirely so) would accordingly seem to be
distortions.[73] By thus accentuating only one part of the Pharisaic
program, they would appear to do violence to its central, political
thrust.

Of the many constitutional arguments which might be dis-
tilled from later collections of Pharisaic teachings, two seem to be
particularly pertinent to an understanding of developments during the Second Commonwealth period. The first was that the union
of the *keter malkhut* and the *keter kehunah* under the Hasmoneans violated the constitutional norm of *ketaric* balance. The
second was that the *keter torah* was inherently superior to the other
domains. Logically (and perhaps also chronologically) these two
arguments could be distinct. They therefore deserve to be treated
separately.

Reference to a required separation of powers between the *keter
kehunah* and the *keter malkhut* are scattered throughout rabbinic
literature. In some cases they consist of oblique *halakhic* regulations emphasizing the distinctions in the prerogatives of the two
domains.[74] In others, they constitute eclectic *aggadic* embellishments of biblical motifs which stress the Divinely-ordained denial of a duality of powers, even to such exceptional figures as
Moses.[75] They are most pronounced, however, in those talmudic
passages which purport to reconstruct events as they actually occurred during the period of the Second Commonwealth itself. Indeed, it is one of these (T.B. *Kiddushin* 66a) which contains a

declaration encapsulating the entire thrust of initial *keter torah* resistance to the Hasmonean assumption of the two other crowns. As such, it might serve as a prooftext for this aspect of Pharisaic political philosophy. "Suffice yourself with the *keter malkhut*," leaders of the party are said to have admonished Yannai (or Hyrcanus I) "and leave the *keter kehunah* to Aaron and his sons."[76]

Implicit in this statement is the second plank in the Pharisaic program: that the *keter torah* was in any case the superior of the three domains. Indeed, it was this facet of their own franchise which authorized the Pharisees thus to pass judgment on their king and high priest. The Hasmoneans, they could claim, did not possess an absolute and unconditional right to either crown, let alone to both. They held office only by virtue of the charters of authorization contained in the Torah, upon whose faithful observance (as interpreted by the instruments of the *keter torah*) ultimately depended both their incumbency and its succession. This was an aggressive doctrine, and one far more appropriate to contemporary political affairs than was the knotty problem of the Hasmonean assumption of a title originally reserved to the Davidic line.[77] The Pharisees, in effect, relegated the issue of the precise locus of power to a position subsidiary to the question of its conferment; who might appoint incumbents to the *keter malkhut* and *keter kehunah*, they argued, was ultimately more important than who might wear the crown. In that way, they projected an image of the *keter torah* as the arbiter of constitutional government in its entirety.[78]

Once such a hierarchy of the *ketarim* had been established, various consequences, all of them revolutionary, seemed logically to follow. In the long term, the hypothesis of *keter torah* supremacy could lead to a complete revision of Jewish history, and to the reconstruction of a chain of tradition from which the other *ketarim* were pointedly excluded.[79] Their immediate practical effect was no less dramatic. By the time of Yoḥanan ben Zakkai (at the latest) — and hence before the destruction of the Temple — the Pharisees had begun persistently to proclaim the rights of the *keter torah* to interfere in the day-to-day affairs of even so sacrosanct a domain as *keter kehunah*. The sons of Aaron, they maintained, could still exercise a cultic monopoly within the Temple; but the procedures whereby they did so had to be in strict accordance with ordinances regulated in the extra-priestly councils of the Pharisaic *keter torah*.[80]

Thus stated, there was more to the Pharisaic program than an attempt to learn some of the priestly tricks of the Temple trade, whose secrets the *kohanim* had hitherto been careful to guard.[81] Neither was it simply a matter of compelling priests to follow Pharisaic stipulations on such niceties as the precise dress of the Levites (Josephus, *Antiquities*, XX, 216-218) or the exact form of water libation on the festival of Sukkot (*Mishnah, Sukkah*, 4:9). At stake, rather, was the rule over Israel's holiest possession and the exclusion from that sanctuary of all persons (including *kohanim*) who did not accept Pharisaic rulings. That is why the Pharisees took such elaborate care over the publication of their own rituals (Mishnah, *Menaḥot*, 10:3). That, too, is why they were adamant in their insistence that opponents of their views be bluntly humiliated.[82] The underlying purpose of such actions was the exercise and demonstration of political power in its most naked form. As much is indicated by the admonition to the *kohen gadol* (on the night of Yom Kippur, no less) that he in effect constituted no more than a "delegate" of the Pharisaic *bet din* (Mishnah, *Yoma*, 1:5).

The destruction of the Temple in 70 CE deprived the *keter kehunah* of the opportunity to formulate a cogent response to such statements of *keter torah* hegemony. Bereft of their principal focus of power, its representatives were no longer in a position to contest the growing influence of the local synagogue service as a possible substitute for the centralized Temple rite.[83] Neither could they defend the exclusivity of their own rigid observance of the laws of ritual cleanliness. The Pharisees, however, experienced no such restraints. Even before the destruction of the Temple they had posited the notion of "the priesthood of all Israel," to the membership of which any Jew could gain entry by the perpetual observance of precisely those rites which the priests considered exclusively their own.[84] After that event, and especially during the period subsequent to the failure of the Bar Kokhba revolt, they pushed the implications of their premises even further. They then came close to positing not merely the superiority of the *keter torah*, but the virtual superfluity of the other two crowns. The Temple was of course still an object of high esteem; indeed, without it the Jewish polity was patently deficient. So, too, was the monarchy; although the messianic emphasis was henceforth decidedly to be on a Davidic king and not a Hasmonean pretender. But, as operational franchises, both could almost be left in the abeyance to which they had been so cruelly condemned by an angry Providence. "The shift," as Neusner has put it, "would be from a perspective founded upon the Temple Mount to a vision formed within the plane of Israel, from a cultic to a communal conception, and from a center at the locative point of the altar, to a system resting upon the utopian character of the nation as a whole."[85]

It was on this basis that representatives of the *keter torah* could claim the right to possession of some of the emoluments originally apportioned to the priests.[86] More significantly, it was also within that context that the study of the law could be raised to a level of sanctity which had formerly pertained solely to cultic activities.[87] Nor was the *keter malkhut* immune to similar encroachments. On earth, the sages took upon themselves the prerogative of debating the pros and cons of the constitutional powers of the principal instrument of that domain.[88] In the heavenly tribunal, rabbinic "elders" (*zekenim*) would certainly take their rightful place as the legitimate successors to King David's heirs.[89] The wheel, so it seemed, had come full circle. By thus claiming to embrace the other two domains, the *keter torah* had done much to upset the very *ketaric* balance in whose defense its spokesmen had originally done battle with the Hasmoneans and the Sadducees.

Conclusion

Eventually, this new situation was itself to change. Divisions within the ranks of the *keter torah* were to appear as early as the first generation after Bar Kokhba. Conflict between the *nesi'im* and the *ḥakhamim* became frequent in *Eretz Israel*, as did tensions between the *Reish Galuta* (Exilarch) and *Rashei Yeshivot* (heads of the academies) in *Bavel*. These developments resurrected many of the earlier distinctions between the *keter malkhut* and the *keter torah*. To a more limited extent, they also allowed for a minor resurgence in the self-awareness of the *keter kehunah*. They thus contributed to the further evolution of all three domains, and to the resilience of their triangular relationship.

Nevertheless, matters did not simply revert to the *status quo ante*. The experiences of the Second Jewish Commonwealth had been too particular to permit their repetition. As far as the three *ketarim* were concerned, the period cannot therefore be regarded simply as another link in their chain of evolution. Rather, it might properly be seen as a watershed in their histories. It had been then that the notion of these three domains had resonated with particular force, and then that their mutual interaction had proven to be particularly consequential. In both respects, the period constituted a crucial stage in their development.

Notes

1. Of the many synoptic studies now available, particularly useful are: M. Avi-Yonah (ed.), *The World History of the Jewish People*: First Series, vol. 7, "The Herodian Period" (Jerusalem, 1975) and vol. 8, "Society and Religion in the Second Temple Period" (Jerusalem, 1977); S. Safrai and M. Stern (eds.), *Compendia Rerum Iudaicarum ad Novum Testamentum*, Section One: "The Jewish People in the First Century" (2 vols., Assen, 1974); E. Schürer, *The History of the Jewish People in the Age of Jesus Christ* (a new English version revised and edited by G. Vermes and F. Millar; 2 vols., Edinburgh, 1973-1979); S. Zeitlin, *The Rise and Fall of the Judean State* (3 vols., Philadelphia, 1968-69).

2. Although the root KTR does occur in the Old Testament (e.g., Judges 20:43), it does not designate a crown until the Book of Esther. The rabbinic preference for the term *keter* over such synonyms as *nezer, mitznefet* and *atarah*, and the symbolism perhaps intended, merits separate study. See this author's article *"Keter* as a Jewish Political Symbol: Origins and Implications," *Jewish Political Studies Review*, vol. 1 (1989).

3. S. Safrai, "Relations between the Diaspora and the Land of Israel," *Compendia Rerum*, vol. 1, pp. 184-187.

4. Schürer, *History*, vol. 2, p. 239.

5. Mishnah, *Kiddushin* 4:3, 3-5, cf. Lev. 21:708. In general, J. Jeremias, *Jerusalem in the Time of Jesus* (New York, 1969), and M.D. Herr, "Yerushalayim, ha-Mikdash, veha-Avodah Bimtziut uve-Toda'ah Bimei ha-Bayit ha-Sheni," *Perakim be-Toldot Yerushalayim Bimei Bayit Sheni* (eds. U. Oppenheimer, et al., Jerusalem, 1981), p. 174.

6. Mishnah, *Ta'anit* 4:2; in general, Schürer, History, vol. 2, pp. 250-256.

7. H.D. Mantel, "The High Priesthood and the *Sanhedrin* in the Time of the Second Temple," *World History*, vol. 7, pp. 273-274; S. Safrai, "The Temple and the Divine Service," *idem.*, pp. 284-323.

8. E.M. Smallwood, "High Priests and Politics in Roman Palestine," *Journal of Theological Studies* 13 (1962), pp. 15, 31-34. On the possibility that the *kohen gadol* was elected by a limited clique

of fellow priests, G. Alon, "Le-Toldot ha-Kehunah ha-Gedolah Be-sof Yemei Bayit Sheni," *Tarbitz* 13 (1941), pp. 14-16.

9. Z. Steinfeld, "Ledinam shel Merubeh Begadim Meshamesh u-Merubeh Begadim Sh'avar," *Sinai* 93 (1983), pp. 43-51; and *idem.*, "Mashuaḥ, Merubeh Begadim, Kohen Meshamesh, ve-Kohen She'avar," *Tarbitz* 52 (1983), pp. 411-434.

10. Schürer, *History*, vol. 1, pp. 125-136; vol. 2, pp. 227-236.

11. Precisely which Hasmonean was the first to place a diadem on his coins has been debated. F. Madden, *A History of Jewish Coinage and Money* (London, 1864), p. 61, opted for Judas Aristobulus; M. Avi-Yonah, in his "Prolegomena" to the 1967 reprint of Madden's work, suggested Yannai (pp. xxiv-xxv); A. Reifenberg, *Ancient Jewish Coins* (Jerusalem, 1940), nos. 9-13 and 20, posited John Hyrcanus. In general, see E.E. Goodenough, "Victory and Her Crown," *Art Bulletin* 28 (1946), esp. p. 147.

12. Known in the Hellenist cities as *boulés*. These cities are listed, and discussed in turn, in Schurer, *History*, vol. 2, pp. 85-183.

13. H. Mantel, *Studies in the History of the Sanhedrin* (Cambridge, Mass., 1961), p. 24. This work also contains an extensive discussion of the various theories which have been advanced and rejected concerning the origins of the body and its development (pp. 54-70). A more recent bibliographical survey is provided in P. Winter, *On the Trial of Jesus* (2nd ed., edited by T.A. Burkhill and G. Vermes, 1974).

14. R. De Vaux, *Ancient Israel: Its Life and Institutions* (London, 1965), pp. 72-74, 92-94.

15. I Maccabees 12:6, 14:20; the Book of Judith 4:8, 11:13-14; Josephus, *Antiquities*, XII, 3:3 (138).

16. Boulé; see also E. Rivkin, "Beth Din, Boulé, Sanhedrin: A Tragedy of Errors," *Hebrew Union College Annual* 46 (1975), pp. 181-199.

17. Y. Efron, "Ha-Sanhedrin ba-Ḥazon u-Vametziut shel ha-Bayit ha-Sheni," *DORON sive Commentationes de antiquitate classica doto viro Benzioni Katz...dedicatae* (Jerusalem, 1967), pp. 167-204.

18. U. Rappaport, "Le-Mashmaut 'Ḥever ha-Yehudim,'" *Meḥkarim be-Toldot Am Yisrael ve-Eretz Israel*, vol. 3 (Haifa, 1975), esp. pp. 62-67.

19. The Mishnaic report of a Pharisaic president (*nasi*) and vice-president (*av bet din*; Ḥagigah 2:2) is either a later interpolation or a reference to an entirely different body. For an analysis of the passage, see S. Lieberman, *Tosefta Kifshutah*, Part V, "Seder Moed" (New York, 1962), p. 1297; cf. Zeitlin, *Rise and Fall*, vol. 2, pp. 385-394.

20. "Just as the holiness of the Temple was not impaired in the estimation of the Sages by High Priests who were unworthy of officiating, so it never entered their minds to repudiate the institution of the Sanhedrin, or to set up a rival to it in the form of a competing court, even if they did not approve of its composition and even if they opposed the High Priests and their entourage. They endeavored rather to exercise their influence, and to introduce their rulings and views even into the ritual of the Temple service and into the Sanhedrin's method of operation." E.E. Urbach, "Class Struggle and Leadership in the World of the Palestinian Sages," *Israel Academy of Science, Proceedings*, vol. 2 (Jerusalem, 1968), p. 52. See also G. Alon, *The Jews in Their Land in the Talmudic Age*, vol. 1 (Jerusalem, 1980), pp. 190-195.

21. Compare, e.g., such traditionalist accounts as are contained in Maimonides' introduction to his Commentary on the Mishnah with the conclusions of J. Neusner, *Judaism, The Evidence of the Mishnah* (Chicago, 1981); and E.E. Urbach, *The Sages: Their Concepts and Beliefs* (2 vols., Jerusalem, 1975).

22. G. Alon, *Jews, Judaism and the Classical World*, (Jerusalem, 1977), p. 437. Later sources which emphasize that the *keter torah*, unlike the other domains, is essentially republican and hence open to all men of talent, are listed in M.M. Kasher, *Humash Torah Shelemah*, vol. 20 (New York, 1957), p. 25, no. 94; Commentary to Exodus 25:10. See also J. Goldin, "Of Change and Adaptation in Judaism," *History of Religions* 4 (1965), pp. 290-291.

23. The principal figures are conveniently described in Schurer, *History*, vol. 2, pp. 346-355.

24. The residual impact of the Maccabee example on later Jewish revolts is traced in W. Farmer, *Maccabees, Zealots, and Josephus* (New York, 1956).

25. On the various facets of this concept, see S. Schechter, *Some Aspects of Rabbinic Theology* (New York, 1923), and G.W. Buchanan, *The Consequences of the Covenant* (Leiden, 1970), pp. 42-90.

26. These developments are most conveniently summarized in M. Elon, *Ha-Mishpat Ha-Ivri: Toldotav, Mekorotav, Ekronotav*, vol. I (Jerusalem, 1973).

27. "In the world of the sages during the Temple period you find no bureaucratic organization — no system whatsoever of appointment, no promotion, no renumeration, not even any real arrangements for training or definition of functions. Likewise, there were, of course, no titles: simply the personal name of the sage was used. The titles 'rabban' or 'rabbi' are of a later time."

E.E. Urbach, "Jewish Doctrines and Practices in Halakhic and Aggadic Literature," in *Violence and Defense in the Jewish Experience* (eds., S. Baron and G. Wise, Philadelphia, 1977), p. 90.

28. See, e.g., the description of the eruption of violence between the schools of Hillel and Shammai in *Tosefta, Ḥagigah* 2:9 and T.B. *Sanhedrin* 886.

29. These events are cogently summarized and analyzed in D.M. Rhoads, *Israel in Revolution, 6-7 CE. A Political History Based on the Writings of Josephus* (Philadelphia, 1976).

30. Schürer, *History*, vol. 2, p. 249-252, 229-232; and T. Rajak, *Josephus, The Historian and His Society* (Philadelphia, 1984), pp. 93-95, 132-133.

31. For a discussion of the talmudic passages attesting to this decline, see B.Z. Luria, *Mi-Yannai Ad Hordus* (Jerusalem, 1975).

32. Jeremias, *Jerusalem*, p. 105-108.

33. On the election by lot of Phannias in 67/8 CE, see C. Roth, "The Constitution of the Jewish Republic of 66-70," *Journal of Jewish Studies* 9 (1964), p. 315.

34. Although Alon thinks not; *Jews, Judaism*, pp. 82-83.

35. Cf. K.W. Clark, "Worship in the Jerusalem Temple after 70 A.D.," *New Testament Studies* 6 (1960), pp. 269-280, and E.M. Smallwood, *The Jews Under Roman Rule* (Leiden, 1976), p. 347, n. 62.

36. On which see L. Finkelstein, *Akiba* (2nd ed., New York, 1970), pp. 217-232; and G. Alon, *Toldot, ha-Yehudi be-Eretz Israel Bitkufot ha-Mishnah ve-ha-Talmud*, vol. 1 (Tel Aviv, 1953), pp. 268-269.

37. M. Avi-Yonah, *The Jews of Palestine; a Political History from the Bar Kokhba War to the Arab Conquest* (Oxford, 1976), p. 26. There was, of course, more to this than mere nostalgia. Without the Temple, Israel was obviously deficient. Hence, even the Pharisaic Mishnah had to "take up the perspective of the work of the priests and Levites. In theme and focus it is mainly, though not solely, a priestly document." J. Neusner, *Judaism, The Evidence of the Mishnah*, p. 224.

38. On Elazar's possible identity, see Jeremias, *Jerusalem*, p. 97, n. 33. The sources do not discuss the possible existence of a priestly structure beneath this personage, but priestly support for Bar Kochba's revolt is posited in D. Goodblatt, "Temikhat ha-Tanna'im o Hashpa'at ha-Kohanim?," *Kathedra* 29 (1983), pp. 6-12.

39. Although, even thereafter, some political pretentions were not lacking. See, e.g., R. Kimelman, "Ha-Oligarkhiah ha-Kohanit ve-Talmidei ha-Ḥakhamim," *Zion* 48 (1983), pp. 135-147.

40. On this topic see T. Ishida, *The Royal Dynasties in Ancient Israel* (New York, 1977).

41. F. Dvornick, *Early Christian and Byzantine Political Philosophy in Original Background*, vol. I (Washington, D.C., 1966), p. 325. "During the exile, kings were only a memory of the past, and not a happy one at that, whereas the priests accompanied the people into exile and provided them with the sole consolation left to them. It was only to be expected that opinions on royalty should suffer in the process."

42. Y. Liver, *Toldot Beit David* (Jerusalem, 1959), p. 37.

43. Neither is it at all certain that their Jewish subjects uniformly wished them to do so. Judaism, even the Judaism of the Pharisees, was in many places affected by Hellenistic traces. See, for the early part of the period, M. Hengel, *Judaism and Hellenism: Studies in their Encounter in Palestine during the Early Hellenistic Period* (London, 1974). And, for specific instances of analyses of rabbinic literature, S. Lieberman, *Hellenism in Jewish Palestine* (New York, 1950).

44. On whom, see D. Schwartz, *Agrippas ha-Rishon. Melekh Yehudah ha-Aḥaron* (Jerusalem, 1987).

45. M. Avi-Yonah, "Historical Geography of Palestine," *Compendia Rerum* 1, pp. 78-115.

46. The conclusions of G.F. Moore's *Judaism* (London, 1927) now seem off the mark. Compare: B. Gerhardssohn, *Memory and Manuscript* (Uppsala, 1961); J. Neusner, "Method and Substance in the History of Judaic Ideas: An Exercise," *Jews, Greeks and Christians: Religion and Culture in Late Antiquity*, (eds. R. Hamilton-Kerry and R. Scroggs, Leiden, 1976), pp. 89-111; and J. Weingreen, *From Bible to Mishnah: The Continuity of Tradition* (Manchester, 1976).

47. Rabbinical traditions to this effect may be found in *Tosefta Sotah*, 13:2; T.B. *Yoma* 9b; *Sanhedrin* 11a. The issue and its consequences are discussed in E.E. Urbach, "Halakhah u-Nevuah," *Tarbitz* 18 (1947), pp. 1-27.

48. See the examples in N.N. Glatzer, "A Study of the Talmudic Interpretation of Prophecy," *Review of Religion*, vol. X (2) (January 1946), pp. 122-123.

49. On the importance which later rabbinic tradition attached to Ezra, see: *Tosefta, Sanhedrin* 4:7; and T.B. *Sukkah* 20a.

50. See the discussion in A. Cody, *A History of Old Testament Priesthood* (Rome, 1969), pp. 114-123. The extent of priestly control over religious instruction is prominent in Philo (*Spec. Legi.* IV 36, 190; discussed in H.A. Wolfson, *Philo, Foundations of*

Religious Philosophy in Judaism, Christianity and Islam, vol. 2, (Cambridge, Mass., 1948, pp. 341-342). It is also illustrated by the evidence of Hecataeus of Abdera (4th cent. BCE): "The High Priest is called by them 'Emissary of God's precepts,' that is, the supreme authority in Torah matters." Cited in Urbach, *Sages*, p. 524.

Not unexpectedly, rabbinic traditions preserve few traditions of *keter kehunah* intervention in matters of *halakhah*. One such instance (Mishnah, *Ma'aser Sheni*, 5:15) is discussed in Lieberman, *Hellenism in Jewish Palestine*, pp. 140-143.

51. On Ben Sira, see M. Hengel, *Judaism and Hellenism*, vol. I, pp. 131-153; E. Rivkin, "Ben Sira: The Bridge between the Aaronide and Pharisaic Revolution," *Eretz Israel* 12 (1975), English section, pp. 95-103. On his identity, J.F.A. Sawyer, "Was Joshua Ben Sira a Priest?," *Proceedings of the 8th World Congress of Jewish Studies* (Jerusalem, 1982), pp. 65-71. For the argument that prophecy constitutes for Ben Sira the link between the teaching authority of the priest and the *sofer's* wisdom tradition, see H. Stadelman, *Ben Sira als Schriftgelehrter* (Tubingen, 1980).

52. E.g., Josephus, *Antiquities*, XIII 10, 6 (297): "The Sadducean group say that only the written regulations are to be esteemed as lawful, and that those which derive from the tradition of the fathers are not to be observed." On independent Sadducean traditions, proclaimed by virtue of priestly authority, see Mishnah, *Makkot* 1:6. In general: J. Blenkinsopp, "Prophecy and Priesthood in Josephus," *Journal of Jewish Studies* 25 (1976), pp. 239-262. On the non-Sadducean High Priest Joshua b. Gamalu, Rajak, *Josephus*, p. 31.

53. For examples, including the outstanding case of Honi, "the circle maker," see W.S. Green, "Palestinian Holy Men: Charismatic Leadership and Rabbinic Tradition," *Aufstieg und Neidergang der Romischen Welt*, vol. 19 (2), (ed., W. Haase, Berlin, 1979), pp. 619-647, esp. p. 625.

54. On *Torah she be'al peh*, see G. Blidstein, "Mekorot ha-Munah 'Torah she be'al peh,'" *Tarbitz*, 42 (1973), pp. 496-498. Also J. Goldin, "The Three Pillars of Simeon the Righteous" *Proceedings of the American Academy for Jewish Research* 27 (1958), pp. 48-50. Early Pharisee claims to possess a tradition independent of Scripture have been noted in Josephus, *Antiquities*, XIII, 293-298; Mishnah, *Moed Katan* 7:4; and Matthew 15:2.

55. On the famous case recorded in T.B. *Bava Metzia* 59a-b, see Y. Engelard, "Tanuro shel Akhnai: Perushehah Shel Aggadah," *Shenaton ha-Mishpat ha-Ivri* 1 (1974), pp. 45-56. The various meanings which might therefore be attached to the term *"Torah"* are discussed in Urbach, *Sages*, chap. 12.

56. The state of present scholarly knowledge is summarized in H.D. Mantel, "The Sadducees and the Pharisees," *World History*, vol. 8, pp. 99-123. Cf. M. Smith, "Palestinian Judaism in the First Century," in M. David (ed.), *Israel, Its Role in Civilization* (New York, 1956); and J. Neusner, "The Fellowship (*Ḥaburah*) in the Second Jewish Commonwealth," *Harvard Theological Review*, 53 (1960), pp. 125-142. The more ancient origins of the title *"haver,"* are discussed in S.J. Spiro, "Who was the Haber? A New Approach to an Ancient Institution," *Journal of Semitic Studies* 11 (1980), pp. 186-216.

57. Hengel, *Judaism and Hellenism*, vol. 1, pp. 308-309.

58. Alon, *Jews, Judaism*, pp. 451-452, and H.D. Mantel, "Ordination and Appointment in the Period of the Second Temple," *Harvard Theological Review* 57 (1964), pp. 325-346.

59. In this view, then, the *Anshei Kenesset ha-Gedolah* was not a court but a non-official religious association — "a federation of the various branches of the *Kenesset* (clubs), corresponding to the Hellenistic 'association of associations' (*Synodoi*)....Like the latter, the *Kenesset ha-Gedolah* probably consisted of delegates from the branches, and was headed by a president" (referred to in later texts as a *nasi* — Mishnah, *Ḥagigah* 2:2). See H.D. Mantel, "The Nature of the Great Synagogue," *Harvard Theological Review* 60 (1967), pp. 69-91.

60. Which Simon did not necessarily do. See W. Wirgin, *On Charismatic Kingship: From Simon Maccabaeus to Simon Bar Kochba* (Leeds University Monograph Series, no. 5, 1964), p. 7.

61. See the discussion in Alon, *Jews, Judaism*, pp. 29-30.

62. On the possible identification of Yannai as the "wicked priest," see W.H. Brownlee, "The Wicked Priest and the Righteous Teacher — the Problem of Identity," *Jewish Quarterly Review* 73 (1982), pp. 1-37.

63. K.G. Kuhn, "The Two Messiahs of Aaron and Israel," *New Testament Studies* 1 (1954-55), pp. 168-170; and J. Liver, "The Doctrine of the Two Messiahs," *Harvard Theological Review* 52 (1959), pp. 149-185.

64. B. Sharvit, "Ha-Kohen be-Kat Midbar Yehudah," *Beit Mikra* 3 (1977), pp. 313-320; and *idem.*, "Ha-Hanhagah shel Kat Midbar Yehudah," *ibid.* (1979), pp. 295-304. J. Neusner has drawn some remarkable comparisons in "Scriptural, Essene and Mishnaic Approaches to Civil Law and Government: Some Comparative Remarks," *Harvard Theological Review* 73 (1980), pp. 419-434.

65. M. Grant, *The Jews in the Roman World* (New York, 1973), p. 44.

66. G. Vermes, *The Dead Sea Scrolls: Qumran in Perspective* (1977), pp. 125-162.

67. A. Schalit, *Konig Herodes: der Mann und sein Werk* (Hamburg, 1969).

68. On the *batei din shel kohanim*, see Mishnah, *Ketubot* 13:1; *Eduyot* 8:3; *Yoma* 6:3; *Rosh ha-Shanah* 1:7.

69. For a refutation of the image of the priests as "collaborators," see Rhoads, *Israel in Revolution*, pp. 88-91, 150-153.

70. See, e.g., the comments of B. Bamberger, "The Dating of Aggadic Materials," *Journal of Biblical Literature* 48 (1949), esp. p. 116.

71. For a form-critical examination of the rabbinic sources, see J. Neusner, *The Rabbinic Traditions about the Pharisees before 70* (3 vols., Leiden, 1970). In *From Politics to Piety. The Emergence of Pharisaic Judaism* (New Jersey, 1973), pp. 45-66, Neusner has argued that the Pharisees, who had been politically active under the Hasmoneans, withdrew from politics in the time of Herod. Moreover, they remained so withdrawn until the Destruction, when they renewed their bid for political power. This view has been contested, most recently by D.R. Schwartz, "Josephus and Nicolaus on the Pharisees," *Journal for the Study of Judaism* 14 (1983), pp. 157-171. See also Schurer, *History*, vol. 2, pp. 381-414.

72. "The interpretations of the Law given respectively by priests and scribes were necessarily colored by their diametrically opposed social connections. The priest in his decisions followed the patrician precedents and sympathies of the Temple, the scribe the inherited ideas of his plebian class." L. Finkelstein, *The Pharisees: The Sociological Background of their Faith* (3rd ed., New York, 1962), p. 265. See also W.W. Buehler, *The Pre-Herodian Civil War and Social Debate* (Basel, 1976).

73. As presented, e.g., in S. Dubnow, *Divrei Yemei Olam*, vol. 2, p. 84; and, albeit in a different form, in E. Rivkin, *A Hidden Revolution* (Nashville, 1978), esp. p. 256. Cf. Alon, *Jews, Judaism*, p. 3.

74. Thus, even King David could be excluded from the Sanctuary, the preserve of the *kohanim*. See, e.g., T.B. *Shabbat* 31a on Numbers 1:51 "*Ve-ha-zar ha-karev yumat.*"

75. See, e.g., Exodus Rabbah 2:7 on Exodus 3:5; "*al tikrav halom.*" Cf. Philo, *De Vita Moysis* 2:2-3: "Moses will be found to have displayed, and more than displayed, combined in his single person, not only those two faculties — the kingly and the philosophical — but also those others, one which is concerned with law-giving [*keter malkhut?*], and the second with the high priests office [*keter*

kehunah?] and the last with prophecy [*keter torah?*]." See W.A. Meeks, "Moses as God and King," *Religions in Antiquity*, (ed. J. Neusner, Leiden, 1978), pp. 354-371.

76. For discussions of this incident, in an ascending scale of utility, see: M.J. Geller, "Alexander Jannaeus and the Pharisaic Rift," *Journal of Jewish Studies* 30 (1979), pp. 202-211; B.Z. Luria, *Mi-Yannai Ad Hordus* (Jerusalem, 1975), pp. 104-106; V. Tcherikover, *Hellenistic Civilization and the Jews* (Philadelphia, 1954), pp. 259-260; Y.L. Levin, "Ha-Ma'avak ha-Politi Bein ha-Perushim la-Tzedukkim Bitkufat ha-Ḥashmon-aim," *Perakim be-Toldot Yerushalayim Bimei Bayit Sheni*, (eds., U. Oppenheimer, *et al.*, Jerusalem, 1981), pp. 71-74; Y. Efron, "Shimon ben Shetaḥ ve-Yannai ha-Melekh," *Sefer Zikkaron le-Gedalia Alon*, (eds., M. Duran, *et al.*, Tel Aviv, 1970), esp. pp. 86-88. Cf. Alon, *Jews, Judaism*, pp. 23-24 and n. 15. For comments on the early language of the passage, see M.H. Segal, *A Grammar of Mishnaic Hebrew* (Oxford, 1927), pp. 72-74 and P. Kieval, "The Talmudic View of the Hasmonean and Early Herodian Periods in Jewish History," unpub. Ph.D. (Brandeis, 1970), p. 48-53.

77. In fact, that was an issue which the Pharisees were content to leave dormant; see J. Liver, *Toldot Beit David*, pp. 115-16. Other circles, however, were less lenient; see, e.g., *Psalms of Solomon*, chap. 17. On the latter and other works, see G.W.E. Nickelsburg, *Jewish Literature between the Bible and the Mishnah* (Philadelphia, 1981).

78. See, e.g., the exegesis of Proverbs 8:15-16 ("By me kings reign...by me princes rule") in *Sifrei*, chap. 119, which makes explicit reference to the three *ketarim*.

79. Most pointedly in Mishnah, *Avot* 1:1: "Moses received the Torah from Sinai, and handed it to Joshua; from Joshua it passed to the elders; from the elders to the prophets; from the prophets to the *Anshei Kenesset ha-Gedolah*." On the absence of the priests from this chain, and others, see M.D. Herr, "Ha-Retzef Sheba-Shal-shelet Mesiratah Shel ha-Torah," *Zion* 44 (1979), pp. 43-56.

80. For details on such encroachments, see J. Neusner, *A Life of Yohanan ben Zakkai ca 1-80 CE* (2nd ed., Leiden, 1970), p. 70-92. A conclusion from the sources which perhaps exaggerates their import (almost to the point of distortion) may be found in E. Rivkin, *A Hidden Revolution.*

    For the thesis that Pharisaic attempts to supervise the Temple ritual were not quite so revolutionary, and that in fact there existed a long tradition in Judaism whereby "a lay man, relying on his own knowledge and interpretation of the sacred law, purifies the Temple from pollution for which the priests have been responsible," see M. Smith, "The Dead Sea Sect in Relation to

Ancient Judaism," *New Testament Studies* 7 (1961), esp. pp. 353-355.

81. B.Z. Luria, "Be-Sodom shel ha-Kohanim," *Beit Mikra* 22 (1977), pp. 283-290.

82. See, e.g., the incident concerning the *Benei Beteirah*, cited in T.B. *Rosh ha-Shanah* 29b and discussed in J. Neusner, *Development of a Legend: Studies on the Traditions Concerning Yohanan ben Zakkai* (Leiden, 1970), pp. 93-94.

83. On earlier priestly sympathy for the synagogue, see S. Safri, "The Temple," in *Compendia Rerum*, vol. 2, pp. 904-905.

84. G. Alon, "The Bounds of the Laws of Levitical Cleanliness," *Jews, Judaism*, pp. 190-234. For a refutation of the claim that a "Kingdom of Priests" (Ex. 19:6) was also a Pharisaic slogan, see D. Schwartz, "Mamlekhet Kohanim ke-Sismah Perushit," *Zion* 45 (1980), pp. 96-117.

85. J. Neusner, *Judaism. The Evidence of the Mishnah*, p. 112.

86. On the evidence provided by such sources as T.J. *Ma'aser Sheni* 5:5, see R. Kimmelman, "The Conflict between R. Yoḥanan and Resh Laquish on the Supremacy of the Patriarchate," *Proceedings of the 7th World Congress of Jewish Studies* (Jerusalem, 1981), p. 13.

87. E.g., *Avot de Rabi Natan*, (ed. Schechter) 4:18: "The study of the Torah is more beloved of God than burnt offerings. For if a man studies Torah he comes to know the will of God...(Prov. 2:5)...hence when a sage sits and expounds to the congregation, Scripture accords it to him as though he had offered up fat and blood on the altar." See also the exegesis on Deut. 11:13 in *Sifre*, chap. 41 (ed. Finkelstein, pp. 87-88).

88. A comprehensive survey of the sources may be found in G. Blidstein, "The Monarchic Imperative in Rabbinic Perspective," *Association for Jewish Studies Review* 7-8 (1983), pp. 15-40.

89. See the references cited in J.M. Baumgarten, "The Duodecimal Courts of Qumran, Revelation and the Sanhedrin," *Journal of Biblical Literature* 95 (1976), pp. 70-71.

Chapter 3

AUTHORITY AND CONFLICT IN POST-DESTRUCTION ROMAN JUDEA: THE PATRIARCHATE, THE RABBIS, THE PEOPLE, AND THE ROMANS

Chaim Milikowsky

Delineating the various spheres of power and authority in post-destruction Roman Judea is a difficult task.[1] Clearly, ultimate power rested with the Roman administration. Though power was also centered in other places, this was delegated power, all reverting theoretically back to the person of the emperor. Fictions pervaded this world of power; to look at Rome itself, the emperors often portrayed the Senate as the depository of ultimate power and themselves, the emperors, simply as the first among equals. Similarly in Judea, a wonderful example of political fiction has been preserved by a coin from Sepphoris. The legend in the coin reads as follows (as reconstructed by Meshorer): "The holy, autonomous and faithful Diocasearea, a covenant of brotherhood and joint help with the Roman people."[2] All this really means is that Diocasearea, which is the Roman name for Sepphoris, had been recognized as a free city and the Roman administration did not meddle in internal affairs, as long as, of course, all taxes were paid on time and Roman rule was never openly opposed.

Therefore, Rome knew how to give its subjects the trappings of freedom and power, and the force of these trappings should not be underestimated. Yet, on the other hand, the trappings of power should not be confused with the reality of power.

Where was power situated and what groups had authority? The question can be more easily applied to Roman Judea than to our own society because of two factors: (1) there is autocratic rule: the people were subjugated politically; and (2) this was a traditional society where it was much easier to identify the elites.

Where, then, were power and authority vested? Four disparate, though inter-related, bases of power and authority can be identified: the Roman provincial administration, the municipal

93

magistrates, the Patriarchate, and the Sages. The Roman provincial administration consisted of the governor and various other officials, mainly concerned with fiscal matters. They were all Roman citizens, sent from Rome for the purpose of governing the province. The municipal magistrates were local inhabitants responsible for the orderly organization of municipal concerns, ranging from normal administrative affairs such as the preservation of law and order or the maintenance of the public water supply to the collection of imperial taxes. The institution of the Patriarchate was a hereditary office whose incumbent was recognized, for at least a good part of the period under discussion, as the leader of the Jewish polity in Judea. The Sages are the most amorphous group of those listed: basically this term refers to those scholars whose proficiency in Jewish law and lore was recognized by their peers and by the people, and who achieved a certain status and standing, sometimes formally recognized but more often not, because of this expertise.

The first two of these groupings have nothing specifically Jewish or Judean (that is, concerning the province of Judea) about them. There does not appear to have been any appreciable difference between Judea and other Eastern provinces of the Roman Empire. The relationship of a province to its governor was very much dependent upon the character and policy of the particular governor sent to that province. In the later Roman Empire, the governor became more of a bureaucratic official and had less freedom of action, but this had more to do with the workings of the Roman imperial administration, and did not necessarily change the basic relationship between the province and its Roman administration.

Every city in the Roman Empire had its municipal magistrates, or *decurions*. City administration was of crucial importance in the Roman Empire, but our knowledge is basically limited to the larger free cities. Roman provincial administration recognized a crucial distinction between the free cities and the rest of the province. Theoretically, the provincial governor had very limited rights in a free city: if the city was paying its taxes and not squandering its resources, he could not interfere in its internal affairs. The rest of the province, on the other hand, was under his direct control. Appreciable differences existed between the western part of the Empire, where the institution of cities was modelled, to a large extent, upon that of Rome itself, and the eastern part, where long before Roman rule the Greek ideal of the *poleis*, city, had taken strong root, and which had, moreover, centuries of prior experience with strong city administration, especially along the Mediterranean coastline (e.g., Tyre, Askalon). Nonetheless, what was common to all cities was the desire of the Roman Empire to leave as much as possible in the hands of local officials.[3]

This desire of Rome had further implications: non-urban territories were often placed under the jurisdiction of the various cities to facilitate the collection of taxes from those areas, so that the central Roman bureaucracy did not have to deal with the inhabitants of each and every village. In Judea, this process seems to have been completed by the fourth century, while in earlier centuries much of the rural area was not under any municipal jurisdiction, and presumably the governor was directly responsible for their affairs.[4] It is clear, though, that also in non-recognized cities, as well as in villages, a large degree of autonomous rule was indeed preferred by the Romans, simply to save it the trouble of having to bloat its provincial administration with extra officials. Similarly, free cities tended to give a fair amount of autonomous decision-making power to the villages under their control.[5] Thus there are references in rabbinic texts to the *bouletai* (Greek: council-members), even when it is clear that neither Tiberias nor Sepphoris is under discussion.[6] There was nothing unique about this situation in Judea; presumably such was the case whenever a province contained a large percentage of territory not included within the boundaries of free cities. In the final analysis, then, it made little difference to the individual Jew if he lived in a small village or in the large capitals of the Galilee: Tiberias and Sepphoris.

It would be interesting to contemplate the possible frictions which developed between the *bouletai* and the other modes of authority in Roman Judea, but it would be merely speculation. If it is recalled, however, that the *bouletai* were always of the wealthier segment of the population, which in a basically agrarian society was generally a hereditary grouping, it would seem likely that tension did arise between them and the new class of Jewish leaders to be discussed below.

It was the Patriarchate and the Sages which represented these elements of the Jewish polity in post-destruction Roman Judea which are specifically Jewish. Though an attempt to delineate the political roles of these two groupings will be made, it must be emphasized that the number of unsolved and, given the paucity and nature of the sources, probably unsolvable problems is legion.

One complex of problems will be analyzed in order to delineate the problematic. No period of history develops within a vacuum, and though the destruction of the Temple is a valid watershed within the structure of the Jewish polity, obviously something must be said about the Patriarchate before the destruction. After all, the rabbinic sources assign the title *Nasi* (Patriarch) to Hillel, a contemporary of Herod whose reign began over a hundred years before the destruction. However, analysis of the contemporary documents, i.e., the New Testament and Josephus, indicates quite clearly that the Patriarchate did not exist as an institution in pre-destruction Judea. In other words, no aspect of power or authority over the Jewish polity in Judea was formally located in the hands of any Pharisaic leader. The Pharisees (among whom Hillel is included) are presented as a religious, and perhaps political, grouping, the opponents of the Sadducees in Hasmonean and Herodian Judea, who at times controlled positions of power, but there was no institutional grounding for Pharisaic authority. At the most they could be said to have comprised a Pharisaic grouping, probably informal, with a recognized leadership role in the hands of a predominant member of this grouping.[7]

Unfortunately, little information exists concerning the relationship between this Pharisaic grouping and the Jewish administration in pre-destruction Judea. This problem is related to the vexing question of the nature of the High Court in Jerusalem, the Sanhedrin: Did a single Sanhedrin exist? Did it follow Pharisaic religious doctrine? Perhaps different venues existed for religious, i.e., *halakhic*, questions and for political questions? All these questions have been discussed endlessly, but the various answers are very far apart and no consensus has emerged.[8] Moving from formal institutions to informal relationships, another important question must be raised: What was the attitude of the people to these Pharisees who clearly are the spiritual and political ancestors of the Sages? One school of thought denies Josephus's claim that the majority of the people followed them, but more recent scholarship has shown that Josephus should be accepted.[9]

In order to emphasize the historical dynamics of the institution of the Patriarchate, it will be useful to look at another period in Jewish history when again there was no Patriarchate. In 429 CE Emperor Theodesius II impounded the *auram coronarian* (Cod. Theo. 16.8.29), a Jewish poll-tax previously paid to the Patriarchate. The law stated that the Jews had to pay the tax to the imperial treasury "after the extinction of the Patriarchate" and debate still reigns whether the Patriarchate was abolished by Roman action or became extinct on its own. From this law and from several others of the late Roman Empire it is clear that the power of the Patriarchate grew exceedingly in the fourth and early part of the fifth centuries; interestingly enough, this was after the Christianization of the Empire. Two laws exemplified this attitude: According to Cod. Theo. 16.8.11 (396 CE), anyone publicly insulting the "illustrious" (title given to members of the senatorial class) Patriarch was to be punished by the state, while Cod. Theo. 2.1.30 (398 CE) asserted that the provincial rulers must execute the judgments given by the Patriarch or anyone he appointed, if the two litigants had applied to the Patriarch or his appointee to serve as judge. From this last law it can be inferred that prior to this rescript the judgments of the Patriarch or his appointed officials were authoritative even if the two litigants did not express their explicit desire to be judged in that specific court (though it is unclear whether these judgments were recognized by the Roman provincial administration *de jure* or only *de facto*).[10]

This very brief overview of the institution of the Patriarchate towards the end of the period under discussion, when taken together with our preliminary observations concerning the non-existence of any formal institution of the Patriarchate at the time of the destruction of the Temple, will serve as the framework for a short synopsis of this institution.

What is known of the institution of the Patriarchate during the first two centuries of the Common Era? As noted earlier, the traditional sources (and some scholars) have projected this institution into the period of the Temple.[11] This is clearly an anachronistic projection from a later political reality into an earlier period. But what about in the years after the destruction? First there is an important distinction to be established relevant to this analysis of the Patriarchate: internal recognition versus external recognition, which in this context means authority versus power. Two of the strongest indications of power are taxation and juridical competence. From the sources cited it is clear that during the later period both of these powers were centered in the person of the Patriarch: the Jews paid him taxes and juridical decisions made by him or his appointees were considered binding by the Roman authorities. From a rabbinic source noted below it seems that general Roman taxation was also channelled through the Patriarchate on its way to the fiscal authorities. These functions exemplify the coercive element of power in the Patriarch's hand. (Not that he necessarily had recourse to coercion, but that he had the capability.) He was recognized by the Roman imperial government as the authority over the Jews and they delegated to him extensive powers.

There is no indication that such recognition or power was to be found in the first century after the destruction. Indeed, it is questionable if the title Patriarch, i.e., *Nasi*, was at all in use at that time. Even though Rabban Gamaliel, who was active at the turn of the first century of the Common Era, is explicitly called *Nasi* at least once in rabbinic literature, it does not appear that he had any political recognition, not even *de facto*, from the Romans.[12] Looking at the situation in the second century, a very interesting fact comes to light. The evidence indicates that two leaders of the Jewish people in Judea were accorded the title *Nasi*, yet moderns unconsciously insist on translating the titles differently: Rabbi Yehuda ha-Nasi (end of second century CE) is termed Rabbi Yehuda the Patriarch,[13] while Shimon Nesi Yisrael (that is, the leader of the second rebellion against Rome who is generally called Bar Kochba) is translated Shimon, Prince of Israel.[14] This unconscious differentiation is legitimate: The *nesi'ut* of Shimon Bar Kosiba was a deliberate attempt to break Roman rule — he rebelled against it — and the English translation "prince" has the correct nationalistic tone to it. R. Yehuda ha-Nasi, on the other hand, led the Jews in their subjugated role under the Romans — indeed the relationship between the Jews and the Roman officials thrived in his day — and so "Patriarch" gives the correct connotation. Indeed, the very use of the title *Nasi* by R. Yehuda ha-Nasi, when everyone knew that it had been used a generation before by the leader of the rebels, may indicate a conscious turning of Jewish sentiment away from the ideals expressed by Bar Kosiba to those R. Yehuda ha-Nasi wished to enshrine.

Thus the use of the title *Nasi* in the context of the institution of the Patriarchate began at the end of the second century. However this does not mean that none of the earlier Sages to whom this title had been given anachronistically had no authority. The point is that the title was not theirs, and, more importantly, there was no formal institutional structure with any sort of external recognition. Nevertheless, clearly the Jews themselves did recognize the authority of these figures, who will be called, for lack of a better term, heads of academy. (However, since the institution of the Patriarchate did develop out of the authority vested in these figures, at times the term "Patriarchate" will be used to include them also.)

As has already been intimated, the question of authority and leadership in the period just before the destruction and the continuity or non-continuity between that period and the post-destruction polity is a complicated one. Without delving into the finer points of this question, certain functions, clearly identified with the central authority before the destruction, are found in the hands of these leaders after the destruction.

The most important of these is the reckoning of the calendar: the evidence is unequivocal that this function was in the hands of the Sages, more specifically tied directly to the academy heads. Thus, for example, the final intercalation could not be approved until R. Gamaliel returned from a trip to Syria (M. *Eduyyot* 7:7). And it is further known that the predecessor of R. Gamaliel, R. Yohanan b. Zakkai, was active in the field of calendar reform.[15]

The term "heads of academy" was used earlier with a specific purpose in mind. In addition to the fact, noted above, that there is no evidence of external recognition of these leaders, there is also no evidence of political interplay between the peoples of the Judean polity and these leaders. This implies that moral, religious, and social authority was actually in the hands of the Sages as a class, and the heads of the academy, as the leaders of this class, exemplified this authority. The function of these leaders as heads of academy will be more evident after an analysis of several texts below which deal with conflicts between these leaders and some Sages.

As noted above, the use of the title *Nasi* for the head of the academy seems to have begun towards the end of the second century, with R. Yehuda ha-Nasi. If so, to what authority does the use of this title attest? It has even been suggested recently that R. Yehuda ha-Nasi was nothing other than "a religious intellectual and his followers were primarily religious zealots."[16]

Against this point of view it must be noted that the sources indicate that much more authority than this was in his hands. Thus, for example, a community applied to him to appoint for them a teacher, judge and preacher; municipal officials (the *bouletai*) came to him to judge a case of theirs; the city of Tiberias complained to him (and not to the governor) that the Sages did not pay their share of the taxes; he instituted certain measures with regard to the payment of Roman taxes; in his testament he advised his son R. Gamaliel regarding judicial appointments; his son-in-law was of the wealthy elite and unlearned.[17] Only with great difficulty can all of these sources be interpreted as referring to a leader of religious zealots. On the other hand, it does not appear that with R. Yehuda the Patriarch's authority was vested in *de jure* recognition by the Roman state.

As is well known, rabbinic literature contains a number of stories about R. Yehuda ha-Nasi and an emperor called Antonius in these texts. Without accepting the historical worth of these legends — one even claims that Antonius converted to Judaism — they should not be considered mere fabrications.[18] On the contrary, the assumption that there was some sort of positive interplay between this emperor, probably Caracalla, and R. Yehuda ha-Nasi is the best explanation for the establishment of the Patriarchate as a formal institution within the context of the Roman administration of Judea. Thus the personal contact between these two persons, as well as the strengthening of internal political and social shifts towards the leaders of the Sages, culminated in the eventual *de jure* recognition of the Patriarchate, which, though it cannot be dated, probably began sometime in the third century.

To summarize: after the destruction of the Temple a fair amount of authority, basically stemming from religio-social sentiment but influencing and expanding into the entire gamut of both personal and collective behavior, was in the hands of the Sages. They had no external recognition nor any power. The broadening of this authority, as well as possible Roman searches for new conduits to the leadership of the Jewish people, expanded the political and economic functions of the head of the academy of the Sages, and this is the beginning of the Patriarchate. This then developed into clear recognition on the part of the Roman Empire, which in turn changed the basic reality of the Patriarchate. From a head of an academy deriving his authority because of his implicit recognition by the people, the Patriarch became the channel whereby the average citizen had contact with the coercive power, i.e., the Romans. Both judicial power and fiscal power were now in the hands of the Patriarch.

One more subject demands attention: the authority of the Sages. On the basis of numerous sources stemming from the time of R. Yehuda ha-Nasi it is clear that official judges with Roman recognition and backing were appointed by the Patriarchate, and many Sages were appointed to these positions. This is not to say that every judge was a Sage — indeed many sources tell of the appointment of non-learned judges — or that every Sage was a judge. Nor does this mean that the authority of the Sage, or better yet, the Sages as a class, was dependent upon their appointment.

Nonetheless, it becomes more difficult to separate their intertwined modes of authority — actually a combination of charismatic and legal authority.

There was an earlier period when the authority of the Sages over the people must have been either charismatic or religious authority. What were the limits of this authority? Was it limited to the religious spheres of life, such as purity, tithing, Shabbat, etc., or did it extend to civil law also? A priori it is difficult to envision a Jewish society almost two thousand years ago which divided its questions into such modern categories. Nonetheless, it can be argued that the existing municipal administration, for generations in the hands of the wealthy elite, fulfilled the function of a civil judiciary, and the people had recourse to the Sages for religious matters only. But this hypothesis cannot be maintained: the texts are clear in ascribing to various Sages the role of judge in civil cases. Though the number of such judgments are not very numerous (case law is not at all common in Tannaitic literature), they are sufficient to belie any claim that the Tannaim dealt only with religious questions.

If the function of the Sage as judge was generated by his authority over the people, how did this manifestation of his authority comply with Roman imperial policy? Judicial authority was in the hands of the Roman governor, and in cities in the hands of the magistrates. Though some tensions may very well have been generated by conflicts or usurpations of jurisdiction, it is probable that in most matters the Romans allowed each subject people to conform to its own ancestral customs,[19] though recourse to the governor was always an option. There is no reason to suppose that the municipal magistrates did not act as judges; it should be remembered that there were not hundreds of Sages available for judicial duties; indeed they saw their main role centered in the academy, not the courthouse. Furthermore, it is quite possible that different classes of people brought their cases for judgment to the Sages and to the municipal magistrates. Regarding all of these questions, the sources simply do not say enough.

From all of the foregoing it is obvious that the relationship between the Patriarchate (using the form in the general sense) and the rabbis must have undergone basic changes as the nature of the authority of the Patriarch changed. There are a number of rabbinic texts which portray conflicts between a Sage (or several Sages) and the Patriarch (or head of academy).

The first text is M. *Rosh Ha-Shana* 2:8-9. The incident related in this mishna developed because of an argument between R. Gamaliel and R. Yehoshua regarding the date of the onset of the new month. The former commanded the latter to come before him with his staff and money on the day that R. Yehoshua reckoned to be the Day of Atonement. R. Yehoshua hesitated, was counseled by two Sages to yield, and, in the end, did so.

On one occasion two witnesses came and said, "We saw it in the morning in the east and in the evening in the west." R. Yohanan b. Nuri thereupon said, "They are false witnesses." When, however, they came to Yavneh, Rabban Gamaliel accepted them. On another occasion two witnesses came and said, "We saw it at its proper time, but on the night which should have been New Moon it was not seen," and Rabban Gamaliel [had already] accepted their evidence. R. Dosa b. Harqinas said: "They are false witnesses. How can men testify that a woman has born a child when on the next day we see her belly still swollen?" Said R. Yehoshua to him: "I see [the force of] your argument." Thereupon Rabban Gamaliel sent to him to say, "I enjoin upon you to appear before me with your staff and your money on the day which according to your reckoning should be the Day of Atonement." R. Aqiva went [to R. Yehoshua] and found him in great distress. He said to him: "I can bring proof [from the Scripture] that whatever Rabban Gamaliel has done is valid, because it says, 'these are the appointed seasons of the Lord, holy convocations, which you shall proclaim in their appointed seasons,' [which means to say that] whether they are proclaimed at their proper time or not at their proper time, I have no appointed seasons save these." He [R. Yehoshua] then went to R. Dosa b. Harqinas, who said to him: "If we call in question [the decisions of] the Beth Din of Rabban Gamaliel, we must call in question the decisions of every Beth Din which has existed since the days of Moses up to the present time. For it says, 'then went up Moses and Aaron, Nadab and Abihu and seventy of the elders of Israel.' Why were not the names of the elders mentioned? To show that every group of three which has acted as a Beth Din over Israel is on a level with the Beth Din of Moses." He [R. Yehoshua] thereupon took his staff and his money and went to Yavneh to Rabban Gamaliel on the day on which the Day of Atonement fell according to his reckoning. Rabban Gamaliel rose and kissed him on his head and said to him: "Come in peace, my teacher

and my disciple — my teacher in wisdom and my disciple because you have accepted my decision."

Nowhere in this story is R. Gamaliel called *Nasi*, nor is the
authority specifically located in his person. Rather it is the Bet
Din (court) of R. Gamaliel which cannot be questioned. Furthermore, from the argument of R. Aqiva cited in the passage, it is
evident that declaring the new month has its own specific ratio-
nale which allows for no deviation once the court has made its decision. No implication can be drawn, therefore, that R. Yehoshua
must always submit to the authority of R. Gamaliel.

The conflict between R. Gamaliel and R. Yehoshua centers on
a question of religious, i.e., *halakhic*, doctrine, but has important
political ramifications as well. Both are members of the academy;
R. Gamaliel has some sort of superior role (his function is not defined, yet the court is called by his name),[20] but R. Yehoshua does
not recognize his authority on *halakhic* matters. Since the authority of the academy, that is, the Sages as a whole, stems from their
expertise in *halakhic* matters, R. Yehoshua feels that his greater
expertise should prevail over R. Gamaliel's formal stature. Other
Sages disagree with him and he yields. The conflict is localized
within the academy; granted that the Sages are vested with
authority by the people, it is only to be expected that the regularization of this relationship will introduce conflict with their
academy.

Another conflict between R. Gamaliel and R. Yehoshua is
found in the Palestinian Talmud, *Berakhot* 4:1 (7c-d).[21] In this
story R. Gamaliel does not emerge victorious. R. Yehoshua and
R. Gamaliel disagreed on a point of law, an anonymous student
told R. Gamaliel of R. Yehoshua's disagreement, and R.
Gamaliel then embarrassed R. Yehoshua in public. As a result of
this action R. Gamaliel was deposed and another Sage, R. Elazar
b. Azaria, was appointed head of the academy. R. Gamaliel then
decided to act: he acknowledged his misdeed before R. Yehoshua
and the other Sages and was restored to his previous position.[22]

And it once happened that a certain student came and
asked R. Yehoshua, "How is the law about the evening
prayer?" He said to him, "Optional." [The student] came and
asked R. Gamaliel, "How is the law about the evening
prayer?" He said to him, "Compulsory." [The student] said to
him, "But R. Yehoshua said 'Optional'!" [R. Gamaliel] said to

him, "Tomorrow, when I come into the meeting-house, get up and ask about this law." The next day that same student got up and asked R. Gamaliel, "How is the law about the evening prayer?" He said to him, "Compulsory." He said, "But R. Yehoshua said 'Optional.'" R. Gamaliel said to R. Yehoshua, "Is it you who says 'Optional'?" He said, "No." [R. Gamaliel] said to him, "Stand on your feet, and let them bear witness against you." And R. Gamaliel sat and taught, and R. Yehoshua remained standing, until the whole assembly shouted and said to R. Huspit the Meturgeman, "Dismiss the assembly!" They said to R. Zenon the Hazzan, "Say..." He began to speak; the whole assembly began, and they rose to their feet and said to [R. Gamaliel], "For upon whom has not come your unceasing evil?"

They went and appointed R. Eleazar b. Azariah to the Academy. He was sixteen years old, and all his hair turned gray. R. Aqiva was sitting sorrowfully and saying, "Not that he is more learned than I, but he is of more illustrious parentage than I. Happy is the man whose fathers have gained him merit! Happy is the man who has a peg on which to hang! And what was R. Eleazar b. Azariah's peg? He was the tenth generation in descent from Ezra. And how many benches were there? R. Yaakov b. Sisi said, "There were 80 benches there of students, besides those standing behind the fence." R. Yosi b. R. Abun said "There were 300, besides those standing behind the fence." [This is the reference of] what we learn elsewhere: "On the day they seated R. Eleazar b. Azariah in the Academy." We learn elsewhere: "There is a midrash which R. Eleazar b. Azariah expounded before the Sages at the Vineyard in Yavneh." But was there a vineyard there?! Rather, those are the students who were arranged in rows, as in a vineyard.

R. Gamaliel immediately went to the home of each person to appease him. He went to R. Yehoshua; he found him sitting making needles. He said to him, "Is this how you make a living?" He said, "And are you just now trying to find out? Woe to the generation of which you are the steward." [R. Gamaliel] said to him, "I submit to you." And they sent a certain laundry-worker to R. Eleazar b. Azariah. But some say it was R. Aqiva. [The messenger] said to him, "The sprinkler, son of a sprinkler, should sprinkle; shall he who is neither a sprinkler nor the son of a sprinkler say to the sprinkler, son of a sprinkler, 'Your water comes from a cave, and your ashes from roasting'?" [R. Eleazar b. Azariah] said to them, "Are you satisfied? You and I shall wait at R. Gamaliel's door." Nonetheless they did not depose [R. Eleazar b. Azariah] from his high dignity, but rather appointed him Av Beth Din.

The major conclusion to be drawn from this story is that R. Gamaliel cannot have been recognized as the focus of authority by the Roman provincial administration and definitely had no official Roman standing. If either of these were true, it is difficult to imagine the Sages deposing R. Gamaliel. Rather this story confirms the earlier analysis presented here. The conflicts between R. Gamaliel and R. Yehoshua were confined to the academy. R. Gamaliel was accepted as the head of the academy and tried to assert a degree of personal power, coercive in nature, which was not accepted by the majority of Sages. They felt the need to remind him that he had no personal power, that authority was collective, vested in the Sages as a social and religious elite, and they have the option of withdrawing their support and removing him from his position as head of the academy.

The head of the academy during the next generation was R. Shimon b. Gamaliel, who, like his father R. Gamaliel, is occasionally called *Nasi* in rabbinic sources (but only in Amoraic texts, never in contemporaneous Tannaitic material). The Babylonian Talmud, *Horayot* 13b, tells of a conflict between him and some Sages. The story details an attempt to depose R. Shimon b. Gamaliel by questioning his competence in abstruse *halakhic* material. However, R. Shimon b. Gamaliel learns of the plot and foils it.

R. Yohanan said: That instruction was issued in the days of R. Shimon b. Gamaliel [II], when R. Shimon b. Gamaliel was the Nasi, R. Meir the Hakam, and R. Nathan the Av Beth Din. Whenever R. Shimon b. Gamaliel entered all the people stood up for him; when R. Meir and R. Nathan entered all the people stood up for them also. Said R. Shimon b. Gamaliel: Should there be no distinction between my [office] and theirs? And so he issued that ordinance.

R. Meir and R. Nathan were not present on that day. Coming on the following day and seeing that the people did not rise for them as usual, they inquired as to what had happened. On being told that R. Shimon b. Gamaliel had issued that ordinance, R. Meir said to R. Nathan, "I am the Hakam and you are the Av Beth Din, let us retaliate. Now, how are we to proceed against him? — Let us request him to discourse upon the tractate of 'Ukzin with which he is unfamiliar, and as he will be unable to discourse upon it we shall tell him: Who can express the mighty acts of the Lord; make all His praise to be heard; for whom is it becoming to express the mighty acts of the Lord? For him who can make all his praise to be heard. We shall then depose him and I shall become Av Beth Din and you the Nasi."

R. Yaakov b. Korshai on hearing this conversation said, "The matter might, God forbid, lead to [the Nasi's] disgrace." So he went and sat down behind R. Shimon b. Gamaliel's study, expounding [the tractate of 'Ukzin], and repeating it again and again. He said, "What could this mean? Did anything, God forbid, happen at the college!" He concentrated his attention and familiarized himself with it. On the following day when they said to him, "Will the Master come and discourse on 'Ukzin," he began and discoursed upon it. After he had finished he said to them, "Had I not familiarized myself with it, you would have disgraced me!" He gave the order and they were removed from the college.

Thereupon they wrote down scholastic difficulties on slips of paper which they threw into the college. That which he solved was disposed of and as to those which he did not solve they wrote down the answers and threw them in. Said R. Yose to them: "The Torah is without and we are within!" Said R. Shimon b. Gamaliel to them: We shall readmit them but impose upon them this penalty, that no traditional statement shall be reported in their names. [As a result] R. Meir was designated 'others,' and R. Nathan 'some say'. In their dreams they received a message to go and pacify R. Shimon b. Gamaliel. R. Nathan went; R. Meir did not, for he said: "Dreams are of no consequence." When R. Nathan came, R. Shimon b. Gamaliel remarked to him: "The honorable position of your father has indeed helped you to become Av Beth Din; shall we therefore make you also Nasi?"

Without accepting the authenticity of the entire story, two points clearly come to light. There was serious conflict between selected Sages in the academy and the head of the academy, which very possibly had to do with the authority vested in the person of the head of the academy as opposed to the academy of the Sages as a whole. The question of religious, i.e., *halakhic*, expertise versus political status played a central role in delineating the area of conflict, just as it did with the conflict between R. Gamaliel and R. Yehoshua.[23]

During the latter part of the second century CE the head of the academy was R. Shimon b. Gamaliel's son, R. Yehuda ha-Nasi. As already noted, he was the first of this illustrious family who is called *Nasi* in Tannaitic sources. Evidence of conflicts between R. Yehuda ha-Nasi and various Sages has been preserved in the Talmud, yet the nature of these conflicts are radically different than those of his father and grandfather.[24]

One set of stories in the Palestinian Talmud, *Demai* 1:3 (22a), tells of the relationship of R. Yehuda ha-Nasi and R. Pinhas b. Yair. Among the different stories cited there, some obviously legendary, one shows explicit disapproval of R. Yehuda ha-Nasi. When R. Pinhas b. Yair was coming to eat with R. Yehuda ha-Nasi, he saw the mules belonging to the latter, and said, "Do Jews feed all these? Perhaps I will never see his face again," and then turned away. Another story in the Palestinian Talmud, *Mo'ed Qatan* 3:1 (81c), focuses on R. Yehuda ha-Nasi's son-in-law, Bar Elishaa,[25] who was very wealthy, but not at all learned. A noted scholar of that day, Bar Qappara, pointed out to him that everyone but him was asking questions of R. Yehuda ha-Nasi, and suggested a question. The question, however, was actually an insult. R. Yehuda ha-Nasi searched around to see who suggested it and saw Bar Qappara laughing. As a consequence of this action, Bar Qappara realized that he would never receive an appointment.

What is most striking about these incidents is that they are completely out of the academy. No longer is there any contention within the academy regarding the position of the head of the academy. This, as pointed out above, had been thoroughly consolidated by R. Yehuda ha-Nasi. His personal authority over the academy, on the one hand, and the people, on the other, had already been established as the basic datum. What, then, generates conflict? These two stories present illuminating examples of just these sort of problems which one would assume to arise when a religious leader consolidates his authority over the people as a whole.

According to the first story, the upkeep of R. Yehuda ha-Nasi's household is financed by the general Jewish populace. When R. Pinhas b. Yair comes to visit, he is overwhelmed by the number of mules and reacts strongly. This is a classic instance of a charismatic, ascetic leader who identifies with the people and is repulsed by apparent personal extravagance at the expense of the people which is exhibited by the regular authority.

The second story has a more specifically Jewish theme: the conflict between different elites in the Jewish people. The members of the academy, the Sages, were an intellectual and social elite, clearly recognized as such by the people for whom their role was crucial in many areas of their life. Another obvious elite was the hereditary wealthy. Though there is little evidence of conflict between these two elites, it cannot be imagined that there was none. It seems that R. Yehuda ha-Nasi, as part of the consolidation of his personal authority over the entire Jewish nation in Judea, wished to generate a new elite class which combined the wealthy and the scholars.[26] Consequently, Bar Qappara's action can be seen as a response of the scholarly elite to R. Yehuda ha-Nasi's elevation of the moneyed upper-class into areas previously the sole terrain of the learned.

Both of these incidents, then, strikingly confirm the earlier analysis of the dynamic change which the institution of the head of the academy underwent in its change to the Patriarchate. There is no attempt at deposition and the authority of the Patriarch is clearly not limited to the academy and the Sages.

The last story to be analyzed centers on the person of R. Yehuda Nesiah, the grandson of R. Yehuda ha-Nasi and active in the middle of the third century CE. The Palestinian Talmud, *Sanhedrin* 2:6 (20d),[27] tells of a sermon delivered by Yosi of Ma'on in the synagogue of Tiberias. The selection he chose was Hosea 5:1: "Hear this, O Priests, attend, O House of Israel, and give ear, O royal house, for right conduct is your responsibility." The Priests who receive the priestly gifts are asked why they do not study Torah, and they respond, "We receive nothing." The house of Israel is asked why they give nothing and say, "The king takes all." The royal house is then condemned to destruction since it does not allow for adherence to the Torah. R. Yehuda Nesiah heard of the sermon, and Yosi of Ma'on was forced to flee until other scholars came to the Patriarch to remonstrate on his behalf. He was then brought to R. Yehuda but continued in his scathing attack on the Patriarchate.

The basis for this conflict is very obvious. The Patriarch has become the channel whereby Roman taxes are collected from the people and transmitted to the Roman administration. Thus the negative aspects of complete *de jure* recognition as the seat of authority by the Romans have become very obvious: The natural resentment felt by any subject people towards the forces that collect taxes by means of coercive power is now addressed to the Patriarch. In a sense the institution of the Patriarch has achieved its final victorious realization: complete internal and external recognition. However, the reality of the situation generated unforeseen repercussions. The range of the Patriarchate's activities now meant that authority was no longer sufficient, and some element of coercive power had to be introduced into the internal Jewish polity in order that the equilibrium between the people, the Patriarch, and the Romans would not be upset.

Notes

1. It will be useful, though not always possible, to distinguish between power and authority. Power implies the ability to command without consent, while the word "authority" generates an alternative image of a polity predisposed towards accepting influence and suggestion because of previous consent. This distinction will help to differentiate between the relationship of the people to the Roman authorities, on the one hand, and the people to their national and religious leaders, on the other.

2. Y. Meshorer, "The Coins of Sephorris as Historical Source," *Zion* 43 (1978), pp. 194-197 (Hebrew). Concerning the use of the term "autonomous" with regard to Eastern cities, see F.F. Abbott and A.C. Johnson, *Municipal Administration in the Roman Empire* (Princeton, 1928), p. 40, note 1.

3. A bibliography of the political institutions of the Hellenistic cities is found in E. Schürer, *The History of the Jewish People in the Age of Jesus Christ*, revised and edited by G. Vermes, F. Millar, and M. Black, Vol. 2 (Edinburgh, 1979), pp. 85-86; see also Schürer's discussion, pp. 86-97, and the works cited in notes 17, 26, and 30. An important study of the later period is A.H.M. Jones, *The Later Roman Empire: 284-602* (Norman, Okla., 1964), 2 vols., especially ch. 19.

4. A.H.M. Jones, "The Urbanization of Palestine," *Journal of Roman Studies* 21 (1931), pp. 78-85, and *idem., Later Roman Empire*, pp. 714-715.

5. See G.M. Harper, Jr., "Village Administration in the Roman Province of Syria," *Yale Classical Studies*, Vol. 1 (1928), pp. 143-

145, for a consideration of the inscriptional evidence from the Eastern Empire indicating that small towns and villages also had councils or *boulai*, and pp. 153-160, for a discussion of the relationship between villages and the cities upon which they were dependent. Concerning this last point, see also Jones, *Later Roman Empire*, p. 456, and Abbott and Johnson, *Municipal Administration*, pp. 22-27. M. Goodman, *State and Society in Roman Galilee, A.D. 132-212* (Totowa, N.J., 1983), pp. 119-128, surveys the rabbinic evidence for local village administration. Though his title specifies Galilee, few of the rabbinic texts he cites are localized by time or person and it is impossible to determine if they refer to Judea or to the Galilee. (For the purposes here, of course, it makes no difference.)

6. See, e.g., the list in M. Kosovsky, *Concordance to the Talmud Yerushalmi*, Vol. 2 (Jerusalem, 1982), p. 373. For some suggestive ideas (though the primary evidence is very thin) concerning local government in Judea after the destruction of the Temple, see G. Alon, *The Jews in their Land in the Talmudic Age*, 2 vols. (Jerusalem, 1980-84), Vol. 1, pp. 176-184, Vol. 2, pp. 485-489. In general, Alon's insistence on the centrality of the Sanhedrin as a political force in the period after the destruction does not seem to be borne out by the sources.

7. The evidence pertaining to the early use of the title *Nasi* was collected by H. Mantel, *Studies in the History of the Sanhedrin* (Cambridge, 1965), ch. 1, "The Title *Nasi* in Jewish Tradition," pp. 1-53. Many of his conclusions, however, are unacceptable. Probably the best study of the political and social standing of the Sages in pre-destruction and post-destruction Judea is E.E. Urbach, "Class Status and Leadership in the World of the Palestinian Sages," *Proceedings of the Israel Academy of Sciences and Humanities* 2 (1966), pp. 38-74. Schürer, *History of the Jewish People*, Vol. 2, pp. 381-382, contains a convenient bibliography of the Pharisees and Sadducees.

8. A partial bibliography (with an overemphasis upon works dealing with the possible role of the Sanhedrin in the trial of Jesus) is found in Schürer, *History of the Jewish People*, Vol. 2, pp. 199-200.

9. D.R. Schwartz, "Josephus and Nicolaus on the Pharisees," *Journal for the Study of Judaism* 14 (1983), pp. 157-171.

10. These laws have been the subject of much discussion; a recent study, with extensive references, is J. Cohen, "Roman Imperial Policy Toward the Jews from Constantine until the End of the Palestinian Patriarchate (ca. 429)," *Byzantine Studies* 3 (1976), pp. 1-29. All extant Roman laws pertaining to the Jews have been

collected by A. Linder, *Roman Imperial Legislation on the Jews* (Jerusalem, 1983) (Hebrew).

11. Mantel, *Sanhedrin*, pp. 2-4.

12. A recent study arguing that R. Gamaliel was recognized by the Roman administration, yet offering an extremely tenuous justification for that recognition, is D. Goodblatt, "The Origins of Roman Recognition of the Palestinian Patriarchate," *Studies in the History of the Jewish People and the Land of Israel* 4 (1978) [In honor of Azriel Schochat on the occasion of his seventieth birthday], pp. 89-102 (Hebrew). (Earlier studies are cited in notes 4-13.) See, however, Schwartz, "On the Pharisees," pp. 167-168.

13. That R. Yehuda was called *Nasi* cannot be doubted; indeed it is his cognomen in rabbinic literature. His role in the Jewish polity of his time will be discussed below.

14. See, e.g., Schürer, *History of the Jewish People*, Vol. 2, p. 544; M. Avi-Yonah, *The Jews of Palestine: A Political History from the Bar Kokhba War to the Arab Conquest* (New York, 1976), p. 12. Y. Yadin, *Bar Kokhba* (New York, 1971), prefers "president." Bar Kokhba assumes the title *"Nesi Yisrael"* in his letters, and on coins appears as *"Shimon Nesi Yisrael."*

15. M. *Rosh Ha-Shana* 4:1, B.T. *Rosh Ha-Shana* 21b.

16. Goodman, *State and Society*, pp. 114-115.

17. See L.I. Levine, "The Jewish Patriarch (Nasi) in Third Century Palestine," *Aufstieg und Niedergang der Romischen Welt*, II.19.2 (Berlin and New York, 1973), pp. 663-676.

18. Followed here are the measured judgments of such scholars as Levine, "The Jewish Patriarch," p. 657 (who also cites further literature), and J.G. Gager, *The Origins of Anti-Semitism* (New York and Oxford, 1983), pp. 89-90.

19. See, among others, Abbot and Johnson, *Municipal Administration*, pp. 52-53, 74-75; A.H.M. Jones, *The Greek City from Alexander to Justinian* (Oxford, 1940), pp. 121-123; Schürer, *History of the Jewish People*, Vol. 2, pp. 218-220; Goodman, *State and Society*, pp. 155-171.

20. The probable reasons for his prominence are outlined by Goodblatt, "Origins of Roman Recognition," pp. 95-97 (though he himself rejects them).

21. P.T. *Ta'anit* 4:1 (67d) contains the same story, almost word for word. A Babylonian Talmud parallel is found in *Berakhot* 27b; compare also B.T. *Bekhorot* 36a. Note that these are all Amoraic sources.

22. Various aspects of this story were discussed by R. Goldenberg,

"The Deposition of Rabban Gamaliel II: An Examination of the Sources," *Journal of Jewish Studies* 23 (1972), pp. 167-190. Though he doubts the veracity of the reports as found in talmudic accounts, he does accept the historicity of Rabban Gamaliel's ouster. Alon, *The Jews in their Land*, Vol. 1, pp. 315-322, assumes that at this time both the Patriarchate and a strong central Sanhedrin existed, and consequently sees the various conflicts between R. Gamaliel and R. Joshua as conflicts between these two institutions.

23. A recent study of this story, with extensive bibliography, is D. Goodblatt, "The Story of the Plot against R. Simeon B. Gamaliel II," *Zion* 53 (1984), pp. 349-374 (Hebrew). Though Goodblatt does prove that several elements in the story are of Babylonian origin, this does not mean, as he claims, that the entire story of a conflict between R. Shimon b. Gamaliel and several Sages is a Babylonian Amoraic fabrication.

24. A.I. Baumgarten, "Rabbi Judah I and His Opponents," *Journal for the Study of Judaism* 12 (1981), pp. 135-172, analyzes several controversies between R. Yehuda ha-Nasi and various Sages from the perspective of rhetoric and polemics.

25. It has been suggested (S. Safrai, "Tales of the Sages in the Palestinian Tradition and in the Babylonian Talmud," *Scripta Hierosolymitana*, Vol. 22 [1971], p. 231) that the Babylonian identification of Bar Elishaa as R. Yehuda ha-Nasi's son-in-law (B.T. *Nedarim* 51a) is dubious. For the purposes here it makes no difference whether he was his son-in-law or simply a wealthy patrician befriended by R. Yehuda ha-Nasi.

26. Urbach, "Class Status," p. 70.

27. *Genesis Rabba* 80:1 (ed. Theodor-Albeck, pp. 950-951) contains a parallel.

Chapter 4

THE POLITICAL DYNAMICS OF THE MEDIEVAL GERMAN-JEWISH COMMUNITY

Ivan G. Marcus

The medieval German Jewish community was formed as merchant families gradually emigrated to the Rhineland from Italy and northern and southern France.[1] Almost at once, political authority was focused on a rabbinical figure whose authority depended on a combination of Torah learning, family prestige, and economic independence. He was a merchant who knew Torah, and he shared leadership with the "board of elders" or *qahal* and its *parnas* (head). These terms are already mentioned in the late tenth century rabbinical answers (responsa) of Rabbi Meshulam bar Qalonimos, an early member of an Italian rabbinic family that migrated to the Rhineland.[2]

Jewish settlements developed in the Rhineland towns because they were the administrative and growing commercial centers of the area. In the middle of the tenth century, Emperor Otto I (936-973) began a policy of appointing bishops and archbishops to serve in the imperial administration, even though this was contrary to Canon Law. In the episcopal towns of Mainz and later Cologne, Worms and Speyer, the local ecclesiastical officials represented the emperor, who offered Jewish merchants protection in return for their economic assistance.

Located at the juncture of the Rhine and Main rivers, Mainz was ideally suited to become an early Jewish settlement. Among the founders of the Mainz Jewish community, some of the French Jewish families traced their lineage back to a wealthy and learned patriarchal founder, Rabbi Abun the Great, from Le Mans in northern France, possibly a branch of a family that was part of the elite of Narbonne in southern France.[3] Another family, the Qalonimides from northern Italy, had a family tradition claiming that a King Charles — that is, Charlemagne (d. 814) — had brought their ancestor from Lucca and resettled him and his important relatives in Mainz. (More will follow about this Carolingian foundation legend first reported by Rabbi Eleazar ben Judah of Worms, d. ca. 1230). Within a short time, members of the Abun clan had intermarried with members of the Qalonimide elite.

From the outset, traces are evident of four key sources of authority among the Rhenish Jewish leadership: family lineage; Torah learning; wealth; and backing — real or imagined — by the Christian government. These sources of authority could confer upon an individual an aura of personal prestige independent of any official elective or appointive office that he might attain in the community. Indeed, these factors serve as the criteria for being elected by the community to be head (*parnas*) or to function as religious judge or head of the rabbinical court (*rav*). Such authority may be called "conventional" to distinguish it from either "institutional" authority, in the sense of elected or appointed office, or "charismatic" authority, strictly understood as involving a claim to being divinely selected to disclose a special revelation or perform a spiritual mission in society.

From the beginning, religious and political authority were intimately associated in the Jewish community, and communal leadership assumed two overlapping but distinct forms. On the one hand, there were the religious judges or rabbis whose expertise in Torah law gave them special authority. On the other hand, communal control over non-*halakhic* (non-legal) public affairs devolved upon the "elders" whose authority derived from their age, wealth, family lineage and other personal qualities. They maintained public order, collected taxes for the Christian authorities and for the support of Jewish social services, and were the liaison with the Christian rulers. To govern effectively over these areas of public life, what was needed was not so much expertise in Jewish law as experience and influence. In the period of first settlement, the religious judges were merchants like the rest of the community, paid taxes, and were among the elders who decided public policy. As communities grew in size and complexity, communal roles became more differentiated, and a paid rabbinate gradually developed in Germany by the thirteenth century.[4]

The immigrant beginnings of the tiny Jewish community of Mainz, its geo-political location on a "Jewish frontier," far from the sway of the Jewish political authority of the Palestinian Gaons or of the Babylonian Exilarch and Gaons or even of European regional leaders such as the Head of the Jews in the Caliphate of Cordova, Hasdai ibn Shaprut — all contemporary with the tenth century early settlement of the Mainz community — gave the nascent leadership there much room to maneuver politically and to improvise and experiment with new patterns of autonomous local governance.

One is struck by the remarkable independence and self-confidence expressed in the responsa of Rabbenu Gershom ben Judah (d. 1028), who was not related to either the Abunides or Qalonimides, but who began his own dynasty and was the dominant figure in Mainz in the last decade of the tenth and the first three of the eleventh centuries. He rarely mentions the decisions and responsa of the Babylonian Gaonim, although he knew of them. Moreover, he often renders decisions by basing himself on the Mishnah or even on a biblical verse, despite an 800-year-old tradition of post-mishnaic legal discussion and codification. In addition, he copied and presumably established his own text of the Hebrew Bible and the Mishnah, a tendency towards textual standardization that continued in the German and especially in the northern French school of Rabbi Solomon ben Isaac (Rashi, d. 1105), who studied in Mainz and Worms in the 1060s. In addition, he exercised his rabbinic authority by issuing ordinances outlawing polygamy and against a woman's being divorced without her consent, both signs of the relatively high standing Jewish women enjoyed in the frontier society of early medieval Germany.[5]

There are also indications of improvisation by the early community boards made up of the communal leaders contemporary with Rabbenu Gershom. Responsible for maintaining law and order, supervising the weights and measures in the market, and providing for the indigent, they reflected the first settlers' occupations as merchants. The institution of *ma'arufia*, an individual Jewish merchant's trade monopoly with a Christian client, was widespread in part of the Rhineland, and community boards adopted measures to protect it. As the Jewish population grew in the eleventh century, community boards placed a ban on new settlements (*herem ha-yishuv*), an innovation designed to protect against excessive economic competition.[6]

After R. Gershom's death in 1028, the head of the Mainz academy and rabbinical court was Rabbi Judah ha-Kohen, Gershom's main disciple, also not an Abunide-Qalonimide.[7] Increased authority rested on the new master. Whereas R. Gershom was sent questions primarily from within the German towns, R. Judah was also regarded as a major authority by Jews living in Champagne in northeast France, as well as further east in Central Europe. The elders of Troyes asked R. Judah to define the limits of local rule. In his answer we have one of the most detailed discussions about the definition and limits of local communal jurisdiction and autonomy in medieval Europe.[8]

R. Judah based his answer on an early rabbinic text which stipulated that the local Jewish "townsmen could compel one another" to conduct local community business such as "to build a synagogue, purchase a Torah scroll" or "to make agreements" such as to regulate the community workers' wages and determine fines in case of damages inflicted on public property.[9] This source had remained theoretical so long as Jews lived in Muslim lands, where Jewish communities were organized under central authorities of Gaons and Exilarchs. R. Judah concluded that each local Jewish community had complete autonomy from any outside intervention of another in matters affecting the religiously neutral areas of public welfare, such as those stipulated in the rabbinic text about the "townsmen." But if members of one community violated Jewish law, then it was the obligation of others to intervene and try to prevent or punish the religious infraction.

In effect, R. Judah was creating de jure recognition for the spontaneous de facto development in northern Europe of local communal self-government. Away from the control and guidance of the Babylonian or Palestinian Jewish leaders, most tiny local Jewish communities, like those in Germany, necessarily acted autonomously, and R. Judah's decision sanctioned this situation by applying to the community in Troyes the rabbinic precedent governing local "townsmen." In this way he made an ancient text into a mandate for the condition of Jewish self-rule that was to characterize hundreds of Jewish communities that emerged in the new towns and settlements in Latin Christendom.

R. Judah also stated that a community may pass ordinances decided upon by the elders even if a majority of the others disagreed. Authority was to be exercised collectively by the rabbinical judges and the *parnasim* acting together with the other elders on the community board. The early Jewish community was not a democratic body, but was an oligarchy run by the consensus of the elite.[10] Still, a theory of association by voluntary consent underlay the Jewish community board's authority "to make agreements." It had the legal force of an oath or vow made by the individual members to follow the community's decisions. This oath, in turn, was theoretically derived from the one the Israelites had taken at Mt. Sinai when the covenantal bond was established with "those that are standing with us this day before the Lord our God and with those who are not here with us this day" (Deuteronomy 29:14).

An additional sign of new communal development occurred in 1084. After a fire broke out in the Mainz Jewish quarter, some of the inhabitants left and were welcomed to Speyer by Bishop Ruediger who issued them a formal charter.[11] Modeled on early Carolingian *privilegia* issued by Charlemagne's son, Louis the Pious, to individual Jewish merchants around 825,[12] the Speyer charter extended guarantees of life, religious protection, and exemption from tolls to a new community of Jewish merchants. In 1090 Emperor Henry IV confirmed it. The patterns of royal protection of local Jewish self-rule that were developed first in the German towns became the model for local Jewish communities in the regions of royal France, Christian Spain, England, and Central and Eastern Europe. State rulers generally continued the Carolingian policy of royal or imperial legal protection of European Jews until late in the thirteenth century.

It should be noted, then, that the Mainz foundation legend crediting a King Charles with the foundation of Mainz Jewry reflects a true collective memory of that community's elite that the Carolingians were the first permanent protectors of the earliest Jewish communities there. In this sense, Charlemagne was the founder of northern European or Ashkenazic Jewry. Rather than speculating on the authenticity of this or that detail in the accounts, it may be understood that at one level at least, the legend recalls the Carolingian origins of the northern European Jewish charter tradition, one of the legend's fundamental historical meanings.

Certain Hebrew sources, including a local Speyer chronicle,[13] recount that the leaders of the new community were members of the Qalonimide elite that began to reassert its political and religious dominance in Mainz and Speyer towards the end of the eleventh and especially in the twelfth centuries. For example, the imperial confirmation of the Speyer charter involved members of the family. Bishop Ruediger initiated it when he was seriously ill. He went to Emperor Henry IV with three local Jewish elders, including R. Judah ben Qalonimos the Elder, to request that he confirm the episcopal charter of 1084. The emperor did confirm it on February 19, 1090, and the bishop died three days later.[14]

It also appears that the second Jewish quarter that was established near the Cathedral at the time of the confirmation was of special significance as a power base of the Qalonimos elite in town. Thus the Speyer chronicle stipulates that R. Judah ben Qalonimos had "his *beit midrash*" there, and this new public area, which included a synagogue building (still partially standing) and an underground ritual bath (*miqvah*), completely excavated, may reflect the general political process of the Qalonimides' re-asserting themselves at this time.[15]

The anti-Jewish riots that broke out in the Rhineland towns in the late spring of 1096 in response to the ferment released by Pope Urban II's call the year before for an armed pilgrimage to Jerusalem — the First Crusade — eliminated many members of the religious leadership in Mainz and Worms, especially the non-Qalonimides, who were martyred there.[16] The one community that survived the attacks without committing temporary mass apostasy[17] was Speyer, where Bishop John (1090-1104), Ruediger's successor, protected most of his Jews and punished the Christians who had killed six or seven.[18]

The fact that most of Speyer Jewry survived and that many non-Qalonimide scholars perished in 1096 gave the Qalonimides who survived the riots in Speyer special opportunities in the twelfth century. Several descendants of that family continued to enjoy positions of leadership. Towards the middle of the century, R. Qalonimos ben Meir of Speyer was active in the court of Emperor Frederick I Barbarossa. His nephew, R. Simha ben Samuel of Speyer, referred to his uncle as being "close to royalty, among the king's courtiers" and recalled that his uncle told the king, "I serve you by making loans and in many other ways."[19] His brother-in-law, R. Judah ben Qalonimos ben Moses of Mainz, was an authority in Mainz, and in Speyer, the older son of R. Qalonimos the Elder, R. Judah, served as *parnas* and his nephew, R. Abraham b. Samuel b. Qalonimos the Elder, was head of the Speyer academy in the late twelfth century.

II

The younger son of R. Qalonimos the Elder, R. Samuel, became known in Speyer as well, not as a legal or communal authority, but as a charismatic link in a chain of esoteric mystical traditional lore derived from the East and transmitted by the Qalonimides from Italy to the Rhineland.[20] This Samuel, born around 1115, just ten years before his father, R. Qalonimos the Elder, died, was later called "the pietist, the holy, and the prophet,"[21] and it was with him and especially with his son, R. Judah the Pietist (*he-ḥasid*; d. 1217), that a fifth major source of political authority appeared in medieval Germany: religious charismatic authority. In each case, it was a younger son who claimed to be a link in the mystical chain of tradition. By laying charismatic claims to their religious authority, these two members of the Speyer branch of the Qalonimide dynasty offered a potential challenge to the bearers of the sources of conventional authority — family lineage, Torah learning, wealth, and Christian governmental support.

After R. Samuel and especially R. Judah developed their charismatic claim to religious authority to project a special religious vision in German Jewish society, a reaction set in when R. Judah the Pietist's disciple and relative, R. Eleazar ben Judah of Worms (d. ca. 1230), effectively ignored or resisted his teacher's charismatic claims to establish a counter-community of pietists. Instead, R. Eleazar returned to asserting conventional claims of communal authority and transformed pietism into a private form of spirituality that was to take place within the conventional Jewish community, not in a surrogate community of religious virtuosi. In the aftermath of the dynamics of the shift from charismatic (R. Judah the Pietist) to conventional (R. Eleazar of Worms) pietism, there are signs that conventional authority itself was beginning to yield to more institutionalized forms of leadership. The appearance in the thirteenth century of newly differentiated community roles was significant.[22] One product of the challenge posed by charismatic authority was a reaction which went beyond merely returning to earlier models of conventional authority and instead moved towards greater professional specialization in several areas of communal life, including the beginnings of the institutionalization of the communal rabbinate, a process that continued into the fifteenth century.

The appearance of charismatic pietists in the middle of the twelfth century in the Rhineland was in part occasioned by the shift from Mainz to Speyer that took place there fifty years earlier during the anti-Jewish riots that accompanied the Popular Crusade in Mainz and Worms. The Hebrew narratives that dwell in length on those riots portrayed Mainz in particular as a newly destroyed Jerusalem and the Jewish martyrs as Temple sacrifices or Holy Things. But in addition to lamenting the loss of Mainz, the edited narratives also portrayed a continuation of German religious leadership in the Speyer community. The Mainz/

Jerusalem that was temporarily rebuilt and destroyed was followed, according to the editor who arranged the manuscript, by Speyer as the new center of Torah learning.[23] In fact, it was in Speyer that the brothers Makhir, descendants of Rabbenu Gershom, collected and preserved the local decisions and customs of Mainz and Worms and added to them those of Speyer, their new place of residence.[24] It was also there that Rabbi Samuel the Pietist, the younger son of a survivor from the 1096 Mainz riots, R. Qalonimos the Elder, began to write down for the first time the elements of an ancient but heretofore privately transmitted vision of the ideal Jew and with it special criteria by which a pietist (*hasid*) could claim to know God's will. Central to the pietist vision was a charismatic qualification for being a good leader and intuitive criteria by which to judge other community leaders.[25]

To be sure, R. Samuel was far from being an outsider in the Rhineland Jewish community. Since his older brother, R. Judah, apparently was the *parnas* in Speyer and had even represented the Speyer community before Emperor Henry IV in 1090, R. Samuel did not lack the connections needed to play a political role in the local communal hierarchy. Yet he took a different path. Apparently, he did not participate in public life as a religious judge or as a *parnas*. Instead, his writings and the near contemporary legends which surround his persona cast him in the role of a religious zealot or *hasid*,[26] an ancient term which began to come into vogue again in the Rhineland as well as in other parts of the Jewish world such as southern France and Egypt.[27]

R. Samuel's few writings thus far identified with some degree of probability dwell on the observance of the neglected commandments, on fasts, and on the avoidance of pleasure.[28] His goal was not focused on society but was turned inward. For him, personal salvation in the next world required not only observance of the religious commandments but also an active search in Scripture for hidden implicit commandments demanded by the will of God only partially revealed in Scripture and rabbinic interpretation. Moreover, it was the pietist who was uniquely qualified to fathom God's hidden will; it was he alone who could lead the good life.

If left by a politically neutral observer as a personal prescription for the salvation of his soul, such writings might have gone unnoticed. In the case of R. Samuel, a well-known figure riding the crest of the new wave of Qalonimide rabbinic influence in the Rhineland, this stance caused a stir but not a social or political crisis. His son's writings on pietism did.

With R. Judah the Pietist, the author of *Sefer Ḥasidim* (Book of the Pietists),[29] a new phase was begun in the political development of the German-Jewish elite. From his writings it is clear that he was a member of the "old boy" network who was also an eccentric religious extremist. He described pietism not only as a program for individual salvation but also as a political program for pietists organized as a counter-elite defined in opposition to the community and its leadership. He conceived of pietism as a sect: pietists alone were the true Jews in opposition to all others whom he called the "wicked"; and he appealed to an intuitive knowledge of God's will, independent of rabbinic exegesis and authority alone.[30]

Whereas his father had also claimed that it was the pietist who knew the hidden will of God, Judah the Pietist drew social and political conclusions from his claim. For him, all Jews were either pietists, or non-pietists, and the latter were "wicked," not much better than Christians. As for pietists, they must look for guidance in this world not to non-pietist communal *parnasim* and rabbis but to the pietist sages (*ḥakhamim*), an ancient term that once referred to the authorities of the rabbinic leadership but now applied to the sectarian leadership of the pietist movement. The sage was to advise the pietist on the hidden meanings of the will of the Creator: tell him which person to marry in accordance with pietist criteria; and, should the pietist sin, the sage knew which penances to prescribe once the pietist had made a personal confession to him.[31]

Judah the Pietist's program may have been carried out for the briefest time or perhaps only very partially, but it should be remembered that his leadership was charismatic, not conventional and certainly not institutional. He was not a *parnas*, a leader of the community board; nor was he a *rav* or religious decisor as was his older brother Abraham.[32] He was elected to nothing. Although he was a member of the Rhineland Jewish aristocracy, he was known for eccentricity[33] — hence, a *ḥasid* — and his peculiar behavior as reflected in his socio-religious program in *Sefer Ḥasidim* was not popular. His followers were ridiculed because of their strange behavior and exclusivism, such as reciting the prayers at exaggerated length[34] or fasting for two consecutive Days of Atonement.[35] R. Judah's charismatic claims for his own authority transformed him from being a potential member of the communal establishment, which he never was, into a God-intoxicated eccentric whose strange behavior appealed only to a few and earned the ridicule of the non-pietist many.

Moreover, it is difficult to understand why a bearer of conventional authority such as Judah would picture his followers as ridiculed in Jewish society if this were not the social reality. After all, as a pietist familiar with the secret will of God, he would have preferred to dominate the rest of the community and force other Jews to follow his ways. That is an underlying assumption in *Sefer Hasidim*. The fact that he pictured them instead as unpopular can best be explained as the result of actual social conflict and resistance to his program. It is circular to argue that his vision of piety and society was a projection of his own mind. If it were, surely he would have projected success rather than failure. There are signs that triumphalism over and withdrawal from the rest of the community were tried and failed;[36] the overwhelming social backdrop of living in, but not of, the Jewish community reflects the sectarian reality. Finally, a few references do exist in non-pietist sources that the pietists were known to be different. Thus, R. Meir ben Baruch of Rothenburg reports that they wore a unique type of prayer shawl all day long;[37] they prayed slowly, as R. Jacob ben Asher records,[38] and R. Judah reportedly wore sackcloth.[39] This indicates a real but eccentric charismatic leader whose way of dealing with his vision and traditions was to act out his exclusiveness and earn the ridicule it so richly deserved.

It is small wonder that R. Judah the Pietist failed to persist in his sectarian expression of pietism beyond his own life. Indeed, his leaving the Rhineland under mysterious circumstances suggests that his lack of popularity showed him that it was futile to remain in Speyer. Instead, he moved eastward to the Bavarian town of Regensburg. Although scholars moved about freely in the Middle Ages, as today, there is a peculiar aspect to the move.[40] It left a trace in the documentary tradition about the rabbinical lines in medieval Germany:[41]

> ...Rabbenu Samuel the Pietist, Holy One, and Prophet who fathered Rabbenu Abraham of Speyer and Rabbenu Judah the Pietist of Speyer who [was][42] (were) exiled from the land of [his] (their) birth to the district of Regensburg on account of a certain incident. His wife touched his box. He had warned her: "Do not come near the box when you are not pure." She forgot and touched it. That box contained holy secrets written on notebooks.

The existence of this story is an indication that R. Judah's move from Speyer to Regensburg was problematic — for the Jews of Speyer. If the occasion were simply the persecution in Speyer in 1195/96, as Avraham Epstein assumed, this type of legend would not have developed. It should be noted that the positive hagiographical legends about R. Samuel take place in the Rhineland, whereas the ones in which R. Judah is a wonder-working hero are almost all set in Regensburg. For this reason, it is likely that the latter represent Regensburg's favorable collective memory in which their R. Judah was pictured as being superior to his older brother, a head of the Speyer rabbinical court. On the other hand, the story about his exile from Speyer may preserve a Rhenish tradition. In general, R. Judah's relationship to the Rhineland and Regensburg requires reexamination.[43]

In addition, R. Judah's move from Speyer to Regensburg may be compared to the contemporary move of the legal scholar and synagogue poet, R. Ephraim b. Isaac (d. ca. 1175). His contentious personality got him into repeated public disputes in Speyer so that he first left for nearby Worms and later moved to Regensburg.[44] Perhaps R. Judah's leaving Speyer for Regensburg is a parallel career move, motivated in R. Judah's case by his eccentricities and unpopular claims to religious superiority over even his kinfolk.

Whatever the reasons, R. Judah translated his social and religious world view into a political program that was a mirror image of the actual Jewish community that he criticized. His model was not Christian apostolic poverty, a desert retreat, or the millennium. Rather, for him, an organized polity was the norm of Jewish life, but he considered only his pietist group to be the legitimate form of Jewish religious polity. His writings directly challenged the existing rabbinic and communal establishment, and when his views were cast aside, it is not surprising that the reaction took the form of the reaffirmation of those institutions that he had criticized.[45]

The most pervasive relationship portrayed between pietists and other Jews is of a series of attempts to live "in, but not of" the rest of the Jewish community in order for the pietist to protect himself from "contamination" from the ungodly.[46] R. Judah the Pietist assumed that if allowed to remain unchecked, the non-pietists would exert a dominant influence over the pietists. Thus, pietists should not live near non-pietist Jews or intermarry with them or give charity to them or permit their children to play with them or even be buried next to them. A compromise was struck between complete separation and pietist concerns about non-pietist dominance. In view of the fact that pietists could not live without the other Jews, they worked out a way to live with them. Pietists had to keep away from the others unless the pietist was in a position of relative strength, for example, as an employer or moneylender; but if he were in a position of relative dependence, the pietist would be vulnerable to being influenced adversely by the non-pietist (or Christian) and should stay away from him.[47]

It is significant that with the death of R. Judah the Pietist in 1217, a more conservative, political phase of German Hasidism became pronounced in the writings of his relative, Rabbi Eleazar ben Judah of Worms. Whereas R. Samuel and R. Judah the Pietist were the younger son and younger grandson respectively of R. Qalonimos the Elder, who had moved from Mainz to Speyer just prior to the 1096 riots, R. Eleazar was a descendant of the Mainz branch of the Qalonimide family that had stayed in Mainz and survived. Unlike R. Samuel and R. Judah, R. Eleazar was a legal authority as well as a pietist, and his efforts brought pietism into line with formal Jewish communal leadership and Jewish legal creativity. It was R. Eleazar who ignored all traces of his teacher's sectarian program of Hasidism. Instead of promoting a sectarian picture of groups of pietists led by sages, Eleazar described Hasidism in personalist categories, appropriate for individual members of the regular Jewish community.[48]

It was Eleazar, too, who prefaced his handbook of Jewish Rhenish law and local custom, *Sefer ha-Roqeah* (Book of the Perfumer), with a summary of the special virtues of the *hasid*, *Hilekhot Hasidut* (Laws of Pietism), and that concluded with a mystical tract on the ecstatic, mystical contemplation of the Divine Unity. He added to that tract a second consisting of lists of sins and penances for the use, not of a sage-confessor, but for the immediate use of the pietist sinner, *Hilekhot Teshuvah* (Laws of Atonement). Moreover, the sins R. Eleazar singled out for special emphasis were not those designed for a penitent who violated sectarian norms in society, but rather the ones corresponding to a list found in the early Jewish mystical text *Hekhalot Rabbati* and which prevent a mystic from being in a state of necessary purity for achieving the mystic vision.[49] The focus in R. Eleazar's writings, then, is on the individual pietist living in the regular Jewish community, not on a surrogate community of pietists. By putting *Hilekhot Hasidut* and *Hilekhot Teshuvah* at the beginning of his book of Jewish law and custom, R. Eleazar sought to incorporate pietism and ascetic atonement into the fabric of Jewish law, the mainstream of Jewish communal and cultural tradition. In short, he was a religious reactionary: his reformulation of pietism reinforced the religious and political institutions existing prior to R. Judah the Pietist's charismatic and sectarian challenge to them.

Moreover, R. Eleazar's neutralization of sectarian elements in R. Judah's program came at the same time as other signs of communal self-affirmation and institutional development among German Jewry, and it was likely that his efforts were part of the same process in the thirteenth century. Thus, shortly after R. Judah's death in 1217, Eleazar participated in a series of Rhenish intercommunal synods that met in Mainz and Speyer in the 1220s, themselves an indication of renewed Jewish political activity initiated by the regular communal leadership.[50] An ordinance passed by that synod appears to contain the earliest reference to the specialized communal office of rabbi, not simply as a member of a community who is proficient in Jewish law, but as some kind of office-holder in the community. One of the ordinances provided that the communal leadership must approve of major communal acts of discipline in the form of the ban of excommunication (*herem*), and that a *parnas* or a rabbi, referred to now as *"rav be-rabbanuto"* (the rabbi in his rabbinical capacity), are not to issue a ban in secret.[51] By the end of the century there were early signs of a rabbi as a salaried official. The responsa of R. Meir ben Baruch of Rothenburg (d. 1293), the most widely recognized authority of German Jewry, tell of a Jew who contributed to the communal charity fund so that the accrued earnings from the fund could be used by the community to hire a rabbi.[52]

It seems likely that the emergence in thirteenth century Germany of intercommunal synods, the earliest signs of an official rabbinic office, and the appearance then of other specialized communal functionaries, such as experts in performing circumcision (*mohelim*), ritual slaughterers (*shohetim*), and scribes (*soferim*), for whom specialized handbooks were written at that time,[53] indicates a reassertion of the legitimacy of the non-pietist communal leadership. At least in part, this process may have been a reaction to the sectarian political claims of the charismatic Qalonimides in Speyer-Regensburg who had challenged the non-pietist community structure.

To support this idea further, it should be noted that it was R. Eleazar of Worms, a descendant of the non-charismatic Mainz branch of the Qalonimides, who wrote down the Carolingian foundation legend of Mainz Jewry. In R. Eleazar's account of the foundation legend, Charlemagne's foundation of Mainz Jewry was presented as part of R. Eleazar's own family history. The text reads as follows:

> They received the esoteric traditions about the arrangement of the prayers as well as the other esoteric traditions, rabbi from rabbi, all the way back to Abu Aaron, the son of R. Samuel the Prince (*ha-nasi*), who had left Babylonia because of a certain incident and he was therefore required to travel all over the world (as a penance). He came to the land of Lombardy, to a certain city called Lucca. There he found our Rabbi Moses who composed the liturgical poem *"'emat nora' otekha,"* and he transmitted to him all of his esoteric traditions. This is R. Moses bar Qalonimos, son of R. Meshullum b. R. Qalonimos b. R. Judah. (Now R. Moses) was the first who emigrated from Lombardy, he and his sons, R. Qalonimos and R. Yequtiel, and his relative R. Itiel, as well as the rest of the people who counted. All of them were taken from Lombardy by King Charles who resettled them in Mainz. There they grew to prodigious numbers until 1096 when the Lord visited His wrath upon the holy communities. then were we all destroyed, utterly destroyed, except for a few of our relatives who survived including R. Qalonimos the Elder. He transmitted (the esoteric traditions) — as we have written — to R. Eleazar Hazan of Speyer. R. Eleazar Hazan transmitted them to R. Samuel the Pietist and R. Samuel the Pietist transmitted them to R. Judah the Pietist. And from him did I, the insignificant one (*ha-qatan*), receive the esoteric traditions about the prayers as well as the other traditions.[54]

Why was it R. Eleazar of Worms who transmitted this legend? The passage was framed in a propagandistic way on several counts. It was not about German Jewry as a whole, but about R. Eleazar's family, and he presented himself as the continuation of a chain of tradition that was authentic because it derived from an ancient Jewish source of authority (R. Samuel the Prince) and from Charlemagne, the Emperor of the Franks and the Romans in the West.

To be sure, R. Eleazar may simply be telling the truth as he knew it when he reported that his teacher, R. Judah the Pietist, had taught him the esoteric traditions he had learned from his father, R. Samuel the Pietist. As R. Eleazar mentions elsewhere,[55] the

126

son to whom he had transmitted the secret traditions had died, and he wrote down the formerly esoteric traditions because he had no one to whom he could transmit them. True, but why does he use the Carolingian motif which is so rare in Jewish writings in the Middle Ages and which lacks even an historical grain of truth?[56]

The Carolingian legend in Christian Europe was developed as political propaganda and R. Eleazar of Worms was close to one of the important sources of that legend. It was the court of Emperor Frederick I Barbarossa that developed and made use of the Carolingian motif for its own political purpose, namely, in order to bolster the Emperor's claims against the French king, Louis VII, as the true heir to the mantle of Roman *imperium* (authority) in the West. By moving to have Charlemagne canonized as his personal saint in 1165, Frederick's chancellor, court poets and chroniclers, among the latter, his uncle Otto of Freising, sought to support German claims against the French monarch. The strategy involved a dual claim of a *translatio imperii* (transfer of authority) and a *translatio studii* (transfer of learning) from East to West.[57]

R. Eleazar's Mainz foundation legend contained both elements of transfer. He argued that the esoteric lore came from Babylonia through Italy to Mainz (transfer of learning), and he also claimed that it was Charlemagne who literally transferred a Qalonimos ancestor who had received authoritative lore from an otherwise unknown, indeed fictitious, R. Samuel the Prince, a title that might be taken to imply Davidic authority (transfer of authority). Moreover, R. Eleazar indicated that the transfer of authority and learning passed through the Speyer descendants of R. Qalonimos the Elder, but then went not to R. Judah's son (R. Moses-Saltman), but to himself, the heir to a branch of the Mainz clan that did not move to Speyer and that did not have charismatics.

R. Eleazar was in a position to know about the Carolingian propaganda in Frederick I's court, for he had close family connections there. His father, R. Judah ben Qalonimos of Mainz, was the brother-in-law of R. Qalonimos ben Meir of Speyer, the court banker for Frederick Barbarossa (the wives were sisters). In addition, the son of that R. Qalonimos ben Meir, R. Judah ben Qalonimos of Speyer, the author of *Sefer Yuhasei Tannaim ve-Amoraim*, was one of R. Eleazar's principal teachers.[58]

When his charismatic teacher died in 1217, Eleazar wrote down most of the esoteric traditions he had learned, and he also wrote down for the first time the Carolingian foundation legend of Mainz Jewry and of his family. Perhaps he was pointing to a reassertion of the prerogatives of the Mainz Qalonimide communal and rabbinic leadership over the role that the Speyer charismatics had played after 1096. Perhaps, too, he was aiming his account, as had Frederick Barbarossa, towards France by insisting on the superior role that German Jewry was destined to play as the continuation of Eastern lore and authority guaranteed by Charlemagne himself, the embodiment of the transfers of authority and learning from the East to the West.[59] His account, it should also be noted, was a functional equivalent of R. Abraham Ibn Daud's "Story of the Four Captives" in his *Sefer ha-Qabbalah* (Book of Tradition), a late twelfth century account that invents a propagandistic tale about the earlier transfer of Jewish authority and learning from the Babylonian Gaons to the rabbis of Cordova in tenth century Muslim Spain.[60]

Thus, by the late thirteenth century, the political factors of traditional Torah learning, family lineage, wealth, and royal support — real or claimed — reasserted themselves over the temporary claims of the Speyer charismatics. At the same time, early signs pointing toward what would later become a professional rabbinate and a series of other communal functionaries emerged there as well. If the 1096 riots marked a temporary shift in the influence of the rabbinic elite away from Mainz and Worms towards Speyer and northern French schools, the chain of events it unleashed, including the appearance of the charismatic pietists in the late twelfth century, ultimately helped consolidate and strengthen the conventional and newly institutionalized leadership in Germany.[61]

Notes

1. On the community's origin, see especially Avraham Grossman, *Hakhmei Ashkenaz ha-Rishonim* (Jerusalem, 1981), and the bibliography in Ivan G. Marcus, "The Jews in Western Europe: Fourth to Sixteenth Century," in *Bibliographical Essays in Medieval Jewish Studies* (New York, 1976), pp. 40-47. On the early German towns, see Fritz Rörig, *The Medieval Town* (Berkeley, 1967) and Horst Fuhrmann, *Germany in the High Middle Ages: c. 1050-1200* (Cambridge, 1986), and their bibliographies.

2. See David Cassel, ed., *Teshuvot Geonim Qadmonim* (Berlin, 1848), nos. 122, 142, etc.

3. See Grossman, *Ḥakhmei*, p. 89, n. 43.

4. See Simon Schwarzfuchs, *Etudes sur l'origine et le développement du rabbinat au moyen âge* (Paris, 1957), pp. 17-38 and cf. below, n. 52. On tax-exemptions, see Israel Ta-Shema, "Exemption of Rabbinic Scholars from Taxes in the Middle Ages," (Hebrew) in Y. Gilat *et al.*, eds., *Studies in Rabbinic Literature, Bible and Jewish History* (Ramat Gan, 1982), pp. 312-322.

5. See Grossman, *Ḥakhmei*, chapter 3 and Alexander Marx, "Rabbenu Gershom, Light of the Exile," in his *Essays in Jewish Biography* (Philadelphia, 1947), pp. 39-60; A. Grossman, "The Historical Background to the Ordinances on Family Affairs Attributed to Rabbenu Gershom Me'or ha-Golah ('Light of the Exile')" in *Jewish History, Essays in Honour of C. Abramsky* (London, 1988), pp. 3-23.

6. On *ma'arufia*, see Irving A. Agus, ed., *Urban Civilization in Pre-Crusade Europe* (2 vols.; New York, 1968), vol. 1, pp. 187-255 for some of the sources. On the ban on new settlement, see Louis Rabinowitz, *The Herem Yayyishub* (London, 1945).

7. See Grossman, *Ḥakhmei*, chapter 4.

8. Kol Bo (Naples, 1490), no. 142, translated with an unsatisfying commentary in Agus, vol. 2, pp. 446-453. Avraham Grossman published R. Judah's book of legal decisions, *Sefer ha-Dinim* (Jeruslem, 1977), the first such book from medieval Germany, with an introduction that appeared separately as "R. Judah ha-Cohen ve-Sifro 'Sefer ha-Dinim,'" *'Alei Sefer* 1 (1975): 7-34.

9. *Tosefta, Bava Mezia* 11:23, ed. M. Zuckermandel (Jerusalem, 1963), p. 396; ed. Lieberman (New York, 1988), pp. 125-126; T.B. *Bava Batra* 8a.

10. Grossman cogently demonstrated this in *Ḥakhmei*, pp. 189-193, against Agus's "democratic" thesis.

11. The Latin original is in Franz X. Remling, ed., *Urkundenbuch zur Geschichte der Bisjchöfe zu Speyer* (2 vols.; Mainz, 1852-53), vol. 1, pp. 57-58, no. 57 (13 September 1084), and is available in English in Robert Chazan, ed., *Church, State and Jew in the Middle Ages* (New York, 1980), pp. 58-59. Note that Chazan's translation on p. 59 of the brief Speyer Chronicle is abbreviated in the middle, thereby omitting the date of the incident (1084), and at the end. The complete text is in Shlomo Eidelberg, ed., *The Jews and the Crusaders* (Madison, 1977) (hereafter, E), pp. 71-72. See p. 161, n. 236 for the date. Physical traces of this first settlement in Altspeyer have disappeared. In the 1960s, Dr. Günter Stein excavated the remains of the second settlement which can be seen today. It apparently dates from 1090, when Henry IV confirmed the episcopal charter (see below). In the fall of 1984, the Stadtmuseum in Speyer mounted a retrospective exhibition on Speyer Jewry to mark the 900th anniversary of the 1084 charter ("1084-1984 — 900 *Jahre Speyerer Judenprivileg*"). On the early settlement of Speyer in general and the question of how significant a change in status the town underwent when Bishop Ruediger admitted the Jews, see Lawrence G. Duggan, *Bishop and Chapter: The Governance of the Bishopric of Speyer to 1552* (New Brunswick, 1978), p. 65.

12. For the three merchant charters issued to individual Jews by Louis the Pious around 825, see K. Zeumer, ed., *Monumenta Germaniae Historica, Formulae Merovingici et Karolini aevi* (Hanover, 1886), pp. 309-310, 325. They are translated in Bernard Bachrach, ed., *Jews in Barbarian Europe* (Lawrence, 1977), pp. 68-71.

13. An editor appended the text to the manuscript which contains the Hebrew First Crusade "Chronicle" attributed to one Solomon ben Samson that was published, with a German translation, in A. Neubauer and M. Stern, eds., *Hebräische Berichte über die Judenverfolgungen während der Kreuzzüge* (Berlin, 1892), (hereafter, NS), p. 31 (Hebrew), pp. 142-143 (German); again in Hebrew in Abraham Haberman, ed., *Sefer Gezeirot Ashkenaz ve-Zarfat* (1945; repr. Jerusalem, 1971) (hereafter, H), pp. 59-60, and in English by Eidelberg, pp. 71-72. The most recent translation, Robert Chazan, *European Jewry and the First Crusade* (Berkeley, 1987) (hereafter, C), does not translate it, since it is not, strictly speaking, part of the Solomon ben Samson narrative. On this short text, see Robert Chazan, "A Twelfth Century Communal History of Spires Jewry," *Revue des Etudes Juives* 128 (1969): 253-257; and on its ideological relationship to the Solomon ben Samson narrative as a whole, see Ivan G. Marcus, "From Politics to Martyrdom: Shifting Paradigms in the Hebrew

Narratives of the 1096 Crusade Riots," *Prooftexts* 2:1 (January 1982), especially p. 51.

14. During the catastrophic fire which broke out in 1084 in the Jewish quarter in Mainz, near the Dom, one outstanding figure was Rabbenu Meshulam b. Moshe b. Itiel who died in 1095. See Grossman, *Ḥakhmei*, pp. 386-387; NS, p. 31; H, p. 59; E, pp. 71 and 161, n. 237. In 1096, the *parnas* there apparently was his son, R. Qalonimos. See Grossman, *Ḥakhmei*, p. 387; NS, pp. 6, 14-15; H, pp. 30, 40-41; E, pp. 30, 44-46. On R. Judah b. Qalonimos (Speyer) in 1090, see the Latin text in Alfred Hilgard, ed., *Urkunden zur Geschichte der Stadt Speyer* (Strasbourg, 1885), pp. 12-14, no. 12 and the translation in Chazan, *Church*, pp. 60-63. For his probable relationship to R. Qalonimos the Elder, see Israel Qamelhar, *Rabbenu Eleazar ben Yehudah mi-Germaiza ha-Roqeah* (Rzeszow, 1930), pp. 9-11. It is also possible that this Judah b. Qalonimos is another part of the family that cannot be connected directly with the rest. The other two delegates, R. David b. Meshullam and R. Moses b. R. Yekutiel, also were Qalonimides. See Grossman, *Ḥakhmei*, pp. 46 and 398. For the twelfth century Qalonimide leaders, see below.

    The Speyer Jewry charter and its royal confirmation contain terms similar to those Henry IV granted in a charter to the chapter of the Speyer Cathedral in 1101. It granted, among other conditions, "the possession and administration of common property (and) certain powers of self-governance and discipline," Duggan, p. 14. Henry IV's concessions to both were part of his effort to gain support during his struggle with Pope Gregory VII ("the investiture controversy"). On Ruediger's illness as the proximate cause for the confirmation's timing, see Sara Schiffmann, "Die Urkunden fur die Juden von Speyer 1090 and Worms 1157," *Zeitschrift für die Geschichte der Juden*, n.s. 2 (1930-31), p. 36.

15. It was the synagogue in this new quarater that was rededicated in 1104. See NS, p. 31; H, p. 60; E, p. 72. On the two quarters in Speyer, see Günter Stein, "Der Mittelalterliche Judenhof und seine Bauten," in *Geschichte der Juden in Speyer, Beiträge zur Speyerer Stadtgeschichte*, Heft 6 (Speyer, 1981), pp. 48-64, especially p. 48 and the bibliography on pp. 63-64.

16. See Grossman, *Ḥakhmei*, p. 436. Among the critical survivors were R. Samuel the Pietist's father, R. Qalonimos (b. R. Isaac) the Elder, and R. Eleazar of Worms' father, R. Judah b. R. Qalonimos b. Moses.

17. Regensburg is portrayed as undergoing forced baptism in the Danube. See NS, p. 28; H, p. 56; E, p. 67; C, p. 293.

18. On the political reasons for Bishop John's success, among them the fact that he was a loyal pro-imperial bishop, see Sara Schiffmann's brilliant analysis *Heinrich IV und die Bischöfe in ihrem Verhalten zu den deutschen Juden zur Zeit des ersten Kreuzzuges* (Berlin, 1931), also published in *Zeitschrift für die Geschichte der Juden in Deutschland*, n.s. 3 (1931): 39-58 and 233-250.

19. See Ismar Elbogen, *et al.*, eds., *Germania Judaica* (2 vols. to date; Tubingen, 1963), vol. 1, p. 341 (no. 17); and R. Isaac b. Moses of Vienna, *Or Zaru'a* (4 vols. in 2; vol. 1, Zhitomir, 1862; vol. 2, Jerusalem, 1887), part 3, p. 37c (*Bava Qama*, no. 460).

20. On R. Samuel, see Abraham Epstein, "R. Shmuel he-Hasid b. R. Qalonimos ha-Zaqen," in A.M. Haberman, ed., *Kitvei R. Avraham Epstein* (2 vols.; Jerusalem, 1950-1957), vol. 1, pp. 245-269; reprinted in Ivan G. Marcus, ed., *Dat ve-Ḥevrah be-Mishnatam shel Ḥasidei Ashkenaz* (Jerusalem, 1986), pp. 25-46.

21. See R. Solomon Luria (Maharshal), *Responsa* (Lemberg, 1859), no. 29, f. 23c.

22. See Israel Ta-Shema, "Qavim le-Ofyah shel Sifrut ha-Halakhah be-Ashkenaz ba-Me'ot ha-13-14," *'Alei Sefer* 4 (1977): 20-41.

23. Marcus, "Politics to Martyrdom," p. 51.

24. See Grossman, *Ḥakhmei*, pp. 358-386, especially p. 383.

25. See Ivan G. Marcus, *Piety and Society: The Jewish Pietists in Medieval Germany* (Leiden, 1981), chapter 2.

26. The Hebrew sources were published in Nehemiah Brüll, ed., "Beiträge zur Jüdischen Sagen und Spruchkunde im Mittelalter," *Jahrbuch für jüdische Geschichte und Literatur* 9 (1889): 1-71 and in English by Moses Gaster, ed., *Ma'aseh Book* (Philadelphia, 1934), nos. 317-318 (pp. 317-396), based on the Yiddish version (Amsterdam, 1723). On the charismatic qualities of R. Samuel, see Brüll, pp. 24-25 and Gaster, nos. 158-165; and on R. Judah, see Brüll, p. 33 and Gaster, no. 166 (Judah will be a "Master of the Name" (*Baal Shem*); Brüll, p. 23, n. 1; Brüll, p. 28 ("he knows the future"); Brüll, p. 43, n. 2 (death bed near revelation of the messianic date).

27. See Isadore Twersky, *Rabad of Posquières* (Cambridge, Mass., 1962), p. 27, and n. 33; S.D. Goitein, "Abraham Maimonides and his Pietist Circle," in Alexander Altmann, ed., *Jewish Medieval and Renaissance Studies* (Cambridge, Mass., 1967), pp. 145-164; and Gershom Scholem, *Origins of the Kabbalah*, R.J. Zwi Werblowsky, ed. (Princeton, 1987), p. 229-231, 238-244 and 254.

28. See Marcus, *Piety and Society*, pp. 136-137.

29. The book exists in two recensions. The long one, found in Heb. MS Parma, 3280, was published by Jehuda Wistenetzki (Berlin,

1891) and again, with an introduction by Jacob Freimann (Frankfurt am Main, 1924). A facsimile edition was published, with an introduction by Ivan G. Marcus (Jerusalem, 1985). The short recension, just as important as the long one, was the basis of all earlier printings (*ed. princ.*, Bologna, 1538). On the relationship between the two and the order of the topical notebooks which constitute the divisions of the book, see Ivan G. Marcus, "The Recensions and Structure of *Sefer Ḥasidim*," *Proceedings of the American Academy for Jewish Research* 45 (1978), pp. 131-153. For a reference to R. Judah's other notebooks, see below. The author is presently completing a critical Hebrew edition and an annotated English translation, the latter for the Yale Judaica Series.

30. Marcus, *Piety and Society*, chapter 4.

31. On the sage, see *ibid.*, pp. 71-78; on the penitentials, see Ivan G. Marcus, "*Ḥasidei Ashkenaz Private Penitentials*," in Joseph Dan and Frank Talmage, eds., *Studies in Jewish Mysticism* (Cambridge, Mass., 1982), pp. 57-83 and *idem.*, "The Political Writings of the Hasidim of Ashkenaz," (Hebrew) in Joseph Dan and Joseph Hacker, eds., *Studies in Jewish Mysticism, Philosophy and Ethical Literature* (Jerusalem, 1986), pp. 369-384.

32. On the contrast between the two brothers, see Gaster, *Maaseh Book*, no. 166, pp. 336-338; and the reference to R. Abraham as one of the "Sages of Speyer" in E.E. Urbach, *Baalei ha-Tosafot* (4th ed., 2 vols.; Jerusalem, 1980), p. 200, n. 48 (R. Isaac b. Moses of Vienna, *Or Zarua ad Avodah Zarah*, par. 182).

33. The author is indebted to Professor Israel Ta-Shema for formulating and documenting this point in a personal conversation.

34. See R. Jacob B. Asher, *Arbaah Turim, Oraḥ Ḥayyim*, par. 113; Marcus, *Piety and Society*, pp. 99-100; and Ivan G. Marcus, "The Devotional Ideals of Ashkenazic Pietism," in Arthur Green, ed., *History of Jewish Spirituality* (2 vols.; New York, 1986), vol. 1, pp. 356-366.

35. The custom is attributed to R. Judah the Pietist and R. Eliezer b. Joel ha-Levi (Ravyah) specifically by R. Moses b. Isaac in his compilation *Or Zarua*, part II, par. 281 (end) who refers to "those people who customarily observe two Days of Atonement." R. Jacob b. Asher also ascribes it collectively to "the German pietists and men of pious deeds" (*ve-ḥasidim ve-anshei maaseh be-ashkenaz*) in *Arbaah Turim, Oraḥ Ḥayim*, par. 624 (end), where he reports that his father, R. Asher b. Yehiel, opposed it. R. Eliezer b. Joel ha-Levi (Ravyah) contains a tradition tracing the practice back to R. Isaac ha-Levi of the Worms academy in the mid-eleventh century. See Avigdor Aptowitzer, ed., *Sefer Ravyah* (2nd ed., 4 vols.; Jerusalem, 1964-1965), part II, p. 659; and

Grossman, *Ḥakhmei*, p. 287 and n. 117 for other references, including that Rashi (R. Solomon ben Isaac, d. 1105) opposed it.

36. Marcus, *Piety and Society*, pp. 89-92. This does not mean that Judah the Pietist's social program was a total fantasy. Cf. the brief and unsupported claim of Joseph Dan in this otherwise admirable study, "Li-Demuto ha-Historit shel R. Yehudah he-Hasid," *Tarbut ve-Hebrah be-Toledot Yisrael Bi-Mei ha-Beinayim* (H.H. Ben-Sasson Memorial Volume), ed. R. Bonfil *et al.* (Jerusalem, 1989), p. 398.

37. R. Meir ben Baruch of Rothenburg, *Responsa* (Prague, 1608), no. 287; translated in Marcus, *Piety and Society*, p. 98.

38. See first reference, above, n. 34.

39. See JTS Mic. 1885, f. 71b from "Sefer Sodot Aḥer" (Another Book of Secrets) copied in a manuscript dated 1413 (f. 76a): "Dress. Sackcloth...we know that the people of Nineveh wore sackcloth and so did the earlier (generations). R. Judah (the) Pietist, may his rest be in Eden, did likewise."

40. A. Aptowitzer dismissed scholarly attempts to explain why R. Judah left the Rhineland for Regensburg: "I do not know why we need to look for a special reason for his going to Regensburg." See his *Mavo le-Sefer Ravyah* (Jerusalem, 1938), p. 346. Aptowitzer assumed that R. Judah travelled there as a student, a common enough practice among Jews and Christians at the time. However, there is no evidence for this assumption.

41. See above, n. 21.

42. The singular is to be preferred, in light of the continuation.

43. See Avraham Epstein, "Das talmudische Lexikon Yehusei Tannaim ve-Amoraim und Jehuda b. Kalonymos aus Speier," *Monatsschrift für Geschichte und Wissenschaft des Judenthums* 39 (1895), part 2, p. 449, n. 5. On R. Judah's legends and their locale in Regensburg, not Speyer, see also Israel Tashema, "Le-Toledot ha-Yehudim be-Folin ba-Me'ot ha-12-13," *Zion* 53:4 (1988), p. 368, where he reached the same conclusion independently.

44. See Urbach, *Baalei ha-Tosafot*, pp. 200-207.

45. The tendency of Jewish religious revivals to mimic the form of the Jewish community but impose its own definition of legitimacy should be compared to Christian and Muslim attitudes towards society at times of religious ferment.

46. There are important similarities between the Jewish martyrs' efforts to avoid being polluted by contact with Christians, as detailed in the Hebrew First Crusade "Chronicles," and the attitude of the pietists towards avoiding any compromising contact with

non-pietist Jews as well as Christians. On the martyrs, see Marcus, "Politics to Martyrdom," *passim*. The pietists' strategy of living among Christians was discussed by Jacob Katz, "The Hasid," chapter 8, in his pioneering *Exclusiveness and Tolerance* (New York, 1961), pp. 93-105. For a revision of Katz's model (theoretical avoidance of contact, practical necessity of contact), see Ivan G. Marcus, "Hierarchies, Religious Boundaries and Jewish Spirituality in Medieval Germany," *Jewish History* (University of Haifa), I:2 (Fall, 1986): 7-26. There the author suggests that the pietists permitted contact with non-pietist Jews or Christians if the pietists were in a position of relative hierarchical strength, i.e., were "on top."

47. See Marcus, *Piety and Society*, chapter 6.

48. On Eleazar's revision, see *ibid.*, chapters 7 and 8.

49. See *Hekhalot Rabbati* 13:2 in Adolph Jellinek, ed., *Bet ha-Midrasch*, vol. 3, p. 93. The significance of this passage for the design and function of Eleazar's penitential will be discussed elsewhere. This influence from late antique or early medieval *Heikhalot* texts is but one sign of the antiquity of much of German pietism that was written down in the twelfth and thirteenth centuries. As such, it is part of a larger socio-cultural transformation in medieval Jewish culture parallel to and in part interactive with what in medieval historiography used to be called "the renaissance of the twelfth century" and more recently is treated in such books as Robert L. Benson and Giles Constable, eds., *Renaissance and Renewal in the Twelfth Century* (Cambridge, Mass.: Harvard University Press, 1977). This is a large subject that the author plans to develop elsewhere as "the renaissance of Jewish spirituality in the twelfth century." For a related aspect of this process whereby early, traditional corpora were written down because of historical factors in the twelfth century, see Moshe Idel, *Kabbalah: New Perspectives* (New Haven: Yale University Press, 1988), pp. 250-253.

50. The proceedings of the communal synods of 1220 and 1223 were published with English translations in Louis Finkelstein, ed., *Jewish Self-Government in the Middle Ages* (New York, 1924), pp. 218-256. The reason these synods met when and where they did (Mainz before 1220, and again in 1220 and in Speyer in 1223) needs further investigation. The new appearance of the Franciscans in the Rhineland might have something to do with it. Thus, the Franciscans began their German activity in 1221 and the new minister general of the Order in Germany, Albert of Pisa, assembled a provincial chapter in Speyer on September 8, 1223. Is there any connection between this initiative and the synod in Speyer that year? See John B. Freed, *The Friars and German Soci-*

ety in the Thirteenth Century (Cambridge, 1977), pp. 26-27 and 38. A separate study will consider the social and political background of these synods.

51. See Finkelstein, p. 228, and Schwarzfuchs, pp. 36-37.

52. R. Meir ben Baruch of Rothenburg, *Sheelot u-Teshuvot*, Prague Edition, M.A. Bloch, ed. (Budapest, 1895), no. 942, p. 133c; Schwarzfuchs, p. 37. In his recent monograph, *Hakhamim be-Doram* (The Religious Leadership of German Jewry in the late Middle Ages) (Jerusalem: Magnes, 1988), Yisrael Yuval discusses earlier scholarship on the question of the origins of the professional rabbinate in medieval Germany and concludes that a fully professional rabbinate, supported by the community, can be traced only to the fifteenth century (pp. 11-20 on the earlier theories, and pp. 322-435 for his conclusions). But, as Yuval correctly notes: "The beginnings of the communal rabbinate are obscured by semantics, guess work, and differing interpretations of the sources" (p. 11). Unfortunately, this applies to Yuval's own brief and unconvincing dismissal of the text cited from R. Meir ben Baruch of Rothenburg and his omission of the text cited in n. 37. The point being made here is that the process of administrative differentiation and professionalization began in the thirteenth century.

53. See above, n. 22.

54. R. Eleazar of Worms, *Sodot ha-Tefillah* (Secrets of the Prayers), Paris, Bibliothèque National, Heb. MS 772, f. 60r; translated in Marcus, *Piety and Society*, p. 67. For the other sources and important discussions, see Grossman, *Hakhmei*, pp. 29-44 and Reuven Bonfil, "Bein Erez Israel le-Vein Bavel," *Shalem* 5 (1987): 1-30.

55. See his introduction to *Sefer ha-Hokhmah* in Oxford, Bodleian Library, Heb. MS Neubauer 1812, f. 53r and published recently in *Peirush ha-Roqeah al ha-Torah* (3 vols.; Bnai Brak, 1978-1981), vol. 1, pp. 9-10, and earlier by Joseph Dan, "Sefer ha-Hokhmah' le-R. Eleazar mi-Worms," *Zion* 29 (1964); reprinted in Joseph Dan, ed., *Iyyunim be-Sifrut Hasidut Ashkenaz* (Ramat Gan, 1975), pp. 44-57.

56. Cf. Grossman, *Hakhmei*, p. 39, n. 50 and the references there.

57. On the Carolingian propaganda in Frederick's court, see Peter Munz, *Frederick Barbarossa* (Ithaca, 1969), pp. 129 and 242-244. The legend of Charlemagne is discussed in detail in R. Folz, *Le souvenir et la legende de Carlemagne dans l'empire germanique médiévale* (Paris, 1950). For the connection between the "transfer" motifs and Frederick, see Ernst Robert Curtius, *European Literature and the Latin Middle Ages* (Princeton, 1953), pp.

28-29. For the Carolingian motif and Jewish history, see Aryeh Grabois, "L'image légendaire de Charlemagne dans les sources hébraïques du moyen âge," *Le Moyen Age* 72 (1966): 5-41; Jeremy Cohen, "The *Nasi* of Narbonne: A Problem in Medieval Historiography," *AJS Review* 2 (1977): 45-76; and Joseph Shatzmiller, "Politics and the Myth of Origins: The Case of the Medieval Jews" in Gilbert Dahan, ed., *Les Juifs au regard de l'histoire* (Paris, 1985), pp. 49-61. The political aspect of R. Eleazar's use of the legend as a reassertion of old German-Jewish claims against the French Tosafists and the *nouveau arrivé* "School of Rashi" will be discussed elsewhere.

58. See Epstein, "Das talmudische Lexikon," pp. 447-451.

59. Compare the suggestion that German pietism was directed at France in Haym Soloveitchik, "Three Themes in the *Sefer Ha-sidim*," *AJS Review* 1 (1976): 318-319, 351-354 and 357; and cf. Marcus, *Piety and Society*, p. 168, n. 80. If we distinguish between the shared ideology of pietism, which is not demonstrably directed at French Tosafism per se, and R. Eleazar's conservative stage in the pietist movement, then the latter can be seen as having an anti-French motivation.

60. See Gerson D. Cohen, "The Story of the Four Captives," *Proceedings of the American Academy for Jewish Research* 29 (1960-1961), pp. 55-129, and the text in Abraham Ibn Daud, *Sefer ha-Qabbalah*, Gerson D. Cohen, ed. and trans. (Philadelphia, 1967), pp. 46-48 (Hebrew) and pp. 63-66 (English).

61. See Mordecai Breuer, "Ma'amad ha-Rabbanut be-Hanhagatan shel Qehillot Ashkenaz ba-Me'ah ha-15," *Zion* 41 (1976): 47-67, and Yuval, *Hakhamim be-Doram*, chapter 6.

PART II –

RENEWAL AND COMMUNITY

Chapter 5

THE POLITICS OF ANGLO-JEWRY
BETWEEN THE WARS

David Cesarani

Anglo-Jewry before World War I was dominated by a small number of men, scions of illustrious families whose power derived largely from their wealth and influence in the non-Jewish world. The Rothschild, Montefiore, Cohen, Samuel, and Montagu families presided over the central institutions of the community — the Board of Deputies, the Anglo-Jewish Association, the Board of Guardians, the United Synagogue and the Federation of Synagogues.[1] It was a lay community in which the rabbinate was respectfully ignored: oligarchy and plutocracy ruled the synagogal institutions as much as those devoted to philanthropy and the political tasks of representing, protecting and regulating the Jewish population.

Since wealth and political clout were the sources of authority in the community, there was little role in it for the Jewish middle class and still less for the recently arrived Eastern European proletariat. Nevertheless, ambitious men of more lowly stature than the Rothschilds were restlessly challenging the ruling hierarchy. These men had their own organizational bases in the B'nai B'rith and the English Zionist Federation in particular. Working class Jews grouped together in *hevras*, Friendly Societies, and trades unions which met their direct needs. They too skirmished with the Anglo-Jewish establishment, but they were too dependent on it and too effectively excluded from the centers of power to have any effect.[2] Despite conflict over the appropriate response to immigration and the Anglicization of the immigrants, the communal leadership acquitted itself well in the resistance to immigration controls and the defense of Jewish aliens. This reinforced its prestige and the legitimacy of its preeminence in the years up to 1914.

During the war, the authority of the Anglo-Jewish leadership was damaged in a number of ways. It alienated immigrant Jewry by encouraging war service and consenting to the "Convention" by which Russian Jews were forced to either return to Russia to fight there, or to enlist in the British army.[3] In 1917, as Stuart Cohen has shown, a large slice of the Jewish middle class, particularly in the provinces, was enraged by the high-handed behavior of the London leadership which publicly rejected the diplomatic activity of the Zionists. As a result of the communal revolution which followed, the influence of the self-appointed Anglo-Jewish Association was curtailed and the electoral base of the Board of Deputies was broadened. For the first time, representatives of non-synagogal institutions were admitted — from the Jewish Friendly Societies and the Union of Jewish Women — as well as delegates from the East End synagogues united in the Federation of Synagogues and the United Synagogue.[4]

The significance of 1917 and the reforms which followed have been exaggerated, but even the qualifications stated so well by Stuart Cohen have themselves to be qualified. The Zionists did not capture the Board; but neither did the B'nai B'rith or the provincial middle class. In 1920, the President of the Board was Sir Stuart Samuel, one of the "cousinhood." He was flanked by two Rothschilds as vice-presidents. The only provincial represented among the honorary officers was Nathan Laski, a figure of pre-war eminence. Of the approximately ninety members of the Board serving on its various committees — and discounting the two Rothschilds who represented Northern constituencies in absentia — only seventeen hailed from parts north of London. Of these, the ubiquitous Nathan Laski accounted for no less than seven, and his son Neville, a further two. The Friendly Societies were awarded only one authentic representative on a Board committee.[5]

A survey of the community in the 1920s reveals the extent to which the ancien regime persisted. At the Board of Deputies, Sir Stuart Samuel replaced the temporarily disgraced D.L. Alexander, and was in turn succeeded by H.S.Q. Henriques in 1922, who was followed by Osmond d'Avigdor Goldsmid, who held office until 1933. They were all figures drawn from the social matrix which supplied the prewar leadership, as were the vice-presidents of the Board — Lord Rothschild (1918-1933), Anthony de Rothschild (1918-1922), Joseph Prag (1925-1928), and Sir Isidore Salmon who took office in 1929. Even the treasurers represented continuity: Nathan Laski, B.S. Strauss, and Jo Prag. The Anglo-Jewish Association (AJA) remained a fief of the "cousinhood" and was ruled in turn by Claude Montefiore, d'Avigdor Goldsmid, and then Claude's son, Leonard Montefiore. At the United Synagogue (US), another Rothschild presided: Lionel de Rothschild, who held the office until 1942, and Sir Robert Waley-Cohen, the real force in the US, who dominated its affairs from the vice-presidency between 1918 and 1942.[6]

The only crack in this carapace of the ancien regime came at the Federation of Synagogues, where a genuine revolution occurred in 1925. The second Lord Swaythling (a Montagu), who had inherited the Federation from his father, was forced to resign by a popular revolt of the East End immigrant membership (see below). Otherwise, the middle and working class elements of the community were penned into the institutions that they had themselves created: the B'nai B'rith (BB), the Zionist Federation (ZF), and the Friendly Societies. A smattering of prominent figures of the B'nai B'rith were elected to serve on committees of the Board of Deputies, but none served as honorary officers until the 1930s. The Zionists were excluded until the closing years of that decade, although individuals were being elected onto Board committees in increasing numbers. The 50,000 Friendly Society members were grossly underrepresented even after the Board's constitution was reformed in 1918-19. They were allotted fifteen seats — as compared to twelve for the London-based United Synagogue Council and the nine seats awarded to the AJA in 1925.[7]

The disparity in representation and the dysfunction between the leadership of these key institutions and the community that they were supposed to represent became a focus of controversy once the crises of the 1920s exposed the failings of the erstwhile leadership. The politics of Anglo-Jewry from this point until 1939 were marked by a dual process. The old leadership suffered a gradual erosion of authority as it manifestly failed to cope with successive crises and to fulfill its appointed function: to lead and protect the community. Simultaneously, alternative leadership cadres arose and proved their mettle. This new leadership was drawn from the Anglo-Jewish middle class and from the immigrant community which was gaining social and financial strength during the same period. Their exclusion became all the more irksome as their wealth accumulated and as they displayed their communal abilities in meeting the challenges of the decades before the war.

Although one Anglo-Jewish historian has commented that the "1920s were a relatively quiet period for Anglo-Jewry," a closer examination reveals a different situation.[8] Far from relative quiet, these were years of crisis and strain, particularly from 1918 to 1925, when the community suffered a triple assault by anti-alienism, anti-Bolshevism, and anti-Zionism.

Immediately after the war ended, the British authorities refused to readmit Jews who had been sent to Russia under the "Convention," and delayed the naturalization promised to alien Jews who had served in the British army. Jews were then caught in the wave of vindictive chauvinism that resulted in the Aliens Restriction (Amendment) Act of 1919. This Act established regulations for the control and supervision of aliens and gave unprecedented powers to immigration officials, the police, magistrates, and the Home Secretary to deport aliens without any judicial proceedings or right of appeal. Jews who reentered England from Russia without visas were frequently trapped by these rules and expelled, even if they had been resident in the country for years, with businesses and families. Others were tried and deported for minor infractions of the regulations, such as not registering a change of address, or for committing petty crimes. At one point in 1923, Jews were being deported from England at the rate of one per day. Also during this period, the state and local governments were practicing systematic discrimination against aliens in the spheres of education, welfare, housing, and employment. The Jews were, not unwittingly, the chief victims.[9]

The animus toward alien Jews was sharpened by their identification with Bolshevism. In the postwar years, the *Morning Post* and the *Times* were propagating the world Jewish conspiracy theory which blamed the Jews for the revolution in Russia, and the *Protocols of the Elders of Zion* were in vogue. Even after the exposure of the forgery, immigrant Jews were viewed with suspicion. At the time of the "Red Scare" in 1924 and the General Strike in 1926, the President of the Board was obliged to reiterate that Jews were not involved with radical movements.[10]

The Balfour Declaration and the Mandate had created a powerful counterforce by virtue of the official association between the Jews and the British government, but its legitimating effect was limited by strong anti-Zionist forces in British politics. Palestine was a subject of extreme controversy in the general elections of 1922, 1923, and 1924. Zionism was debated repeatedly in the Houses of Parliament, debates in which anti-Zionists drew on anti-alienism and anti-Bolshevism. If anything, the question of Zionism exacerbated anti-Jewish feeling.[11]

The travails of the 1920s were a severe test of the leadership of

Anglo-Jewry: its claim to represent and serve the community was shaken by a succession of failures. One section of the old elite failed at the first hurdle: those who congregated in the League of British Jews. Formed in 1917 to oppose the claim that all British Jews were Zionists, the League's membership read like a roster of the "cousinhood." Many of those on its national committee held communal office prior to 1917 and for years afterwards, despite the antipathy that it attracted. The League openly denounced Zionism and also identified itself with the anti-alien, anti-Bolshevik campaign. In May 1919, ten of its leading figures wrote to the *Morning Post* — at that time leading the campaign against Zionism and proclaiming the world Jewish conspiracy with fervor — condemning the pro-Bolshevism of foreign Jews in England, as alleged by the *Post*, and disassociating themselves from this supposed activity. This gesture was condemned at the Board of Deputies, by the Zionist Federation, the Federation of Synagogues (where Swaythling, one of the ten, was president), Friendly Societies, and synagogues all over the country. *The Zionist Review* probably reflected the general mood in the community when it judged that the letter of the ten and its anti-Zionism had "stripped the League of its last shred of reputation."[12]

The more temperate leadership of the Board also suffered a loss of prestige and legitimacy during these years. The Board failed to achieve any modifications of the Aliens Act, an agony of powerlessness that was repeated annually since the Act had to be renewed each year by Parliament. Jewish MPs were reluctant to oppose the measure: several were members of the League, which maintained its own discrimination against alien Jews. But the main reason for the Board's lack of success lay in the prevailing anti-alien atmosphere and the intransigence of the Home Secretary from 1924 to 1929, William Joynson-Hicks, a well-known protagonist of anti-Zionist and anti-Jewish causes. However, to the immigrant section of the community and its champions, the Board was simply not functioning in its chief role as intercessor and protector. Friendly Society representatives on the Board, whose members were most directly affected by the aliens legislation and discrimination, were indignant at the repeated failures to win any amelioration. Their frustration led in 1925 to demands for direct representation on the Board. The annual report of the Association of Jewish Friendly Societies stated that the neglect of Friendly Society and working class interests and "the totally unsatisfactory representation in the past had created a strong feeling in the movement and had begun to undermine sympathy for the Board...."[13] Despite improvements in lobbying and some successes in 1928, one Friendly Society leader still complained that the Board was too complacent about the delay in the naturalization of aliens — a crucial matter, since this perpetuated the vulnerable, second-class status of many Jews.[14]

Nor was the Board's authority enhanced in the eyes of Zionists by its treatment of the Jewish National Home. Despite the official sanction Zionism had obtained through the Balfour Declaration and the 1922 White Paper, the old families of Anglo-Jewry did little more than pay obeisance to their new, patriotic duty to support the British-patronized Jewish enterprise in Palestine. While the Board passed declarations welcoming the Mandate, there was no lead from the top to give teeth to these expressions of sympathy. When the Zionists on the Board tried to pass resolutions that would oblige the Board to work with the Zionist Organization, they were defeated. Formally, the Board joined the Jewish Agency in 1924; informally, its leaders refused to contribute what the Zionists needed most — their personal advocacy of the cause and their money.[15]

Over four years after the Balfour Declaration, the *Zionist Review* complained that "Our columns have month after month testified to the unceasing flow of donations from every part of this country. A striking feature, negative but sadly significant, nevertheless, in these lists is the almost entire absence of the names of those blessed above all with worldly goods and insistent on their claims of communal leadership in British Jewry."[16] The abstention of the rich and the influential was not changed by the creation of the Jewish Agency. Some leading members of the community, like Sir Robert Waley-Cohen, patronized the economic development of Palestine and d'Avigdor Goldsmid, in his role as a member of the Jewish Agency, was supportive of Zionist work, but this was more out of a sense of duty to Britain than to any affinity with Jewish nationalism, and also to a fear that if the National Home experiment failed, it would reflect poorly on Jews in England. In 1924, the *Zionist Review* lamented that Anglo-Jews "may congratulate themselves on the fact that they have been privileged to receive the Balfour Declaration on behalf of the Jews of the world, and that it is this country which has undertaken to establish the Jewish National Home in Palestine. We fear that this is all that English Jews can say in their own favor in that respect."[17] To the Zionists it was apparent that the leadership was failing in its communal duty. Their constant criticism of the Board's leaders and the democratic rhetoric directed against the Board, the AJA, and other central institutions of the community further eroded the authority of the traditional leadership.

The loss of authority was evident in the events which shook the Federation of Synagogues — the only genuine "revolution" in the governance of a communal institution in the 1920s. Zionism and democracy were pivotal features of the conflict here. *Di Tsait* celebrated the success of Davis and his allies by reflecting that previously, Lord Swaythling had "used standing orders so that the Federation had nothing to do with the Zionist Movement...."[18] A similar democratic rhetoric was present in the struggle for Zionist influence in the United Synagogue (US). Despite repeated resolutions passed by constituent synagogues, the honorary officers of the US refused to countenance the recommendations for a voluntary levy on seatholders to raise money for the Jewish National Home. Anthony de Rothschild, Robert Waley-Cohen, and Samuel Moses used the constitution of the US ruthlessly to declare all but strictly religious matters *ultra vires*, beyond the competence of the US Council.[19] By 1926, however, there was a majority on the Council of the US for some kind of pro-Zionist gesture: meetings became increasingly stormy and the behavior of Waley-Cohen increasingly autocratic. After one exchange, Herbert Bentwich was moved to write to the *Jewish Chronicle* that "it is necessary that public protest should be made against this overbearing procedure on the part of a responsible Executive, wielding temporary powers, and presuming to defeat by a maneuver the deliberate decisions of the Council and Delegates on large constitutional questions."[20]

Through their opposition to Zionism, the erstwhile leaders of Anglo-Jewry appeared to be setting their faces against democracy in the defense of outworn ideas. Their methods were often high-handed and unscrupulous, and the repeated assaults by Zionists only exposed the archaic and undemocratic nature of communal authority. Every clash highlighted the distance between the leadership and the rest of the community.

Prior to 1911, the traditional leadership of the community had been able to rely upon the support of its spiritual arm, the chief rabbinate. Chief Rabbi Adler, for example, had banned Zionism from the synagogues.[21] The election of J.H. Hertz in 1911, however, had saddled the leadership with a truculent personality who was strongly disposed towards Zionism. Hertz attempted to exercise some leadership in this direction, but he was hampered by the

Erastianism of the United Synagogue and the poor state of the rabbinate. The Anglo-Jewish ministry was not a powerful force before the war and, despite Hertz's efforts to raise the prestige of the clergy and increase the scope of their activity, it remained lame. It was widely felt that the average rabbi was little more than a synagogue secretary and not a spiritual leader — or leader of any kind. Criticism came from across the spectrum of the community. In 1919, the *Jewish Guardian*, voice of the old families, ascribed the low repute of the ministry to its composition: "The spiritual future of the Anglo-Jewish community cannot be considered to be secure as long as our ministers are drawn from, or appeal to, that section of the community which may be described as its foreign element."[22] A few years later, the *Zionist Review*, which might have been expected to show greater favor to such a rabbinate, complained that "Our ministers have, hitherto, with some notable exceptions, proved to be mouthpieces of their *parnassim* rather than the exponents of teaching and tradition on the *mitzvot* of the *yishuv* in Eretz Israel."[23] Hertz was one of those notable exceptions, along with Dayan Feldman, a leading figure in Jews College for many years. Both held positions in the Mizrachi Organization, Hertz actually acting as President. But they were the only members of the United Synagogue establishment to side with Zionism.

The ministry tried to raise its profile by means of a series of bi-annual conferences for "Anglo-Jewish preachers." These congregations deliberated on Zionism, education, welfare, and matters relating to the immigrant population. But sections of the community were averse to the rabbinate entering the mundane sphere. The *Jewish Guardian* took Hertz to task for supporting fund-raising to aid pogrom victims in the Ukraine. On the other hand, it took a benevolent view when one of the leaders of Liberal Judaism in England, Rabbi Israel Mattuck, denounced Zionism in the *Spectator* in 1926.[24] Clearly, the rabbinate was not valued for its autonomy: the traditional sources of its authority, learning, and the law, applied only to the devotees of strict Orthodoxy such as members of the Machzike Hadas in East London. For the wider rabbinate, presiding over the vast majority of the community, its role in leadership was almost non-existent.[25]

Education was one of the issues that most preoccupied Hertz. This was the Cinderella of Anglo-Jewry, but it became an ever more pressing issue as the children of immigrants began to grow up in a milieu that did not automatically inculcate Jewish knowledge. The Jewish War Memorial Council, founded in 1919, was intended to remedy the deficiencies of Jewish education in England, but the million pounds proposed to finance the enterprise never materialized and the scope of the project had to be curtailed. In 1922, the Jewish Religious Education Board launched the first of several appeals for funds, marking a renewed concern for education. At the end of the 1920s, a full-time worker for the Board was appointed for the first time. It is significant that Noah Morris was a Zionist and prominent as a founder of Zionist youth groups.[26] To Robert Waley-Cohen, a member of the Council for Jewish Education, instruction was a means to Anglicize and to instill the virtues of citizenship. For the Zionists, many of whose activities could be called educational, the aim was to raise national consciousness and to undermine precisely the values of the prewar community. The growth of the Zionist youth movements from the start of the 1930s revealed the extent to which Zionist endeavor and the force of circumstances succeeded in achieving this. But the metamorphosis evident during the course of that decade was due to more than ideology.

By 1940, the politics of Anglo-Jewry was transformed. The President of the Board, Selig Brodetsky, was foreign-born and an active Zionist. One of the two vice-presidents was Dr. Israel Feldman, a professional man who had long been associated with the Zionist movement. A more democratic executive had been created to replace the autocratic system of rule by the honorary officers, and in 1943 the relationship with the AJA was finally terminated. Zionism was hegemonic: the fact that from 1933 onward, every president of B'nai B'rith was also a prominent member of the ZF was indicative of the preeminence of Zionism in the new suburban communities.[27]

Other important developments had taken place outside the ambit of the Board and the familiar institutions of Anglo-Jewry. New organizations had been set up in response to events in Germany and Fascism in England, the most important of which were the Jewish Representative Council for the Boycott of German Goods and Services and the Jewish Peoples' Council Against Fascism and Anti-Semitism. These bodies comprised delegates from synagogues, Friendly Societies, Jewish trades unions, trades associations, and Zionist groups. They represented those who were barred from the Board of Deputies and their existence was a standing reproach to the notion that the Board was either democratic or representative. It is also significant that the constituents of these councils had been less politically active prior to the 1930s, but that their activation, when it came, could not, or would not, be accommodated by the existing institutions, forcing them out to the "left" both in strictly intra-communal and also general political terms. Zionists, but more prominently socialists and communists, supplied a brand new leadership to sections of the community who no longer felt served by the old leaders.[28]

During the 1920s, politics in the community had reached a stalemate. The Zionist movement and the Friendly Societies were unable to alter the power structure or were mollified by various concessions so that they felt no need to press for change. The old leadership held onto power. In 1933, however, Osmond d'Avigdor Goldsmid was replaced as President of the Board by Neville Laski. Laski represented that class which had rebelled in 1917: he was a barrister from Manchester whose family had long been involved in pro-Palestine activity. The Zionists thought that he would be a natural ally, and actually asked him to join the Council of the Zionist Federation upon his assumption of office at the Board.[29] But Laski proved to be a huge disappointment. Instead of closing the gap that had grown between the leaders and the community, he adopted the policy and practices of the old establishment, ranging himself alongside Lionel Cohen, Anthony de Rothschild, and Waley-Cohen.

While Laski assumed the governing style of the plutocrats, he lacked the money, power, or the prestige and influence that they had carried in the non-Jewish world. By contrast, he faced an opposition that drew its numbers from the newly rising sectors of the community: the suburbanites, the professionals, and the communal workers who had won their spurs in the Friendly Society and Zionist movements. A potential alternative leadership stood in the wings when Laski took the stage: his failure, in their eyes, to meet the challenge of the crises that were to rain upon the community destroyed his political career.

Neville Laski was elected the new President of the Board of Deputies on 15 January 1933. The following month he was confronted by the critical situation arising from Hitler's assumption of power. Laski's policy was formulated in close cooperation with Leonard G. Montefiore, the President of the AJA, with whom he was joint chairman of the Joint Foreign Committee (JFC). Together they were able to dominate the JFC which then presented policy to the Board, so that Laski and Montefiore began with an inordinate degree of power and authority. In fact, 1933 witnessed a steady erosion of the respect in which they and their offices were held and a drastic loss of influence in the community.

Initially, Laski and Montefiore counselled inaction. Despite anxious questions at the Board, they were practically passive until March 1933 when there were raids on Jewish organizations in Germany, wholesale dismissals of Jews, violence, and an anti-Jewish boycott. At the end of March there were demands in the Jewish community in England for a public protest and a boycott of German goods and services. But Laski and Montefiore disdained these urgent requests for action. They told JFC and Board meetings throughout April and May that they were advised by the German community that demonstrations would have severe repercussions in Germany. Furthermore, Laski warned the Board that since the public demonstration was their only weapon, it would be foolish to use it at once, and without making sure it would be of impressive aspect.[30] The impatience of the Jewish community finally exploded in a series of marches, demonstrations, and an anti-German boycott. In the midst of this welter, Laski appeared time and again before the JFC and the Board advising caution, promising that he was trying to arrange a truly impressive public protest, and strongly deprecating most forms of spontaneous demonstration. He intervened actively to prevent a march by Jewish trades unionists in May and leaned on Lord Melchett to cease patronage of the *Jewish Economic Forum*, a journal devoted to orchestrating the boycott. It seemed that Laski was not only inactive, but that he was trying to frustrate the activity of others.[31]

The result was a storm of criticism that was ad hominem and also aimed at the institutions over which Laski and Montefiore presided. Michael Levy, a leading Zionist and Friendly Society worker, complained that "After fourteen years as a member of the Deputies, I have arrived at the conclusion that the Board does not represent the opinion of Anglo-Jewry, although it may represent the opinion of a miserable minority who are always against coming to the front lest their social standing suffer."[32] The Friendly Societies objected to the conservatism of the Board and Laski's divisive style of leadership, which turned any criticism of policy into a vote of no-confidence in his presidency. The *Jewish World* reported that the two largest Friendly Societies were contemplating cooperation at the Board to form a united opposition. "It is undeniable that ever since the crisis brought about by Hitlerism, the unity of the Board has been broken and the rupture seems to get more serious," wrote the *Jewish World*, but hoped that this would force the leadership to modify its stance "in line with those who would prefer to fight Hitlerism rather than utter high-sounding formulas." The Friendly Societies were debating whether they could continue to follow the old leadership: "There is a feeling that the Board's and the Joint Foreign Committee's administration is weak, and that insufficient information is being vouchsafed, that mandarin-like characteristics are becoming noticeable, and that the community as a whole is not being mobilized in one common effort, either for money or for services."[33]

This soon led to questions regarding the representative nature of the Board, whether it included the best or the right elements in the community. Demands were raised by the end of the summer for the inclusion of Jewish trades unions, the enlargement of representation for the Friendly Societies, and a review of the system of election via synagogues. Zionists often led this onslaught. The *Monthly Pioneer* excoriated the secrecy of the leadership and the "unnatural and humiliating quiescence on the part of Anglo-Jewry."[34] Yet the ZF itself followed the Board's line until 26 March, and when it did take independent action, it was more in the wake of general events than in the vanguard, and even then for a mixture of reasons. The ZF wanted to insist that protests on behalf of German Jews should stress the Zionist moral about the need for open immigration to Palestine. ZF leaders like Barnett Janner were also worried that left-wingers were making inroads into the Jewish community, especially in the East End. For these reasons, claiming that it wished to offer guidance to the various protests, the ZF set up a committee of Zionists and non-Zionists to coordinate anti-Nazi activity. The committee was criticized by Laski, who regarded it as a rival to his authority, although its accomplishments were not notable. If anything, it seems to have formed a lever on the Board which resulted in the enlargement of the JFC and the co-option of several prominent communal leaders, including leading Zionists like Brodetsky.[35]

By the end of 1933, the Board had been subjected to a barrage of criticism. The Association of Friendly Societies had issued a demand for its reform, echoed in the *Jewish Chronicle*. Left wingers attacked the Board for its exclusivity since it did not adequately represent the East End, trades unions, or the broad Jewish lower-middle class. In early March 1934, the new *Zionist Review* issued a series of damaging articles delegitimizing the old leadership. Robert Waley-Cohen was characterized as a "dictator";

Montefiore, a follower of bankrupt assimilationism; Otto Schiff, a philanthropist doing the work of the anti-Semites. The explicit message of the Zionist critique was that the assimilationist policy of these men, their autocratic temper and methods disqualified them from leadership.[36] At the same time, the ZF began its campaign for the democratization of the Board and thus donned the mantle of populist advocate.[37] The struggles over Fascism and Zionism reinforced this challenge to the old pattern of authority.

Laski's attitude to the Fascist menace is well-known.[38] In essence, he advocated a pacific response, relying on the authorities to protect Jewish persons and property. To the Jews he advocated self-restraint and self-improvement, the latter so as not to give grounds for anti-Jewish allegations. As early as July 1933, the Friendly Societies were dissenting from this approach and suggesting independent action. On their own initiative, they set up a campaign of open-air meetings to combat Fascist propaganda in East and North London. The establishment of the left-dominated Jewish Peoples' Council (JPC) in 1936 split the Friendly Societies over the appropriate attitude. The most Zionist, the Grand Order Israel (GOI), affiliated; the most conservative, the Order Achei Brith (OAB), condemned the JPC for setting itself up as a rival to the Board.[39] But even the pro-Board magazine of the OAB, *The Leader*, could understand the growing frustration with Board policy. It editorialized in August 1936 that "There is no doubt that the hesitant and over-cautious attitude of the leaders is tending to make Jewry look elsewhere for the championship of Jewish rights."[40] The Board had failed to give a lead on the boycott, defend Jews on Sunday trading, and now it was failing to cope with the Fascist challenge. The role of the Friendly Societies and the trades unions in opposition to Mosely emboldened their demands for a greater say in the affairs of the community. They demanded direct representation on the Board from early 1937 onwards, with increasing vigor after the leadership's ineffective role in the resurgence of Fascist violence in the East End in early 1938. The normally temperate *Leader* reflected the disenchantment with the old leadership when it protested that "while you play bridge in Golders Green, old people are living in the shadow of impending terror in Bethnal Green."[41]

The Leader was coy in its reference to alternative champions of the Jewish people, but the inference was clear: Jews were turning to the Communist Party (CP) in increasing numbers. It is at this time that the CP assumed a leadership role in the East End, often through the activity of prominent Jewish personalities, renegades from the great families like Ivor Montagu, or Jack Gaster, the son of Haham Moses Gaster.[42] Zionists were particularly alarmed by this trend. It appeared that the best of East End youth were gravitating towards a philosophy and a party that was anti-Zionist. The Federation of Zionist Youth (FZY) felt the competition most keenly and deployed extensive resources to win back ground in the East End lost to the left.[43]

Because of their front-line position, the Zionist youth groups articulated this discontent most loudly. Aubrey (Abba) Eban, writing for the *Young Zionist* in April 1936, commented that "The greatest obstacle in the face of Zionist and all progressive movements in the community is the antiquated tradition of Anglo-Jewish aristocracy with its concommitants of assimilation, servility, social push and conventional orthodoxy."[44] Eban, along with the leadership of the Young Zionist movement, advocated affiliation to the JPC and a united anti-Fascist front with the left. He condemned the "suicidal neutrality of the Board of Deputies" which refused to engage in political struggle against Fascism.[45] The undemocratic nature of the Board seemed to be confirmed when in July 1937 it refused the affiliation of the FZY. After that, Young Zionist conferences and publications systematically derogated the Board, disclaiming its representativeness and influencing the elite of a rising generation of Anglo-Jewry.

Although the Zionist youth movements were loudly and effectively anti-Fascist, the senior movement made no public declaration on the issue of Fascism until after October 1936, when it demanded the enforcement of the Public Order Act. Silence followed again until the *Zionist Review* began to report on the situation in the East End in 1938, where Fascist violence reached a new peak. Zionist spokesmen Barnett Janner and Morris Myer criticized the leadership for its ignorance of affairs in the East End and its apparent lack of concern. Zionist deputies were prominent in the establishment of a defense fund, set up in November 1938, after prolonged agitation.[46]

Despite the ZF's tardiness on the matter of anti-Fascism, Zionism was the ultimate reason for Laski's downfall. Although the ZF had welcomed Laski's election and looked forward to close harmony between the Board and the Zionist movement, Zionists were soon disillusioned. When the ZF wanted to organize a public campaign against the proposal for a legislative council for Palestine in 1935, he declined to give his support and concerted the opposition of the honorary officers on the Board and powerful members of the community.[47] After the outbreak of rioting in Palestine in 1936, he soft-pedaled when the Zionist-dominated Palestine Committee of the Board drafted a protest resolution. When the resolution was finally put to the Board in July 1936, it was denounced by Waley-Cohen, one of the vice-presidents. In the event, Waley-Cohen's intervention did more harm than good to the old leadership. The *Zionist Review* commented that "The result was all the more significant in view of the opposition of a distinguished honorary officer of the Board who, at the last moment, moved an amendment which was defeated by so large a majority that it must have come as a shock to the mover who, by virtue of his position in many communal institutions, is unaccustomed to his suggestions being treated in so summary a fashion."[48]

This resolution had a serious long-term impact on the balance of power between the old leadership and the Zionist opposition and its allies. Since the Zionists controlled the Palestine Committee which formulated policy for the Board and now appeared to be able to command a majority on the Board for that policy, Laski and his colleagues were forced increasingly to operate outside the established institutions. In order to forward their views and to frustrate Zionist initiatives, the non- and anti-Zionists resorted to various forms of backstairs diplomacy with the Colonial and Foreign Offices, alliances with non-Zionists abroad, and private negotiations with Arab leaders. This only aggravated the Zionists still further and added venom to the conflict.

The private diplomacy of Anglo-Jewish non-Zionists reached its apogee during the Partition crisis of mid-1936 to the end of 1937. Anglo-Jews who found the prospect of a Jewish state anathema were placed in a dilemma by the recommendations of the Peel Commission. Since they had to accept loyally the policy of the government, their only recourse lay in either dissuading the government or proving that the Mandate remained workable. Pursuing the first course, they considered a 1917-style demarche in an attempt to scuttle Partition by the weight of their collective influence. In July 1937, a meeting took place at New Court that was reminiscent of events two decades earlier: Lionel and Anthony de Rothschild, Osmond d'Avigdor Goldsmid, Robert Waley-Cohen, Lionel Montagu, Leonard Montefiore, Bukeley Johnson, Sir Isidore Salmon, and Neville Laski congregated together to draft a letter to the *Times* insisting on the viability of the Mandate and the undesirability of a Jewish state. The letter was never sent —

perhaps with 1917 in mind. Instead, Laski concentrated on the diplomatic activity of Albert Hyamson and Col. Newcombe who were trying to work out a formula acceptable to Arab leaders who would then announce their willingness to live with Jews under British rule.[49]

This private diplomacy led to the censure of Laski by the British Section of the Jewish Agency, of which he was a member, and the passing of the resolution by the Board which announced its support for the creation of a Jewish dominion within the British Empire. The background to these two events is tortuous. Weizmann had attempted to win over leading members of the old ruling families — Lord Reading, Lionel Cohen, and d'Avigdor Goldsmid — by offering them a role as advisors on a political committee. They accepted on condition that they could state their reservations to the Colonial Office. The memorandum which they submitted to Weizmann stating the conditions under which they would work with the Zionist Organization was a classic statement of anti-Zionism and totally unacceptable. Laski had appended his name to the declaration. In addition he was encouraging Hyamson and Col. Newcombe who were seeking ways to forestall Jewish statehood. For this, he was publicly rebuked by the British Section and the Palestine Committee.[50] He and Lionel Cohen were humiliated; the memorandum was suppressed. The Palestine Committee then put to the Board a resolution pledging Anglo-Jewry to a Jewish state within the British Empire. The function of the resolution was mainly domestic: to put the lid on opposition to the Zionists. After it was passed, Lionel Cohen resigned as vice-president.[51] Moshe Shertok, who observed this Zionist victory, commented in a letter to Brodetsky that "the resolution passed by the Board of Deputies is of great political importance. It represents a victory of democratic Zionism over assimilationist 'gvirocracy.'"[52]

From this point onwards, Zionism was ascendent in the Board. The election to replace Cohen resulted in the success of Dr. Israel Feldman, long-serving chairman of the Palestine Committee and close ally of the Zionists. In the campaign, his rival, the philanthropist banker Otto Schiff, was smeared as an anti-Zionist and attitudes to Palestine were made the determining factor in a contest without precedent in the history of the Board.[53] Laski and Montefiore were forced back on their position in the JFC, where they seemed to the Zionist majority to be obstructing even attempts to secure the entry of 10,000 German children into

Palestine in 1938. The *Zionist Review* launched ferocious attacks on the JFC and the old leadership: "Their policy of assimilation is bankrupt. The JFC, for example, survives like an antedeluvian relic in a world in which its outlook, its methods, and its machinery have become irrelevant. It still conducts its activity, such as it is, on the basis that there is no Jewish problem and no Jewish people. Why then is it kept alive? Because it holds the fort for assimilationism. Because it keeps official Anglo-Jewry out of the integrities of Jewish life."[54] In order to overcome the JFC, Zionists had demanded its reform and had worked on several committees which investigated ways of reorganizing the Board between 1934 and 1936. None of these came to fruition, but the sense of frustration and the democratic thrust climaxed in 1939 and together led to Brodetsky's irresistible triumph.[55]

Brodetsky's victory only acknowledged formally what had been the case in fact for the previous four to five years. The Board and its leaders had ceased to represent the majority of Anglo-Jewry. This might not have mattered if their social distance and divergent interests had not coincided with what was widely perceived to have been a dereliction of duty — a failure to protect the community from the storms of the 1930s. By contrast, the Friendly Societies, Jewish trades unions, and the ZF had shown themselves to be closely attuned to popular feeling and able to act effectively in response to it.

The leadership of these groups had always been more reflective of the social character of the community. However, it was only when the social transfiguration of Anglo-Jewry took place that the alternative cadres acquired the wealth and influence necessary to actually seize the leadership. This movement can be charted in several ways, first by contrasting the leadership groups and secondly by showing how social and economic trends strengthened their claim to authority. In the 1920s, of nearly half the members of the BZF Council whose biographical details can be readily identified, 15 percent were professionals, nearly 10 percent were manufacturers or engaged in finance and service occupations, and just over 4 percent were women. Of those whose place of birth has been identified, over 50 percent were immigrants. These proportions were reflected in the composition of the executive and honorary officers of the ZF. By comparison, every honorary officer of the Board, the US, and the AJA from 1920 to 1939 was born in the United Kingdom. There were no women in the hierarchies of any of these organizations. Moreover, the leadership with but a few exceptions, like Waley-Cohen, derived its income from nineteenth century sources: often the holders of power were simply rentiers living off fortunes accumulated by Jews who were closer to the *hof-Juden* than to the Jewish middle class of the twentieth century.[56]

In addition to occupation and sources of income, the two factions were distinguished geographically and by virtue of style. The Friendly Societies, the B'nai B'rith, and the ZF were becoming essentially suburban organizations, reflecting the dispersal of the East and Central London communities north and northwestwards. In 1918, of thirty-two Zionist societies in London, eighteen were in East London postal districts, with a further nine in adjacent areas of West and North London. Twenty years later, of fourteen societies, four were located in the Northwest and only one in the East End heartland. Three clung to the periphery of the East End, but the accent had changed decisively. The same was true for the Friendly Societies. The first new lodge to be formed by the OAB after the war was in 1927, in Brondesbury and Cricklewood. This lodge soon became the fastest growing, most active, and richest of all the lodges.[57]

It must also be noted that the suburban communities were acquiring a spiritual leadership that was more in tune with their social and political outlook. Rabbi Louis Rabbinowitz was the first United Synagogue rabbi to come from an immigrant background and a traditional yeshiva education. He served the Cricklewood area as a minister, but this did not prevent him from engaging forcefully in Zionist politics. He was frequently in conflict with the hierarchy of the US, but was loyally supported by his congregants. In Stoke Newington, another new area of settlement, another young rabbi, Bernard Cherrick, incurred the wrath of even the chief rabbi for "pulpit tirades" in which he scored the leadership of the community for its attitude toward the boycott. A similar accusation was levelled against Saul Amias, the young rabbi of the new community in Edgeware.[58]

Accompanying the move to the suburbs was an upward movement in income and a predisposition to dispose of it in new philanthropic ventures. The old leadership had always derived power from its ability to finance welfare and education in the community. In the 1920s, large sums were collected for the Board of Guardians, the Jewish Religious Education Board, and the London Jewish Hospital. Totals ranged from £10,000 to £50,000. But these were as nothing compared to the munificence of Bernhard

Baron, the immigrant cigarette magnate, who in 1925 alone gave away £70,000, followed by another £50,000 in 1926, to the Keren Hayesod exclusively.[59] And when the plight of German Jewish refugees led to the formation of the Central British Fund, the new money of the community showed itself decisively. The Marks-Seiff-Sacher family out-donated even the Rothschilds. For the first three appeals of the CBF, the family gave £10,000 per year. Robert Waley-Cohen, by contrast, gave £1,000 and then dropped out, Claude Montefiore managed a total of £3,000, the Sassons and the Samuels did better, but could not exceed the Marks and Spencer juggernaut. In a community in which the old regime had inculcated a gross respect for money power, this was tantamount to a humiliation.[60]

The old families, deriving wealth from old, outmoded and declining sources, were on the wane. The new men, mostly Zionists, were waxing on incomes flowing from new industries and enterprises — the Burtons, Mond, Baron (Craven 'A'), the Goldbergs of Glasgow, Marks-Seiff-Sacher, Isaac Wolfson (mail order), Oscar Deutsch (Odeon), and Sigmund Gestetner, to name the most prominent.[61] The rise of Zionism was the rise of these men and their fortunes. The burgeoning of suburban Jewish communities in which social life was heavily oriented around Zionist and Friendly Societies that gave political work a prominent place led to the creation of a large, assertive middle and petit bourgeoisie. These class fractions had more in common with each other than with the grand bourgeoisie. Moreover, the incompetence of the latter threatened to deliver Anglo-Jewry into the hands of Communists who encouraged class warfare within the community. They rallied to the call of democracy, because this offered them a role in communal government, and nationalism, because this explained the crisis of Jewry and offered solutions without requiring radical action. Zionism also exposed most penetratingly the weaknesses of the ancien regime. To them, Laski was a class traitor. He had been co-opted into a barely reformed communal leadership, which he then defended. Instead of allowing the process that began in the war years to work itself through gradually, Laski dammed up the tension until it swept him away along with the prewar hierarchies.

The result was the smashing not only of the old leadership, but the representative of the victory of 1917, which makes these events seem so contradictory. A further consequence of his behavior was the efflorescence of Jewish political activism outside pre-existing communal channels and the development of a quite different leadership. At first this dual power was confined to the Zionist Federation and the Board; by 1936 authority had splintered still further so that several representative bodies claimed to represent Jewry. But the events of 1939 were not due to these insurgent forces: they were peripheral to the actual process, even if they helped to fuel it. Brodetsky's victory was the triumph of Zionism, of the new men, the new money, and the suburban communities.

Notes

* A later version of this essay which incorporates further research, with a different emphasis and a substantially revised conclusion, appears in D. Cesarani ed., *The Making of Modern Anglo-Jewry* (Oxford: Blackwell, 1989).

1. On the Anglo-Jewish community before 1914, see Israel Finestein, "The New Community, 1880-1918," in V.D. Lipmann, ed., *Three Centuries of Anglo-Jewish History* (London, 1961); Chaim Bermant, *The Cousinhood* (London, 1971); and V.D. Lipmann, *A Social History of Anglo-Jewry, 1850-1950* (London, 1954).

2. The politics of Anglo-Jewry in this period are dealt with admirably in Stuart Cohen's *English Zionists and British Jews. The Communal Politics of Anglo-Jewry, 1895-1918* (Princeton, 1982). The politics of immigration and immigrant politics are well-treated in Lloyd P. Gartner, *The Jewish Immigrant in England, 1870-1914* (London, 1960), and Geoffrey Alderman, *The Jewish Community in British Politics* (Oxford, 1983).

3. The latest and most detailed investigation of this episode is in Julia Bush, *Behind the Lines. East London Labour, 1914-1919* (London, 1984), pp. 165-191. It is also mentioned in Colin Holmes, *Anti-Semitism in British Society, 1879-1939* (London, 1979), pp. 126-138.

4. *Board of Deputies of British Jews, 67th Annual Report, December 1917-December 1918*, pp. 23-24. (Hereafter, *BOD, Annual Report* etc.).

5. *BOD, 69th Annual Report, December 1919-December 1920*, pp. 18-19.

6. See *Anglo-Jewish Yearbooks, 1918-1939* and *Annual Reports of the United Synagogue*, 1918-1939.

7. See the *Annual Reports of the Board of Deputies, 1918-1939.*

8. Lipmann, *A Social History of the Jews in England*, p. 165.

9. The problem of Jewish aliens is chronicled in the *Annual Reports of the Board, 1918-1929.* Material pertaining to government policy and the response to Jewish lobbying can be found in Public Records Office, Kew, HO/24765.

10. On the anti-Jewish wave, see Colin Holmes, *Anti-Semitism in British Society*, pp. 141-174, and Gizela Lebzelter, *Political Anti-Semitism in England, 1918-1939* (London, 1978). Osmond d'Avigdor Goldsmid made the statement concerning Jewish working class opinion and the strike at the Board meeting on 21 June 1926, *Board of Deputies Minute Book*, 21 June 1926.

11. For the controversy over Zionism, see Chaim Weizmann, *Trial and Error* (London, 1949), pp. 350-354, 360-362; Martin Gilbert, *Exile and Return* (London, 1978), pp. 142-148; and Bernard Wasserstein, ed., *Letters and Papers of Chaim Weizmann*, Vol. II (London, 1978), pp. x-xiii.

12. *Zionist Review* 3:2 (June 1919), p. 19. On the League of British Jews, see Stuart Cohen, *English Zionists and British Jews*, pp. 303-310.

13. *Association of Jewish Friendly Societies Annual Report, 1925.*

14. "Friendly Societies Supplement," *Jewish World*, 8 November 1928.

15. See *BOD Minute Book*, 20 November 1921, when cooperation with the Zionist Organization was agreed to, and 18 December 1921, when practical action was spiked. A year later the Board thanked the government for the Mandate, 19 November 1922, and agreed to join the Jewish Agency after amending the Board's constitution, 21 December 1924. In May 1927, the leadership was asked if anything practical had been done about the Board's Agency membership.

16. *Zionist Review* 5:10 (February 1922), p. 155.

17. *Ibid.* 8:6 (October 1924), p. 61.

18. *Di Tsait*, 15 January 1926.

19. The saga of Zionist lobbying inside the United Synagogue is documented in the United Synagogue Archive, Permanent File 426A, and in the Minutes of Honorary Officers, Executive Council and Council meetings of the US from 1921 to 1927.

20. *Jewish Chronicle*, 17 December 1926.

21. See Stuart Cohen, *English Zionists and British Jews*, pp. 188-189.

22. *Jewish Guardian*, 14 November 1919.

23. *Zionist Review* 8:3 (July 1923), p. 32.

24. For criticism of Hertz, see *Jewish Guardian*, 19 October 1923 and its review of *Affirmations of Judaism* by Hertz (London, 1927), which contained extracts from the writing of Herzl and Brenner on 28 January 1927. For the Mattuck affair, see *Jewish Guardian*, 24 December 1926.

25. On ultra-Orthodoxy, see Bernard Homa, *A Fortress in Anglo-Jewry* (London, 1953).

26. *Report of the Central Committee for Jewish Education, 1928-1929.*

27. For the transformation of the Board, see "Selig Brodetsky and the Ascendency of Zionism in Anglo-Jewry (1939-1945)," *Jewish Journal of Sociology* 22:2 (December 1980) and *BOD Annual Report, 1939-1940*, pp. 18-20. On the B'nai B'rith, see Walter Schwab, *B'nai B'rith, The First Lodge of England: A Record of Fifty Years* (London, 1978).

28. On the Representative Council, see *Jewish Chronicle*, 22 September 1933, p. 24 and editorial comment, p. 6, and Alderman, *Jewish Community in British Politics*, p. 121. The Jewish Peoples' Council is dealt with in Lebzelter, *Political Anti-Semitism in England*, pp. 139-143. An account of the surge in support for the Communists can be found in Alderman, *The Jewish Community in British Politics*, pp. 115-119.

29. Paul Goodman, Honorary Secretary of the Zionist Federation, to Neville Laski, 27 January 1933, Board of Deputies Archive, E1/111.

30. The *Jewish Chronicle* reported that it was flooded with letters calling for a boycott, 24 March 1933. But at the Board, Laski refused to give official endorsement to or leadership of the boycott movement, *Jewish Chronicle,* 31 March 1933.

31. See, for example, Laski's defense of prevarication at the Board on 9 April 1933, reported in the *Jewish Chronicle*, 14 April 1933, and his intervention against the protest march organized by the United Jewish Protest Committee, reported by the *Jewish Chronicle*, 14 July 1933. The march was a huge success: on 20 July, 50,000 Jews walked from Stepney to Hyde Park, an impressive show of solidarity with German Jewry. See *Jewish Chronicle*, 21 July 1933.

32. *Jewish Chronicle*, 31 March 1933.

33. *Jewish World*, 24 August 1933.

34. *Monthly Pioneer* 5:6 (March 1933), p. 4.

35. There is an account of the ZF's reaction in the *Zionist Federation of Great Britain and Ireland 34th Annual Report, 1933*, pp. 21-22.

36. The articles appeared consecutively in the *Zionist Review* 1:1 (March 1934), 1:2 (April 1934), 1:3 (May 1934), 1:4 (June 1934), and 1:5 (July 1934). Waley-Cohen was described as "a dictator in

an age of dictators" who steered clear of any involvement in democracy. To Otto Schiff was applied Herzl's apothegm that "Many an apparent friend of the Jews turns out on careful inspection to be nothing more than an anti-Semite of Jewish origin, disguised in the garb of the philanthropist."

37. For calls to democratize the Board of Deputies, see *Zionist Review* 1:4 (June 1934), p. 53; 12 May 1938, p. 2; and 19 May 1938, pp. 3-4.

38. See Lebzelter, *Political Anti-Semitism in England*, pp. 139, 144-154, and Alderman, *The Jewish Community in British Politics*, pp. 116-117, 121-123.

39. The Grand Order Israel joined the Jewish Peoples' Council, possibly under the influence of Joel Slutsky, a former Young Zionist activist, *Jewish Chronicle*, 30 July 1937. *The Leader* dubbed the Council "a rebel army," condemned its arrogance in dividing the community, and expressed fears that Anglo-Jewry would seem to be identifying with "one party," *The Leader*, December 1936.

40. *The Leader*, August 1936. In January 1937, *The Leader* urged the reform of the Board in order to bring in the Jewish trades unions and so end the necessity of their association with a "political" body, i.e., the Jewish Peoples' Council.

41. *The Leader*, November 1938.

42. See Alderman, *Jewish Community in British Politics*, p. 115. See also such personal accounts as Joe Jacobs, "Out of the Ghetto. My Youth in the East End." *Communism and Fascism, 1913-1939* (London, 1978) and Phil Piratin, *Our Flag Stays Red* (London, 1978).

43. The *Zionist Review* ran a series of articles on "The Communist Challenge" in 1935. They were prefaced by a short statement that "This subject is of growing importance, especially in the East End of London, where great difficulties are experienced in Zionist organizations, particularly among the youth, who, impelled by circumstances, regard everything only from the economic and material point of view." *Zionist Review* 2:6/7 (August-September 1935), p. 89. The series was later issued as a pamphlet by the Federation of Zionist Youth as *The Community Challenge and the Zionist Reply* by Joseph L. Cohen (London, 1936).

44. *Young Zionist* 11:4 (April 1936), p. 1.

45. *Young Zionist* 12:3 (March 1937), p. 3.

46. *Zionist Review*, 19 January 1939, p. 6.

47. Laski wrote to Waley-Cohen that he wanted to "avoid all the paraphernalia of a raging, tearing campaign." Laski to Waley-Cohen, 13 January 1936, Board of Deputies Archive (BDA), E3/233.

48. *Zionist Review* 3:5/6 (July-August 1936), p. 80. For the opposition

of Laski and the honorary officers, see the Minutes of the Palestine Committee of the Board, 16 July 1936, and "Memorandum re Palestine Committee," 16 July 1936, BDA, E3/233. In January, Laski had circulated a letter to Louis Gluckstein, d'Avigdor Goldsmid, and Waley-Cohen expressing his opposition and seeking their support, Laski to Waley-Cohen et al., 30 January 1936, BDA, E3/210.

49. A record of these proceedings can be found in "Memorandum of Meeting at New Court," 19 July 1937, BDA, E3/237.

50. For the censure of Laski, see *British Section of the Jewish Agency Minute Book*, 23 November 1937. The discussions of the Palestine Committee, which include various versions of the affair from the chief actors, are recorded in the *Palestine Committee Minute Book*, 1 December 1937. Details of Laski's private diplomacy with Albert Hyamson can be found in his correspondence files, BDA, B4/HU15 and E3/236-237.

51. *Board of Deputies Minute Book*, 16 January 1938. Cohen's resignation was explained as due to pressure of work, *BOD 108th Annual Report, 1938*, p. 32.

52. Moshe Sharret to Selig Brodetsky, 24 January 1938, Weizmann Archive.

53. The *Jewish Chronicle* covered the contest and participated in it by forcibly putting the case for Otto Schiff in its editorials, *Jewish Chronicle*, 11 February 1938 and 18 February 1938. The *Zionist Review* promoted its candidate, *Zionist Review* 5:2 (January 1938), pp. 19-29.

54. *Zionist Review*, 30 December 1938, pp. 10-11.

55. Various reports on the workings of the Board and proposals for reform are to be found in the records of Board discussions, for example, *Board of Deputies Minute Book*, 18 June 1933, 5 July 1933, 23 August 1933, 15 April 1934, 1 July 1934, and 17 February 1935. The prime mover behind the reform campaign was S. Rowson. He was finally driven to resign from the committee investigating the Board's management after the prolonged tergiversation led him to believe that the Board's leadership was not taking the issue seriously. See *BOD Minute Book*, 23 June 1935.

56. This analysis is based on lists of personnel in the *Annual Reports of the Zionist Federation, 1918-1930*, biographical details in the *Anglo-Jewish Yearbook, 1918-1970*, the *Zionist Yearbook, 1950-1970*, and obituaries in the *Jewish Chronicle*. Many Jews chose not to signify place of birth; occupation, when given, was often vague. A full sociological analysis would be a monumental but rewarding task.

57. For the location of Zionist societies, see *Anglo-Jewish Yearbook*,

1918 and *Zionist Federation of Great Britain and Ireland 39th Annual Report, 1938*. On the foundation of the Robert Waley-Cohen Lodge, see *The Leader*, July 1927 and *Order Achei Brith 39th Annual Report, 1926-1927*.

58. "Pulpit Tirades," a section of the Minutes of United Synagogue Honorary Officers Meeting, 24 April 1939, United Synagogue Archive. Chief Rabbi Hertz's response was contained in a letter to Sir Robert Waley-Cohen, 4 May 1939, Minutes of Meeting of US Honorary Officers, 8 May 1939.

59. These figures are culled from "Notable Events" in the *Anglo-Jewish Yearbooks, 1917-1927*.

60. J.L. Cohen Private Archive, Central Zionist Archive, A173/39.

61. Harold Pollins, *Economic History of the Jews in England* (London, 1982), pp. 194-208. This work contains a wealth of information which can be related to political changes in the community.

Chapter 6

THE DEMOCRATIZATION OF
THE AMERICAN JEWISH POLITY

Jonathan S. Woocher

In November 1969, a young Jewish graduate student, Hillel Levine, stood before several thousand delegates to the General Assembly of the Council of Jewish Federations and delivered a ringing indictment of the Jewish communal "establishment." Jewish Federations, the dominant institutions in the Jewish power structure in America, were, he charged, out of touch with the real needs of Jewish life in America. "Federations must seek not only the financial support, but also the guidance and leadership of a broader constituency from the American Jewish community. It can no longer be run by a few generous men or the patrons of particular projects whose concerns do not transcend their project. Rabbis, people involved in Jewish education, Jewish scholars, students and concerned Jews should participate on all levels of decision-making and allocations."[1]

Levine's call for broadened participation in Federation decision-making reflected a common perception among critics of Jewish communal organization during that turbulent period of the late 1960s. Writing during that same year, another long-time Jewish activist and professional, Judah Shapiro, put the matter even more boldly: "In a comparison with industry, the Jewish Federations come out a poor second, even with respect to the superficial aspects of democratic procedures...in Jewish Federations there is no election in which the shareholders have a voice with respect to the selection of leadership, the approval of policy, or the choice of alternatives. There is not even a poll of sentiment with respect to actions taken. This means, in fact, that there is no accountability of the leadership to the contributors, to the Federation's constituency."[2]

* A somewhat different version of this chapter was published in *Contemporary Jewry*, vol. 8 (1987).

The judgment that American Jewish Federations are un- (if not actually anti-) democratic has not been limited to a handful of political activists. Marc Raphael, a prominent American Jewish historian, has been no less forceful in his evaluations; "Most Federations make little or no pretence of democracy, viewing it as an impediment to efficient operation....Democratic democratization — where as broad as possible a basis of participation is involved in the process (small and large contributors equally) — remains what 'ought' to be, nowhere what 'is'."[3]

The underlying theme and premise of these indictments — that the American Jewish community both heads and lacks "democratic" institutions — long antedates the burst of activity which again brought it to the forefront of the communal agenda more than a decade ago. The debate over "democracy" in American Jewish life has a long and honorable history. Both in the local and national arenas, attempts to organize democratically-based representative organizations to unify, serve, and speak on behalf of American Jews began more than a century ago. The histories of the most famous endeavors in this direction — the establishment of the Kehilla in New York City in 1908 and of the American Jewish Congress during the First World War — illustrate its inherently problematic character.

The call for the creation of the Kehilla, made by Judah Magnes and his colleagues, was as bold and direct as the proclamations of his counterparts sixty years later. "We need an organization that shall derive its authority from the people and that shall give expression to the will of the people."[4] Yet from its very inception, the Kehilla which emerged was linked inextricably to the very Jewish establishment — as embodied in the American Jewish Committee — which most strongly repudiated the validity of the democratic concept as the organizing principle for American Jewish life as a whole. Though the organizers of the Kehilla averred that their efforts would push the Committee itself to move in the direction of "democratization" on a national scale,[5] when the opportunity for such a national representative body appeared, Magnes found himself caught between his establishment allies and the more radical democrats of the day. In the end, Magnes was unable to bring the two camps together, and his own carefully constructed effort to balance democratic and oligarchic forces in New York was weakened in the process.

Magnes' dilemma reflected a larger one which has persisted throughout American Jewish history: How can democratic forms be institutionalized in a community which is both voluntary and pluralistic? Despite the efforts of men like Steven Wise, who "hammered away at the 'oligarchic' control of Jewish life,"[6] the Zionists and the so-called "Congress party," who championed a permanent democratic American Jewish organization during this period, were unable to achieve such a major restructuring. With the collapse of the Kehilla and the reorganization of the American Jewish Congress in the early 1920s as simply one among the many national Jewish agencies which can speak on behalf of segments of the American Jewish populace, the era of what might be termed "radical democratizing" in American Jewish life drew to an end.

The debate about "democracy" — and efforts to find ways of injecting democratic elements into the evolving system of communal governance — did not. Although such efforts on a national scale were troubled and short-lived,[7] the gradual emergence of Jewish Federations and Welfare Funds as the "framing institutions" of the American Jewish polity[8] provided a new focal point for both the controversy and the process of democratization.

That Federations were the primary target of those like Hillel Levine who called in the 1960s and 1970s for greater participation and accountability in American Jewish organizational life bespeaks their increasing prominence within the American Jewish communal system. The conceptualization of Federations as political institutions constitutes in its own right a transformation of no little significance. Beginning as confederations of established (and by and large establishment) local charities joining together for more effective and efficient fund-raising, Jewish Federations stood by and large outside the initial struggles over "democracy" noted above. It was not long, however, before the leadership of these Federations, generally of German-Jewish origin, were faced with demands for broadening participation, primarily in the form of incorporating immigrant charities as constituents and beneficiaries of their communal fund-raising. This demand for inclusion led in the course of events to a second: for expanded participation by the newer immigrants themselves in the governance of the Federations. Three factors pushed the Federation leadership of the 1920s and the 1930s toward accommodation of these pressures. The first was the ideological substructure of the Federation movement itself which emphasized community and inclusiveness. The second was the practical need to involve larger numbers of donors, and to cultivate new major contributors from the ranks of the Eastern European immigrants. The third, which operated perhaps on a more subtle level, but which has colored the evolution of the American Jewish community from the outset, is the democratic ideal which is such a pervasive element of American culture in general.

Thus, the issue of "democratization" began to find its way increasingly into the discussions of leaders of the Jewish philanthropic system. "There must be…a democratization of the Federation as to make it wholly representative of the people who support it….All our charitable institutions belong to the Jewish people of Philadelphia, therefore, the boards of directors which govern their activities must be representative of the Jewish community — must, as far as possible, be selected by the Jewish community." So urged the President of Philadelphia's Federation in 1926. The theme was echoed by another leader two years later: "Adequate representation on Federation and agency boards and committees, a policy of rotation of office, giving leadership opportunity to the many instead of confining it to the few, will soon dispel a criticism, so often heard, that Federation is a closed corporation serving vested and inherited interests."[9]

When Ben Selekman, one of the major architects of the Federation movement in America, surveyed that movement's condition a few years later, he concluded that democratization of "the Federation structure so that all governances of the Jewish community will be represented in the governing body" was a vital ask for the immediate future.[10] These pleas did not go entirely unheeded, although it is evident from the continued vitality of contemporary critics that "democratization" was by no means fully or universally achieved. During the 1930s and 1940s, other community-wide instruments — Welfare Funds raising money for overseas and sectarian Jewish needs and Community Councils — were created in many localities, sometimes in alliance and sometimes in muted competition with the local Federations, and provided alternative points of access and influence for those who could not or would not achieve power within the Federation itself. Nor did the Federations lack their defenders when it came to the degree of democracy and representativeness they incorporated. Harry Lurie, a leading Federation executive and historian of the movement, wrote in 1938: "The charge is sometimes made that Federations and philanthropic agencies are not democratic. They are not, it is true, under the control of the 'Jewish community'...but they are under the democratic control of the organization of contributors."[11] The debate, as it has developed, has had two components — one perceptual and one evaluative. On the first count the question has been: "Are Federations (and the Jewish polity in general) democratic?" The second question is perhaps more difficult to answer: "To what extent is 'democracy' the appropriate model for Federation (and Jewish communal) governance?" And underlying both is a third question: "What do we mean by 'democracy' when we apply the term to the American Jewish community and its organizational system?"

In truth, the term "democracy" has limited utility unless we can specify the political processes which we mean to identify with it. Typically, one might begin with formal characteristics: election of office holders, decision-making by majority vote, open debate. By these criteria, Federations and nearly every other American Jewish organization are undeniably democratic. But the existence of formal democracy, though obviously critical as the infrastructure without which a more substantive, operational democracy could not exist, is obviously not what concerns the critics of the Jewish communal system. Rather, what is important are a set of political conditions and processes which are often lumped together under the term "democracy," but which should be distinguished more clearly. In order to answer adequately both the perceptual and the evaluative questions about the state of "democracy" in the America Jewish polity, and especially in seeking to assess recent trends, we should consider seven different (albeit often related) aspects of the communal political process:

1) Access — Who is heard in the political process? What channels are available for reaching decision-making centers? What are the modes for making one's views and concerns known?

2) Participation — Who is actually involved in decision-making, for what range of issues, and in what ways?

3) Representation — To what extent do decision-makers represent the members of the community? How are various interests, ideologies, and sub-communities represented? What type of representation does the system embody?[12]

4) Debate — Are policy alternatives considered and openly discussed by decision-makers?

5) Accountability — To whom or what are decision-makers accountable in their actions?

6) Communication — How are members of the community made aware of decisions? What mechanisms exist for providing feedback on the effectiveness of policies to decision-makers?

7) Political development — To what extent does the system build political community? How effective is it in the tasks of political socialization and recruitment?

Before undertaking any assessment of the American Jewish polity based on these questions, an important caveat must be offered. The governance system of the America Jewish polity is extraordinarily complex and variegated. The polity itself is in many ways more an intellectual construct than a functioning reality; this is certainly so for many of its citizens. It is a "multidimensional matrix of institutions and organizations,"[13] all voluntary, most operating independently of one another, in a variety of arenas ranging from the neighborhood to the world. The polity has no formal center, no overall leadership, no overarching structure. If we choose to concentrate in the discussion below on Jewish Federations, it is because by common consent they are the most important elements in the organizational matrix, but by no means the only important ones. To a large extent, because the American Jewish community generally shares a single political culture, the comments and observations made below will be applicable to more than just the Federation sphere. That domain will, however, be the focal point of concern here, and since the generalization even within that sphere is risky, it is all the more so beyond its boundaries.

What, then, can be said about the state of "democracy" in the American Jewish polity? The truth, it would seem, probably lies somewhere between the dismal picture painted by critics and the relatively sanguine reassurance offered by some defenders of the current system. A case can be made for both points of view. Indeed, as one begins to examine the evidence, one is struck by the extent to which it supports the central claims of both parties in the debate. The differences, it appears, lie more in the expectations of the participants than in their estimation of how the system functions today.

A number of facts seem beyond dispute. One is that the community is run "on elitist lines."[14] Substantial participation in key decision-making is limited to a relatively small segment of the Jewish community. What is more, this leadership elite tends to be drawn from a relatively homogeneous population of the well-to-do and well-connected (businessmen, professionals) with a sprinkling of academics and individuals with "Jewish credentials" (rabbis, Judaica scholars) thrown in.[15]

Acknowledgement of the existence of this governance elite — what Daniel Elazar, the American Jewish polity's most authoritative analyst, terms a "trusteeship of givers and doers,"[16] does not in itself, however, mean that the polity as a whole is either "undemocratic" or, as we shall see below, "un-Jewish." Several other factors must be considered. One is the question of how the elite achieves its position of power. Here too there is general agreement on the facts, but less on their meaning. By and large, the members of the elite are co-opted, rather than selected by any grass-roots electoral process. Elections do take place, to be sure, but as Elazar notes, "though not always formalities, [they] are usually simply means of formally ratifying the choices of nominating committees, and even when contested they are rarely contested by candidates representing seriously different characteristics or points of view."[17]

In this sense, it is fair to characterize the typical leadership pattern within the American Jewish polity as "oligarchic." One must go further, however, and recognize that the leadership elite, while relatively small and not the product of democratic selection, is neither monolithic nor exclusive. The cosmopolitan volunteers who dominate Federations and other Jewish communal organizations linked to the Federation system do not constitute "an oligarchy that extends itself through all spheres of Jewish life."[18] Synagogues, fraternal and membership organizations, and a host of other religious, educational and special interest agencies within the Jewish community both enjoy effective autonomy and are led by rather different elements of the Jewish populace. At best, one can speak, as Peter Medding does, of a "multi-element oligarchy" in which elites "often coalesce rather than operate separately," at least within certain recognizable spheres of communal activity.[19]

Those who defend the current system against the charge of "elite domination" often point as well to the fact that far from seeking to exclude individuals from leadership opportunities, Federations and their allied agencies are often engaged in a fruitless search for new volunteers willing and able to assume positions within the system. Sidney Vincent, one of the most thoughtful and influential leaders of the Federation system in recent years, has written of this problem:

All of us are committed to democracy by our entire training and our way of life. We mean it when we talk at our annual meetings about how eager we are for more participation by our citizenry, even in decision-making. But all democratic institutions struggle with the problem of how to involve their constituencies responsibly in decision-making....In Jewish life, involvement is even harder to achieve. All our institutions are voluntary; very little is decided by general elections and no one needs to pay Jewish taxes. The great majority of our constituents know little or nothing about the great communal issues that absorb us. Indeed, the organized community is frequently perceived as a closed corporation, where the elite makes the decisions. Many of us vigorously refute that charge, claiming that the portals of entry into communal service and promotion are open to all those willing to devote themselves to communal service. To claim otherwise, we say, is a copout....[20]

This position is not without merit. As Elazar puts it, "the cosmopolitan voluntary leaders represent an oligarchy, but it is a voluntary one as much as or more than it is self-perpetuating."[21] Nevertheless, it is also important to note that the objective conditions required for entrance into the leadership elite — ability and willingness to expend sufficient time and energy on communal affairs and a readiness to play by the "rules of the game" which emphasize avoidance of conflict — serve to eliminate or discourage many who might otherwise be both qualified and eager to have greater input into communal decision-making.[22]

One empirical question which is in dispute between critics of the communal system and other observers is the extent to which the leadership elite is representative of and fairly represents the Jewish community as a whole. For those like Shapiro, the answer is clear: "It is too obvious that the goals of the people and of the Federation leadership are by now far apart."[23] Raphael, citing evidence from Columbus, Ohio, reaches a similar conclusion: contributor preferences are largely ignored when allocations committees do their work.[24] Yet there is substantial evidence, both impressionistic and empirical, to support an alternative perspective: organizational leaders are by and large "representative" of their ostensible constituents; indeed, if they are "unrepresentative," it is in maintaining higher levels of Jewish activism and concern. Based on data from the National Jewish Population Study conducted in 1970-71, Alan York concludes that a broad sample of

Jewish leaders "participate more than non-leaders in Jewish organizations, they tend to give more to charity, to have higher occupational status, and to attend synagogue more frequently, but they are neither marginal in their Jewish practice and identification nor exceptional: they are as observant and identifying as the average American Jew."[25] The American Jewish historian Melvin Urofsky summarizes the results of his study as follows: "Today's leaders are not atypical cf their followers, but archetypical."[26] Even if one focuses on the "cosmopolitan volunteers" who lead the major institutions of the Jewish polity, the situation seems much the same. Elazar writes that "the trusteeship is representative of American Jewry in that it reflects the attitudes, values, and interests of the community — except perhaps in one respect: the leaders are probably more positively Jewish than the community's rank and file."[27] Charles Liebman, indeed, describes the leaders of New York's Federation of Jewish Philanthropies, the largest in America, as "not representative of New York's Jews, or of Federation's own contributors," precisely because "by and large, they are more Jewishly concerned and committed."[28] Thus, even where critics and more neutral observers might agree on the existence of some differences between the attitudes and interests of communal leadership and the rank and file (and these should not be exaggerated), the critics might well be disappointed with the results of a shift from a "trusteeship" to a "mirror image" model of representation.[29]

One might, therefore, justifiably conclude that the narrow base of participation in decision-making and the lack of meaningful input by the larger community in the selection of leaders are not in and of themselves fatal barriers to the leadership's capacity to fulfill the representative function which democratic theory demands. In other respects, however, the system which the critics of the last two decades have decried, does fall well short of a democratic ideal. The most serious liability, many would agree, is the lack of mechanisms for providing regular communication between the leadership elite and the community rank and file. Accurate representation, when it occurs, is more the result of the lack of serious ideological diversity within the American Jewish community than of deliberate efforts to channel constituent concerns to leadership cadres. Again, this is not, by and large, due to a desire to ignore such expressions. Rather, it is the lack of initiatives by either the leaders or the average members of the community which is so debilitating. The problem is in part structural —

formal channels of access are either non-existent or inefficient —
but it is also more broadly systemic. Medding notes that especially
at national levels of policy-making "there exist no democratic or
representative integrative mechanisms for joining rank and file
members to their leaders." "The views, ideas, goals and aspirations of the Jewish grass roots and rank and file, reach the top, if at
all, only as interpreted and presented by various sub-leaders who,
presumably, have their own personal and institutional interests to
promote, which must clearly influence their transmission of the
views of their constituents."[30] The major problem, however, goes
beyond these structural limitations. The American Jewish community today suffers from a paucity of what Elazar calls
"publics," groups of Jews actively committed to participation in
communal affairs on an ongoing basis. It is this lack which men
like Sidney Vincent point to when they cite open doors through
which no one is walking. It is not a question here of a total absence
of inputs to and demands on the political system. Individuals and
institutions do come with their positions and concerns. But they do
so often as pressure groups and self-proclaimed populists, almost
in a posture of antagonism, rather than as elements in a set of
publics prepared to engage in an orderly process of interest aggregation and representation.[31] The problem is both one of the quan-
tity of participation and of its quality. With neither a tradition of
nor mechanisms for regular debate on matters of policy and program, leaders tend to hear either opinions which only confirm the
established "consensus" or opposing views which represent a
"disturbance" of that consensus and, hence, may be both offered
and received in a quasi-confrontational atmosphere. Where to
place blame for this state of affairs is largely a moot point;
clearly, a vicious cycle can, and probably has taken hold. What is
evident is that, as Elazar warns, a "republican" system of communal governance cannot long endure without "publics" prepared
and permitted to take part in its affairs as a matter of course.[32]

The depressed level of public participation and access also un-
dercuts the possibility of establishing genuine accountability
among the leadership for its decisions. Once more, it is not that
leaders wish to arrogate all power to their own hands and to ignore
the community's interests. It is that even as trustees, some mechanisms must exist for determining when policies are in fact
meeting with the approval of and meeting the needs of the community whom the trustees purport to serve. Without contested elections or broad public participation in decision-making, such

mechanisms are lacking and accountability is theoretical rather than operational. Leadership elites believe that they are acting responsively and responsibly, but the only way of judging whether this is so is the rather crude measure provided by annual fund-raising campaigns. Even by this criterion, it is not clear that the community at large is satisfied with either the substance or process of communal decision-making, but efforts to increase direct accountability for specific policy choices are almost non-existent. The ultimate danger for the community in the distance which exists between leadership and constituency is that it will at some point simply be unable to mobilize the relatively apathetic masses for even the minimal levels of support which are necessary for the communal enterprise itself to endure. In this sense, greater "democracy" is not merely a normative ideal, but a requisite for the polity's survival. As Medding put it: "Whether Jewish communities, organized as they currently are, and without more responsive and representative leadership and executive bodies, will continue to be able to mobilize the vast majority of members of Jewish communities and command their loyalty is an open question."[33]

This concern, as we have seen, finds echoes even within the leadership establishment itself. In the decade and a half since the last wave of critics began their assault on the communal system, the situation decried then has not remained static. Transformations in both the composition of the leadership cadres and, in a more limited extent, in the processes of communal governance have taken place which have affected the state of "democracy" within the polity.

These changes have not all been deliberate, nor have they necessarily taken place with "democratization" as their goal. In fact, as we shall see, their impact in this respect has been ambiguous in some respects. But they do constitute the polity's best efforts thus far to respond to the implicit warning in assessments like that of Peter Medding, and they do establish the direction along which future changes are likely to take place.

Three areas of change in the recruitment, composition and characteristics of the leadership elite in recent years should be taken note of. The first is a notable effort to recruit and advance leaders from previously "underrepresented" segments of the community. Three groups in particular have been targeted for these efforts (in some instances following or concurrent with their own demands for greater representation): youth, women, and the

Orthodox. The success of these efforts has been mixed. A number of women have broken out of their segregation into "women's divisions" to become Presidents of Federations, campaign chairpersons, and, most recently, head of a national agency. Representation of women on major committees and in other positions of responsibility does seem to have been increased. And new provisions are being made to recruit and involve professional and business women (alongside what are now often called "professional volunteers") in ways that are roughly equivalent to those targeted at their male counterparts. Whether these changes have brought new viewpoints into leadership circles is less certain, but they have symbolized an opening of the elite across what has heretofore been one of its major boundaries.[34]

Efforts to involve larger numbers of young people, from whose ranks many of the establishment's most vocal critics were drawn, have been on the whole less successful. Many Federations and other organizations have made places on their boards and committees for youth/student representation. Many have increased their allocations or programming for what are defined as student or youth-oriented concerns.[35] These steps have not, however, brought more than a handful of those under the age of twenty-five into active participation. The focus of polity outreach has been on a somewhat older and, realistically, more potentially productive group — those referred to as "young leadership," between the ages of twenty-five and forty (see the discussion below). The modest achievements in involving and responding to the concerns of those between eighteen and twenty-five should not be discounted entirely; a bridge has been created where none existed before. But neither has it brought any revolution to community life and to the patterns of power and influence which shape it.

The third group which has been both a critic and more recently a recruitment target of the polity establishment is the Orthodox community. For many years the Federation was regarded as a "secular" institution led largely by assimilated Reform Jews. In more recent decades, the latter proposition has lost its validity as Conservative Jews have come to share leadership positions alongside those who identify with the Reform movement.[36] The former characterization as well is, as we shall note below, increasingly inapt, but what has remained true until quite recently is that few Jews who identified themselves as Orthodox were in positions of lay or professional leadership in the Federation system. It is difficult to know to what extent this situation has changed. It is clear that many Federations have become more responsive to concerns traditionally identified with the Orthodox community, e.g. support for Jewish day schools (although this also reflects the overall "Judaization" of the polity discussed below). Recently, some signs of a "counter-movement" have developed, with increasing complaints being heard that "concessions" to the Orthodox have not produced a concommitant increase in their commitment and contributions to Federation. At the same time, some Orthodox and other synagogue sphere leaders continue to decry what they perceive as tokenism in both the involvement of and responsiveness to the religious community.

In general terms, it seems reasonable to conclude that there has been a broadening of the leadership elite of the polity in recent years, with greater opportunities for participation by members of underrepresented segments of the community. Even where decision-making power is still largely in the hands of more traditional leadership types, the meeting of demand and outreach has produced some corollary advances in the "democratization" process. Better communication has been established with these constituencies (youth and the Orthodox tend to be better organized as such then are women). In addition, polity agencies do feel a stronger sense of accountability to these groups, even where mechanisms for ensuring that they are actually held accountable are missing.

In assessing the impact of these changes, one must take account of two other processes which have been occurring simultaneously. The first of these, alluded to above, is a general "Judaization" of the polity. This constitutes the latest phase in the longer-term consolidation of the polity's "civil religion" of "Jewish survivalism."[37] As a world-view and ethos, this "civil religion" focuses on countering threats to Jewish continuity, security, and well-being, while promoting an ethic of exemplary Jewish moral responsibility. Whereas it was once possible to find Jewish communal leaders whose basic ideological commitment was to "the melting pot," to "charitable work," or to an ideal of "universal social justice," these values have now been subordinated (where they remain present at all) to the overriding values of Jewish survival and mutual responsibility. As the comments above concerning the levels of commitment found among leadership cadres indicate, recent years have seen a movement toward a greater congruence between public ideology and personal behavior as the "civil religion," with its utilization and positive valuation of Jewish myth, symbol and ritual forms, has taken hold. What has emerged is a new model for the Jewish polity leader — one who works for the continuity of the Jewish people and its tradition in every arena: the personal-familial, the community-institutional, and the public-political.

Helping to propel the spread of this new model, and thereby of the polity's "Judaization," is the third major area of recent change in the realm of leadership: the dramatic spread of institutionalized programs for the recruitment and socialization of new leaders. "Leadership development" programs are now a staple not only of Federations, but of nearly every major national Jewish organization. Some of these programs do serve as one means of bringing women, Orthodox, and other "atypical" Jews into the leadership "pipeline." They are also the prime means of trying to induce younger business and professional leaders to follow in the footsteps of their active elders. But even more, and in some respects countering the "democratizing" influence of such programs, they socialize these "young leaders" into the regnant "Jewish survivalist" ideology. Participants in the programs are sensitized to critical Jewish issues, oriented to the agencies and the way they operate, and given increasingly important roles in carrying on the work of the polity. "Young leadership" cadres have had an impact on the Federation world in spearheading the movement toward greater "Judaization" and a broader definition of leadership responsibilities. In so doing, they have become an elite within the elite, in many ways even less "representative" of the community at large than their elders.

Here we confront again one of the major dilemmas in any discussion of "democratization" of the American Jewish community. Taken literally, such a program might well involve a slowing or even a reversal of the trends toward heightened Jewishness among polity leaders. Yet somewhere between a project of this type, which even most critics would view with great skepticism, and the current trend toward the promotion of a more Jewishly concerned but ideologically homogenous leadership, there may well be a system for recruiting and training leadership which would bring positive but diverse Jewish commitments to inform the polity's self-definition and policy deliberations. For all of its merits, the "Jewish survivalism" which dominates the attitudes of current and emerging leaders alike is an ideology which supports, rather than challenges, the already powerful consensual biases of the communal governance system.

In fact, the powerful emphasis within communal rhetoric on "unity" and on adopting a "community-wide" perspective on problems has probably resulted in some dilution of the representational aspects of the system. Whereas it was once not uncommon for individuals to speak on behalf of particular agencies, interests or ideologies within decision-making councils, this type of representation appears to be diminishing. Instead, leaders seek to anticipate the "community consensus" which presumably represents a synthesis of all interests and viewpoints. This high-mindedness reflects the fact that there is, as we have seen, a broad consensus on many issues, certainly among the leadership cadres, but it also tends to foreclose vigorous debate and makes aggressive representation of sub-communal interests appear somewhat suspect. Many instances have been recounted of occasions when issues have seemingly been decided by majority votes, only to have the "winners" draw back because the decision did not command a full consensus. The quest for consensus is, on the one hand, a sound and "democratic" means of insuring that minority viewpoints are protected. It can, however, also be debilitating for the democratic process, forcing premature compromise and pushing truly dissenting viewpoints outside of the process altogether.

In raising this issue of how increasing ideological homogeneity can work subtly to weaken some of the representational elements built into the polity's governance process, we should not overlook other changes that may be counterbalancing this effect. One of these is the expansion of the "public agenda" of Jewish communal life itself. In recent years, more and more areas of Jewish activity have come to be seen as requiring "public" attention as opposed to being left for individual or "private institutional" action alone. The polity is now called upon to be increasingly involved in Jewish education, in the quality of Jewish family life, in the support of religious activities, and in public affairs. These new responsibilities are in many ways an outgrowth of the "survivalist" ideology we have discussed above. Their pursuit has required that the polity interact with a wider range of Jews than in the days when it was primarily devoted to providing health, welfare, and recreational services. Synagogue leaders, day school supporters, children of young parents, Jewish political activists, and others who previously were not foci of attention and concern are now perceived as constituencies which must be incorporated in some fashion within the polity.

The desire to involve new segments of the community in the

overall communal system is most apparent in the frequent discussions among leaders of the need to "reach out to the unaffiliated." Most polity leaders are well aware of the fact that a substantial majority of Jews are only tenuously (if at all) involved in the Jewish communal network. The desire to bring these marginal Jews into the system is in many respects a survival requisite for the system, as implied by Medding above. But the motivation for outreach efforts is idealistic as well. Polity leaders believe in the concept of "community," and their concern for the future of Jewish life is both genuine and personal. What have not yet been developed are strategies and techniques of outreach which are effective in bringing the unaffiliated in. Most continue to seek to develop better understanding of the system and its goals, which will presumably lead to commitment, and eventually to participation. Only quite recently have new approaches began to be attempted which seek to appeal to the unaffiliated in terms of their specific concerns and patterns of involvement, which may or may not be similar to those already active within the Jewish polity. Finding different points of access and new types of participation for the presently unaffiliated, perhaps even the development of new structures — with the assumption that commitment may follow upon rather than precede such involvement — is a major challenge to the polity just beginning to be addressed.[38]

The final, and perhaps ultimately the most important factor in propelling the American Jewish community towards greater "democratization" today is the growing awareness of its own political character. The idea that the Jewish organizational matrix constitutes a polity has never been entirely absent from the self-consciousness. Nor, as we have seen, did concern for its democratic character await this awareness. But the greater sensitivity of leaders to the fact that they are engaged in a political process and a growing sophistication in their understanding of how the nature of this process relates to the success of their endeavors, focuses attention on the issues of access, participation, representation, decision-making, and accountability which we have emphasized above. The gradual redefinition of the polity mission from service provision alone to community development helps to engender this heightened political consciousness. Professional leaders can play a critical role in this regard. The historical alliance of Jewish communal service to the social work profession, which has emphasized democratic process and community organization, is weakening today for a number of reasons. If it is replaced by a purely managerial self-definition, some of the impulse toward "democratization" may be muted. If, however, the evolving professional identity of the Jewish communal worker includes a strong awareness of his/her position as one within a voluntary Jewish political system, such workers could become prime architects of a more "democratic" effective polity.

Implicit here are the outlines of a response to the key questions posed earlier. Are Federations — and the Jewish polity in general — "democratic"? More so than they have been in the past, we would suggest, and less so than they could be. To what extent is democracy an appropriate form of Jewish communal governance today? If by "democracy" we mean a system which provides substantial opportunities for access and participation by all those who seek involvement, in which there are some mechanisms for representing diverse interests and viewpoints, in which polity alternatives are openly debated, in which leaders are accountable for their actions, and in which efforts are made to develop "publics" and enhance the quality of citizen participation in political processes, then we would answer that communal democracy is a goal worth pursuing.

In offering these judgments we must, at the same time, offer several qualifications. What seems neither feasible nor desirable in American Jewish life are some of the more radical schemes for "democratization" which have been suggested. National representative bodies, or even communal elections on a local scale, seem unlikely to prove workable in the forseeable future. As Elazar notes, and Medding's researches confirm, "Those modern Jewish communities which have experimented with communal elections have not found them any better a solution to the problem of representation, because the turnout in these elections tends to be extremely low. Moreover, a voting procedure does not guarantee the election of statesmen to communal leadership either."[39] As long as the American Jewish polity is a voluntary one, with a multiplicity of organizations, there will probably always be a tendency for central or framing institutions like the Federations to place a high premium on the maintenance of consensus and the avoidance of conflict. Other arenas exist for those who wish to pursue particular interests and concerns in the many sub-communal organizations. Thus, vigorous contest over policy or office at the core of the polity is unlikely to become the norm, and the American model of representative democracy to remain an inapt one for the Jewish community.

Even more important, perhaps, the political tradition of the Jewish people, one which has served it well across a broad expanse of time and space, is not itself a radical democratic one. Rather, it rests on a philosophy which Elazar has labeled "aristocratic republicanism," and which Mordecai Roshwald has called "democratic elitism."[40] The polity belongs to the people, not to its rulers, but actual leadership is vested in a group of trustees — responsible both to the people and Jewish law — who are selected on the basis of their qualification to serve. As Elazar describes it:

> Political life in Jewish communities and polities has usually involved the following factors:
> (1) the initial consent of the members to the community's authority and to the authoritative structures and processes of governance within it;
> (2) a commitment toward participation in communal affairs on the part of a relatively substantial percentage of the citizenry;
> (3) the utilization of various forms of representation...where direct participation was not feasible; and
> (4) a system of dispersed decision-making with different tasks assigned to different bodies often involving the same individuals wearing many different hats, moving from body to body in their leadership capacities.[41]

In broad terms, the American Jewish polity today works within this framework, and the criteria it suggests seem appropriate ones for evaluating the polity;'s continued progress towards the proper blend of "democratic" and "aristocratic" principles.

There are, then, avenues along which "democratization" can and should proceed which would conform with both the limits imposed by the environment within which American Jewish organizations must operate and the norms of the Jewish political tradition. Many are relatively simple to conceive, though perhaps more difficult to execute: rotation of office holders, creation of formal channels for receiving "citizen" input, more vigorous efforts to educate and inform the Jewish community about issues and the political process, insurance that no single criterion — such as wealth — becomes the sole qualifying factor for recruitment into the leadership elite. More far-reaching measures can also be envisioned. Elazar, for example, has suggested that drawing the synagogues more directly into the public domain might provide a basis for an electoral process through congregations which would enhance the representative character of Federation leadership and provide new courses for recruitment.[42] Nearly all — critics, observers, and defenders of the current system alike — agree that the prime requisite today is the increased participation in communal affairs by the Jewish rank and file. This means not only proclaiming the system's openness, but providing incentives and new structural designs for such involvement. Here, current experiments with such "constitutional" change as regionalization, mail ballots to elect a portion of governing boards, and various proportional representation schemes, may be pointing the way forward. One should not expect such changes to produce dramatic or even entirely beneficial effects, but without them, the danger of a gradual loss of legitimacy by polity instruments looms as a larger threat.[43]

In the final analysis, the transformations which have taken place in American Jewish communal governance over the past several decades may not appear dramatic, but they are nonetheless real and potentially significant. American Jews are fated to play the central role in determining whether Jewish communal self-governance within the "aristocratic republican" framework of the Jewish political tradition and amidst the challenges and constraints of the modern diaspora can endure. We will achieve no democratic utopia. But if those who step forward to assume the mantle of leadership do so truly as the representatives of a community which cares about and pursues its destiny as a part of the Jewish body politic — what in Hebrew is called *Adat Yisrael*, a commonwealth — then, as Elazar asserts, "we will have achieved a great thing."[44]

Notes

1. Hillel Levine, "To Share a Vision," in *Jewish Radicalism*, Jack Nusan Porter and Peter Dreier, eds. (New York: Grove Press, 1973), pp. 192-193.

2. Judah J. Shapiro, "The Philistine Philanthropists: The Power and Shame of Jewish Federations," in *Jewish Radicalism*, pp. 203-204.

3. Marc Lee Raphael, "Federated Jewish Philanthropy and Communal Democracy: In Pursuit of a Phantom," in *Understanding American Jewish Philanthropy*, Marc Lee Raphael, ed. (New York: Ktav), pp. 153, 158.

4. Norman Bentwich, *For Zion's Sake: A Biography of Judah L. Magnes* (Philadelphia: Jewish Publication Society, 1954), p. 78. The history of the Kehilla and of the difficulties in establishing a representative democratic organization for New York's Jews is recounted in great detail in Arthur A. Goren, *New York Jews and the Quest for Community: The Kehilla Experiment, 1908-1922* (New York: Columbia University Press, 1970).

5. Bentwich, p. 80.

6. Howard Morley Sachar, *The Course of Modern Jewish History* (New York: Dell, 1958), p. 529.

7. The second notable twentieth century effort to establish a roof organization for American Jewry on democratic representative principles was the American Jewish Conference, set up in 1943 in response to the wartime crisis. Like the Congress during World War I, it almost surely would not have come into existence without the stimulus of the extraordinary events of the day. Also like the original Congress, it sought to combine institutional representation with direct election of delegates from local communities. It too was unable to sustain itself as a representative organization in the face of opposition from (and eventual secession by) several key national agencies which opposed its Zionist policies. The Conference eventually dissolved in 1949.

8. The phrase is Daniel Elazar's. See his *Participation and Accountability in the Jewish Community* (New York: Council of Jewish Federations and Association of Jewish Community Organization Personnel, 1982), pp. 12-13.

9. The quoted statements are from Alfred J. Kutzik, "The Social Basis of American Jewish Philanthropy," Unpublished Ph.D. Dissertation, Brandeis University, 1967, pp. 718-719, 689.

10. *Ibid.*, p. 689.

11. *Ibid.*, p. 691.

12. It is important to recall that within the history of democratic theory there have been notable debates about what "representation" means and what the responsibilities of a "representative" are. Is the representative to serve merely as a mirror-image of his/her constituents' views, or to use his/her own best judgment as to what is in their (and the political system as a whole's) best interests?

13. Daniel J. Elazar, *Community and Polity: The Organizational Dynamics of American Jewry* (Philadelphia: Jewish Publication Society, 1976), p. 13. Elazar's work is the definitive description and analysis of the American Jewish polity. The discussion below is heavily indebted to his account and conceptual framework.

14. Peter Medding, "Patterns of Political Organization and Leadership in Contemporary Jewish Communities," in *Kinship and Consent: The Jewish Political Tradition and Its Contemporary Uses*, Daniel Elazar, ed. (Ramat Gan and Philadelphia: Turtledove Publishing, 1981), p. 281.

15. One should, perhaps, also include the cadre of professional Jewish communal workers, especially agency executives, within this leadership elite. A number of observers regard these professionals as the single most influential force in communal governance. (See, e.g., Shapiro and a number of articles in Raphael.) The question which must be addressed is whether these professionals constitute a "democratizing" force within the polity. Some do indeed come from social strata and religious backgrounds not well represented among the volunteer leadership, but it is unclear whether this has any substantive impact on their policy preferences or attitudes on communal process. More relevant, in all likelihood, is their professional training and identification, some possible implications of which we discuss further below.

16. Elazar, *Community and Polity*, p. 336.

17. *Ibid.*, p. 285. The one major organization in the American Jewish community which prides itself on holding contested elections for the office of International President — B'nai B'rith — illustrates this point. It is usually difficult, if not impossible, to find any significant differences, either in background or general policy orientation, between the several candidates.

18. *Ibid.*, p. 286.

19. Medding, p. 283.

20. Sidney Vincent, *Personal and Professional: Memoirs of a Life in Community Service* (Cleveland: Jewish Community Federation of Cleveland, 1982), p. 259.

21. Elazar, *Community and Polity*, p. 286.

22. It is no longer necessary to be extraordinarily wealthy to ascend to a leadership position within Federation. Nor will the simple possession of wealth, or even a substantial contribution in absolute terms, guarantee an invitation to assume an active leadership role. Today's rhetoric emphasizes the need to make a "quality" gift, in proportion to one's means. Nevertheless, a measure of affluence remains an almost necessary if insufficient condition for leadership advancement, both because it helps to insure that the "quality" of one's gift is noted, and because fulfilling communal responsibilities often involves travel, time taken out of work, and other ancillary expenses which require "disposable income."

23. Shapiro, p. 204.

24. Raphael, pp. 153-163.

25. Alan S. York, "American Jewish Leaders from the Periphery," *Jewish Journal of Sociology* 23 (June 1981): 25-36.

26. Melvin I. Urofsky, "American Jewish Leadership," *American Jewish History* 70 (June 1981): 406.

27. Daniel J. Elazar, "Decision-making in the American Jewish Community," in *The Jewish Community in America*, Marshal Sklare, ed. (New York: Behrman House, 1974), p. 109.

28. Charles S. Liebman, "Leadership and Decision-making in a Jewish Federation: The New York Federation of Jewish Philanthropies," *American Jewish Year Book*, vol. 79 (1979), p. 65.

29. This should not be taken as implying that contributor and constituent preferences ought to play no role in determining policies and priorities. One of the difficulties in this regard is developing appropriate ways of presenting policy options or priorities (e.g., in Federation allocations) to the Jewish public. Allocations are made to agencies and programs, not to "goals" and "priorities," and determining how the two are related in specific terms is often a difficult matter of analysis and judgment. The application of public opinion polling and "market research" techniques to Jewish communal affairs is only in its nascent stages in the United States, and its potential impact on decision-making and communal democracy is unknown.

30. Medding, pp. 277-279.

31. Elazar, *Participation and Accountability*, pp. 10-11. Jay Stern also alludes to the problem of insuring that participation is mediated through an integrative process, rather than coming in the form of demands from outside the system in his discussion of American Jewish communal governance models. Jay Stern,

"Some Thoughts on the Polity of Jewish Organizational Life," *Journal of Jewish Communal Service* 59 (Winter 1982): 111-15.

32. Elazar, *Participation and Accountability*, p. 4.

33. Medding, p. 285.

34. On the changing position of women within the polity, see Deborah Lipstadt, 'The Changing Nature of Power and Policy-Making in the American Jewish Community: The Case of Women," unpublished manuscript, 1980.

35. The North American Jewish Students Appeal, which receives allocations from many Federations, is one example of this. Another is the establishment of a Student Advisory Board within the national United Jewish Appeal. The increasing role of Federations in funding Hillel Foundations and other campus programs has naturally raised questions of "co-optation" and "tokenism." Some student groups prefer to remain outside the "system" in order to maintain their "autonomy." The entire area of youth and student involvement is marked by ambivalence and occasional recriminations on both sides.

36. The author's research on Young Leadership groups indicates that Jews who call themselves "Conservative" may be on the way to assuming a preponderant role in Federation leadership circles.

37. On the polity's "civil religion," see the author's *Sacred Survival: The Civil Religion of American Jews* (Bloomington: Indiana University Press, 1986). See also, "Civil Judaism in the United States" (Philadelphia: Center for Jewish Community Studies, 1979); "The Civil Judaism of Communal Leaders," *American Jewish Year Book*, vol. 81 (1981), pp. 149-169; and "'Jewish Survivalism' as Communal Ideology: An Empirical Assessment," *Journal of Jewish Communal Service* 57 (Summer 1981): 291-303.

38. One effort in this direction was the New Gifts Program of the United Jewish Appeal. Utilizing state-of-the-art attitudinal research and marketing methods to supplement traditional approaches, the New Gifts Program attempted to develop alternatives to the appeals which have long dominated UJA fund-raising. Many Federations are now pursuing similar efforts to attract new local donors.

39. Elazar, "Decision-making," p. 109; cf. Medding, pp. 279-280.

40. Elazar, *Participation and Accountability*, p. 1f.; Mordecai Roshwald, "Democratic Elitism: The Ideological Framework of Jewish Community," *Judaism* 27 (Winter 1978): 47-62.

41. Elazar, "Covenant as the Basis of the Jewish Political Tradition," in *Kinship and Consent*, pp. 49-50.

42. Elazar, *Community and Polity*, pp. 337-338.

43. One undertaking which might help the process of "democratiza-tion" along would be the collation and evaluation of the initiatives developed by the various local communities in this direction. This would be a logical assignment for the Council of Jewish Federations, the umbrella body for the Federation movement. Of local efforts thus far initiated, those in Los Angeles, which has developed a major regionalization program, appear to be both the most sophisticated and carefully evaluated. The highly decentral-ized structure of the American Jewish polity serves both as a boon by permitting experimentation on a modest scale and as a barrier by making communication of the results of such experiments more difficult.

44. Elazar, *Participation and Accountability*, p. 29.

Chapter 7

THE DEMOCRATIZATION OF A COMMUNITY: THE CASE OF FRENCH JEWRY

Ilan Greilsammer

The problem of the relationship between Judaism and democracy has been much debated. As Daniel J. Elazar has noted, many writers have tended to present Judaism as an essentially democratic tradition,[1] disregarding those elements of Jewish religious thought which may be of an oligarchic or even autocratic nature.

It is true that over the past several years various studies have tried to reappraise the relationship between Judaism and democracy and have shown that they are not necessarily cut from the same cloth.

This question, which is in the realm of religious and political philosophy, will not be discussed here; rather, Judaism will be viewed from the perspective of existing Jewish communities, organizations and associations. Such diverse comparative studies as those of Moshe Davis, Seymour M. Lipset, Daniel J. Elazar, Charles S. Liebman and others have emphasized the different functions fulfilled by the various Jewish organizations. These studies stress the fact that the Jewish organizations are of the same order as other social groups functioning within a given territory or nation. In particular, they are constituted and directed according to the same political criteria as other forms of social organization (clubs, parties, labor unions, churches, etc.).

The fact that the great majority of Jewish organizations in the diaspora are at present governed according to oligarchic principles (that is, by small groups of prominent citizens and notables) is understandable: these notables are probably the only ones having at their disposal the time and the material means necessary to attend to the administration of the community; they are often the

---

* This chapter previously appeared in the *Jewish Journal of Sociology*, Vol. 21, No. 2 (December 1979).

most well-known Jews in non-Jewish society, and therefore perhaps the best suited to politically represent their respective communities before the authorities; being often the largest contributors to the Jewish Appeal, they seek to ensure the proper utilization of these funds; they enjoy the respect of the majority of their fellow Jews; and so on.[2]

The case of the Jewish community and its institutions in France is a good illustration of the power of the notables, where the factors listed above have been reinforced by a number of causes specific to the French context:

1) The organizational system established by Napoleon (the Consistoires) aimed explicitly at assigning the conduct of the Jewish community to prominent members of the moderate bourgeoisie who were loyal to the central authority.[3]

2) Within the community, certain "great families" have always been active, through filial loyalty, in the Jewish organizations and enterprises.

3) As a result, on the one hand, of the separation of church and state (1905), and the rapid assimilation of French Jewry, on the other, the financial means of the community were significantly reduced (we can note the generally low level of contributions as compared to those of certain neighboring communities, such as Belgium and Switzerland), thus increasing the social and political influence of several large donor families.

4) Following the exceptional economic and social improvement of the Jews of France, they found that they had more and more in common with their leaders, and had no real cause to contest them.

This model of government by the notables has recently been called into question and undermined by a process of democratization which has taken place over the course of the last 10 to 15 years. This process ultimately resulted in the replacement of the previous system by what appears to be a classical parliamentary regime. Why did this process begin? How did it develop? What were its results? This brief study will try to answer these questions as it describes the organizational change that has taken place within French Jewry.

The Process of Democratization

First of all, it should be indicated that the process to be described here deals with only one of the institutions of the French community: the Fonds Social Juif Unifie (United Jewish Welfare Fund — FSJU). Nevertheless, one can speak of the "democratization of the community" in that the Fonds has truly become the central organization of French Jewry, with its role and functions steadily being broadened over the last 25 years. It distributes the funds collected and allocated to the community,[4] it makes the important choices and lays down the major orientations, and, in effect, determines the evolution of the various sectors of the life of French Jewry. Only three domains are outside its sphere of activity: that of religious worship, administered by the Consistoire Central and the Orthodox and Reform organizations; the Zionist domain, run by the Jewish Agency and the Zionist Movement of France; and the domain of political representation, which belongs to a federative organization, the Conseil Representatif des Juifs de France (CRIF).

However, the Fonds Social tends to extend even into these three domains, since it subsidizes the religious schools and takes an active part in all the activities of identification with Israel and in the political demonstrations of the CRIF. In short, to use the terminology suggested by Daniel J. Elazar, the Fonds Social Juif Unifie is at the same time a "government-like institution" and a "general-purpose, mass-based organization."[5]

Until several years ago, the government of the Fonds corresponded quite closely to an oligarchic-type model. The people who directed it and, through it, the community, enjoyed various kinds of authority (authority of trust, authority of identification, authority of legitimacy, authority of sanction); they were few in number and owed their power essentially to their position as notables of the community. Socially, they all belonged to a limited number of socio-professional categories: industry, commerce, banking, and the academic world.

According to its statutes, the FSJU did indeed possess a formally representative system of government, with a General Assembly, a National Council, study commissions, etc., but these institutions had fallen into disuse and the management of the Fonds was in practice entirely in the hands of its Executive Committee.

On the level of political sociology, there is clearly room to underline the oligarchic characteristics of this model. Of course, it also contained more democratic elements. It is true, for example, that the Council appointed qualified advisors, competent in various social and cultural fields. It is equally true that the Council frequently co-opted independent personalities known for their scholarship (rabbis, professors). But this does not seem to have noticeably altered the nature of the administrative system of the Fonds Social.

The process of democratization which was initiated in the late 1960s had both immediate and remote causes. The central factor in this evolution has undoubtedly been the demographic change which occurred within the community with the arrival of approximately 120,000 repatriates from Algeria (1961-1962), and of the refugees from North Africa in general. Whereas the community had previously been relatively homogeneous (French Jewry being quite closely identified with the sociological characteristics of its leaders: Ashkenazic, bourgeoisie), the gap between the new community and its administrators soon became very large. The repatriates were Sephardic, they belonged in many cases to the middle or even lower social strata (minor officials, employees, small merchants), they had their own priorities in the communal domain, and, most importantly, their Judaism was younger, perhaps more militant and dynamic. This crisis of identification with the existing institutions did not immediately manifest itself, and it has in fact never been openly or blatantly exposed. On the contrary, for several years the newcomers did not challenge the structures of the Jewish organizations in France, and they were even quite well integrated.[6] Nevertheless, this sociological rift between the new community and the older leadership can be seen as one of the deep-rooted causes of the process of democratization.

These events were followed by the shock of the Six-Day War, the reawakening of the community (in large measure prompted by the young Sephardim), and the confrontation with a fundamentally changed political climate. The new Gaullist policy aroused the opposition of almost the entire Jewish community, leading to the adoption of a militant attitude, radically foreign to the habits and modes of action of its leaders.[7]

However, it was, above all, the events of May 1968 which came into play, when the students, as well as other strata of the French population, demanded greater participation. These events, which constituted a part of the national environment of the Jewish community, played an important role in its future reorganization. In the words of Moshe Davis: "What is striking is the fact that the multi-patterned communal structures...take form to a large extent from the socio-political organization of the respective societies in which they function."[8]

During the May riots, the premises of the FSJU and the Consistoire were also occupied. (Curiously, the occupation of the Consistoire was organized by a group of young Orthodox Jews who demanded the discontinuation of the use of the organ in the Synagogue de La Victoire, presenting this demand as a criticism of the religious establishment.) While these occupations and demonstrations had few immediate consequences, they marked a clear climate of contestation.

In 1969 a group of young Jewish graduates of the Grandes Ecoles (the Polytechnic School, the National School of Administration, and others), belonging to what is considered the technocratic elite of the French political and economic system, demanded a place in the management of the FSJU. This movement, which aroused considerable interest in the Jewish press, and even in *Le Monde*, called itself "Point 1970." These young Jewish technocrats sought to contest the community decisions which they considered arbitrary, and to rationalize the functioning of the community. Following a strong reaction by the notables, the young technocrats were defeated, and "Point 1970" ceased to exist. It was only three years later, in the wake of a new crisis, that a democratic reform succeeded.

The circumstances which led to the democratization of the Fonds began when its leaders decided to set up a gigantic, multifunctional center in the heart of the Latin Quarter of Paris. The decision was no doubt an excellent one, but very strong criticisms were expressed on all sides against the decision-making process within the Fonds, especially as the sums involved were so huge that they would have tied up the budget and the future activities of the whole Jewish community for several years. In reaction, a strong movement, animated by former members of "Point 1970," academics, youth movement leaders, administrators of the Fonds, and some of the notables themselves, set out to force the FSJU to reform its constitution in a democratic direction. After long preparatory work, the new constitution was adopted on November 1, 1972.

In order to understand the substance of the reform, it is useful to briefly compare the old constitution (1966) with that adopted in 1972. The principal innovations dealt with the membership and institutions of the Fonds. According to the constitution of 1966, the FSJU included, in addition to "active members," also "associate members," "honorary members," and "corresponding members" (international organizations). In the new constitution, this last category was eliminated.

While the old constitution reserved the status of "active member" to those who had contributed to its fund-raising drives for three consecutive years, the new constitution conferred this status on anyone over 18 years of age who joined the FSJU by paying a membership fee. This provision is obviously the key element of the reform.

As for the "associate members," this group included various organizations of the community. But whereas the old constitution was concerned only with social, cultural and educational organizations, the new constitution opened membership in the FSJU to any Jewish association, regardless of its character (even if purely political).

Finally, although the new constitution did not go so far as to radically discontinue the category of "honorary members" (people who had rendered important services to the community), it granted them only a consultative voice in the National Council.

According to the constitution of 1966, the FSJU comprised several organs, certain of which found themselves in competition with one another, their respective domains being ill-defined: the General Assembly, the National Council, the Executive Committee, the Action and Fund-Raising Committees, the study commissions, etc. After 1972, the FSJU was to be composed of three governing institutions: the National Council (*Conseil National*), a kind of "Jewish parliament," which is the sovereign organ; the Board of Directors (*Comite Directeur*), which must follow community policy as defined by the Council; and the Executive Bureau (*Bureau Executif*), a kind of cabinet to which the Board of Directors delegates authority and which administers the community.

The emphasis was thus placed on the National Council, which is composed of 120 delegates elected for six years from among the "active members" and 40 delegates elected from among the "associate members." In order to be eligible, it is sufficient to have been a member of the FSJU for two years. The members of this parliament can be reelected. The elections are conducted by a single round uninominal ballot, on the basis of a geographic division into regional districts. The Council meets at least once a month.

The constitution of 1972, drawn up by well-known jurists, virtually copied all the institutions and statutes of classical parliamentarianism. The Board of Directors comprises 30 members elected for four years by the Council by a secret uninominal ballot. Its members may be reelected once, but they are eligible for reelection to a third term only four years after the end of their second mandate, thus avoiding perpetual government by the notables.

The Executive Bureau is composed of seven members: five elected by the Board of Directors from among its members, and the other two being the secretary general and the treasurer of the FSJU.

The directors of the Fonds themselves presented the change in the following manner:

> The FSJU, since it represents the community as a whole, was best suited to do away with a policy of closed doors, which is no longer practical. Its leaders had the courage to take the lead in an undertaking prompted by young academics who took it upon themselves to propose a radical reform....A radical reform, a calculated risk, for the present leaders will have to submit to the Jewish electorate, a first step in the direction of a Jewish parliament....Either we will be left on the sidelines and disappear, or we will form this living, democratic and strong community which the new generations demand and which Israel needs.

The Results of the Reform

The different organizations of French Jewry and the Jewish press (mainly *L'Arche, Tribune Juive, Information Juive*, and *Les Nouveaux Cahiers*) greeted the reform of the Fonds with great satisfaction.[9] Such diverse organizations as the Consistoire Central and the Zionist Movement of France called upon their members to join the FSJU, stand for election, and vote in the upcoming elections. An extensive membership campaign was conducted in 1973-1974.

The Membership[10]

If one takes into consideration the extent of the campaign conducted and the substantial means employed, the results were quite modest. The FSJU in effect registered only 16,341 members (for a community estimated at 525,000-700,000).[11] The membership was divided as follows: Paris 6,332; Paris suburbs 3,739; and provinces 6,270. The greater metropolitan Paris area embraced 10,071 members, or two-thirds of those Jews who can be considered militant or involved. Two provincial regions, the Provence-Languedoc region (2,029 members) and the Rhone-Alps region (1,465 members), contained the majority of the provincial membership. In two provincial regions, North (165 members) and West (88 members), the membership was negligible. These figures may be said to provide a good account of the distribution of those Jews who are most willing to engage in acts of militancy for Jewish causes in France today.

However, judging these results to be still very insufficient, it was decided that at the next by-election to the National Council (November 1978), the principle of membership would be abandoned and the right to vote be granted to all those who contributed financially to the Fonds Social. Thus, in 1978 there were a much larger number of voters, 38,702, distributed as follows: Paris 15,654; Paris suburbs 8,509; and provinces 14,539.

The Candidates

The following analyses are based on the 1978 elections, the basic data furnished in 1975 being very incomplete. In addition, it should be emphasized that the percentages indicated below provide only an approximate indication of the situation since they are computed on the basis of very small overall figures. And, even in 1978, the candidates often provided incomplete information about themselves, frequently neglecting to mention their age or profession.

With regard to one of the most interesting questions, that of how many Sephardim stood for election, the study can only be onomastic, and therefore partial and highly inadequate.[12] It appears that in 1978 the percentage of Sephardim among the candidates was as follows: Paris — 40 percent; Paris suburbs — 75 percent; and provinces — 60 percent. These figures seem to indicate that the reform succeeded in attracting a considerable fringe of the North African refugees, certain of whom had undoubtedly long aspired to more active participation.

The division of candidates for the FSJU by sex seems less satisfactory: Paris had the highest percentage of women candidates (21.3 percent), but there were only 10.6 percent in the Paris suburbs and 14.1 percent in the provinces. There seems to be a fairly clear correlation here with the proportion of Sephardic candidates in each zone: the more Sephardic candidates in a given district, the fewer women candidates, and vice versa.

An analysis of the candidates' professions[13] reveals that a large proportion of the candidates still belong to the liberal professions (particularly medicine and law): Paris — 15.5 percent; Paris suburbs — 15.1 percent; and provinces — 14 percent.[14] This is understandable given the social composition of French Jewry.

Setting the liberal professions aside, the differences between the three zones are quite significant. In Paris, many of the candidates were retired (15.5 percent), executives (11.4 percent), or high school and university teachers (10.6 percent). The same proportion of teachers (10.6 percent) was evident among the candidates in the Paris suburbs, but here executives constituted the largest group (18.1 percent). As can be expected in a region where Algerian repatriates are dominant, 7.5 percent of the candidates in this area were minor and intermediate grade civil servants. In the provinces, the candidates' professions as a whole were more varied. Notably, 15.3 percent were tradesmen.

Conversely, certain professions were very poorly represented. In Paris as well as in the provinces, none of the candidates were manual workers or technicians (whereas this group represented 4.5 percent of the candidates in the Paris suburbs); employees were relatively few (4 percent in Paris, 1.5 percent in the Paris suburbs, 3.8 percent in the provinces); manufacturers and bankers were poorly represented in the suburbs, whereas they accounted for 8.1 percent of the candidates in Paris. Finally, on the whole, there was a particularly low percentage of students: 0.8 percent in Paris, 3.3 percent in the suburbs, and 6.4 percent in the provinces.

Although the ages of a number of candidates is unknown,[15] it may be noted that the candidates were much older in Paris where 51 percent were 50 years of age or older, while in the Paris suburbs this age group constituted only 15.1 percent, and in the provinces 28 percent of the candidates. The candidates in the provinces were clearly the youngest: 29.4 percent were 40 years old or less (27.2

percent in the suburbs, 22.1 percent in Paris). There were few candidates under 30 years of age (4.9 percent in Paris, 4.5 percent in the suburbs, 10.2 percent in the provinces). In the three electoral zones, the age group which supplied the largest number of candidates was the 40-49 year old age group (23.1 percent in Paris, 30.3 percent in the Paris suburbs, 24.3 percent in the provinces).

In conclusion, it may be noted that while the democratization campaign seems to have succeeded in arousing the desire of the Sephardim to participate in the management of community affairs, it does not seem to have led to increased involvement among women, youth, and "underprivileged classes" of French Jewish society (workers, employees, minor civil servants, etc.) on the candidate level.[16]

Before examining the candidates' orientations, it should be emphasized that the method of voting adopted was in fact half-way between voting by ticket, with the option of splitting one's ticket, and a uninominal ballot. In effect, while the voters cast their ballots for individuals, the candidates could form tickets reflecting their common views on community affairs and Israel. Thus, both in 1975 and 1978 we find in Paris four major "currents": a "central" current including most of the notables and leading personalities in the community, who, while essentially oriented towards the development and reinforcement of the institutions of French Jewry, also declared their loyalty to Israel;[17] a current made up of former members of the youth movements and of people who, while more or less well-known, were not included for personal reasons on the "central" list; a current essentially representing the repatriates from Algeria and other North African Jews; a leftist current (including Bernard Lazare's group, former communists, and people connected with Hashomer Hatzair). A comparison of the platforms of these different tickets does not reveal any significant differences between them. On the contrary, there is a clear uniformity on all the important issues (community and Israel).

Ostensibly democratic, this ticket system could not give entirely satisfactory results. For although, in theory, it is possible to split one's ticket, the individual Jewish voter tends to cast his or her ballot for a particular ticket as a whole (especially as the candidates are unfamiliar). The results were exactly the same in 1975 and 1978: almost all those elected were from a single ticket, that of the "central" current, comprising the best known figures and personalities of the Jewish community. The new candidates who appeared on other tickets or who stood for election independently had in fact no chance of being elected. Thus, in the 1975 elections in Paris, all those elected belonged to the "central" ticket known as *Am Ehad*. Similarly, in 1978 all those elected (except one)[18] belonged to the same ticket, renamed *Ahavat Israel*. This system may well discourage new candidates from running in future elections.

The Vote

In 1975, 6,700 people participated in the elections, or 41.1 percent of the registered voters. Thus, there were clearly two levels of "activism": the act of membership and the act of voting. In 1978, 7,798 people voted, or 20.1 percent of the "registered voters" (who in this case were in fact all the contributors to the Fonds). If we assume that almost all those who voted in 1975 voted again in 1978, this represents an increase of roughly one thousand voters (+16 percent).

As regards voter participation, important differences may be noted from one electoral zone to another. The general tendency seems to be that the more "registered voters" there are in a particular zone, the smaller the relative turnout.

	1975		1978	
	Registered Voters	Voter Turnout (%)	Registered Voters	Voter Turnout (%)
Paris	6,332	33.7	15,654	19.3
Paris suburbs	3,739	43.1	8,509	22.5
Provinces	6,270	48.1	14,539	19.6

This statement is confirmed most clearly in the different electoral districts in the provinces. Thus, in 1978 the average turnout in those provincial districts having the largest number of potential voters (400 to 12,147) was only 17.3 percent, while the turnout in those districts having less than 400 registered voters was 26 percent.

Another interesting correlation is that between the percentage of votes cast in each district and the percentage of "blank" or "disqualified" votes.[19] The greater the number of votes, the fewer blank and disqualified votes were found, and vice versa. Thus, in the two suburban districts having the largest voter turnout, Val d'Oise 3e (33.6 percent) and Val de Marne 4e (31 percent), only 2.4 percent and 2 percent of the votes respectively were either blank or disqualified. Conversely, the two districts where the turnout was the smallest, Val de Marne 2e (16.5 percent) and Seine-Saint Denis 1e (17.2 percent), were also those where the proportion of blank and disqualified votes was the largest: 7.4 percent and 7.9 percent.

We find the same correlation in the provinces, where the districts with the highest voter turnout were Bretagne-Vallee de la Loire 1e (36 percent, with 2.3 percent blank or disqualified votes) and Est 1-1e (28 percent, with 6.4 percent blank or disqualified votes), while those with low voter turnout were, for example, Est 1-2e (12.6 percent, with 19.6 percent) and Nice-Cote d'Azur 1e (12.6 percent, with 20 percent).

The Elected Deputies

A detailed analysis of the 1978 results reveals clearly what must be seen as a certain conservative or cautious tendency on the part of the French Jewish electorate in choosing its representatives. In fact, some of the positive trends toward diversification and regeneration which were noted on the candidate level are absent or diminished within the elected body.

It is true that the percentage of Sephardim elected was about the same as that among the candidates (though it should be recalled that the data on the subject is not very accurate): 33 percent (as opposed to 40 percent among the candidates) in Paris, 73 percent (as opposed to 75 percent) in the suburbs, and 60 percent (60 percent) in the provinces.

While in the suburbs the percentage of women elected was higher than the percentage of women candidates there (17.3 percent versus 10.6 percent), it was less in Paris (14.2 percent versus 21.3 percent), and strikingly less in the provinces (3.3 percent versus 14.1 percent). In all the provincial districts there was a clear preference for male candidates. It is probably in this domain that one finds the most apparent regression in comparison to the 1975 elections, when the percentage of women elected was 30 percent in Paris and 8 percent in the provinces.

With respect to age, significant differences appear. In Paris there was a clear trend towards seniority: not a single candidate under 30 was elected, while the age group providing the largest number of delegates was the 40-49 group (42.8 percent), with an additional 42.8 percent who were 50 or older. In effect, practically none of the "new" or young members of the *Ahavat Israel* ticket were elected.

The situation was slightly different in the provinces, where 28.5 percent of those elected were under 40 (of whom 7.1 percent were under 30). However, at the same time, 21.3 percent of those elected were 50 or older (of whom 3.5 percent were over 70). It was only in the Paris suburbs that younger delegates were elected, reflecting the composition of the Jewish population in that area: 43.3 percent of those elected were under 40 (8.6 percent under 30), and only 8.6 percent were 50 or older (with none over 60). It should be added that these results correspond with surprising accuracy to what is known of the distribution of French Jewry by age.[20]

Conclusions

The events and the reform which took place within the French community were marked by elements peculiar to the French national context, elements characteristic of any process of democratization of a Jewish institution, and elements characteristic of any institutional change. First of all, there is no doubt that the changes which took place within the community were to a great extent related to the events which occurred in France during 1968, and to the general anti-authoritarian revolt which affected the society at large as well as individual groups within it. The French context is also reflected in the role of the "technocratic elites." This can undoubtedly be attributed in part to the immense prestige enjoyed by the graduates of the Grandes Ecoles, and in particular of the National School of Administration, among all sectors of the population. Several of the most brilliant French Jewish technocrats played a central role in the organization of the reform. In a final reflection of the French context, the reform failed to affiliate the radicals of the extreme left through the "new community." Unlike the American case, where certain groups of young radicals remain strongly concerned with their Judaism and with *clal Israel*, the French Jewish radicals are in general totally disinterested in any form of community life or organization.[21]

What seems characteristic of any process of change within a

Jewish institution is the striking permanence of the structures of authority and influence. The notables possess what can truly be described as "paternal authority." And if the community is, to cite Peter Y. Medding's expression, a "family" or a "family of families,"[22] it is to be expected that the authority of these "family heads" will remain dominant; in other words, that the electorate of the newly democratized community will continue to reelect their notables, old and new. Thus, in 1978 almost all the outgoing delegates of 1975 were reelected. In fact, since the leadership, being voluntary, demands a considerable investment of time, it is quite probable that, despite all attempts to diversify the leaders through democratic elections, they will continue to be recruited from among those who have the material means to dedicate themselves to this task.

Finally, in the circumstances of the reform there were elements characteristic of any institutional transformation, which is related to two other important kinds of change:

— A change in the surrounding system of values and political culture. If the Napoleonic era, with its principles of hierarchy, centralism, authority, faith in the notables, conformism, and the omnipotence of Paris, was favorable to the establishment of such institutions as the Consistoires, it may be understood how the post-war period, and especially the post-1968 period, with its themes of autonomy and participation, encouraged a change like that which has been analyzed above.

— An institutional transformation is also often related to a change in the existing social and economic structures. In the case of the Jewish institutions in France, a direct link has been noted between the advent of the reform and the prior arrival of immigrants with a social and professional composition clearly different from that of the indigenous Jewish population.

Notes

1. Daniel J. Elazar, "American Political Theory and the Political Notions of American Jews: Convergences and Contradictions," *Jewish Journal of Sociology*, vol. 9, no. 1 (June 1967): 22, n. 6.

2. Charles S. Liebman has dealt with the question of the basis of the community leaders' authority in "Dimensions of Authority in the Contemporary Jewish Community," *Jewish Journal of Sociology*, vol. 12, no. 1 (June 1970): 29-38; and "Sources of Authority in the Contemporary Jewish Community," *Jewish Digest*, no. 17 (November 1971): 1-7.

3. See Simon Schwarzfuchs, *Les Juifs de France* (Paris: Albin Michel, 1975); and Bernhard Blumenkranz, ed., *Histoire des Juifs en France* (Toulouse: Privat, 1972).

4. The collection is carried out by the United Jewish Appeal of France (AUJF), and allocated to the community in France by the FSJU.

5. Daniel J. Elazar, "The Institutional Life of American Jewry," *Midstream*, vol. 17, no. 6 (June-July 1971): 35.

6. The case was clearly different with the immigrants from Eastern and Central Europe who began to arrive at the end of the nineteenth century and established their own networks and community organizations in France, separate from those of the indigenous Jewish population.

7. See Alain Greilsammer, "Jews of France: From Neutrality to Involvement," *Forum*, nos. 28-29 (Winter 1978): 130-146.

8. Moshe Davis, *Jewish Communities in World Perspective* (New York: Council of Jewish Federation and Welfare Funds, 1964): 9.

9. A detailed study of the community's four major journals reveals a rare unanimity in enthusiasm for the reform. On the attitude of the principal organizations, see the dossier published by the FSJU: *Reforme des Structures du Fonds Social Juif Unifie — Positions des Organisations Juives* (1974).

10. See the brochure *Resultats des Elections au Conseil National — Scrutin du 26.1.75*, FSJU, 1975.

11. These two extreme estimates must be quoted. In fact, the numerical size of the Jewish population of France has been the subject of an interesting controversy between specialists in Jewish demography. A team from the SOFRES (an important French polling institute) under the direction of Emeric Deutsch proposed the hypothesis that the Jewish population of France is about 700,000; see *Bulletin Quotidien d'Information — Agence Telegraphique Juive*,

no. 1527 (February 11, 1977). This figure and the methods used in establishing it were strongly contested by Professors Sergio Della Pergola (Hebrew University) and Doris Bensimon (C.N.R.S.) who have suggested the figure of 525,000; see "Enquetes socio-demographiques sur les Juifs de France," *Dispersion et Unite*, no. 18 (1978): 190-212.

12. Since this was the first occasion on which the North African Jews could really make their presence and participation felt, it was important to know the origin of the candidates. As no document mentioned their place of birth, onomastic criteria had to be utilized. However, aside from the fact that certain names are common to both Ashkenazim and Sephardim (Cohen, Levy, etc.), it is impossible to distinguish among the Sephardim themselves between those who were repatriates or recent refugees and those, for example, who originated from Salonika or who had long been integrated into French society.

13. There were, however, a substantial number of candidates whose profession was unknown.

14. E. Deutsch estimates the percentage of French Jews belonging to the "liberal professions and managerial staffs" at 16 percent; *op. cit.*, p. 2. See also Sergio Della Pergola and Doris Bensimon, *op. cit.*, pp. 207-209.

15. 1.6 percent in Paris, 27.1 percent in the Paris suburbs, and 17.9 percent in the provinces.

16. One of the "revelations" of the questionable survey conducted by the SOFRES was that 22 percent of the French Jewish population was composed of "workers" (10 percent skilled workers, 8 percent semi-skilled or unskilled workers, and 4 percent domestic staff). Della Pergola and Bensimon give much lower figures; *op. cit.*, p. 207.

17. The candidates on this ticket reflected a broad sample of all the trends in the community: Diasporists, Zionists, Orthodox, Reform, etc.

18. This was Serge Klarsfeld, Beate Klarsfeld's husband, who is famous for his role in the pursuit of former Nazis (a member of the *Atidenou* ticket).

19. It has been French electoral practice to compute blank and disqualified votes together. This practice is particularly open to criticism in the case of elections to Jewish community institutions since the blank vote and the disqualified vote designate completely different attitudes. In the case being examined here, a blank vote may, for example, signify a lack of confidence in the candidates, the tickets, or the general structure of the organized community, while the invalid votes are "those ballots which

include more names than the number of seats to be filled in the district, those ballots including a name that does not appear on the list of candidates, and those ballots that bear any sign whatsoever."

20. Della Pergola and Bensimon have pointed out the differences between the distribution of the Jewish population by age in Paris proper and in the Paris suburbs. They note a clear aging of the population in Paris, in contrast with the "youthful" character of the suburbs. In Paris, for example, the average age of the Jews is about 41, as opposed to 30 in the suburbs; *op. cit.*, pp. 200-201.

21. The gulf which separates the American Jewish radicals from their French counterparts on the question of their relationship with the Jewish community (opposition to the community establishment in the U.S. as opposed to a rejection of the community as a whole in France) is noted in Jack Nusan Porter and Peter Dreier, eds., *Jewish Radicalism* (New York: Grove Press, 1973) and Annie Kriegel, "Judaisme et Gauchisme," in *Communismes au miroir francais* (Paris: Gallimard, 1974): 219-225.

22. Peter Y. Medding, "A Contemporary Paradox: Israel and Jewish Peoplehood," *Forum*, no. 26 (1977): 5-6.

Chapter 8

THE DYNAMICS OF THE THREE *KETARIM* IN THE POLITICAL TRANSFORMATION OF CONTEMPORARY FRENCH JEWRY

Shmuel Trigano

The history of the Jewish community in France since the end of the Second World War and more precisely since the beginning of the Fifth Republic (1958) is such that in it we can almost see the inner workings of the process of reconstruction of a Jewish community.

During that period, two antagonistic processes of Jewish history in France intersected. A communal model imposed from outside, but totally taken up and internalized by the Jews, disintegrated under the blows of external events and its own historic exhaustion. Meanwhile, a new model came together piece by piece, emerging from the workshop built on the ruins of the first.

Consequently, the French example serves as a touchstone for the models and analytic prisms recently constructed to more coherently analyze the phenomenon of the Jewish community. We propose conducting this analysis through the theory of the "three crowns." The implications of the analysis will enable us to test the validity of the theory.

I. The Exile of *Keter Malkhut*: The Genealogy of Communal Political Authority

The founding criterion of every political authority in Jewish history has always rested on the concept of the *brit*, the Covenant, from the origins of the Jews through ancient times and the Middle Ages. One might have expected that with the coming of modern times, this foundation would crumble and disappear under the

A version of this chapter previously appeared in French in the journal *Pardes*, 6 (1987).

jealous universalism of the democratic state, and especially the modern constitutional mechanisms which it established. What makes the Jew modern, in fact, is democratic citizenship which he enjoys within the framework of a constitution, which serves as a substitute "covenant." In this sense, modern contractual political systems contrast with the charters and statutes of the *ancien regime* insofar as they no longer consecrate agreements between a collectivity and a monarch, but take on a "universal" validity. It is through this aspect (although it may be necessary to reexamine the limits of the comparison, since the universal tone of the Sinai constitution has quite another meaning) that they approach the *brit* of Sinai and through this angle that the Jews were able to see a reflection of themselves in modern constitutions.

For the past two centuries, Jews have erected political authority on the basis of the constitutional norms of the society as a whole. Most often, they have reproduced the essential features of the political culture within which they were living.[1] It has already been noted by Elazar that the structure of Jewish organizations in the diaspora follows the model of the state where they are located. There is no doubt that the organization of French Jewry is marked by Jacobin centralism, just as the American Jewish federations follow the model of the federal state. In fact, in spite of the lack of its original content, the *brit* as a criterion has preserved its relevance. It has survived symbolically with a two-fold character: exteriorization (being turned outwards) and substitution.

In the collective imagination of French Jewry, as expressed in writing and speech, the Declaration of the Rights of Man replaced the Torah of Moses, through a total identification of the first with the second.[2] As a result, Republican France was raised to the level of a "chosen people," the continuation of the original chosen people.[3] In this way, the *brit* was preserved with all its philosophic and behavioral connotations, but as a purely abstract symbol, an empty Hebraic form henceforth filled with French republican ideology. Hence, the Declaration of the Rights of Man was represented in art as inscribed on two tablets, like the Tablets of Sinai. The *brit* endured, but deprived of its internal dynamics, devoid of its relevance; it had been turned outwards. Thus the Jews of France conceived of and forged their adhesion and allegiance to the rules of French citizenship and nationality as a function of the form of the *brit* (as an empty, purely symbolic form, to be sure). It no longer symbolized belonging to the House of Israel, but to the House of France.[4] This phenomenon becomes very important for understanding continuity and change in the Jewish political tradition in modern times.

Quite logically, a substitute messianism developed simultaneously, transferring the "chosenness" of Israel to the "chosenness" of France, the new Chosen People charged with bringing civilization to the ends of the earth. Thus, the *brit* was accompanied by its counterpart, "chosenness" ("election"), that is, the experience of the divine among men and in history, here transformed into an exaltation of the French nation which had wed the "spirit of history."[5] We can find parallel mechanisms in the history of every modern Jewry, in Germany, England, the United States, and the early period of Soviet Russia.

In its foundations, modern Jewry was still connected with Hebraic messianism which, however, had been diverted, led astray, made into a gesture, "universalized," and cut off from its historic dimension and meaning. This explains why the Jews have been the great artisans of meaning in modern politics, among the most important alchemists of modern ideologies and revolutionary messianisms. They infuse the domain of modern politics with all the power of Jewish messianism. In this respect, the Hebraic dimension — whether authentic or perverted — of socialism and communism among modern Jews has not been pondered enough. What is significant for this analysis is that the *brit* and the concept of chosenness are still the basis of political authority among the Jews, even if they have been infused with a new meaning.

Now here is a decisive feature of modern Jewish politics which we find linked with the new configuration of power in the modern Jewish community. Its outstanding and fundamental trait seems to be the hypertrophy of the *keter kehunah* (the crown of the priesthood) or priestly authority. The Sanhedrin convoked by Napoleon imposed an extreme model for turning Jews into a religious denomination.[6] By this means, all the old privileges of the centers of authority and power in traditional Jewish society, *keter malkhut* and *keter torah* (civil authority and Torah authority), became vestigial and what remained of their attributes were transferred to the office of Chief Rabbi. He was supposed to represent and join together the whole Jewish community and Jewish wisdom, but his main characteristic, nevertheless, was to possess only religious authority in such a manner that the *keter malkhut* and *keter torah* disappear while Jewry and Judaism vanish as society, history, and way of thinking.

Here perhaps is a principle of every Jewish polity: when

malkhut is eliminated, the *kehunah* remains the most powerful nucleus of power. It is interesting to note in this regard how much the authority of the Chief Rabbi in France was presumed, in the representations made of it, to repeat the ancient pattern imposed on the Second Jewish Commonwealth when, deprived of its political sovereignty as a result of foreign domination, all Hebraic authority was concentrated in the office of the High Priesthood, except that then there existed a semi-autonomous Jewish society. This is particularly interesting, considering that it was installed and legitimized by a "Sanhedrin" created out of whole cloth by Napoleon after an interruption of nineteen centuries. Even in its self-dissolution, the Jewish political tradition was still powerful. But again, we find the same feature of exteriorization/substitution, insofar as the Chief Rabbi derived his identity from Napoleon's will, whereas the High Priest derived his from Sinai. Things are the same, but everything has changed.

However, the French-Jewish model itself underwent rapid development which for us verifies the insurmountable character of the "three crowns" pattern of triple authority: it secreted, almost despite itself, a new center of power and representation, secular and political in nature. This was the Alliance Israelite Universelle (AIU), a reconstitution of the *keter malkhut* of this civil authority, legally abolished by the Consistory system established by Napoleon's Sanhedrin. Civil authority in the Jewish community reappeared, however, only on condition that its effect be directed outside the community. Its legitimacy was considered international rather than intranational. The AIU intervened abroad to defend and safeguard Jewish life in places where it was threatened. It possessed political power, since its interventions took place on the government level concerning political issues, by deploying the whole range of powers within the capacity of pressure groups. But this new power still fit into the general pattern, since the arena of this civil authority, secular and obviously non-denominational as it was, was located abroad, outside France, in such a way that it respected the primacy of the denominational dimension and "priestly authority" within France. In short, its legitimacy was defined negatively, since it was the existence of "threatened" Jewry — and in principle Jews were not supposed to be threatened in France — that the AIU basically aspired to defend and support. *Malkhut* was not taken up in its profundity and consciousness of self, even if it often presented traits of broad scope and the attributes of its identity.

Turning the authority of *kehunah* and *malkhut* outwards constituted the criterion validating those two authorities. Exteriorization was national, that is, immersion in French society, as far as priestly authority was concerned. It was international, fitting into relationships with governments, as far as civil authority was concerned.

The fields of application of these two authorities were mutually exclusive and derived their validity from that exclusion. Compared with them, the *keter torah* was extremely weak; each of the other two "crowns," each authority, tried to appropriate the *keter torah* to itself, as if to provide itself with letters of nobility and legitimacy. The Central Consistory, aside from the institution of the Chief Rabbi, comprises the Rabbinical Seminary charged with training rabbis. In addition to its task of international political representation, the Alliance (AIU) took upon itself the major role in the Jewish and secular education of Mediterranean Jewry by building up a whole educational network.

The purposes of these two networks were selective: rabbis for the Seminary, non-French Jewish communities for the AIU. In this situation, we find the characteristics of both authorities (intra-French denominational and extra-French civil), each one of which tried to join Torah authority (*keter torah*) to itself. Thus each one cancelled out Torah authority within its exclusive sphere. In essence the eclipse or absence of *keter torah* characterized the system. Here, too, a mechanism of exteriorization was at work, since *keter torah* here was a purely formal, nominal category, insofar as, in the case of the AIU, it had to do above all with transmitting French culture (did not France take over the role of "chosen people"?) and, in the case of the Seminary, with a denominational form that had been drastically shrunken in scope. Exteriorization was thus simultaneously a mechanism of alienation. The same goes for the two other authorities: turning them outward considerably altered and denatured the very basis of their identity and validity. Everything tended to be more theatrical than real. The true ancient logic of the "three crowns" was lost, even if their structure remained.

II. Modern Jewish Political Reality

Exteriorization was to have different consequences for each of the domains. For the priestly authority it set off a debilitating process. Conversely, for the civil authority it was to have very important results in the sphere of Jewish political history. For the first time in ten centuries, since the end of the sway of the Babylonian Exilarchate, civil authority was measured on a worldwide scale involving the Jewish people in the totality of its communities. The ban on Jewish civil authority in French society and Jewish life in France produced its paradoxical deployment on the outside, where it sketched with dotted lines a worldwide, transnational Jewish political entity which first of all affirmed itself negatively (in efforts to save persecuted Jews) and also for the grandeur of France. But already taking shape within this transnational synthesis was Zionism, the aspiration towards renewed nationality, beyond the Jews' adopted nationalities. The basic and exclusive goal of Zionism was the restoration of the power of *keter malkhut*. Quite logically, the AIU founded one of the first agricultural institutions in Israel: the Mikveh Israel School.

We also have a negative measure of this whole movement in the anti-Semitic suspicion of a "worldwide Jewish conspiracy" to gain power over all other peoples. The idea of Jewish "power" is central here. It is the notion of a power which crosses national boundaries. But this demonstration of political power in the Jewish world was then, of course, totally perverted by the anti-Semites.

In fact, the AIU was the first worldwide Jewish organization to be institutionalized. It was a historic innovation, synthesizing all the aspects of modern Jewish life. It was the prototype for all modern Jewish institutions, in which the future Jewish state was already present in outline. What is certain in any case is that the inevitable worldwide spread of *keter malkhut* awakened the Jews as a people and reintroduced the French Jewish community into the Jewish people as a whole.

We must consider the paradox here. The whole Napoleonic model was aimed at annihilating the *keter malkhut* within the Jewish communal system. This did not mean destroying Jewish life totally, but letting so little exist as to condemn it to something worse than non-existence: insignificance. The system erased the relevance of Jewish communal life by institutionalizing it in a new way.

The proof of the power and durability of Jewish communal life is that there was need for a dramatization of its continuity through an ersatz Sanhedrin at the very moment it was being cut off from history.

This leads us to think a good deal about the meaning of modern Jewish institutional life, which is scarred by the absence of the community. One might define the sphere of modern Jewish politics in this way. But it is by profoundly assuming its logic that the French Jews have outwitted the pitfall and avoided the fatal trap. This came at the price of a subtle equilibrium, since the principle which ensured their survival on the outside, denied it on the inside.

This paradox is the sign that Jewish political authorities (priestly, civil, and Torah) have lost their authenticity in the very midst of their continuation. The *keter malkhut* was forbidden within the restricted national framework of the countries where the Jews lived, yet by spreading worldwide, it was to ensure its continuity. This process of spreading worldwide is illustrated of course in the early experience of an international Jewish organization with a political (i.e., humanitarian) mission. But we must also see the worldwide spread of *malkhut* in the committed political and intellectual participation of the Jews in the life of the West, most often through the great messianic ideologies of the nineteenth and twentieth centuries.

Internationalism and ideological-political universalism opened powerful channels for assimilation and erosion of identity for numbers of modern Jews. But their secret principle actually involved Jewish survival in a modern society which made Jewish survival almost impossible. This is why we must trace the Jewish genealogy of assimilated Jewish personalities such as Karl Marx, insofar as a certain logic (*the* logic?) of modern Jewish destiny has worked through them. Might we define this secret survival through apparently entropic paths as a sort of compensation, as a superinvestment on the outside of a forbidden inside? It seems not, and the explanation is not psychological, since forbidden on the inside, the *keter malkhut* quite simply went outside.

Here is an illustration of the *intrinsic* power of the civil dimension of authority in the Jewish world. It remains, nevertheless, ambiguous due to the very paradox of its situation. The becoming-a-collectivity of Jewish life throughout the world was in fact the paradoxical product of the modern system which aimed at foreclosing — in every European state in particular — the dimension of Jewish historical collectivity. Moreover, this becoming-a-collectivity drained the real, historic content of the civil authority which was now only a "crown" that one placed on the head of a political leader as a function of a purely circumstantial political balance of power without regard to the "contract" itself and to the traditions adhering to this authority. Its purpose had become purely negative, to defend persecuted Jews. This of course is an important prerogative of every political authority, but it is of secondary importance, for erecting a political authority basically aims at laying the basis for a political community living on earth and in human history.

This occurred in such a way that although the Jewish collectivity in modern times has something very real and powerful about it, it is also hollow within, lacking substance, inauthentic. Jewish leadership lost its solidity insofar as leadership flows from a configuration of power which is external to the Jewish political domain and insofar as the position which it acquires there is a replication of its situation on the outside. In a word, the notables of the community were first of all notables of the surrounding society. Replication meant that modern Jewish political authority was no longer authentic; it was born neither in the midst of the community nor through explicit, discursive, and procedural consensus. What happened was the superimposition of a political configuration which has been crystallized elsewhere.

Due to the very structure of its modern identity, the *keter malkhut* was cut off from its historicity. It is not at ease with its historic complexion. It has something artificial about it. It aimed at reaching the universal, but it produces in fact Jewish "particularism." Thus, even when the *keter malkhut*, which emerged in nineteenth century France with the heralds of the AIU, sets itself down somewhere and especially in Zion with political Zionism, it is as if it has remained absent from itself, as if even in the Land of Israel the *keter malkhut* remained outside, in the West, in exile. This is what characterizes Jewish political reality in modern times. By particularizing itself on "universalist" (Western) foundations which, in fact, turned it outwards from itself, the intrinsic universality of the *keter malkhut* was eclipsed. Within its own logic, Jewish political authority became its own stage set, the stage set of its own universality, a stage set occupied by a void.

This process has been accompanied by a far greater process of the disappearance of the *edah* whose existence was made impossible, like that of the *keter malkhut* (for which the *edah* is the sphere), by the modern system of national citizenship that effectively outlawed the Jewish collectivity. The *edah* over the course of time has provided the universal framework for the historic existence of the Jewish people, as much in its political dimension as in its interior dimension. Indeed, the notion of *edah* is illuminated by the notion of "testimony" ("*ed*" means "witness") in which we may see, from our perspective, not the "declaration of faith" but rather, more generally, the overall transmission of a tradition. The *edah* is larger than the sum of its parts: it is not a voluntary association but is inscribed in space and time, independent of psychological states. That is what underlies its dynamic activity.

From the point of view of its internal economy, the *edah* was deprived of, exiled from, its own inwardness, removed from Jewish existence. Placed outside of itself or alongside itself, the *edah* was no longer taken as a matter of course with its own historic strength. Its existence was no longer possible except through an effort, except by means of an intermediary. Thus the *covenant* only exercised authority and power by virtue of an ideology, by proxy. The Jewish collectivity gathered together internationally — or even nationally — only through external intermediaries: universalist humanitarianism, identification with the nation and the state, which were the exclusive vehicles of this gathering together. Likewise, to voice approval of Jewish existence, individual Jews secreted the need to commit themselves to an ideology, an intermediary for their identification with Jewish destiny in all its dimensions. This mediation and exteriorization in the relation of Jewish existence to itself constituted the dynamics of modern Jewish political reality: the falling away of universality from the Jewish political sphere, particularization (as to the domain of application and the identity) of political authority, the intercession of ideology in the very production of political reality.

III. The Return of Kingship

Two events shattered the slow progress of the exile of civil authority, of "kingship." One event was external: the Vichy regime put the finishing touches on and institutionalized an anti-Semitism already lurking below the surface and much debated, of which the Dreyfus Case was a high moment. Thus Vichy vitiated the presupposition of the universality of citizenship and the disappearance of the historic Jew within its bosom, which necessarily accompanied it. Hence, the turning outward of the *keter malkhut* became null and void. Vichy designated the Jew by name, cut him off from the universal, and left him in his particularity, his singular solitude.

Moreover, the experience of Vichy, as of genocide in general, worked to create an environment propitious for the birth of a neo-messianism, of a creative effervescence of social existence, when the State of Israel was created. The image of resurrection surged forth from the graves of the abyss. This neo-messianism was made possible by an event (the Six-Day War) and a newly created situation (the massive arrival of North African Jews in France in the 1960s which created the "social density" necessary for such an effervescence).

Neo-messianism is the most exact term there is for this kind of event. The Six-Day War marked a radical turning point in the history of the Jewish people, insofar as it brought about a collective, worldwide coming into self-awareness of the whole Jewish people, even of those farthest away from and most forgetful of their origins. It was accompanied by a feeling of universal singularity and solitude. The neo-messianic declarations of faith after Israel's victory, notably in France, could fill whole books.

From the point of view of this analysis, it is the appropriateness of *keter malkhut* — its validity and its present relevance — which has been found again, beyond disuse, after Vichy, beyond its old criteria of validation (exteriority and ideological universalism), and by virtue of the new sphere where it operates: no longer the highways of the universe, but the inside of the dwelling: a *keter malkhut* which is intimately joined to itself. Hence, what was reversed was the classic dialectic of the universal and the particular.

The universal, perceived as inauthentic, was broken in pieces and the *keter malkhut* surged forth, or rather, appeared in the eyes of French Jewry as possible in its singularity and properly internal validity, but nevertheless still through the intermediary of ideology: no longer universalism (its final defeat was that of post-Stalin Jewish Communism), but Zionism (the present reality of which is a *keter malkhut* returned to itself and taking itself into itself). The nuance bears some importance, since there was only an "evocation" there of the relevance of the *keter malkhut* insofar as its return took place through an ideological mediation (Zionism) and in the manner of a symbol (what was involved was the return of the *keter malkhut* to Jerusalem). The effervescence of political Zionism furnished the ideological background for the return of the *keter malkhut*.

The Three Ketarim in Contemporary French Jewry

Here we have traced the general background and dynamics of the return of the *keter malkhut*, but we can also analyze it in the institutional history of French Jewry which more specifically formalizes it in two quite distinct sequences. First, in January 1944, during the Second World War, the CRIF (Conseil Representatif des Institutions Juives de France) was founded as an underground body. This was the first time that a French Jewish institution saw itself as having a political and communal mission to represent the French Jews to public authorities. The founding charter of the CRIF defined the new organization as the "only one entitled to speak for French Jewry, before the authorities, public opinion, the Jewish organizations of other countries, and international bodies." This was the very moment which put an end to the "Age of the Alliance" and sealed the end of the latter's sway.

In fact, it was the whole Consistory system that sank down. The CRIF, due to the very nature of its domain of application (political and in confrontation with governmental bodies) and due to the very basis of its legitimacy (representing all Jewish organizations, up to and including the Consistory), overshadowed the Consistory, even if, according to the rules prior to March 1982, the President of the Central Consistory of France was also the President of the CRIF or designated him. (Since March 1982, that is no longer necessarily the case.) This first return of civil authority thus tended to eliminate the supremacy of the priestly authority.

The slow decline of the Consistory was reinforced with the founding of "Fonds Social Juif Unifie" in 1949. Here the new political dimension which emerged with the CRIF was paralleled by a social and cultural dimension, as the Fonds made itself into the solid, substantial focus of Jewish life. Article 2 of the "By-laws" of the FSJU of 1950 declares that the Fonds Social has the mission of "promoting throughout the territory of the French Union...the cultural, social, and educational activity of French Jewry."

The *keter malkhut* was reinstituted in the Jewish community and French society in general on this double foundation. Let us note its functional bipolarity operating on the principle of the political nature of the body or institution with which it deals: the state (for the CRIF) or the community (for the Fonds Social). Here is a remnant of the old cleavage between inside and outside, but we must temper this evaluation by noting how fragile the CRIF still is in comparison to the FSJU, and the extent to which the FSJU has more and more made itself into the partner of ministries of the state in order to carry out its plans. The FSJU was formally recognized by the government as an "association of public utility," which gave it the privilege of being financed through the state budget.

This process (decline of priestly authority/rise of civil authority) seems to have undergone a pause with the election of Chief Rabbi Rene Sirat in 1981. He, at least in his declared intentions, aspired to restore the luster of the Central Consistory and the office of Chief Rabbi. His view of matters was almost political and quite within the framework of *keter malkhut*. He spoke at his investiture of the "separation of powers favored by Montesquieu," and went on, "I would say that in the French Jewish community, there is also a legislative power, a judicial power, and an executive power." The first derives of course from the texts of the tradition. The second is exercised by the Rabbinical Court of Paris "which has jurisdiction for everything concerning the problems of religious life." The third is exercised by the Council of Rabbis which must "gradually" become "the government of the French rabbinate and assume its responsibilities within a structure of major ministries...." Three spheres of activity are distinguished: religious (Central Consistory and regional consistories directed by democratically elected assemblies), political (the CRIF), and social and educational (the FSJU).[7]

The new Chief Rabbi chose a two-fold strategy: taking away the representational function of the CRIF through access to the media, and creating a "Chief Rabbinate" apparatus within the Consistory, thus breaking out of the mold of the Consistory and conferring an Israeli style on the French Rabbinate. But this ambition came to an abrupt end. For many reasons, the Chief Rabbi encountered hostility from a large part of the Consistory, notably from its secular component which was troubled by losing its representative function, and the distrust of other Jewish institutions. He did not stand for reelection to the office of Chief Rabbi in 1987. His abortive attempt threatened the political system of French Jewry (where the *keter malkhut* had just been reestablished) with a restored hegemony of the *keter kehunah*, a return to its classic domination.

Was such a return possible, historically speaking? The question is still to be answered; the events are too recent. Indeed, the *keter kehunah* tried, in order to recover its sway, to combine the ways and procedures of the *keter malkhut*, on the model of the state (cf. the Chief Rabbi's statement). Yet, this policy might be interpreted in another way. Rather than the domination of the priestly authority over the civil authority, one might see in it an attempt by the priesthood to break out of its consistorial mold and come back to itself as priestly office, as *keter kehunah*, passing through the screen of the model of civil authority, the *keter malkhut*.

A revival of the authenticity of the *keter kehunah*? A revival of the authenticity of the *keter malkhut*? Is there an attempt to leave modernity and the problematics of exteriorization? There is still only one single criterion by which to judge: the state of the *keter torah*.

Now at the end of this development, of this process of reestablishing a Jewish body politic, the *edah* in France, we realize to what extent this process is unfinished and its future still uncertain when we consider the state of the *keter torah*.

Its domain is still objectively non-existent. No institution accepted by communal consensus, no leader either represents it or embodies it. And, as before, the *keter kehunah* and the *keter malkhut* try to appropriate it to themselves in order to lay a basis for their own legitimacy. This is an even more important step for them when they are located in the diaspora. Modern Western Jewish communities do not really have a decisive political scope, but concentrate more often on cultural and religious purposes. Moreover, the legitimacy of the two *ketarim* is dubious, since the majority of the Jewish community does not take part in communal voting and does not identify itself with the Jewish institutions.

The great stakes or the great temptation in every Jewish political system has always been the exercise of domination over the *keter torah*. This derives from the fact that Hebraic society has been "textocentric." Its framework and dynamics were based on a relationship to the text of Sinai.[8] He who attaches it to himself, attaches to himself legitimacy. This is even more important when the processes of legitimacy are fragile. So the Fonds Social has created a structure of community centers throughout France, the Centre Universitaire des Etudiants Juifs (CUEJ) in Paris where courses in Judaism are given, and some Jewish primary and secondary schools.[9]

The Central Consistory, for its part, still controls the Rabbinical Seminary, but it has no intellectual sway over the community. Chief Rabbi Sirat undertook, before his ouster, to create an Institute of Higher Jewish Studies, under government aegis, which would be aimed at doctoral candidates. Thus it would be of a totally academic nature. The Chief Rabbi, himself a university academic, defined the validating criterion of Jewish studies by academic standards. His ambition at one point was to try to align the rabbinical diplomas with the national university diplomas. This is a classically modern phenomenon. The validity of Jewish activity is always to be sought in an external set of values.

The *keter torah* is devoid of institutions and recognized premises. It thus occupies an informal domain with poorly drawn outlines within the sphere of Jewish intellectual life, a sphere currently not shaped by any system of intellectual and social ethics, by any collective consensus. It is interesting to note that under the auspices of the World Jewish Congress an "Annual Colloquium of French-Speaking Jewish Intellectuals" has been regularly held for about twenty years. It has almost become an intellectual institution. It was founded on the basis of a non-French Jewish institutional network very eager to develop its influence in France.

Beginning in 1985, there was a new development in this intellectual domain. Under the impulse of its new president, Ady Steg, who wanted the Alliance "to do *teshuva*," the oldest Jewish institution created a College des Etudes Juives where many young intellectuals assemble, trying to bridge between lay intelligence and Jewish studies, and which every year organizes a colloquium which competes in fact with the WJC's colloquium. Is this a new Alliance interest in *keter torah*?

For their part, the several classic centers of tradition have chosen silence and total abstention with regard to the major communal and Jewish issues. Their Jewishness is totally religious, though it is not related to the Consistory. The Napoleonic rabbi today wears *peyot* and a hat. Only the psychological and behavioral modalities have changed. An Orthodox sector more radical than the Judaism of the Consistory has established itself with a powerful infrastructure: financial companies, a network of schools and *yeshivot*, and even a food supply network (the *kashrut* is "*glatt*" and not "*bet din*").[10] This sector totally avoids the jurisdiction of the Consistory and dependence on the Fonds Social; nor is it represented on the CRIF; it has no press, and does not issue statements on any issue. This is why it cannot be considered a locus of the *keter torah*. It is completely alienated from the community and shows no political responsibility toward Jewish life as a whole and to the French Jewish collectivity. It should be seen as a community separate from the organized community.

Consequently, the *keter torah*, or what takes its place

structurally, is the locus of "war lords" where influence is decided not as a function of the ethical integrity of a cultural discourse, but rather of the power acquired by any means possible in relation to the public. This is a charismatic structure. Hence, authority no longer follows any rules or procedures. This is an extremely noteworthy development, given the centrality of the *keter torah* among the Jewish people throughout the centuries, one which decisively characterizes the modern Jewish communal system.

Here and there, great intellectual figures appear with enough aura to crystallize around themselves several sectors of the community which grant them some legitimacy. But here again, the criterion of aura is the judgement of the surrounding society and the success which an individual does or does not obtain in it, only then winning over the community. In order to acquire authority within the framework of the *keter torah*, one must first acquire authority within French society, gain access to the media, and reach the Jewish public by ricochet. The value system of the community, which represents the unwritten constitution of the *keter torah*, is hence totally "outer-determined." Intra-Jewish discussion is mediated by primary reference to the outside and technically shaped by access to the communications media: to the radio, television, and print media. A new kind of power has been established, that of the "media Jews," very similar to the power of the medieval "court Jews."[11]

The law of functioning of the value system of the *keter torah* can be stated in the form of a theorem which I propose calling "Mendelssohn's Law," after Moses Mendelssohn's theory and life story.[12] It contains five propositions:

— the more you speak to non-Jews
— the more the Jews pay attention to you
— the less they hear you since you are really not speaking to them
— the more communications chaos and disorder increase
— the more non-Jews are suspicious of you since, in fact, you are not addressing them while you are speaking to them.

The recent establishment of Jewish mass communications media following the 1981 liberalization of the law to permit private radio stations has opened a new area within the nebulous *keter torah*, but it is much too early to judge its development. This new media dimension is in fact very important insofar as it obtains for the community a continuous presence for itself at the very moment when it is splintered and dispersed. This no doubt was the creation of an extremely effective process of collectivization, given the nature and very structure of the community. It was really adapted to its needs, much more than the classic institutions.

It would be an error to mistake the informal and amorphous character of *keter torah* in France as an inevitable feature of the *keter torah* in general. Even the prophets who seem to form the vaguest part of the Jewish political system enrolled themselves in a lineage and tradition which were transmitted among the "sons of the prophets" (I Kings 20:35), by means of accepted, organized procedures which no doubt gave us the prophetic books of the Bible and a great part of Jewish literature, notably including the Kabbalah which claims to be a direct continuation of that tradition.

The current absence of a minimal code of "professional" ethics for its adepts is thus not to be understood as a normal feature of *keter torah*. On the contrary, this is a sign of its deviation from tradition and the crisis in which it finds itself. Here we have a determinative criterion for evaluating the Jewish political system, since Jewish society has always crystallized around a text, the text given at Sinai, and its very structure has been woven around that text. The Jewish people is the only example of a "textocentric" society. Every historic step in Jewish society thus immediately becomes a step within the text, a movement in a process of textual interpretation.

The Hebraic social bond is established by a relationship to the text, a hermeneutical relationship of interpretation. Hence we can read the history of Jewish society in the history of Jewish hermeneutics and its successive crises.[13] Jewish hermeneutics, in all its many schools, has always obeyed very precise rules. The ineffectiveness of any code of professional behavior within the process of producing commentaries and the Jewish intellectual and cultural style — which have made the *keter torah* into a true "*hefker*," property without an owner — is an overall indication of the situation of the Jewish communal system.

This enables us to correctly evaluate the condition of the three *ketarim*. As we have seen, the *keter torah* is at the mercy of the other two authorities within the system. Nevertheless, it remains the system's nerve center and no doubt it is within its arena that the future development of the system will be decided. It is especially in this arena that Jewish institutional creativity seems most probable either through the appearance of new institutions or the updating of old ones.

IV. Within and Without: The Social-Communal Link

Several questions must be asked about such a configuration of power and authority within the community. What is the nature of communal existence if the *edah* has been eclipsed within the Jewish collectivity, even as that collectivity, formerly outlawed, has been reestablished in practice, but without the *keter torah* recovering its legitimacy and status? In view of the normative void which characterizes Jewish collective existence, without the clear awareness and formulation of the *keter torah*, what can communal coalescence accomplish? If communal coalescence is to be explained by voluntarism, then must one believe that at the heart of the community there is a "non-community" which happens to be a majority, since the voluntary adherents of communal institutions represent a minority?[14]

If modern Jewish institutional life is defined as a paradoxical instance of the absence of the *edah* and of the "presence" of the Jews in modern society, then the institutional disaffection of the Jews would be a beneficial sign, since it would mark the rebirth of the *edah*, the return of its presence to itself, beyond the institutional dimension. In fact, the situation is somewhere in between. We have seen how the classic authorities tend to reconstitute themselves or survive through new institutions. There may well be today a borderline situation between exile and the return of the *edah*.

Belonging to the *edah* does not depend on individual will, or on a militant commitment. That is an ideological conception. The presence of every Jew in the *edah* is objective and historic. It is better understood from the point of view of the *ketarim*. The apparent schism and differentiation between organized Jews and those who are absent from organizational life derives quite simply from the fact that the scope of diaspora Jewish institutions is not universal, as a government is, and that the *ketarim* do not enjoy undisputed recognition from all sectors of the community. This is why some think that what is involved is "voluntarism," whereas what is involved is not the choice of individuals but an overall breakdown of the Jewish collectivity as reflected in the narrowness of the domain of validity of the Jewish authorities. The ideological perspective, which is satisfied with facile appearances, is easily transcended when we take into consideration the disappearance and reappearance of the *edah* in France, which enables us to better understand the relativistic character of the criterion of belonging. We must develop a typology of the fall and rise of the *edah* which, twice in the past, reappeared only with the unexpected arrival of a wave of Jewish immigration: from Eastern Europe in the 1930s and from North Africa in the 1960s. These two movements from the "periphery" to the "center" led to a return of the *keter malkhut* to the place where it was forbidden.

Meanwhile, the form of the *brit* is still hardy, but its nineteenth century "republican" face has been replaced by a Zionist face. Unity around Israel is what seals the unity of the community and determines its integrity and the effectiveness of its authorities.[15] Communal Zionism thus plays the role of a legitimizing criterion in place of the *keter torah* (and under the sign of *keter malkhut* since it involves the image of a state). The cause of Israel is what orders the authorities and assigns them their functions. Consequently, every conflict over authority occurs as a function of the criterion of Zionism. Communal conflicts unfold around the issue of whether or not one conforms to the Zionist norm. This was the case with "Renouveau Juif."

The emergence of a logic of the *edah* in the absence of the *edah* entails, as we might suspect, a conflict situation. This takes shape in the idea of voluntary belonging to the community which presumes that Jews who do not declare themselves and do not participate, institutionally speaking, are outside the community. Hence there is conflict on the overall level of communal coherence and cohesion. This conflict is three dimensional. First there is the political dimension of Zionism: the institutions are avowedly Zionist, so that certain political sectors are excluded from the communal domain. Next there is the dimension of the Consistory: there Orthodox and "Liberal" (affiliated with the Reform movement) communities that reject the imperative rules of the consistorial consensus have established themselves outside the Consistory. Moreover, in certain provincial communities, schisms sometimes take place vis-a-vis the recognized consistorial communities, when the authority of the local *bet din* over *kashrut*, and especially the payment of the taxes which this presumes, is not accepted. Thus, recently, in cities like Toulouse, Montpellier, and Grenoble, two rival religious communities have been formed. This is a process which has since levelled off. Finally there is the intellectual dimension: a "secular," "enlightened" sector seeking an identity, which rejects reference to what has to do with Torah and tradition and which identifies itself with the Israeli left wing in the Israeli political debate. This identification with the Israeli left wing became even more noticeable after the war in Lebanon when the internal debate in Israel spread to the Western diaspora.

In a word, each of the three authorities in the community is riven by conflicts which challenge their legitimacy. These intra-communal conflicts are accompanied by "inter-*ketaric*" conflicts among the classic authorities themselves: the whole purpose of this analysis serves to demonstrate this. Communal belonging is defined quite simply by voluntarism because there is no majority consensus on the authorities and the legitimacy of their institutions and leadership.

To complete the picture, there is "intra-*ketaric*" conflict within each authority. Within the civil authority, the Fonds Social passed through a malaise when its leadership was to be renewed. A conflict also developed between the AUJF, the fund drive apparatus, and the leadership of the Fonds Social, revolving around the *L'Arche* press organ of the Fonds Social and the right to criticize Israeli policy. The assistant editor, Jean-Luc Allouche, was forced to resign in 1983, initiating a crisis that ended in the departure of the press director of the Fonds Social, Adam Loss, former director-general of the FSJU, in 1985.

Within the CRIF, there was also a conflict between the new president (Theo Klein) and a camp of different political coloration led by Emile Touati, president of the Paris Consistory.[16] This came on top of an old controversy over the exact representative nature of the CRIF which brought together very old organizations and overlooked the new layers of the community which are not active in those organizations or which come from North Africa where communal commitment was not based on the associational mode. At the beginning of the 1980s, a violent conflict also shook the foundations of the CRIF when a powerful Jewish movement supported by the Jewish "street," Renouveau Juif, challenged the representative nature of the CRIF and the softness of its support for Israel, and advocated encouraging the "Jewish vote" to influence the French government towards a policy in favor of Israel.

The representative of priestly authority, Chief Rabbi Sirat, was able to appeal charismatically to a media audience, but within the Consistory he engendered very strong opposition. This was reflected in the open conflict between the Paris Consistory, which is very powerful financially, and the Central Consistory which is the home base of the Chief Rabbi but is almost entirely lacking in financial means.[17]

It is useless to speak of conflicts within the Torah authority since, as we have seen, it almost does not exist, politically speaking. We must simply note that Jewish institutions seek Jewish intellectuals a great deal today. They try to organize the intellectuals around the institutions, as is done around the central institutions of the Jewish people in Jerusalem.

Hence, conflict appears as a general principle throughout the whole system of Jewish authority in France. Its meaning must be understood in the context of the reemergence in a negative way, to be sure, of the *edah*. Its reemergence dislocates the Napoleonic model, which was based on suppression of the *edah*, in such a way that a flow runs through the system as a whole, with its scars found everywhere. More directly, the disequilibrium of the system derives from the *keter torah* which does not yet have a solid base, reality, or effectiveness. In fact, the community has no communal "charter," no civil constitution, on the model of the *haskamot* or *taqanot hakahal* which were characteristic of the medieval Jewish communities and which governed questions of consensus, of relations between the authorities, and the communal "rules of the game." This was a necessity for a system of Jewish authority based on the *brit*.

The community has secreted a simulation of consensus and an unwritten charter through the defense of Israel which is inscribed in all the by-laws of the Jewish institutions, but these by-laws are not "charters"; they are internal, private regulations specific to each institution. The only case of a transinstitutional charter is that of the CRIF which, theoretically, is to concern all Jewish institutions, given the nature of the CRIF. But in fact, it involves a declaration of intention of an ideological type, classically aimed at French, not at Jewish, society. It is a reaffirmation of attachment to liberty, to the struggle against racism, against terrorism, for Israel. The only innovation involves the concept of "Jewish community within the city," which is almost nullified in fact by the defensive reiteration of the individualistic character of Jewish destiny in France, e.g., "without claiming any political authority, without substituting itself for the personal responsibility of each of its members, the organized Jewish community refuses to act as a partisan pressure group...."

The defense of Israel has the effect of affirming the *edah*, but the latter is purely symbolic since it presumes the negation of the existence of the *edah* in France and its exclusive identification with the State of Israel. One must see in communal Zionism an ambiguous, paradoxical rationalization of the fact that the *edah* has returned, but that it is still elsewhere (Zion). Thus we verify the artificial, symbolic (embryonic?) dimension of the *edah* and of the system of Jewish authority in France today.

Perhaps there was a junction point where a model emerging from within — but which did not yet have the means to assert itself — replaced the Consistory model imposed by the state. In the course of the development and beyond the metamorphoses of the communal domain, we can thus recognize the relevance of the existence of a system of authority and of political relations within Jewish communal life in France. But even though this system reflects a structural continuity with the past (the *ketarim*), the continuity is more symbolic than historic.

Structuralist approaches have run into difficulty in apprehending historic development and, thus, especially the break represented by modernity. Nevertheless, the very fact that we have been able to carry out this study attests that the breach of modernity has not erased, as one might too easily believe, the vitality and power of the models and values of Jewish society before modern times. It attests in a certain way to the durability and permanence of Israel in the most apparently contradictory situations.

Notes

1. From this constitutional perspective, a comparison ought to be made between countries with a written law and countries with customary law as to the kind of influence each kind exercises on the Jewish political system. Cf. Daniel J. Elazar, "Covenant as the Basis of the Jewish Political Tradition," in Elazar, ed., *Kinship and Consent* (Lanham, Md.: Jerusalem Center for Public Affairs and University Press of America, 1981).

2. One typical expression of this attitude is "The Revolution of 1789 is our second Law from Sinai, the only banner around which we Jews must rally." Isidore Cohen in *Les Archives Israelites*, 4 Novembre 1880, p. 363.

3. The French, the "chosen people of modern times," J.H. Dreyfus, *Sermons et allocutions* (Paris, 1908-1913) I, pp. 277-283; or "France is the land, of all lands, that You (God) seem to prefer, because it is more worthy of You" in "La Priere pour la France" ("Prayer for France") by Lazare Wogue, *Le guide du croyant israelite*, 2nd ed. (Paris, 1898), pp. 515-519.

4. Cf. Maurice Bloch in "La societe juive en France depuis la revolution," *REJ*, vol. XLIII (1904), p. xli, "The new Jerusalem will be everywhere that the French idea of the Revolution triumphs."

5. Id., p. 20, "The time of the Messiah had come with that new society which replaced the old Trinity of the Church with another Trinity...Liberty! Equality! Fraternity!"

6. The Sanhedrin held its first session on 9 February 1807 and ratified the conclusions of the labors of the Assembly of Notables convoked by Napoleon on 26 July 1806. This transformed Jewish existence in France into that of a religious denomination.

7. Cf. Jewish Telegraphic Agency, Paris, 1/9/81.

8. It did so with the help of the Joint Distribution Committee, without which the creation of the Fonds Social would have been hardly conceivable. The creation — on 1 April 1947 — of a "Comite Consultatif des Oeuvres" affiliated with the Joint was a decisive moment for the later establishment of the Fonds Social.

9. Cf. infra and, more generally, Shmuel Trigano, *La demeure oubliee: Genese religieuse du politique* (Paris: Lieu Commun, 1984), or "Comment on ecrit l'histoire juive," in *Pardes*, no. 1 (May 1985), Paris, Lattes.

10. The financial companies are united through the Refuge, a powerful financial group which derives its revenues from a legal stipulation allowing businesses to pay out one percent of their income

for social purposes. It builds schools, nurseries, and yeshivot, among its many activities.

11. I coined the term "media Jews" for this purpose, cf. my book, *La Republique et les Juifs* (Paris: Presses d'Aujourd'hui-Gallimard, 1982), p. 112, *"Les mirages du Juif Mediatique."*

12. Mendelssohn's theory tried to define Jewish existence as a function of the needs of the external environment rather than in terms of its internal logic, so as to promote the integration of the Jews into the dominant society. True to his theory, the life of a Mendelssohn developed in the milieu of the Berlin Jewish philosophic salons.

13. Cf. *La Demeure Oubliee..., op. cit.*

14. According to *L'Information Juive*, March 1981, the 1980 fund drive comprised 24,000 donors. One may suppose that they represent 24,000 out of 180,000 Jewish households in France. With such a small number of Jews institutionally organized, one must then include in the "community" — if only in a negative way — those Jews who are not organized.

15. The "Charter of the CRIF," entitled *"La communaute juive dans la Cite,"* declares as follows: "The Jewish community in France recognizes in Israel the favored expression of Jewish existence. Any threat to the existence of the State of Israel is felt by the Jewish community as an attack on its well-being, on its collective memory, on its faith, its hope, its dignity" (Paris, 25 January 1977). The by-laws of the FSJU state in Article 2: The FSJU "favors for this goal, the maintenance and development of Jewish life in France, the relations of the French Jewish community with Israel" (By-law of 3/4/84).

16. Cf. *L'Information Juive*, June 1985.

17. This conflict was illustrated in September 1985 (cf. *Agence Telegraphique juive* (Paris), 2, 3, and 20 September 1985 and *Le Monde*, 4 and 15/16 September 1985), when the Chief Rabbi publicly denounced the laxity of the Consistory with regard to conversions. (What triggered the issue was a conflict between the Chief Rabbi and the consistoral lay leaders about the easy conversion of a Rothschild's non-Jewish wife.) The presidents of the Central Consistory and the Consistory of Paris answered him in the negative. But it seems that this was a pretext for a deeper conflict.

PART III –

PERENNIAL ISSUES

Chapter 9

LEADERSHIP IN THE JEWISH POLITY: EARLY RABBINIC VIEWS

Stuart A. Cohen

The hypothesis of this essay is that Jewish political traditions, particularly as they find expression in the bench-mark sources of the talmudic period, articulate an ambivalent attitude towards the issue of leadership in Jewish public life.

At a purely pragmatic level, those traditions do recognize that Jewish society, indeed any society, requires leaders. Accordingly, they make provisions (some of which are extremely detailed) for the appropriate regulation of appointments to positions of leadership; successions of leaders; the definition of leadership tasks; and the designation of leadership roles. One of the earliest rationales for such legislation was provided by Sa'adyah Gaon (882-942). Summarizing much of talmudic thinking on the topic, his *Book of Beliefs and Opinions* (folios 387-8) argues that the ambition to attain leadership status is both innate and positive. "Were it not for this aspiration towards leadership, there would be no means of keeping the world in order or of looking after its welfare. It is thanks to its authority that kings are able to conduct wars and take charge of their countries' defense, that judges can manage law-abiding men and the overseers correct the incorrigible among them....For the orderly control of the world can be affected only by the application of wisdom (in government)."[1]

Notwithstanding its frequency, the point of view thus expressed does not seem to articulate an ideal. Rather, it represents a concession. It acknowledges, in effect, that it is the fallibility of human nature which necessitates the appointment of human leaders, just as (according to the biblical account in I Sam. 7:7-9) it was the weakness of the Children of Israel during the period of Samuel which set in motion the process which eventually led to the appointment of a human king.

There are various reasons why the rabbis should have adopted this ambivalent, perhaps even suspicious, attitude towards leadership. One, and in many respects perhaps the most obvious, was their awareness that power tends to corrupt. Ample support for that axiom could be found in the recent Jewish history of their own times (and I refer not merely to the dictatorships of such kings as Yannai and Herod, but also to the authoritarianism of one of their own class, Rabban Gamliel II, whom a clique of rabbinic malcontents is reported to have deposed from his office of *nasi*).[2] A second cause of their ambivalence, this one perhaps more sensitive, was their recognition of the heavy burdens which high office imposes on its incumbent. "Uneasy lies the head which wears a crown," although not itself a rabbinic dictum, nicely expressed much of rabbinic feeling.[3]

But these notions, although undoubtedly present in the rabbinic attitude, are not really its central theme. It is here posited that what ultimately accounts for rabbinic ambivalence vis-a-vis the notion of leadership is the sense that the phenomenon of a human leader, selected from among the totality of Jewry, in effect strains against another Jewish notion, whose paramountcy is unquestioned, that of covenant. When the rabbis studied the numerous biblical records of ancient Israelite covenantal association, they saw in those transactions the means which had made possible the ideal form of government which they designated *malkhut shamayim*.[4] The Sinai covenant, in particular, had transformed what had been God's rule, originally manifest at the Creation, into God's realm. At Sinai, Israel had become the instrument whereby Divine government was in a sense to be publicly proclaimed, confirmed and legitimated.[5]

Of the many implications of this perception, one is of particular interest in our present context. The Israel which covenanted at Sinai was a totality. In relation to the rest of the world, it might have constituted only a small band of initiates, but in relation to itself the group was one. All Israel was present at Sinai, as equals, and all had, equally, taken upon themselves the rights and obligations which flowed from that event. According to Numbers 16:3, this argument was first expressed against the leadership of Moses and Aaron by Korach and his band: "All the congregation are holy, every one of them, and the Lord is amongst them. Why then do you raise yourselves up over the assembly of the Lord?" It was echoed and expanded in some of the rabbinic *midrashim* on that passage.[6] In both categories of texts the central axiom is very similar. By virtue of their common covenantal experience, all Israel (to be precise, all Israelite males) had attained an equal right to share in the management of the *malkhut shamayim*. It was only a subsequent fall from grace, exemplified by the sin of the golden calf, which necessitated the introduction of various classes of leaders into the system. Moreover, even that concession must be considered temporary. The rabbinic messianic perspective envisions the reestablishment of the true covenantal status, with the attendant removal of all distinctions between leaders and led.[7]

II

The extent to which this ambivalence towards leadership permeates rabbinic discussions of the topic can be illustrated by reference to three aspects of the topic: paths to leadership, prerogatives of leadership, and patterns of leadership. This essay will attempt to show that in all three instances the formulators of the Jewish political tradition and its *halakhic* expressions were deeply conscious of the tensions resulting from their own perceptions of leadership as necessity and their aspiration towards the absence of leadership as an ideal. It was this consciousness which accounts for the nature of several of their provisions on the subject.

Paths to Leadership

As is well known, the rabbis did not have to invent a checklist of the qualities expected of a leader. For one thing, they had several biblical paradigms on which to draw (and in particular the example of Moses). For another, they had on hand a convenient biblical formula suggested by Jethro (Exodus 18:21): "able men, such as fear God, men of truth, hating unjust gain." All subsequent rabbinic specifications of the personal criteria needed for leadership basically constitute amplifications of and embellishments on this proof text.

There is, however, far more to the rabbinic discussions on the paths to leadership than a mere repetition of these requirements. Indeed, the latter, although frequently echoed, are never considered sufficient criteria. On the contrary, where the rabbis seem to have concentrated far more attention was on the *mechanics* whereby those qualities could be granted public recognition, and thus regulate orderly appointments to office and standardize the procedures of accession. The result was a shift in emphasis, from the personal characters of individual leaders to the general principles upon which their rights to office are made to depend. It is this shift which explains the concentration in the sources on such mechanistic topics as: the uniqueness or otherwise of the office in question; the precise moment of accession; the selection of the successor; and the relationship between successive office-holders.[8]

The author's previous work on the three *ketarim* has explored the different procedural criteria demanded of office-holders in each of the spheres of the *torah*, the *kehunah* and the *malkhut*.[9] Yet there are also commonalities in those procedural criteria, particularly where they are of a ritualistic nature. A review of the sources suggests that in none of the *ketarim* is accession, nor even succession, made dependent solely upon the possession of the personal qualities referred to above. These, in effect, are taken for granted.[10] Appointment (*minui*) is the implication, not a matter of inherent right, but of public acquiescence (*haskamah*). It is this which accounts for the care which is taken over such issues as the genealogy of the candidate (his *yiḥus*; is he of the appropriate tribe, or family?; is he the first-born within his family?) and the manner of appointment (by anointment — *meshiḥah*; or ordination — *semikhah*).

It is characteristic of the inherently ambivalent attitude of the Jewish political tradition to public appointments that all such procedures and rituals involve (quite apart from the candidate for office himself) the participation of two separate parties. One is the congregation over whom he is to exercise leadership; the other is God (whether directly or indirectly, via His various laws). Basing themselves on ample biblical precedents, the rabbis stressed the necessity for the convergence, in ritual, of both sources of authority.[11] Interestingly, it seemed difficult to determine hard and fast rules from these instances, particularly regarding the respective weights which were to be accorded to Divine sanction and public selection (sometimes, Divine selection and public sanction). Even on a purely chronological level, which was prior to which? But what is significant, especially in view of the tensions already referred to, is that no single source was ever deemed sufficient. *Minui* to office, precisely because it represented a regression from the high ideal of Sinai, could only be legitimated by rites which somehow compensated for the failings of those over whom authority was to be exercised. Rituals of investiture, therefore, cannot be regarded merely as instances of diplomatic finesse. Their observance, and only their observance, restores order to a system which has been warped by the necessity for their enactment.

Prerogatives of Leadership

Once their covenantal rights to leadership had been confirmed, office-holders were considered virtually unassailable. In that respect, their positions and power were considered prior to their active political behavior. It was inconceivable that any person other than an attested member of Aaron's family might perform priestly rituals in the sanctuary,[12] just as it was imperative that all claimants to the "crown" of kingship demonstrate their direct descent from the royal Davidic line.[13] In neither sphere did early rabbinic political traditions ever advocate democracy.[14] High priests, even though they be sinners, could not altogether be stripped of their distinctive (and everlasting) sanctity.[15] Kings, similarly, could not be summarily dispossessed of their offices.[16]

Nevertheless, the rabbinic texts of the talmudic period do not express any tolerance for despotism. What they attempted to do, rather, was to define the constraints which had to be observed if human leadership was to function correctly (in a constitutional sense) as well as effectively. Starting from the hypothesis that leadership is a matter of assignment, they came to the conclusion that public authority cannot be arbitrary. Instead, they came close to the position that the prerogatives of leadership are dependent on the manner of its exercise.

One expression of this attitude is to be found in the frequent talmudic injunctions admonishing all leaders to take account of the wishes and capacities of their publics. Quite apart from being sound pieces of practical advice, such aphorisms were sometimes elevated to the status of constitutional maxims. As much is illustrated by those texts which intimate that leaders, once they had assumed office, were no longer to be regarded as private individuals. Hence, they were not at liberty to relinquish their offices. Genetic abdication is not at all an option open to priests; similarly, no cognizance is taken of the action of a king who might wish to forego the honor due to his particular domain.[17] Underlying these stipulations is the concept that such office-holders, once they had undergone the appropriate rituals of investiture, had in some definable way changed their character. In effect, they had relinquished their previous identities and attained a status which categorized them as pieces of public property.[18]

What is more, as institutional descendents of the original holders of their particular offices,[19] public leaders had also entered into a distinctive relationship with God. In addition to their individual obligations, therefore, they now also had to fulfill the particular covenantal duties of their particular domains. Indeed, from the point of view of Heaven, their continued possession of their offices could be considered contingent upon the degree to which they did so. Although various views on this matter may be found in the talmudic literature,[20] the weight of opinion seems to have been distinctly limiting over the course of time. Support for the extreme view on this issue was found in those biblical chapters (particularly Psalm 132) which appeared to stress that continued Divine support for the original incumbent of an office (or his successors) was made strictly dependent upon the degree to which they fulfilled the terms of the covenant to which they had originally been parties.

One conclusion from this discussion was the notion that leaders have to behave in accordance with the constitutional charters of their own demesne (of which the best-known is perhaps that pertaining to kings recorded in Deut., chap. 18). The sacred prerogatives of leadership, this passage suggested, are strictly conditional upon the proper exercise of those prerogatives. But a second and potentially more far-reaching conclusion was the possibility of distinguishing between two facets of leadership in public office. One was to regard the post as an everlasting possession; the other to view it as a temporary trusteeship. This was a distinction which cut to the very heart of the rabbinic ambivalence with regard to leadership; and it is a measure of the tensions which it generated that the talmudic sources do not entirely solve the issue one way or the other. As the insistence on *yiḥus* showed, the sages of the time could never quite reconcile themselves to an abandonment of the idea that leadership was indeed everlasting. Hence their insistence on the need for prayers which specifically referred to a restoration of the royal Davidic house and of the priestly Aaronide line. But they were also sensitive to the difficulties in this approach, and hence to the contrasting virtues of the conception of leadership as a trusteeship. Quite apart from all else, this idea seemed best suited to the republican notion that at some date in the messianic future all public offices would in any case revert to the entirety of the house of Israel. If that were the case, leadership would simply become superfluous.[21]

Patterns of Leadership

The uncertainty which ensued also served to dictate rabbinic views on appropriate patterns of leadership. Here the essential conceptual distinctions were not between different tasks and functions, nor even between separate leadership domains. Rather, the choice seems to have been between what some modern students of the topic have termed leadership "strategies" (see, notably, Gunnar Myrdal's discussion of "leadership by accommodation" vs. "leadership by protest") and leadership "styles" ("charismatic leadership" vs. "bureaucratic leadership").

The traditional Jewish inclination (again, as reflected in early rabbinic texts) seems to have been preponderantly conservative: the preferred strategy being that of "accommodation" and the preferred style that of "bureaucratic management." To say that is not, of course, to overlook the ample evidence which indicates that various outstanding personalities at various points in Jewish history managed to break previous molds and thereby imprint their own highly individual stamps on the course of their people's history. Such, indeed, was the case with all of those whom Professor Elazar and myself have referred to as "constitutional architects."[22] In playing a pivotal role in shaping and designing the periodic constitutional referents and systems of the Jewish polity, these men indubitably deserve to be defined as "leaders." Their work (indeed their very personalities) were quite unlike those of other mortals; and it was by virtue of their idiosyncratic distinctions that they ultimately shaped the entire course of Jewish constitutional development for longer or shorter spans of time. Judah ha-Nasi and Rav Ashi (respectively, the editors of the Mishnah and the Babylonian Talmud) were therefore seen to fit into the exceptional mold first cast by Moses.[23] Like the latter, they were considered to have deflected the constitutional arrangements of the Jewish polity into channels which had previously been uncharted, if at all imagined.

But even when the magnitude of their achievements is thus acknowledged (as it must be), several cautionary comments seem to be in order. First, such "constitutional architects" were not regarded as paradigms. By their nature extraordinary, they were not held up as examples whose patterns of leadership had to be emulated by all subsequent aspirants to Jewish public office. On the contrary, many luminaries (contemporary and historical) were often mistrusted, regarded almost as much as an influence to overcome as to cherish. Particularly was this so when they were self-proclaimed visionaries, in receipt of their revelation directly from God. Individuals in that class obviously presented intractable problems of recognition. Aware that charlatans were not easily distinguishable from men inspired (and even if they were so inspired, was it by God?), most talmudic sages preferred a policy of caution. It was this which accounts for the skepticism with which they handled such ecstatics as Honi ha-Me'agel.[24] More fundamentally, it also led them to pronounce that prophecy, like the sacrificial service, had in their time ceased, and had been replaced as the principal medium of constitutional expression by the rite of learning.[25]

Clearly, there was more to this than a suggestion that a shift in emphasis had transpired. The real thrust of that rabbinic statement was a declaration that the pneumatic experience (which is necessarily sudden, unexpected and granted only to the select few) was no longer to be regarded as a salient test of communal leadership. Rather, public office was henceforth to devolve only upon those who had undergone a lengthy process of scholastic apprenticeship.[26] This may have been a tough and exacting course, designed to produce a meritocracy, but it was not one which transformed leadership into a closed preserve, with a corporate style and substance unattainable by a wide public. On the contrary, the distinguishing feature of the *keter torah*, as portrayed by its own spokesmen, was that entry into its ranks did not depend upon either appropriate lineage (as is the case in the *keter kehunah*) and/or material advantage (as in the *keter malkhut*). It was open to all men of proven devotion and ability, any one of whom was entitled to participate in the activities of its accredited schools and academies.[27]

At one level, the establishment of that educational network can be seen to have reflected rabbinic sensitivity to what we have already referred to as the covenantal equality of the entire Jewish polity. At the same time, it also served to reinforce the corollary of that perspective: an ambivalent attitude towards the exceptional leader. In effect, it thereby further strengthened the leaning towards a conservative style in leadership, which eschewed innovation in favor of the typical. Together with the simultaneous evolution of the process of rabbinical ordination (*semikhah*), and the formulation and then inscription of the *torah she be'al peh*,[28] the foundation of the academies facilitated the institutionalization of the *keter torah*. The bureaucratic consequences of that development were themselves potentially enormous (at the very least, it provided the domain of the *torah* with an independent infrastructure which could rival that once possessed by those of the *kehunah* and *malkhut*).[29] So too were its implications for the future patterns of the polity's scholastic leadership. By thus regulating the *keter torah* and ensuring its primacy, the rabbinic sages also determined the tone and style of subsequent Jewish political discourse. Henceforth, leaders in all three domains were to conform to the style and patterns which tanna'itic and amoraic exegetes derived from their reading of the biblical sources. Rights and obligations of leaders were thenceforth to be rooted in real or imagined (sometimes forged) antiquity, novelty being suspect. What was vital, in this view, was the preservation of tradition, in the sense of a continuous and shared experience of proper modes of leadership, together with its required institutional forms and ritual norms.

Ultimately, as post-talmudic history was to show, that thrust towards conservatism was to meet with only partial success. Various influences — the breakdown of Jewry's centralized institutional frameworks, the experience of contact with other (gentile) styles of leadership and government, the emergence of new constitutional issues and problems — combined to result in a renewal of the drive towards radical change in this sphere, as in others. Although much of what transpired was often described (not least by Jewish constitutional architects themselves) as a reaffirmation of previous principles, much that passed for tradition was really revolution in disguise. Nevertheless, the fact that such camouflage was for so long considered necessary remains a tribute to the resilience of the conservative patterns of leadership fostered by the Jewish political tradition as formulated in late antiquity. That pattern, it has here been suggested, was not the product of a fear (abstract or real) of outrageous leadership. Rather, it was the outgrowth of a central ambivalence towards the entire notion of the relationship between human leaders and their human constituents within the framework of a covenantal community.

Notes

1. See also the saying attributed to R. Akiva (second century) in Leviticus *Rabbah* 11: "Israel are compared to fowl. Just as fowl cannot fly without wings, so Israel can do nothing without their elders [*zekenim*]."

2. Babylonian Talmud (hereafter TB), *Berakhot* 27b-28a. This and other passages relevant to the episode are analyzed in R. Goldenberg, "The Deposition of Rabban Gamaliel II: An Examination of the Sources," *Journal of Jewish Studies* 23 (1972): 167-190.

3. See, e.g., the well-known passage in Exodus *Rabbah* 27.

4. Literally, "the kingdom of heaven," the term might best be rendered "the holy commonwealth." On its origins and meanings, see S. Schechter, *Some Aspects of Rabbinic Theology* (New York, 1923), chaps.7 and 8. On the rabbinic understanding of covenant, see G. Freeman, *The Heavenly Kingdom* (Lanham, 1986).

5. See, e.g., the sources and their analysis in G.E. Ladd, "The Kingdom of God — Reign or Realm?," *Journal of Biblical Literature* 81 (1962): 230-238.

6 M. Ber, "Meridat Koraḥ u-Meni'ehah be-Aggadot Ḥazal," *Mekhkarim...le-Zekher Yosef Heinemann*, (ed. E. Fleischer, et al.; Jerusalem, 1981), pp. 9-33.

7. See, e.g., the *aggadah* cited in *Seder Eliyahu Zuta* (84), which reports the miraculous emplacement of two crowns (*ketarim*) on the head of each Israelite at the moment of the theophany at Sinai, and their removal after the incident of the golden calf. Commenting on Isaiah 35:10, the passage concludes with the assurance that the Almighty will Himself restore all of Israel's crowns with the advent of the Messiah.

8. For a survey of the social science literature on these topics, see J.R. Goody's introduction to *Succession to High Office* (Cambridge Papers in Social Anthropology, no. 4; Cambridge, 1966).

9. S.A. Cohen, "The Concept of the Three *Ketarim*: Its Place in Jewish Constitutional Thought and its Implications for a Study of Jewish Constitutional History," *AJS Review*, vol. 9 (1984): 27-54.

10. Indeed, their absence automatically disqualifies candidates for office, whatever their other claims. Hence *Tosefta's* ruling (*Shekalim* 2:15): "Whosoever has precedence for [purposes of] inheritance has precedence for rulership [*sererah*], provided that he follows the customs of his fathers." See also S. Lieberman's comments in *Tosefta Kifshutah: Moed*, p. 694.

11. See, most explicitly, the exegesis on Exodus 35:30 in TB *Berakhot* 55a, reporting the procedures whereby Bezalel's appointment was confirmed, and the extended commentary on Deut. 1:13 in *Sifrei* 13.

12. See, e.g., the exegesis on Numbers 1:51 in TB *Shabbat* 31a.

13. On this claim and its authenticity, see D. Liver, *Toldot Beit David* (Jerusalem, 1959).

14. Nor, for that matter, in the sphere of the *torah*. See, e.g., the injunction to follow the dictates of the sages, "even if they tell you that right is left and left is right," Jerusalem Talmud, *Horayot* 1:1.

15. *Ibid.*, 3:1.

16. On the problems which the incidents described in I Kings 11 and 12 raised in this regard, see the discussion in M. Aberbach and L. Smolar, "Jeroboam and Solomon: Rabbinic Interpretations," *Jewish Quarterly Review* 59 (1969): 118-132.

17. *Kevodo aino maḥul*, TB *Kiddushin* 22b; contrast the position of a *talmid ḥakham* in *idem*. 32a.

18. On terminological reflections of this attitude, see S. Leiter, "Worthiness, Acclamation and Appointment," *Proceedings of the American Academy of Jewish Research* 41-42 (1973-74): 137-168.

19. On institutional continuity, see, e.g., the exegesis on I Sam. 12:6, 11 in both *Tosefta, Rosh ha-Shanah* 2:3 and TB *Rosh ha-Shanah* 25a.

20. For a review of both talmudic and medieval literature, see G. Blidstein, *Ekronot Medini'im be-Mishnat ha-RAMBAM* (Ramat Gan, 1983), esp. pp. 65-90 and 168-177.

21. See above, n. 7.

22. D.J. Elazar and S.A. Cohen, *The Jewish Polity: Jewish Political Organization From Biblical Times to the Present* (Indianapolis, 1985), p. 30.

23. See, e.g., the comparisons of these three personalities, all of whom are said to have combined *Torah* with "greatness" (*gedulah*), in TB *Gittin* 52b.

24. W.S. Green, "Palestinian Holy Men: Charismatic Leadership and Rabbinic Tradition," *Aukfstieg und Niedergang der Romischen Welt*, vol. 19 (2), W. Haase, ed. (Berlin-New York, 1979), pp. 619-647.

25. TB *Megillah* 17b. On the aura of piety gradually attached to intellectual endeavor in rabbinic scholarship, see J. Neusner, *Torah: From Scroll to Symbol in Formative Judaism* (Philadelphia, 1985).

26. N.N. Glatzer, "A Study in Talmudic Interpretations of Prophecy," *Review of Religions* 10 (1946): 114-137.

27. See, e.g., the exegisis on Deut. 33:4 in TB *Sanhedrin* 91b. On the efforts made by the great Babylonian academies of the fourth and fifth centuries to introduce wider audiences to the fruits of their scholarship by means of the *pirqa* (public sermon) and *kallah* (study seminar), see: I. Gafni in *Yad la-Talmud*, E.E. Urbach, ed. (Jerusalem, 1984), pp. 39-42, and J. Neusner, *A History of the Jews in Babylonia*, vol. 4 (Leiden, 1969), pp. 384-386.

28. See, respectively, J. Newman, *Semikhah (ordination): A Study of its Origin, History and Function in Rabbinic Literature* (Manchester, 1950), and E.E. Urbach, *Ha-Halakhah: Mekorotehah ve-Hitpathutah* (Jerusalem, 1984).

29. On the emergence of a new form of established academy in third century Eretz Israel (the *yeshivah*) and in Babylonia (the *metivta*), see, respectively: Y.L. Levine, *Ma'amad Ha-Hakhamim Be-Eretz Israel Bitkufat Ha-Talmud* (Jerusalem, 1986), pp. 10-12, and Y. Gafni, "Yeshivah u-Metivta," *Zion* 43 (1978): 12-37. On the latter, however, compare D.M. Goodblatt, *Rabbinic Instruction in Sasanian Babylonia* (Leiden, 1975).

Chapter 10

THE ETHICS OF NATIONAL POWER: GOVERNMENT AND WAR FROM THE SOURCES OF JUDAISM

Reuven Kimelman

The Problem of Nationalism

The first section of this study of national power and ethics is concerned with the role of moral judgment in political decisions. It asks what, according to the prophets, is the prime cause of international conflict and what avenues are open for mediating between national sovereignty and international authority.

By their very nature, nations possess ambiguous moral status. The ambiguity grows out of the drive toward self-preservation. On the one hand, in safeguarding themselves, nations secure the lives of their members. On the other hand, under the guise of national security, nations may compromise the rights and lives of the very same people. Seeking to secure their own interests, nations position themselves to exploit the vulnerabilities of their neighbors. Although the moral status of nations involves both internal and external vectors, this study focuses on national power as the grist for the mill of international conflict.

Among the moralists of antiquity, the contribution of the prophets to discourse on international morality lies in underscoring the role of unrestrained nationalism in sowing the seeds of international conflict. For them, unqualified national sovereignty paves the way for international anarchy as international anarchy paves the way for war.

The prophetic understanding was aptly encapsulated by Robert Gordis who wrote:

Just as no man can regard his own desire and interest as overriding all other principles in his relations with his fellows, so nations, whose existence is equally legitimate, cannot make national honor, self-interest, or military superiority the ultimate arbiter of their destiny. Unlimited sovereignty is as immoral for nations as for individuals.[1]

According to the prophets, people not only do not lose their moral dimension as they coalesce into national entities but assume an added collective moral status rendering them responsible for one another. As such, nations are at least as subject to moral review as individuals. For the prophets, the uncritical acceptance of the doctrine of national sovereignty is naught but a disguise for the denial of legal or moral responsibility. They sought to unmask it and strap sovereignty with moral constraints.

Their version of limited national sovereignty challenges the *realpolitik* tradition from Machiavelli through Hobbes and Spinoza which holds, in the words of Spinoza, that just as "each individual should endeavor to preserve itself as it is without regard to anything but itself," so should nations.[2]

Both positions, however, assume a continuum from the individual to the nation, except the prophetic view holds that just as individuals are subject to moral scrutiny, so are nations. *Realpolitik* philosophy maintains, to the contrary, that since the highest value for the individual is self-preservation, the highest value of the nation is likewise self-preservation. The belief that the interest of the state alone constitutes the highest good can facilely render deleterious national commitments ipso facto non-binding. While not totally rejecting considerations of state, the prophetic stance opposes the cavalier spurning of any appeal to moral considerations in the calculus of national interests. On the contrary, moral considerations must be factored into political judgments. Indeed, the prophetic insight is that ethics are constitutive of self-interest.

The opposing stances of the prophets and *realpolitik* theorists constitute the antipodes between which American foreign policy has traditionally oscillated. This is readily observable from the differences between the policy formulations of George Kennan and Grover Cleveland.

George Kennan, the leading scholar-architect of American foreign policy in the post-war era, believed that "the most serious fault of our past formulations lies in...the carrying over into affairs of states the concepts of right and wrong, the assumption that state behavior is a fit subject for moral judgment."[3]

The American position that Kennan deplores is reflected in President Grover Cleveland's denunciation of American intervention in the internal affairs of Hawaii. In defense of his refusal to recognize the new government which was imposed by American forces, Cleveland said:

> I suppose that right and justice should determine the path to be followed in treating this subject. If national honesty is to be disregarded and a desire for territorial extension, or dissatisfaction with a form of government not our own, ought to regulate our conduct, I have entirely misapprehended the mission and character of our Government and the behavior which the conscience of our people demands of their public servants.[4]

Just as one strain in American political thinking is an extension of classical European *realpolitik* theory, so the other is an outgrowth of prophetic political thinking.

From the table of nations in Genesis, chapter 10, through Isaiah's visions of the End-Time, the Bible presents the history of humanity as revolving around national poles. Despite the fact that Genesis traces the etiology of nations back to the sin of the Tower of Babel, the messianic vision of Isaiah does not seek to redress the situation by projecting a future of nationally undifferentiated humanity. Rather, Isaiah (2:2-5) foresees a future where nations gazing on the House of the Lord say, "Come, let us go up the mountain of the Lord." Not only will the Temple Mount be an international, as opposed to a universal, house of prayer, but the law which shall go forth from Zion will set standards by which the Lord "will judge among the nations and arbitrate for the many peoples." This prophetic vision fosters the internationalization of divine authority.[5]

Once there is an international house of prayer and supernational way of resolving conflict, the prophet can envisage a day when "nation shall not take up sword against nation, neither shall they learn war anymore."

Nonetheless, the prophet does not presume that in the days to come nations will automatically be irenic. Since the prophet foresees nations appealing to an international court for resolution of conflict, it is assumed that nations jockeying for power will continue to dominate the international scene. There is no illusion of a divine harmony which absolves nations from the need to provide machinery for accommodation and resolution of conflict. Indeed, since conflicts of power are intrinsic to the political process, there is an ongoing need for crisis management. The future is not a world devoid of power-politics.

So then we can ask, why will nations not make war anymore?

The prophetic answer lies in its program designed to prevent conflicting interests from becoming so exacerbated as to spill over into war. This requires a consensual mode of conflict resolution with at least an authoritative international law adjudicated by a recognized tribunal. The prophet, as Robert Gordis noticed:

> ...does not depend on good will or on love to guard the peace, nor does he expect that all differences of outlook and self-interest among nations will miraculously disappear in the End-Time. Before peace can be a reality, there must be a law which shall go forth from Zion, which will be accepted as binding among the nations and will be enforced among the people.[6]

This connection was extended by the prophets into the realm of international relations. Beginning with Amos (1:3-2:3), it informs their assessment of contemporary political events. For them, the exercise of power, no matter how justified, is no excuse for its abuse. War is not *carte blanche* for mass brutality. Accordingly, Amos finds Damascus (Aram) culpable for its outrages against neighboring Gilead. Neither is mass population expulsion acceptable as national policy. Thus Amos threatened Gaza (Philistia) with retribution "because they carried off an entire population to sell as slaves to Edom." Nor may international agreements be broken with impunity. So Amos warns Tyre (Phoenicia) of an impending conflagration "because they sold an entire population to Edom ignoring the covenant of brotherhood."[7] Similarly, he threatens Edom with devastation "because he pursued his brother with the sword and repressed all pity."

Holding both leader and people responsible for national infamies, Amos envisioned God pouring out His wrath on Ammon and exiling her leaders "because they ripped open pregnant women in Gilead in order to extend their frontiers." Supporters bear responsibility for the atrocities of their leaders. In the case of Moab, both leader and followers will be destroyed because they "burned to lime the bones of the king of Edom."

Why do nations act as though they are exempt from moral restraints? Why is the brutality which is condemned in interpersonal relations condoned in international relations? According to Habakkuk 1:11, the origin of national savagery lies in the idolatry of might — in the "guilty men, whose own might is their god." In a similar vein, Jeremiah (23:10) condemned the ancient version of the "might makes right" doctrine, while Hosea (chapters 10 and 13 condemned militarism as a religio-ethical sin. Prophetically speaking, since nations are not morally autonomous entities, the doctrine of national sovereignty was not allowed to become a code word for the lack of international accountability. In a God-ruled world, feelings of unlimited authority verge on idolatry.

More than any other prophet, Isaiah illuminated the correlation between national arrogance and international barbarism. Assyria, the first world-power, is his case in point. Assyria's ruthlessness, according to him, springs out of its national pride:

> Assyria thought:
>   By the might of my hand have I wrought it,
>   By my skill, for I am clever:
>   I have erased the borders of peoples;
>   I have plundered their treasures,
>   Even exiled their vast populations.
>   I was able to seize, like a nest,
>   the wealth of peoples;
>   As one gathers abandoned eggs,
>   So I gathered all the earth:
>   Nothing so much as flapped a wing
>   Or opened a mouth to peep (10:13-14).

Even if Assyria as a world conqueror had license "to take spoil and seize booty" (10:6), it was not authorized to wreak havoc with the civilized world. Mass deportation was not its only crime. Its warfare abounded in atrocities. After it plummeted from the dizzying heights of power, Assyria was long remembered as the conqueror "who made the world like a waste and wrecked its towns, who never released its prisoners to go home" (Isaiah 14:17 — JPS translation).

Conquering nations is one thing; "destroying and wiping them out" (Isaiah 10:7) is another. According to Isaiah, Assyria's ignominious downfall was its comeuppance for having "destroyed countries and murdered nations" (14:20). Even conquest has its moral constraints. The Isaiah of the exile extended his namesake's analysis to the next world-power, Babylonia. Although faithfully executing God's sentence against Israel, Babylonia was castigated for exceeding its mandate. Isaiah sensed the divine wrath which had led to the defiling of His heritage by delivering His people into the hands of the Babylonians. The charges he levels against Babylonia do not deal with conquest per se, but with the unwarranted attendant cruelty, especially to the aged:

You showed them no mercy.
Even upon the aged you made
Your yoke exceedingly heavy (47:6).

Since it expected to reign forever, Babylonia felt it could act with impunity.

You thought, "I shall always be the mistress..."
You were secure in your wickedness
You thought, "No one can see me" (47:7).

Babylonia not only suffered from the same national arrogance as Assyria, but was deluded into believing that its superior technology justified its claim to supremacy:

It was your skill and your science that led you astray.
And you thought to yourself, "I am, and there is none but me" (47:10).

But Babylon is ineluctably accountable.

Evil is coming upon you
Which you will not know how to charm away.
Disaster is falling upon you
Which you will not be able to appease... (Isaiah 47:11).

Similarly, Jeremiah saw Babylonia getting its comeuppance:

I will punish the king of Babylon and that nation and the land of the Chaldeans for their sins...
They too shall be enslaved by many nations and great kings.
And I will requite them according to their acts and according to their conduct (25:12, 14).

In the same vein, Habakkuk, upon seeing the fierce impetuous Chaldeans "cross the earth's wide space to seize homes not their own...and amass captives like sand...slaying nations without pity," pronounced the following verdict:

Because you plundered many nations,
All surviving peoples shall plunder you —
For crimes against men and wrongs against lands,
Against cities and all their inhabitants (2:8).

Neither Isaiah nor Jeremiah categorically proscribe the use of force in the international arena. Yet they hold nations responsible for its abuse. Univocally, they denounce unauthorized aggression.

The key word here is "unauthorized." Discerning no intrinsic antimony between morality and power, they did not disguise defeatism in lofty utopian ideals. After all, "To make the avoidance of tragedy dependent upon a condition that has no chance of fulfillment is a counsel of despair."[8]

To sum up, this biblical perspective realizes that there can be no national security without a world order. Indeed, the rules of world order affect national security. The solution to the moral failings of nations lies not in the abolition of national entities, but rather in the moralization of national power. The prophets do not attempt to solve the problem of the abuse of national power by calling for the dissolution of nations. Rather by subjecting nations to legal restraint they seek to civilize them. In this manner the morally preferable can become the politically possible.

The Limits of Government

This section asks whether the biblical theory of government is republican, monarchial, or something akin to a constitutional monarchy. It also delves into the religio-ethical stipulations for rulership and asks whether these requirements are primarily personal or political. Lastly, it asks how Jewish political theory maintains the balance between the power needed to secure the state and the limitations on its exercise to secure the liberties of its citizens.

Jewish political theory, which bases itself on the Bible, seeks a system of government which is both politically workable and morally acceptable. Much of the content for this theory evolves out of the interplay between two blocks of material. The first, which serves to undergird a *realpolitik* perspective, is the selection in the Book of Samuel on the power of kings. Apparently, Samuel held that divine sovereignty excludes human sovereignty. Therefore, when the people began to clamor for a temporal king, Samuel tried to dissuade them by delineating common royal prerogatives and their abuses with the following:

This will be the practice of the king who will rule over you:
1) He will take your sons and appoint them as his charioteers

and horsemen, and they will serve as outrunners for his chariots.
2) He will appoint them as his chief of thousands and of fifties; or they will have to plow his fields, reap his harvest, and make his weapons and the equipment for his chariots.
3) He will take your daughters as perfumers, cooks and bakers.
4) He will seize your choice fields, vineyards, and olive groves, and give them to his courtiers.
5) He will take a tenth part of your grain and vintage and give it to his eunuchs and courtiers.
6) He will take your male and female slaves, your choice young men (or cattle — LXX) and your asses, and put them to work for him.
7) He will take a tenth part of your flocks, and you shall become his slaves (I Samuel 8:11-17).

The second block, which serves to empower and delimit royal authority, is the setting forth of the laws of kingship in the book of Deuteronomy. The first part mentions the request for a king along with the conditions, qualifications, and restrictions on an Israelite monarch:

If, when you have entered the land that the Lord your God has given you, and have occupied it and have settled in it, you decide, "I will set a king over me, as do all the nations about me," you shall be free to set a king over yourself, one chosen by the Lord your God. Be sure to set as king over yourself one of your own people; you must not set a foreigner over you, one who is not your kinsman. Moreover, he shall not keep many horses, or send people back to Egypt to add to his horses, since the Lord has warned you, "You must not go back that way again." And he shall not have many wives, lest his heart go astray; nor shall he amass silver and gold to excess (Deuteronomy 17:14-17).

The second part stipulates the conditions for dynastic perpetuation.

When he is seated on his royal throne, he shall have a copy of this Torah written for him by the levitical priests. Let it remain with him and let him read from it all his life, so that he may learn to revere the Lord his God, to observe faithfully every word of this Torah as well as these laws. Thus he will not act haughtily toward his fellows or deviate from the Mitzvah to the right or to the left, to the end that he and his descendants may reign long in the midst of Israel (17:18-20).

The classical discussion of kingship, based on these passages, seeks to resolve whether the establishment of an Israelite monarchy is a commandment or a concession.[9] A gallant defense of monarchy as biblically mandated is mounted by the renowned twelfth century legal philosopher, Maimonides. His treatment of government appears in the fourteenth book of his *Mishneh Torah*, called *Judges*, in the section entitled "The Laws of Kings and Their Wars."

Although not denying that Samuel intended to deter the people from requesting a king, Maimonides saw in Samuel's delineation of royal powers an accurate account. He holds that for the proper discharge of royal responsibilities, the law accedes to the king significant latitude in the exercise of his office.[10]

Maimonides' position is in contrast to those of the Franco-German school who claim that Samuel's statement on kingship was not intended to spell out the norms of government, but rather to deter the people.[11] As such, the statement does not sanction these as appropriate governmental norms.

Be that as it may, both of the above schools looked positively upon the establishment of the monarchy and considered it a biblical commandment.

The third position in the Talmud, that of Rabbi Nehorai, however, minces no words regarding the desirability of a king. For him, provision for appointing a king is only an accommodation to the anticipated insistence of the people. Accordingly, Deuteronomy 17:14 is understood not as a commandment but as a grudging concession. Even then, the mandate for monarchy is contingent upon popular demand. Should the Israelites be unable to resist the political models of the gentile nations surrounding them, the Torah demands of them adherence to the aforestated directives lest the emulation of gentile political institutions lead to the emulation of their religious structures.

Once Maimonides codified the position that kingship is mandatory, however, subsequent legal opinion followed suit. Nevertheless, Maimonides has been taken to task for deviating from the normal rules of codification which would indicate that the Nehorean position should be the norm.[12]

Other midrashic positions which oppose monarchy pick up on the biblical theme which hears in the request of a human king a rejection of divine sovereignty. One source glosses the verse, "I will set a king over me," by reporting that God responded, "In this world you asked for kings, and kings arose in Israel and caused you to fall by the sword."[13] The midrash goes on to enumerate the national tragedies precipitated by Saul, David, Ahab, and Zedekiah. It concludes with the following denigration of human kingship in contrast to divine sovereignty:

> When Israel saw what befell them on account of their kings they all began to cry out: "We do not desire a king, we desire our first king," (as it is said), "For the Lord is our judge, the Lord is our law-giver, the Lord is our king; He will save us" (Isaiah 33:22). Whereupon God replied: "By your life, I will do so." How do we know this? For it is said, "And the Lord shall be king over all the earth..." (Zechariah 14:9).[14]

A similar tack is adopted by the eleventh benediction of the daily Amidah prayer. Although seeking the restoration of political sovereignty, it emphasizes that God alone is to reign. Ostensibly, this position is receptive to various forms of government as long as they do not interfere with divine sovereignty. As it stands, this version of the antimonarchial position fails to provide counsel on how society should structure its power through government and thus reverberates little in the subsequent literature.

The antimonarchial Nehorean position, however, is given a specific political dress by the fifteenth century savant and government intimate Abravanel. Abravanel espoused such a fervid republican position that in his Commentary to I Samuel (8:7), he dubs monarchy "a malignant plague."

In his Commentary to Deuteronomy 17, he expounds the reasons for his antimonarchial position:

> Even if we should admit that a king is beneficial and necessary for other peoples for the improvement and maintenance of political order — which actually is contrary to the truth — such reasoning does not make kingship necessary for Israel. The general proposition advances three arguments in favor of kingship:
>
> 1. As supreme commander of the armed forces, the king provides the people with help and comfort against the enemy, and he leads them in the fight for their country;
> 2. As supreme legislative authority, he provides his people with a constitution and laws as the occasion warrants;

3. As supreme judicial tribunal, he sentences and punishes, often without justice, as called for by the circumstances.

Abravanel counters the three arguments that a king is necessary to maintain security, initiate legislation, and adjudicate conflict by maintaining that: 1) God is Israel's help against their enemies, and that judges like Joshua, Gideon, Samuel and others were sufficiently competent to lead them in battle; 2) that the Torah and not the king is the source of legislation; and 3) that the supreme court or Sanhedrin is primarily authorized to administer judicial functions and not the king.

Although Abravanel would countenance a constitutional monarch,[15] his own preference is for authority to be vested in judges, not kings. Even should one accept that necessity of kings for other peoples, it still, he argues, would not apply to Israel:

Experience teaches us that we can even more forcefully point to the lesson of the kings of Israel and Judah about whom it is said, "They were rebels against the light" (Job 24:13). They turned Israel's heart backward, as you know of Jereboam, the son of Nebat, as did all the other kings of (the northern kingdom of) Israel, as well as most of the Judean kings, who brought about the Judean exile....Such was not the case with Israel's judges and prophets, who were all competent rulers who feared God, all men of integrity, who hated unjust gain....All this demonstrates that the leadership of judges is a good thing, whereas the leadership of kings is bad, harmful and extremely dangerous. This accounts for Hosea prophesying in God's name, "I give you kings in my ire..." (13:11).[16]

According to Abravanel, it is precisely the political pluses of monarchy which are its moral minuses. The advocates of monarchy praise it for its unified or singular leadership, cross-generational stability, and absolute power. Abravanel, on the other hand, advocates collective leadership, subject to limited terms. A rotational leadership, he contends, allows subsequent administrations to check the probity of their predecessors and hold them accountable for wrongs committed during their rule. The mere awareness of accountability, it appears, serves to dampen excesses and to alleviate suspicions of misconduct. Threatening to compromise the principle of accountability, dynastic succession can undermine the moral stature of government. Thus it is not surprising that a generation after Abravanel, the Italian exegete,

Sforno, identified the hereditary aspect of monarchy as most objectionable. Were it not for the obstanacy of the people, he asserted, such an idea would never have been entertained.[17]

Whatever be the attitude to monarchy, Jewish political theorists, both pro- and anti-monarchialists, had to grapple with the problems resulting from the centralization of authority. By focusing on the uses of power, the issue, as we shall see, shifts from kingship per se to that of the appropriate restraints on the exercise of all duly constituted authority.

The Constraints of Power

Jewish political philosophy is preoccupied with the problems of power. From Deuteronomy on, it forms the leitmotif for discussion of governmental structure. In fact, the same biblical book which entertains the option of monarchy is the very one to circumscribe its power. The greater the centralization of power, the greater the potential for abuse. Therefore, even as Chapter 17 of Deuteronomy legislates for the possibility of monarchy, it proscribes despotism. The result is a precursor to the doctrine of constitutionally-limited monarchy.

What are the constitutional limitations on biblical monarchy? "Constitutionally," the monarch (in Deuteronomy 17:14-20) is enjoined from multiplying horses, wives, silver and gold, and obliged to have his own copy of the Torah. Of the two major explanations for the royal proscriptions, one school of thought deems them intended primarily to limit the king, the other to restrain the government.

The first position, most ably represented by Moses Maimonides in his aforementioned Code, the *Mishneh Torah*, views the restrictions as safeguards against the moral dissolution of the king. It is improper for a king to be involved in non-functional ostentation, or vainglorious acquisition of possessions, or indulgence in sexual excess, "so that his heart turn not away" (Deuteronomy 17:17), "for his heart is the heart of the whole community of Israel."[18] Being preoccupied with the heart of the people he will, as the verse says, "turn not away," i.e., be not diverted from the affairs of state.

This concern with the moral and political stature of kingship induces Maimonides to append to the Deuteronomic restrictions one other regarding intoxication. He states:

The king is forbidden to drink to the point of intoxication as it is written: "It is not for kings to drink wine" (Proverbs 31:4). He shall be occupied day and night with the study of the Law and the needs of Israel, as it is said: "And it shall be with him, and he shall read therein all the days of his life" (Deuteronomy 17:19).[19]

The connection between the moral life and political duty is here tied tightly. Incapable of attending to the needs of the people, a sottish monarch becomes a political liability. Maimonides lines up with earlier Gaonic thought in grasping the prohibitions as means of preventing the ruler from being distracted from the responsibilities of leadership.[20]

Maimonides prefers to deal with the threat of the abuse of power by cultivating a king more resistant to the enticements of power than by infringing on the authority of the king. His tactic is two-fold: on the one hand, he grants the king wide-ranging authority up to and including the judicial office of final court of appeals; on the other hand, he stresses the moral role of kingship. His presentation of royal prerogatives ends with the following charge to the king to exercise moral leadership:

> Whatever he does should be done by him for the sake of Heaven. His sole aim and thought should be to uplift the true religion, to fill the world with righteousness, to break the arm of the wicked, and to fight the battles of the Lord.[21]

This last rhetorical flourish is made all the more poignant by echoing motifs found in the description of the messianic king by the prophet Isaiah (11:14). There is nothing like a sense of mission to abate the craving for power.

The idea that the ideal king must have adequate power to subdue enemies as well as execute justice has a long tradition. It is based on the biblical belief that royal power should secure the realm from external aggression as well as from internal oppression.[22]

Following Maimonides' lead, Abravanel also explains the restrictions imposed on the king as directed at containing royal excesses. For him, the prohibition against multiplying horses counters that royal drive for self-glorification which is frequently promoted by military exploits. The limitation on the number of wives corresponds to the temptation of royalty to over-indulgence and the sating of lust. And finally in order to thwart the royal proclivity of becoming immersed totally in amassing great wealth, there is the rule against the excessive acquisition of gold and silver.[23]

Abravanel maintains that the power and visibility of the king imposes upon him a special obligation to serve as moral exemplar. A king must appear reluctant to resort to violence, above self-indulgence, and not enmeshed in the pursuit of self-aggrandizement. As most subject to the commandments, he is not only to commission his own copy of the Torah, but to make provision to be accompanied by one in all of his endeavors.

Abravanel supplies three considerations for the special role of the king as religious model. As the most visible and admired person in the realm, both his virtues and defects will be magnified manifold among the people. As a public figure, his position educationally becomes a public trust. Abravanel realized that whatever a king does, for good or for ill, takes place on a grand scale.

Secondly, as the most subject to the temptations and vertigo of power, he is most in need of edification and restraint. Long-term, intensive character education is a royal prerequisite. Lastly, as the most exalted of men in this world, he should cultivate those spiritual qualities which will allow him to be and remain above the transience of this world.[24] If a ruler cannot remain above the fray, the exigencies of the moment will preclude the possibility of far-sighted statesmanship.

The other school of political philosophy holds that the limitations on the king are aimed less at his personal development than at inhibiting that arrogation of power which leads to tyranny. According to Josephus, the ideal Jewish government is under God, mediated through those most qualified to lead. If, however, the people do appoint a king, he must be a native son, and be committed to promoting virtue, especially justice. He is also enjoined from initiating policy without prior consultation with the high priest and elders.

Since a government of law is the best bulwark against despotism, Josephus sees the prohibitions against amassing wives, possessions, and horses as stemming the royal bent to spurn the law. For him, the ideal polity is in possession of the requisite means to govern effectively, yet free of the excesses which pave the way for oppression.[25] His understanding of the biblical polity is best summed up in Lincoln's famous question: "Must a government of necessity be too strong for the liberties of its own people or too weak to maintain its own existence?"

From this perspective, the limitation on horses pertains

especially to war or chariot horses.[26] By impeding the accumulation of martial might, this restriction places brakes on the militarization of society, thereby minimizing the potential for dragging the people into war unnecessarily. For an ambitious king, a large standing army may prove irresistible.

The limitation on wealth follows similar lines. As the medieval Bible commentator Abraham Ibn Ezra noted,[27] it keeps the king from exacting oppressive taxes. Philo, over a thousand years earlier, was probably the first to note that such measures serve "to prevent him from...storing up great wealth all unjustly wrung from the poverty of his subjects."[28] Burdensome, especially military, taxation is particularly prone to promote the malignant growth of an imperial monarchy.

Finally, the limitation on wives can arrest the formation of entangling alliances which in the ancient world were often sealed through marriage.[29] Such marital diplomacy facilitates not only the importation of foreign practices, but also the forging of intergovernmental ententes for mutual support in the event of popular uprisings. How often are security forces created under the guise of protection from foreign incursion deployed to suppress internal dissension? This prohibition also serves to counter the strong correlation between alliance involvement and war proneness.[30] The world has seen many such unholy alliances. In a world of tyranny, a United Governments is not a United Nations.

The special injunction of inditing a copy of the whole Torah, or as some say, a summary of it such as Deuteronomy, concretizes the idea of the ruler as servant of the law rather than its master. The constant intercourse between king and Torah was meant to produce a law-abiding king. As Joshua was told upon being installed as Moses' successor, "Let not this Torah-book cease from your lips, but recite it day and night, so that you may observe faithfully all that is written in it" (Joshua 1:8). The link between Torah and king is further promoted by the mishnaic requirement of the king to read prescribed selections of the Torah before the whole people at the septennial national assembly.[31]

Because of his broad discretionary powers, the king must be inculcated in the rule of law lest he forget his own Sovereign and lord it over the people. Such is the paradox of authority: the more power, the less freedom to follow one's whims.

Cognizant of the connection between the rise to authority and the need for a heightened awareness of royal limitations and responsibilities, a midrash pictures a herald reminding the king of each of the latter two as he ascends the six steps of the throne (see I Kings 10:19). At the first three steps, the herald proclaims: "He shall not have many wives." "He shall not keep many horses." "Nor shall he amass silver and gold in excess" (Deuteronomy 17:17). At the last three steps, the herald announces: "You shall not judge unfairly." "You shall show no partiality." "Neither shall you take a bribe" (Deuteronomy 16:19). Finally, as the king is about to take his seat on the throne, the herald cries out, "Know before whom you sit."[32] By combining the prohibitions against the amassing of monarchial power of the first three steps with those against judicial turpitude of the last three steps, attention is drawn to the links between government draining of the economy and militarization, on the one hand, and the corruption of the rule of law, on the other.

While Aristotle's *Politics* underscores that "if laws aim at anything, they aim at the maintenance of power," the Torah aims at circumscribing those in power for the sake of those who are not. This conforms with the rabbinic as well as Philonic view that the purpose of a royal Torah is to lend prominence to the idea of royal authority as derivative of, and subject to, the Torah.[33]

Assuming that these regal directives are aimed at tempering the potential abuses of monarchy, the biblical idea of postponing the appointment of a king until after the conquest of the land takes on added sense. Were the king to lead the people in conquest, they might become inured to rendering him absolute fealty. Were he subsequently to oversee distribution of the land, they might become totally beholden to him. Such habits of obeisance and feelings of gratitude to one who has exercised absolute authority in time of war have all the makings of tyranny in time of peace. There is nothing like imperial responsibility for creating an imperial rule.

As the sixteenth century Italian exegete Abraham Menahem Porto notes, Deuteronomy (17:4) makes provision for a king only after stating that the people had already resided in the land and that God had granted it to them. It thereby guarantees that this ruler, unlike other kings, will not be accredited with the conquest of the land.[34] The natural proclivity of a people to attribute their security and domestic tranquality to the military genius of the king will be blunted. Since the king had neither conquered nor parcelled out the land, they would not have become accustomed to total submissiveness nor feel completely in his debt.

Precluded from laying title to the land, a non-conquering

king would be hard-pressed to exercise economic control. Moreover, the biblical perception of God as sole proprietor of the land[35] precludes any comparable claim by the king. A healthy distance between the locus of political power and that of economic power thwarts the temptation for abuse which is well-nigh irresistible when the two coincide.

Concern with the capricious use of power moves the Bible not only to limit royal power, but to curb the natural bent of the people to relinquish their own power to the king. The problem is two-fold: the usurpation of power by the king, and the unconditional renunciation of power by the people. The temptation to exchange responsibility for tranquility or to barter freedom for security is everpresent.

Since the time of Montesquieu, it has become popular to argue that the balance between the need for adequate power to govern and the need for safeguards against its arbitrary use can be maintained through the doctrine of the separation of powers. Dispersing sovereignty over several institutions of government enables them to monitor each other, thereby containing each other's excesses.

The twentieth century biblical commentator David Zvi Hoffmann has argued that a similar concern with the abuse of power accounts for the rulings on kingship in Deuteronomy 17:14-20 cropping up in the midst of the whole corpus of ancient biblical officialdom. Prior to the rules on monarchy, the rulings on the judicial and legislative offices appear in Deuteronomy 16:18-20 and 17:8-12. Afterwards come the rulings on priests and levites (18:1-9), prophets (18:10-22), and war leaders (20). By guaranteeing the diffusion of authority, the separation of powers minimizes abuse. Hemmed in by the "constitutional" functions of others, the king is directed to his primary responsibility of enforcing the law.[36] The result is that coercive sovereignty is not to be confused with legislative or other types of sovereignty.[37]

In sum, both schools of thought on royal power focus on king and government. Together they make the point that bad men are as likely to corrupt good institutions as bad institutions are likely to corrupt good men. While power may be morally corrosive, it is also the great enabler. The institutionalization of the distribution of power limits the latitude for abuse by any single person or branch of government without diluting the sum total of power available to government as a whole.

What is the minimal distribution of power in Jewish political theory? The fourteenth century legal thinker Rabbenu Nissim required the separation of executive and judicial functions. He apportioned to the Sanhedrin the judicial function while leaving to the king the responsibility for the stability and security of the political order. Since the strict demands of justice are not always in consonance with overall political needs, there is, he argues, a need for two arms of government. Merging the two slights either the requirements of strict justice or the needs of the social order.[38]

Derivative of the monarch's responsibility for the security of the political order is his military role. Here political theory assimilates the idealism of Deuteronomy with the realism of Samuel's description. The primacy of the monarch as both ruler and protector is thrown into relief by the request of the people for a king in I Samuel 8:20: "Let our king rule over us and go out at our head and fight our battles." Realizing that the Bible mandates that as chief executive a king must also serve as commander-in-chief explains why Maimonides entitled his treatment of kingship, "The Laws of Kings and Their Wars."

Nonetheless, a hereditary monarchy is not the only method for producing a chief executive. Maimonides, for example, understood Joshua to be serving as king.[39] In a similar vein, he considered the Hasmoneans to be legitimate kings[40] and had no reservation in designating Bar-Kokhba "a great king."[41]

Rabbi David Ben Zimra, in his commentary to Maimonides' Code, states explicitly that when Maimonides mentions "king," it denotes not only one crowned by a prophet, but anyone who rules by consent of the people.[42] Long before, Philo had already understood the biblical injunction of "you shall establish a ruler over yourself" to entail "appointment by election...made by the whole people."[43] It follows that since the king represents sovereign authority, a sovereign who duly assumes the reins of power is entitled to those powers of kingship which express such authority.[44]

A good biblical example of the sovereign=king equation is the case of the aforementioned public reading of the Torah at the septennial assembly of the king. According to II Kings (23:1-3), King Josiah performed this role. Before there was a king, Joshua, according to several commentators, was envisioned as performing the role in Deuteronomy 31:11. Afterwards when kings had ceased to rule Israel, a somewhat similar ceremony, according to Nehemiah (8), was carried out by the Persian king's emissary, Ezra the scribe. Thus it is not surprising that in the post-biblical period, Josephus reports that this public recitation of Scripture was a function of the high priest.[45]

Once the overlap of functions between king and executive authority is established, one can, as Nahmanides did, conclude that war may be undertaken not only by a king, but also "by a judge or whosoever exercises jurisdiction over the people."[46]

In the twentieth century, Abraham Kook, the former Chief Rabbi of (pre-state) Israel, was most influential in promoting the idea of a king as chief executive. He saw the monarch as the embodiment of national sovereignty. In the absence of a king, he contended, sovereignty reverts back to the people. Thus a leader who represents the people and administers their affairs for their general well-being assumes the authority of a king.[47] Rabbi Kook's position on the nature and authority of the chief executive has been adopted by subsequent Israeli rabbinic authorities[48] and serves as the *halakhic* basis for legitimating the security decisions of the Israeli government.

The test case for any political theory of checks and balances is war. Since it also tests the outer limits of the ethical deployment of power, it forms the next subject.

Jewish Ethics of War

Types of War

The Jewish ethics of war focuses on two issues: its legitimation and its conduct.

The Talmud classifies wars according to their source of legitimation. Biblically mandated wars are termed mandatory (*milhemet mitzva* or *milhemet hovah*). Wars undertaken at the discretion of the Sanhedrin or its legal equivalent such as the modern Israeli Knesset are termed discretionary wars, (*milhemet reshut*).

There are three types of mandatory wars: 1) Joshua's war of conquest against the seven Canaanite nations; 2) the war against Amalek; 3) a defensive war against an already launched attack. Discretionary wars are principally composed of expansionary efforts undertaken to enhance the political prestige of the government or to secure economic gains.[49]

The first type of mandatory war retains only historical interest. Having lost their national identity already in ancient times, the Canaanite nations have been removed from the postbiblical agenda. This ruling, which appears in both mishnaic and talmudic sources,[50] is part of a tendency to blunt the impact of the seven-nations ruling. The Bible already points out that these policies were not implemented even during the zenith of ancient Israel's power.[51] An ancient midrash explicitly excludes the possibility of transferring the seven-nations ruling to other non-Jewish residents of the Land of Israel.[52] Maimonides is just as explicit in emphasizing that all trace of them has vanished.[53] This limiting of the jurisdiction of the seven-nations ruling to the conditions of ancient Canaan precludes it from serving as a precedent for contemporary practice.

The second category of mandatory wars, viz., that of the war against Amalek, has been rendered operationally defunct by comparing them with the aforementioned Canaanites,[54] or by viewing them as the embodiment of sheer evil and postponing the battle to the pre-messianic struggle.[55]

The two remaining categories, defensive wars (which are classified as mandatory) and expansionary wars (which are classified as discretionary) remain intact. So, for example, King David's response to the Philistine attack is termed mandatory,[56] while his wars "to expand the borders of Israel" were termed discretionary.[57] Intermediate categories such as preventive, anticipatory or preemptive wars defy so neat a classification. No only are the classifications debated in the Talmud,[58] but commentators disagree on the categorization of the differing positions in the Talmud.

The major clash among the commentators occurs between the eleventh century Franco-German scholar Rashi and the thirteenth century Franco-Provencal scholar Meiri. According to Rashi, the majority position in the Talmud deems preemptive action to be *discretionary* while the minority position expounded by Rabbi Judah considers it to be *mandatory*.

According to Meiri,[59] a preemptive strike — which he describes as a military move against an enemy who it is feared might attack or about whom it is already known is preparing for war — is judged to be *mandatory* by the majority of the rabbis, but only deemed *discretionary* by Rabbi Judah. According to this reading, Rabbi Judah defines mandatory wars only as those responding to an already launched attack. Maimonides, for his part, also limits the mandatory classification to a defensive war launched in response to an attack.[60]

Since subsequent discussions are variations on these themes, the rest of the analysis focuses on the following four issues: 1) May the classification of a defensive war as mandatory be extended to include preemptive strikes? 2) Which branch of government makes the decision to wage war? 3) How may war be conducted? 4) And finally, who is subject to the draft?

Preemptive Strikes as Self-Defense

It is widely held that the right of national self-defense is as much a moral right as is personal self-preservation. Not only Machiavellians view the security and survival of the state as non-negotiable. The question rather is whether the inalienable right of self-defense is limited to an already launched attack. This apparently is the majority talmudic position according to Rashi, and that of Rabbi Judah, according to Meiri. This position is seconded by Article 51 of the United Nations Charter which states:

> Nothing in the present Charter shall impair the inherent right of individual or collective self-defense if an armed attack occurs against a member....

On the other hand, the minority position of Rabbi Judah, according to Rashi, and the majority position, according to Meiri, hold that a preemptive strike against an enemy amassing for attack is sufficiently similar to a defensive counterattack to be categorized as mandatory. This position holds that to wait for an actual attack might make resistance impossible. Such an argument was championed by Lord Chancellor Kilmuir before the British House of Lords when he remarked with reference to the aforementioned Article 51:

> It would be a travesty of the purpose of the Charter to compel a defending state to allow its opponents to deliver the first fatal blow.[61]

This judgment lies behind the endorsement by the United States House Appropriations Committee of the concept of a preemptive attack. Its conclusions were formulated as follows:

> In the final analysis, to effectively deter a would-be aggressor, we should maintain our armed forces in such a way and with such an understanding that should it ever become obvious that an attack upon us or our allies is imminent, we can launch an attack before the aggressor has hit either us or our allies. This

is an element of deterrence which the United States should not deny itself. No other form of deterrence can be relied upon.[62]

This understanding of anticipatory defense allows for a counterattack while the initial blow is yet to fall.

Under the terms of modern warfare, for example, if the Soviet Union were to launch a missile attack, the United States could legitimately retaliate even if Soviet missiles had yet to exceed Soviet borders and penetrate the airspace of the United States or its allies. Even more, the doctrine of anticipatory defense would allow for a preemptive strike even if the missiles were still on their launching pads as long as the order had been issued for their launching.

The Decision to Wage War: Who is Authorized to Declare War?

A mandatory war is declared by the chief executive. A discretionary war requires the advice and/or consent of the Sanhedrin[63] or, as noted above, its judicial legislative equivalent.

There are several considerations for requiring the involvement of the Sanhedrin in the decision-making process of a discretionary war. The first is its role as the legal embodiment of popular sovereignty, the *edah* in biblical terms.[64] Maimonides, who understands this to imply that the high court was the legal equivalent of "the community of Israel as a whole,"[65] uses interchangeably the phrases "according to the majority of Israel" and "according to the high court."[66] This equivalency enabled former Chief Rabbi Shlomo Goren to explain that the requirement to secure the Sanhedrin's approval in a discretionary war derives from its representative authority.[67]

The second consideration for involving the Sanhedrin is due to its role as the authoritative interpreter of the Torah-constitution. Since the judicial interpretation of the law is structurally separate from its executive enforcement, the Sanhedrin can serve as a check on executive power.

The involvement of the Sanhedrin in a discretionary war safeguards the citizenry from being endangered without the approval of those who represent them. That citizens should be obliged to fight in a discretionary war at all is based on the biblical perspective which considers the people and the monarch to be bound by a covenant,[68] each side of which possesses certain obligations.

Statehood involves a mutual security pact. The people commit themselves to the state which protects them as long as the state resists risking their lives unnecessarily. Ideally, the people are obliged to support the king just as he is forsworn to uphold the constitution.[69] Allocating some war-making authority to the Sanhedrin guarantees the presence of a countervailing force to the ruler in order to preserve the inviolability of the social contract.

Prior to granting authorization to wage war, the Sanhedrin must weigh the probable losses, consider the chances of success, and assess the will of the people. Since wars are always costly in lives, the losses have to be measured against the chance of success. Calculations of victory alone are not determinative; the price of victory must be considered. The great third century Babylonian talmudic authority Mar Samuel condoned the loss of up to one-sixth of the fighting forces before subjecting a government to charges of misconduct.[70] Thus a government is not only required to project future losses, but to take precautions to limit them. Nonetheless, precision is well-nigh impossible. The gap between plan and execution characterizes the best of military calculations. Linear plans almost always fail to deal with the nonlinear world that rules strategy and war. Already in talmudic times, Rabbi Eleazar noted, "any war which involves more than sixty thousand is necessarily chaotic."[71] Modern warfare has not significantly changed the equation. In the words of Prussian Field Marshall von Moltke, "No plan can survive contact with the battle."[72]

Still, preventive warfare is unwarranted if the number of lives saved does not significantly exceed the number of lives jeopardized. As David Bleich writes:

> The Sanhedrin is charged with assessing the military, political and economic reality and determining whether a proposed war is indeed necessary and whether it will be successful in achieving its objectives.[73]

These calculations are the province of that body whose objectivity will enable it to represent the people best. The ruler, for his part, may be insufficiently disinterested, predisposed as he is to perceive war as an opportunity for enhancing personal prestige, for stimulating the economy, or for consolidating his political base. As the Talmud notes, nothing diverts public attention and deflects the opposition while simultaneously creating the need for a strong leader as war.[74] Reflecting a similar insight, Josephus —

well aware of the machinations of opportunistic rulers — pointed out that the biblical laws of warfare are meant to deter conquest by preventing war "wage(d) for self-aggrandizement."[75]

The ruler may also be reluctant to commit his army out of fear of compromising his living standards in the defense of the citizenry. In fact, the exclusion of the king from certain official decisions is attributed by the Talmud to the concern that the expense of maintaining a standing army would unduly influence his judgment.[76]

In sum, before the populace may be endangered, the ruler's considerations to wage war or not should be checked by the Sanhedrin's assessment of the people's interest. Through such a system of countervailing powers, the interest of the state and the interest of the people can be balanced.

The obligation of the citizen to participate in a mandatory defensive war flows from three assumptions, of which the first two are that national defense is based on an analogue of individual self-defense,[77] and that national defense is required by the verse, "Do not stand idly by the blood of your neighbor."[78] The implication is that the duty to come to the rescue of compatriots under attack is comparable to the duty to intervene in order to rescue an individual from an assailant.[79]

These two assumptions alone prove inadequate. After all, if escape is available, self-defense is optional. Moreover, classical legal opinion is divided on the obligation of risking one's life for another.[80] The upshot is that the domestic analogy alone remains insufficient. The right of national defense cannot be facilely extrapolated from the right of home defense.

Justifying risk of life in the name of national defense calls for an additional consideration, viz., the assumption that the duty to save the community *is* sufficient to authorize risk of life. As Maimonides notes at the end of his *Epistle to Yemen*, "the public welfare takes precedence over one's personal safety."[81] This responsibility to defend the community increases when the community involved is the state whose mandate includes the protection of the total citizenry.[82]

In a defensive war, the lives of the citizenry are imperiled with the first attack. The counterattack constitutes an effort to diminish the risk to life. Such is not the case in discretionary wars which seek to extend the political or economic influence of the government. Even in a preemptive attack, according to one school of thought, the lack of imminent danger to the population prevents the executive from independently endangering the lives of the citizenry. Whether a policy of war should be endorsed is left to the discretion of the Sanhedrin.

The Ethical Conduct of War

The estimation of one's own losses and one's own interests are insufficient for the determination of discretionary war. The total destruction ratio required for victory must be considered. This assessment involves a "double intention," that is, the "good" must appear achievable and the "evil" reducible.

Thus, for example, prior to laying siege to a city, it must be determined that it can be captured without destroying it.[83] There is no warrant for destroying a town "in order to save it."

The other rules for sieges follow similar lines of thought. Indefensible villages may not be subjected to a siege. Negotiations with the enemy must precede subjecting a city to hunger, thirst, or disease for the purpose of exacting a settlement. Emissaries of peace must be sent to a hostile city for three days. If the terms are accepted, no harm may befall any inhabitants of the city. If the terms are not accepted, the siege is still not to begin until the enemy has opened hostilities. Even after the siege is laid, no direct cruelties against the inhabitants may be inflicted. In fact, a side must be left open as an escape route.[84]

Philo warns that national vendettas are not justifications for wars. If a city under siege sues for peace, it is to be granted. Peace, albeit with sacrifices, says Philo, is preferable to the horrors of war. But peace means peace. "If," he continues

> the adversaries persist in their rashness to the point of madness, they (the besiegers) must proceed to the attack invigorated by enthusiasm and having in the justice of their cause an invincible ally.[85]

Although the purpose of an army at war is to win, both Philo the Alexandrian and the ancient rabbis rejected the claim of military necessity as an excuse for military excess. While victory is the goal, indeed victory with all due haste, aimless violence or wanton destruction is to be avoided. As the Spanish commentator Naḥmanides makes clear, acts of destruction are warranted only in so far as they advance the goal of victory.[86] Clearly, weapons calculated to produce suffering disproportionate to the military advantage cannot be licensed.

Since there are times when excessive concern with moral niceties can prove to be morally counterproductive, it is imperative that moral compunctions not appear as timidity, and that moral fastidiousness not be seen as squeamishness, lest such misunderstandings serve to actually invite aggression. To ensure that it be perceived as issuing from a position of strength, moral preparedness must go hand-in-hand with military preparedness.

Well-aware of the military ambiguity of moral concerns, Philo sounds a note of caution in the following summary of the biblical doctrine of defense:

> All this shows clearly that the Jewish nation is ready for agreement and friendship with all like-minded nations whose intentions are peaceful, yet is not of the contemptible kind which surrenders through cowardice to wrongful aggression.[87]

One of the scruples that cannot be sacrificed on the altar of military necessity is the immunity of noncombatants. Such a principle discriminates in favor of those who have done no harm. As Philo notes:

> The Jewish nation, when it takes up arms, distinguishes between those whose life is one of hostility, and the reverse. For to breathe slaughter against all, even those who have done very little or nothing amiss, shows what I should call a savage and brutal soul.[88]

Philo extends the prohibition against axing fruit-bearing trees (Deuteronomy 20:19-20) to include vandalizing the environs of the besieged city. He says:

> Indeed so great a love for justice does the law instill in those who live under its constitution that it does not even permit the fertile soil of a hostile city to be outraged by devastation or by cutting down trees to destroy the fruits....Does a tree, I ask you, show ill will to the human enemy that it should be pulled up roots and all, to punish it for ill which it has done or is ready to do to you?[89]

In a similar vein, Josephus expands on the biblical prohibitions to include the incineration of the enemy's country and the killing of beasts employed in labor.[90] Despoiling enemy countryside for no military advantage comes under the proscription of profligate destruction.

Maimonides takes the next step in extending the biblical prohibition to categorically exclude wanton destruction. He states:

> Also, one who smashes household goods, tears clothes, demolishes a building, stops up a spring, or destroys articles of food with destructive intent, transgresses the command "You shall not destroy."[91]

If one succeeds in reining in the destructive urges provoked by the war-time situation against non-human objects, there is a chance of controlling the destructive urge against humans. The link between these two forms the basis of two *a fortiori* arguments for the immunity of noncombatants.

Since the prohibition against destroying trees is formulated in a rhetorical manner, namely, "Are trees of the field human to withdraw before you under siege?" (Deuteronomy 20:19), it is deduced that just as a tree — had it fled — would not be chopped down, so a person — were he to flee — should not be cut down. As the fifteenth century Spanish-Italian exegete Isaac Arama notes, after mentioning the prohibition against the wanton destruction of trees, "all the more so is it fitting to take care that no preventable injury come upon humans."[92]

The immunity of noncombatants is further supported by the ruling that a fourth side of a besieged city be left open. Commentators are unclear whether the motive here is humanitarian or tactical. In either case, the opportunity of escape, willy-nilly, saps the resolve of the beseiged to continue fighting.[93] Thus it is important that the option to flee not be allowed to be exploited for regrouping in order to mount rear attacks.[94] Whatever the case, if (unarmed) soldiers have the chance of becoming refugees, then all the more so noncombatants and other neutrals. Thus the prohibition of weapons directed primarily at civilian targets. This position precludes the military option of counter-people warfare in conventional war as well as mutually assured destruction (MAD) in nuclear warfare. Multi-megaton weapons whose primary goal is civilian slaughter and only secondarily military targets would be totally proscribed. As there are unacceptable weapons, so there are unacceptable targets.

These ethical intrusions in the waging of war have two major foci: to safeguard the moral character of the soldier, and to preserve the human image of the enemy.

Any system which appreciates both the realities of the moral life and of the military faces a dilemma in promoting the moral perfection of the individual while allowing for military involvement. Some systems forswear war as the price of moral excellence. Others apportion the moral life and the military life to different segments of the population. If the two are mutually exclusive, then a division of labor is a possible solution.

Neither alternative is acceptable in Jewish ethical theory. Regarding forswearing war, Maimonides pointed out that to renounce defense is to guarantee occupation, conquest and exile. Realizing that dispersion is an unnatural political condition for Israel, Maimonides, in his *Epistle to the Sages of Marseille*, attributed the loss of the Second Jewish Commonwealth to the neglect of the art of war. Clearly Maimonides would find it, in the words of Abba Eban, "hard to see why the advocates of unilateral renunciation are more 'moral' than those who seek to prevent war by a reciprocal balance of deterrents and incentives." Solutions to conflict have to be judged by their effectiveness, not only by their virtue. Indeed, there is no reason to concede, as Eban continues, "that prevention of conflict by effective deterrence [is] less moral than the invitation to conflict by avoidable imbalance." For deterrence to be credible, the capacity to make war must be credible. Paradoxically, as Raymond Aron notes, "the possibility of unlimited violence restrains the use of violence without any threats even being proffered."[95]

Unilateral disarmament cannot be judged more moral if it invites attack. A policy of abdication of power which results in condemning others to subjugation has a questionable moral basis. For a leader of a beleaguered nation, political naivete can result in moral sin. Thus Maimonides concludes his critique of the political sagacity of ancient Israel's leaders by lamenting, "Our fathers have sinned, but they are no more."[96]

With regard to a division of labor on ethical lines, Jewish theorists have generally been inclined to reject solutions which are predicated upon the exemption of the ethical elites from the maintenance work of society. Instead, they have been struggling with the challenge of sustaining the moral stature of the soldier. As far back as the first century, Philo, as mentioned above, already explained that the prohibition against slaying the defenseless derives from a concern with the savagery of the soul of the soldier. Since there is never license for indiscriminate killing, it should be of no surprise that even kings were condemned for their ruthlessness in the slaying even of enemies.[97]

For centuries ethicists have been concerned with the

brutalization of character which inevitably results from the shedding of blood in wartime. In the thirteenth century, Naḥmanides, who elsewhere expressed his apprehension that "the most refined of people become possessed with ferocity and cruelty when advancing upon the enemy,"[98] opined that the Torah wants the soldier to "learn to act compassionately with our enemies even during wartime."[99] As Isaac Arama noted two centuries later, "war is impossible without murder and hatred of humanity....There is nothing like it to undermine all sense of right and wrong."[100] In the eighteenth century, Ḥayyim Attar underscored how killing, however justified, "gives birth to a brutalization of sensibilities" which requires special divine grace to be palliated.[101]

In the nineteenth century, Samuel David Luzzato argued that since the Torah's purpose is to strengthen the forces of compassion and to counter the natural drive for only self-serving acts, it is concerned that we not become ingrates by casting stones into the well from which we drank. Such would be the case if, after eating the fruit of a tree, that very tree were to be chopped down.[102] Jewish agonizing over the moral stature of the soldier is summed up, in the twentieth century, in the following words of Justice Ḥaim Cohen of the Israel Supreme Court: "It seems that constant violence, even in self-defense, is not easily compatible with moral sensitivity."[103] All the more reason for an ethic of soldiery.

The concern with the humanity of the enemy has also engaged Jewish ethical reflection. Two of the most poignant comments hark back to the first century. Referring to Deuteronomy 21:10ff, Josephus says the legislator of the Jews commands —

> showing consideration even to declared enemies. He...forbids even the spoiling of fallen combatants; he has taken measures to prevent outrage to prisoners of war, especially women.[104]

Consideration for the humanity of the enemy forms the basis of Philo's explanation for the biblical requirement in Numbers 31:19 of expiation for those soldiers who fought against Midian. He writes:

> For though the slaughter of enemies is lawful, yet one who kills a man, even if he does so justly and in self-defense and under compulsion, has something to answer for, in view of the primal common kinship of mankind. And therefore, purification was needed for the slayers, to absolve them from what was held to have been a pollution.[105]

Since, alas, there are times when evil has to be used to hold evil in check, the problem, as Rabbi Abraham Kook noted in his book *Lights*, is how to engage in evil without becoming tainted. One tactic, as noted here by Philo, is the requiring of rites of expiation even after necessary evils. There is no such thing as a war that does not require penance. According to some, this approach was implemented after the slaying in the Golden Calf episode.[106]

The ongoing tension between the demands of conscience and the exigencies of the hour was caught by Buber in the following words:

> It is true that we are not able to live in perfect justice, and in order to preserve the community of man, we are often compelled to accept wrongs in decisions concerning the community. But what matters is that in every hour of decision we are aware of our responsibility and summon our conscience to weigh exactly how much is necessary to preserve the community, and accept just so much and no more; that we do not interpret the demands of a will-to-power as a demand made by life itself; that we do not make a practice of setting aside a certain sphere in which God's command does not hold, but regard those actions as against His command, forced on us by the exigencies of the hour as painful sacrifices; that we do not salve, or let others salve our conscience when we make decisions concerning public life....[107]

Necessary evils remain evils.

These concerns for the moral quotient of the soldier and the life of the enemy inform the "purity of arms" doctrine of the modern Israel Defense Forces. The doctrine of "purity of arms," an expression apparently coined by the Labor-Zionist idealogue Berl Katznelson, limits killing to necessary and unavoidable situations.[108] How successfully it has been maintained under wartime conditions is illustrated by the following account of an Israeli unit entering Nablus during the Six-Day War:

> The battalion CO got on the field telephone to my company and said, "Don't touch the civilians....Don't fire until you're fired at and don't touch the civilians. Look, you've been warned." The boys in the company kept talking about it afterwards....They kept repeating the words..."Their blood be on your heads."[109]

According to Israeli Colonel Meir Pa'il, the "purity of arms" doctrine is able to maintain the moral stature of the soldier without seriously compromising his fighting capacity. He writes:

> There can be no doubt that the turning toward extreme and consummate humanism can endanger the I.D.F.'s [Israel Defense Forces] ability to function, but experience has proved that the proportions of this danger are extremely small and that it does not constitute a phenomenon that really endangers the operative capacity and the efficiency of the defense forces.[110]

There is a consistent thread weaving its way through Jewish ethical thought from biblical ordinance to modern practice as noted by ancient as well as medieval and modern observers. Just because an army is legitimately repelling an aggressor does not allow it to recklessly violate civilian life. The warrior is the enemy, not the noncombatant civilian. A just war does not justify unjust acts. If peace is the goal, the reality of war is to be conditioned by the vision of the reconciliation between the warring populations. Education for peace is also part of military preparedness.

Many of these considerations for maintaining the moral stature of the soldier and the humanity of the enemy received their initial stimulus from those biblical passages on war which have been categorized as discretionary. Nonetheless, they seem as applicable to mandatory wars. Although the better known tendency distinguishes between the two types of war, the inclination to underscore the overlap of considerations between discretionary and mandatory wars also figures prominently in the classical discussion.[111]

This drive toward moral convergence between the two types of war finds its roots in the Bible. Thus, provisions are made in I Samuel 15:6 to evacuate neutrals from the battle area even in the biblically-mandated war against Amalek.

In addition to some moral considerations, the two types of war share some strategic considerations. Since the aforecited statement by Rabbi Eleazar in the midrash with regard to the chaotic nature of warfare derives from the numbers involved in the conquest of the Land of Israel, it follows that even the mandatory war of the original conquest of Israel required a weighing of victory against losses not unlike those of discretionary wars.

A midrash traces the blurring of the distinctions between the two types of war back to the Torah itself. It finds in the following dialogue a way of parrying the assumption that overtures of peace are limited to discretionary wars.

> God commanded Moses to make war on Sihon, as it is said, "Engage him in battle" (Deuteronomy 2:24), but he did not do so. Instead he sent messengers...to Sihon...with an offer of peace (Deuteronomy 2:26). God said to him: "I commanded you to make war with him, but instead you began with peace; by your life, I shall confirm your decision. Every war upon which Israel enters shall begin with an offer of peace."[112]

Since even a divinely-commanded war must be preceded by an overture of peace, Joshua, according to the midrash, extended such an offer even to the Canaanites.[113] Indeed, Numbers 27:21 underscores the need for applying to the priestly Urim and Tumim for assessing the chances of victory. Apparently, not even in mandatory wars do chief executives have *carte blanche* to commit their people to war.

The move to impose upon mandatory warfare the procedural or moral restraints of discretionary warfare counters "the sliding scale argument," namely, the belief that "the greater the justice of one's cause, the more rights one has in battle."[114] The move from convictions of righteousness to feelings of self-righteousness is slight. The subsequent move of regarding the enemy population as beyond the pale of humanity is even slighter. Since this tendency is especially pronounced in ideologically and religiously motivated wars, any countermove is especially salutary.

The greater the blurring of distinctions between discretionary and mandatory war, the greater the chance of removing from the military agenda the option of total war. Only a sliding scale of limited warfare is ethically feasible. An ethic of unlimited warfare is a contradiction in terms.

Exemptions from Military Service

The Sanhedrin is also to weigh popular support in its endorsement of a war policy. This does not imply a government by referendum. Even those who maintain that sovereignty ultimately rests with the community hold that during their tenure, representatives are authorized to express the collective will.[115] Even democracy, the contemporary *halakhist* Eleazar Waldenberg notes, does not necessarily entail government by referendum.

Representative government is not government by the people, but government by its agents.[116]

Nonetheless, concurrent with theories of majority rule are provisions for minority rights.[117] As there is general agreement that the majority cannot impose unfair rules which discriminate against the minority, so is there a consensus on the right of the majority to impose on the minority in matters which are clearly for the benefit of the community. Legal opinion, however, is split on whether the minority can be imposed upon in those discretionary areas (*devar hareshut*) which though desired by the majority are not clearly for the benefit of the community as a whole.

Whether such provisions would apply in war is open to question. It would appear that once the government has complied with proper procedure, the individual would have no recourse but to fight. After all, if the duly-constituted authorities have determined the necessity of war, how could the prerogative of reviewing the government's decision be left to the individual? This surely holds in defensive wars where none is exempt from the obligation of self-defense, the duty to rescue others, and the need to come to the defense of the state whose very existence shields all.

The question is whether these considerations apply equally in discretionary wars or is majority rule limited by the discretionary nature (*devar hareshut*) of the war and thus must meet the requirement of benefit to the community as a whole. Although these considerations are not made explicit, they may help us understand the peculiar biblical rules of warfare with regard to exemptions from military service.

According to the Torah, before commencing hostilities, the officials must address the troops as follows:

> Is there anyone who has built a new house but has not dedicated it...or planted a vineyard but has never harvested it...or spoken for a women in marriage but has not married her....Let him go back home, lest he die in battle and another...(do) it.

> The officials shall go on addressing the troops and say, is there anyone afraid and tender-hearted: Let him go back to his home, lest the courage of his comrades flag like his (Deuteronomy 20:5-9).

Individuals in these categories are required to report for duty first before being assigned alternative service.

There is another category which not only is exempt from

reporting for duty, but is also excused from all alternative service such as provisions and weapon supply, road repair, special security expenditures, or even oversight of defensive installations.[118] This category derives from the following verse: "When a man has taken a bride, he shall not go out with the army or be assigned to it for any purpose: he shall be exempt one year for the sake of his household, to give happiness to the woman he has married" (Deuteronomy 24:5). According to the Mishnah, the absolute exemption of one year for one who has consummated his marriage applies also to "one who has built his house and dedicated it" as well as to "one who has planted a vineyard and harvested it."[119]

All the exemptions are characterized by their universal access. There are no exemptions based on birth, education, or professional class, not even on religious status.[120] This fits the moral purpose of conscription which is to universalize or randomize the risks of war across a generation of men. By not creating a special exclusion even for religion, the Torah underscores that when life is at stake, there can be no respecting of persons.

The purpose of all of the exemptions is not made explicit. One factor which is alluded to is the consideration of removing from the field those who cannot concentrate on the battle. The presence of such people increases fatalities resulting from disarray and failure of nerve. Other suggestions include the need to mitigate individual hardship, to give courage to those who remain, to maintain the sanctity of the camp,[121] or to prevent depopulation of urban areas.[122]

At any rate, the talmudic rabbis, by grasping each case as illustrative of a principle, extended the exemptions to cover four categories of handicaps: the economic, the familial, the psycho-moral, and the physical.[123] Claims for economic and familial exemptions are subject to substantiation. The other two are assumed to be self-evident.[124]

Although the psycho-moral exemption does not require independent confirmation, its meaning is far from self-evident. The Torah mentions two categories: "afraid" and "tender-hearted." According to Rabbi Yose HaGalili, "afraid" means apprehensive about his sins; "tender-hearted" means fearful of war lest he be killed. According to Rabbi Akiva, "afraid" means fearful of war; "tender-hearted" means compassionate — apprehensive lest he kill.[125] Taken together, there would be grounds for exempting the psychologically timid as well as the morally scrupulous.[126]

Besides having to be substantiated, the economic and familial exemptions share another common denominator. Projects such as starting a house, beginning a vineyard, or getting engaged mostly affect men in their prime which is the age of maximum combat readiness. These are also the people who would be most willing to fight a necessary war and most reluctant to fight an optional one. A large number of exemptions for this age group can so hamper mobilization efforts as to impair the military effort. Naḥmanides says it in so many words when he notes that "Were it not for [the requirement of substantiation], a majority of the people would seek exemption on false pretenses."[127] Naḥmanides' fears were borne out by the experience of the biblical judge Gideon who, upon making provisions for the psycho-moral exemption, lost two-thirds of his fighting force.[128]

But this is precisely the point. There is a loophole in the war legislation — a loophole so gaping that it allows those not convinced of the validity of the war to reassert their sovereignty through legal shenanigans. Doubts about the validity of the war will stir up their own social momentum and induce many to seek wholesale exemptions. The result is a war declared by the executive and approved by the Sanhedrin, which sputters for failing to persuade the populace of its necessity.[129]

Mobilization cannot succeed without a high degree of popular motivation. Many will express their half-heartedness by dragging their feet in the hope of being, as the Talmud says, "The last to go to war and the first to return."[130] Through expressing their reluctance to fight, the populace retains a semblance of sovereignty. By allowing them to, however indirectly, pass judgment on whether the military venture is both necessary and legitimately serving political ends, the Torah underscores the interdependence between military readiness and popular readiness. Indeed, in order for conquered territory to enter the public domain, according to Maimonides, the military venture must command the approval of the majority.[131]

The upshot is that both mandatory and discretionary wars require both a moral and a political base.[132] Otherwise, the war effort threatens to be undermined by the morale of that community which constitutes the resource of power. David Ben-Gurion summed it up well when he said, "two-thirds of military prowess is popular morale."[133]

In the final analysis, the issue is not the justice of the war (*jus ad bellum*) nor the conduct of the war (*jus in bello*) but the ends and purposes for which war is used. Just because a war can be justified both by cause and by conduct does not make it necessary. While final judgments of necessity are always retrospective, life-and-death decisions in the interim remain subject, in part, to review by the governed.

In sum, it is not enough that wars be justified by reference to ends and means. They must also be justified in the eyes of those who are called upon to make the supreme sacrifice.

The Wars of Modern Israel

After clarifying the classical categories of warfare, we are in a position to ask whether the wars between Israel and her neighbors are to be classified as discretionary or mandatory. The wars under discussion are, in order, the 1948 Israeli War of Liberation, the 1967 Six-Day War, the 1973 Yom Kippur War, and the 1982 Lebanese incursion.

Based upon the aforementioned position that the Israeli executive assumes the role of the ancient monarch, and the Knesset in security matters serves as the contemporary Sanhedrin, we can apply the same procedural and ethical categories to the contemporary situation.

The War of Liberation and the Yom Kippur War qualify as mandatory wars. In both cases, the invading armies had crossed their military borders into Israel; in the former — Egypt, Jordan, Syria, Lebanon and Iraq, and in the latter — Egypt and Syria. Since Israel had no choice on the timing of the war, the Israeli counterattack needed to be authorized solely by the Israeli executive without securing the approval of the Knesset.

The Six-Day War was a bit different. From a military point of view, Israel launched a preemptive attack. From a legal point of view, Egypt's blockade of Eilat by closing the Straits of Tiran was the *causus belli*. Since Egypt had not only announced that its objective was "to destroy Israel," but had also begun amassing forces along Israel's border, and was effecting an economic stranglehold, Israel acted within the bounds of self-defense when she launched an interceptive attack.

While many authorities consider this a mandatory war, others contend that as long as Egypt and its allies had not yet penetrated Israeli territory, it remained a discretionary war. As such, it was incumbent upon the government to secure the approval of the

Knesset, which it did, and to ensure that it had solid popular support, which it had.

The Peace for Galilee incursion into Lebanon in 1982 is yet of a different order. At the time of the Israeli move into Lebanon, there was no evidence of an enemy force being positioned for invasion. Not only was the state not threatened, but even its northern border had not yet been subject to the type of aggression which frequently precedes conquest or annexation, a situation which could meet one of the talmudic criteria for a mandatory war.[134] The fact that there was constant shelling, even sporadic killing, may call for a military response, but does not render that response a mandatory war.[135] The nature and the timing of the response remained at the discretion of the Israeli government. This holds whether the purpose of the war was to destroy a PLO committed to Israel's destruction or whether the intent was to extend Israeli political influence into Lebanon in order to insert a wedge between Israel's sworn enemies.

As long as the timing of an incursion is a function of Israeli initiative, the executive and military must secure the solid backing of the Knesset. Insofar as the decision to go to war is left to the executive and the military, it fails to meet this safeguard. As popular support falters and enthusiasm flags, doubt about the validity of the enterprise grows. Unpopular ventures are as poor candidates for mandatory wars as they are for discretionary ones.

The more a culture resists granting the executive the exclusive prerogative to declare war, the more ethical considerations have to be factored into the political process to ensure popular participation. Lacking a moral basis, wars tend to lose their political will. Without the requisite political will, governments are not authorized to risk their citizenry. Thus, wars that cannot be politically justified to the populace turn out to be morally unjustified wars, all the more so if they lack moral justification from the start.

Epilogue

In answer to the question why the Torah records those occasions when God's orders on the conduct of war were rescinded in favor of Moses' counsel of restraint, the midrash states, "even war is recorded for the sake of peace."[136] If the reality of war is to be conditioned by the vision of peace, then restraint in both the recourse to, and the conduct of, war are imperative to keep ajar the openings of peace.

Notes

1. Robert Gordis, *The Root and the Branch; Judaism and the Free Society* (Chicago: University of Chicago Press, 1962), p. 187.

2. Spinoza, "A Theological-Philosophical Treatise," in *The Chief Works of Benedict de Spinoza*, ed. R.H.M. Elwes (New York 1955), p. 200.

3. George F. Kennan, *American Diplomacy, 1900-1950* (Chicago: University of Chicago Press, 1951), pp. 95-100. One of the classic statements of this realist school in international relations can be found in Hans Morgenthau, *Politics Among Nations: The Struggle for Power and Peace* (New York: Alfred Knopf, 1985), pp. 3-14.

4. Grover Cleveland in *Documents of Modern History, The Diplomacy of World Power: The United States, 1889-1920*, eds. Arthur S. Link and William M. Leary, Jr. (New York 1970), p. 15.

5. The link between an international house of prayer and a supernational mode of conflict resolution is not made explicit. It is possible, as *The Sibylline Oracles* (3.755-758) predict, that universal peace will result from amity among rulers and "a common law for men throughout the earth," or as Daniel (7:14) envisioned — violent conflict will be dissolved in the universal worship of God. Whatever the case may be, a universally accepted vision of a political order unified by law, but ethnically diverse, needs visible symbols of human solidarity.

6. Above n. 1, p. 186, cf. R. David Kimchi ad Micah 4:3. For a contemporary defense of this position, see the Introduction of Grenville Clark and Louis B. Sohn to *World Peace Through World Law*, third ed. (Cambridge: Harvard University, 1966), pp. xv-xvii.

7. See I Kings 5:26; 9:12-13.

8. Abba Eban, *The New Diplomacy: International Affairs in the Modern Age* (New York: Random House, 1983), p. 321.

9. Moshe of Coucy, Joseph Bekhor Shor, Menaḥem HaMeiri, Nissim Gerondi and Joshua Ibn Shu'ib, for example, hold that it is mandatory, while Josephus, as well as Saadia Gaon, Ibn Ezra, Sforno, and Zvi David Hoffman (all ad Deuteronomy 17:14)

maintain that it is concessive. The ambiguous positions of Gersonides, Naḥmanides and Baḥya ben Asher are pointed out by Gerald J. Blidstein, *Political Concepts in Maimonidean Halakhah* (Hebrew) (Ramat Gan: Bar Ilan University, 1983), p. 21, note 5, who also highlighgts the complexities of Rashi's position in the annual *Eshel Beer-Sheva III* (Beersheva: Ben-Gurion University, 1986), p. 138, n. 3. On the assumption that all public appointments require popular consent, several early modern commentators have resolved the ambiguity by explaining that monarchy is mandatory only if the people take the initiative in asking for it; see Netsiv (Rabbi Zvi Naftali Berlin), *Ha'emeq Davar* and Malbim ad Deuteronomy 17:4 along with the responsa of Ḥatam Sofer, *Hoshen Mishpat*, No. 19.

10. Maimonides, *Mishneh Torah, Hilkhot Melakhim* 4:1. The entitlements of the monarch are further expanded by Meiri, *Beit HaBehirah ad Sanhedrin* 20b. Both positions are based on that of the *tanna* Rabbi Yosi and the *amora* Mar Samuel in *B. Sanhedrin* 20b.

11. See, e.g., Gersonides (Ralbag) to I Samuel 8:11. This position is based on the dictum of the *tanna* Rabbi Judah and the *amora* Rav as found in *B. Sanhedrin* 20b. In *Sifre Deuteronomy* 156, ed. Finkelstein, p. 208, Rabbi Judah's position is juxtaposed to that of the to-be-discussed Rabbi Nehorai's. For an analysis of the controversy in its own terms, see Gerald J. Blidstein, "The Monarchic Imperative in Rabbinic Perspective," *AJS Review* 7-8 (1982-83): 15-39.

12. See Yeruḥam Perlow, *Sefer HaMitsvot of R. Saadia Gaon* (Hebrew) reprint (Jerusalem: Keset, 5733), pp. 230ff.

13. *Deuteronomy Rabbah* 5:11.

14. *Ibid.*

15. Abravanel, *Commentary on the Early Prophets* (Hebrew) (Jerusalem: Torah VeDa'at, 5715), pp. 204b-205a.

16. Abravanel, *Commentary on the Torah* (Hebrew) ad Deuteronomy 17:14 (Jerusalem: B'nai Arbael, 5724), p. 166b. Abravanel, above n. 15, pp. 93-95, lists the differences and similarities between government by king and government by judge. These points of convergence and divergence are summarized by Martin Sicker, *The Judaic State: A Study in Rabbinic Political Thought* (New York: Praeger, 1981), p. 92, who concludes, "...that the fundamental distinctions between king and judge rest more on the question of political status than on political function." A concerted effort to counter Abravanel's objections to viewing kingship as biblically-mandated is mounted, a century later, by Moses Alshekh, *Torat Moshe* (Warsaw 1865); facsimile edition

(New York 1966), ad Deuteronomy 17:14ff., vol. 2, pp. 124-126, cited by Sicker, *ibid.*

17. Sforno, *Commentary on the Torah* (Hebrew) ad Deuteronomy 17:14, ed. Gotleib (Jerusalem: Mossad HaRav Kook, 1980), p. 337. I Samuel has also been read as a critique of filial succession; see Moshe Garsiel, *The First Book of Samuel: A Literary Study of Comparative Structure, Analogies and Parallels* (Hebrew) (Ramat Gan: Rivivim, 1983), pp. 66f. The hereditary principle has been deemed the sine qua non of monarchy (see *Genesis Rabbah* 83:2; *Exodus Rabbah* 15, end of 4).

18. Maimonides, *Hilkhot Melakhim* 3:6.

19. *Ibid.*, 3:5.

20. *Otzar HaGeonim: Sanhedrin* (Jerusalem: Mossad HaRav Kook, 5727), no. 329, p. 159.

21. *Hilkhot Melakhim* 4:10.

22. For the extensive biblical material, see Moshe Weinfeld, *Justice and Righteousness in Israel and the Nations: Equality and Freedom in Ancient Israel in Light of Social Justice in the Ancient Near East* (Hebrew) (Jerusalem: Magnes, 1985), pp. 26-44.

23. Abravanel, *Commentary to Deuteronomy*, p. 168b.

24. *Ibid.*, p. 170.

25. Josephus, *Antiquities* IV.8.17 (223-224).

26. Following Isaiah 31:1 and 2:7, see Joshua 11:9 and II Samuel 8:4, along with Zachariah 9:10. See Yutaka Ikeda, "Solomon's Trade in Horses and Chariots in Its International Setting," in *Studies in the Period of David and Solomon and Other Essays*, ed. Tomoo Ishida (Winona Lake: Eisenbrauns, 1982), pp. 215-238.

27. Ibn Ezra ad Deuteronomy 17:17; see R. Meir Halevy Abulafia, *Yad Ramah ad Sanhedrin* 21b.

28. Philo, *The Special Laws* IV.158.

29. So A. Malamat, "Aspects of the Foreign Policies of David and Solomon," *Journal of Near Eastern Studies* 22 (1963): 1-17, esp. 8-10; see *idem.*, "A Political Look at the Kingdom of David and Solomon and Its Relations with Egypt," in ed. Ishida, above n. 26, pp. 189-214, esp. 198f.

30. As shown by J.D. Singer and M. Small, "Alliance Aggregation and the Onset of War, 1815-1965," in *Quantitative International Politics: Insights and Evidence*, ed. J.D. Singer (New York: Free Press, 1968); and J.D. Singer and M. Wallace, "Intergovernmental Organization and the Preservation of Peace, 1816-1964: Some Bivariate Relationships," *International Organizations* 24 (1980): 520-547.

31. *M. Sotah* 7:8, based on Deuteronomy 31.

32. *Numbers Rabbah* 12:17. See Philo, *The Special Laws* IV.169, and *The (Qumran) Temple Scroll* 57:19-21.

33. *Genesis Rabbah* 6:9 and Philo, *The Special Laws* IV.160, 161, 164.

34. Abraham (Rapo of) Porto, *Minhah Belulah* (Verona n.d.); facsimile edition (Jerusalem 1972). The development of this insight follows David Zvi Hoffmann, *Sefer Devarim* (Hebrew translation) (Tel Aviv: Nezach, 1961) II, p. 332.

35. Leviticus 25:23.

36. Hoffman, above n. 34, p. 329. Long before, Josephus, above n. 25, underscored the significance of a separation of power doctrine. With regard to the actual practice under the Davidic monarchy, see Abraham Malamat, "Origins of Statecraft in the Israelite Monarchy," *The Biblical Archaeologist Reader*, eds. E. Campbell, Jr. and D. Freedman (Garden City: Anchor Books, Doubleday, 1970), pp. 163-198, esp. 173f.

37. As opposed to those biblical kings who exercised both judicial (II Samuel 8:15-15:2; I Kings 3:9-7:7; 3:15-28; II Kings 8:3-15:3; Jeremiah 22:15-17) and priestly functions (I Samuel 13:9-16; II Samuel 6:14-18; 24:18-25; I Kings 8:25; 12:28-35; II Kings 16:12-16). Only II Chronicles 26:17-20 reflects the Deuteronomic view on the separation of royal and hieratic powers. This tendency to restrict the exercise of royal power reaches its extreme in the *Temple Scroll* of the *Dead Sea Scrolls*; see M. Hengel, J.H. Charlesworth, D. Mendels, "The Polemical Character of 'On Kingship' in the Temple Scroll: An Attempt at Dating 11Q Temple," *Journal of Jewish Studies* 37 (1986): 28-38.

38. Rabbenu Nissim of Gerondi, *D'rashot HaRan*, reprint Jerusalem 5734, pp. 191-195; cf. R. Isaiah Horwitz, *Shnei Luḥot HaBrit*, (Amsterdam edition) part 2, *Parshat Shoftim*, p. 24b. For discussion, see Menachem Elon, *Jewish Law: History, Sources, Principles* (Hebrew) I (Jerusalem: Magnes, 1973), pp. 44f.

39. Commentary to *Mishnah Yoma* 7:5; *Hilkhot Melakhim* 3:8; *Hilkhot Terumah* 1:2.

40. *Hilkhot Hannukah* 3:1.

41. *Hilkhot Ta'aniot* 5:3.

42. *Ad Hilkhot Melakhim* 3:8.

43. Philo, *The Special Laws* IV.157. From Philo (following Harry Austryn Wolfson, *Philo II* [Cambridge: Harvard University, 1968], pp. 328-333) to Rashi (following Blidstein, *Eshel Beer-Sheva*, p. 138f), the qualification of popular approval as well as that of merit has been perceived as sorely circumscribing the principle of dynastic succession.

44. See Meiri, *Beit HaBehirah, Sanhedrin* 52b. For such an understanding of the social contract, see Elon, above n. 38, p. 46, n. 143.

45. Josephus, *Antiquities* IV.8.12 (209).

46. Ramban's addenda to Rambam's *Sefer HaMitsvot,* ed. Chavel (Jerusalem: Mossad HaRav Kook 1981), p. 409.

47. Abraham Kook, *Mishpat Kohen* (Jerusalem 5725), section 144, pp. 336ff. See end of *M. Yoma* 7:5. Similarly, both "Hazon Ish" and R. Aaron Kotler allow for discretionary war under a nonroyal executive; see *Sefer Hazon Ish, Orakh Hayyim* (Bnei Braq 5717) *Hilkhot Eruvin, Siman* II4, letter alef, p. 332, and Aaron Kotler, *Beit Midrash* (Jerusalem 5741), cited by Shlomo Yosef Zevin, *LeOr HaHalakha* (Tel Aviv: Abraham Zioni, n.d.), p. 24.

48. For example, Shaul Yisraeli, *Yad Yemini* (Tel Aviv 5726), ch. 9, especially pp. 76-81; Eliezer Waldenberg, *Sefer Hilkhot Medinah* (Jerusalem 5712), I, pp. 175f; Zvi Magence, *Sefer Kedushat HaArets* (Jerusalem: Gross Brothers, 1979), pp. 252-263; and former Chief Rabbi Shlomo Goren, *Torat HaShabbat VeHaMoed* (Jerusalem: WZO Dept. for Torah Education and Culture in the Diaspora, 5742), p. 451.

49. *B. Berakhot* 3b, *B. Sanhedrin* 16a, and Maimonides, *Hilkhot Melakhim* 5:1.

50. *M. Yadayim* 4:4; *B. Berakhot* 28a.

51. I Kings 9:20-21; II Chronicles 8:7-9.

52. Following David Hoffman, *Midrash Tannaim* ad Deuteronomy 20:15, p. 121, n. 10. On the non-transferability of the seven-nation rulings to others, see Joseph Babad's commentary *Minhat Hinukh,* to *Sefer HaHinukh,* mitsvah no. 527 (New York: Pardes, n.d.), pp. 154-155.

53. Maimonides, *Hilkhot Melakhim* 5:4.

54. Babad, *Minhat Hinukh,* mitsvah no. 604, p. 213.

55. Moses b. Jacob of Coucy, *Sefer Mitsvot Gadol* (SeMaG), negative mitsvah no. 226, and the *Maimonidean Glosses ad Hilkhot Melakhim,* chapter 5, letter alef.

56. *Midrash Samuel* 22:2, ed. S. Buber, p. 110.

57. *Midrash Lekah Tov,* ed. S. Buber, Deuteronomy, p. 35a.

58. *B. Sotah* 44b, and *J. Sotah* 9:10; 23a.

59. *Beit HaBehirah ad Sotah* 42a; see the leniency of the *Or Zaru'a* as cited in the gloss to the *Shulkhan Aruk, Orakh Hayyim* 329:6.

60. Maimonides, *Hilkhot Melakhim* 5:1, according to Avraham Karelitz, *Hazon Ish, Al HaRambam* (B'nei Brak 5729), p. 841.

61. Cited in Barry Feinstein, "Self-Defence and Israel in International Law: A Reappraisal," *Israel Law Review* 11 (1976): 531.

62. *Ibid.*, p. 533.

63. *Mishnah Sanhedrin* 2:4, see Maimonides' Commentary ad loc.

64. *B. Sanhedrin* 16a. For the biblical material, see Abraham Malamat, "Organs of Statecraft in the Israelite Monarchy," *The Biblical Archaeologist Reader* 3, ed. E.F. Campbell, Jr. and D.N. Freedman (Garden City: Doubleday, Anchor Books, 1970), pp. 167f.

65. Maimonides, *Commentary to the Mishnah, Horayot* 1:6, ed. Kafiḥ, *Nezikim*, p. 309; see Gerald J. Blidstein, *Political Concepts in Maimonidean Halakha* (Hebrew) (Ramat Gan: Bar-Ilan University, 1983), p. 58.

66. Following Gerald Blidstein, "Individual and Community in the Middle Ages," in Daniel J. Elazar, ed., *Kinship and Consent: The Jewish Political Tradition and its Contemporary Uses* (Ramat Gan: Turtledove, 1981), p. 247, n. 62.

67. Shlomo Goren, *Mashiv Milhamah* I (Jerusalem: Idra Rabbah, 5743), pp. 127ff. See Blidstein, *Political Concepts*, p. 58, n. 19.

68. II Kings 11:17 and II Chronicles 23:3 along with II Samuel 5:3. On the problems involved in the issues of covenant, see Malamat, above n. 64, pp. 164f, and Hayim Tadmor, "'The People' and the Kingship in Ancient Israel: The Role of Political Institutions in the Biblical Period," *Jewish Society Through the Ages*, ed. H.H. Ben-Sasson and S. Ettinger (New York: Schocken, 1971), pp. 59-62; and F.M. Cross, *Canaanite Myth and Hebrew Epic* (Cambridge: Harvard University, 1972), p. 221.

69. See the example in Josephus, *Antiquities* IX.7.4 (153).

70. *B. Shavuot* 35b, following *Tosafot*, s.v., *deqatia*. Cf. *Responsa Hatam Sofer ad Orakh Hayyim* (Hebrew) no. 208 (Wien 1895), p. 77a.

71. *Midrash Song of Songs Rabbah* 4:4.

72. For the so-called "Clausewitzian friction" that distinguishes the fluid and chaotic nature of real war from war on paper, see Gordon Craig in *The Makers of Modern Strategy from Machiavelli to the Nuclear Age*, eds. Peter Paret with Gordon A. Craig (Princeton: Princeton University Press, 1986), pp. 481-509; and Edward N. Lutwach, *Strategy: The Logic of War and Peace* (Cambridge: Harvard University, 1987).

73. David J. Bleich, "Preemptive War in Jewish Law," *Tradition* 21,1 (1983): 25. According to one source, assessing the chances of victory falls within the province of the priestly Urim and

Tumim, while the endorsement of a war policy falls within the jurisdiction of the judiciary (*B. Eruvin* 45a, see *M. Sanhedrin* 2:4).

74. *B. Temurah* 16a. Cf. Plato's *Republic* 50b and Aristotle's *Politics* 1313b.

75. Josephus, *Contra Apion* II.272, 292. Similar thinking apparently lies behind Rashi's comment to *B. Gittin* 8b, *s.v., kibush yahid*.

76. *B. Sanhedrin* 8b, following *Arukh, s.v., apsania*. In a similar vein, the *Midrash* (*Numbers Rabbah* 22:6) notes how executive dilly-dallying can be a ruse to extend one's tenure in office.

77. *Midrash Tanhuma, Parshat Pinhas*, section 3, p. 90.

78. As Leviticus 19:16 was understood. See Reuven Kimelman, "Judging Man by the Standards of God," *B'nai B'rith International Jewish Monthly* (May 1983): 12-18.

79. See Reuven Kimelman, "Torah Against Terror — Does Jewish Law Sanction the Vengeance of Modern-Day Zealots?," *B'nai B'rith International Jewish Monthly* (October 1984): 16-22; and Itamar Warhaftig, "Self-defense in the Crimes of Murder and Injury," (Hebrew) *Sinai* 81 (5737): 48-78.

80. The debate concerning the duty to risk one's life for another revolves around the opinions of David Ben Zimra, *Teshuvot Radbaz* III, n. 1052, who denies such a duty, and Joseph Karo, *Kesef Mishnah ad Hilkhot Rotzeah* 1:14, who affirms it.

81. See Abraham Halkin and David Hartman, *Crisis and Leadership: Epistles of Maimonides* (Philadelphia: Jewish Publication Society, 1985), p. 131. Cf. *Genesis Rabbah* 91 which contends that it is preferable that "one be placed in doubtful danger than that all be placed in certain danger."

82. Following Abraham Avidan (Zemel), "Risking Oneself in the Saving of Another in the Light of the Halakha," (Hebrew) *Torah SheBa'al Peh*, vol. 16 (Jerusalem 5734), p. 133; and Abraham Kook, *Mishpat Kohen* (Jerusalem 5724), sections 142-144. For a discussion of the special prerogatives of the community, see Shaul Yisraeli, "Mandatory War and Discretionary War," (Hebrew) *Torah SheBa'al Peh*, vol. 10 (Jerusalem 5728), pp. 46-50. A key biblical text here is Judges 5:23.

83. *Sifre Deuteronomy*, section 203, ed. Finkelstein, p. 239, with *Midrash HaGadol* ad Deuteronomy 20:19, ed. Fisch, p. 451f.

84. *Ibid.*, following David S. Shapiro, "The Jewish Attitude Towards Peace and War," *Israel of Tomorrow*, ed. Leo Jung (New York 1946), p. 239.

85. Philo, *The Special Laws* IV.221.

86. Naḥmanides, *Commentary* ad Deuteronomy 20:19.

87. Philo, *The Special Laws* IV.224.

88. *Ibid.*, 224-225.

89. *Ibid.*, 226-227.

90. Josephus, *Contra Apion* II.212, 214.

91. Maimonides, *Hilkhot Melakhim* 6:10. See also his *Sefer HaMitzvot*, negative mitzvah no. 57.

92. Isaac Arama, *Akedat Yitzhak*, ch. 81, reprint (Jerusalem 1961), p. 97b.

93. Ramban's addenda to Rambam's *Sefer HaMitzvot*, ed. Chavel (Jerusalem: Mossad HaRav Kook 1981), the fifth mitzvah, p. 246.

94. Based on *Targum Onqelos, Targum Pseudo-Jonathan*, and *Midrash Leqah Tov* ad Numbers 33:55.

95. Abba Eban, *The New Diplomacy: International Affairs in the Modern Age* (New York: Random House, 1983), p. 325. Raymond Aron, *Clausewitz, Philosopher of War* (Englewood Cliffs, N.J.: Prentice Hall, 1985), p. 345.

96. Maimonides' *Collected Epistles and Responsa*, II (Hebrew), ed. A.L. Lichtenberg (Leipzig 1859), p. 25. Maimonides is alluding to Proverbs 20:18 which significantly concludes saying, "and we bear their iniquity." Note that Hecataeus of Abdera (ca. 300 BCE) in his *History of Egypt* (in Diodoras Sicalas, Library of History 40,3) writes of the Jews as follows: "Their lawgiver was careful also to make provision for warfare and required the young men to cultivate manliness, steadfastness, and generally the endurance of every hardship." The Galut-reluctance to deal with the realities of power is so deep-seated that it informs even the political thought of Zionist thinkers as diverse as Herzl, Kook, and Magnus. Theodor Herzl's *Altneuland* makes no provision for a professional army. Rabbi Abraham I. Kook argues that the exile had been extended so long to allow for the advent of a time "when government could be conducted without ruthlessness and barbarism" ("The War," in *The Zionist Idea*, ed. A. Hertzberg [New York 1959], pp. 422-423). Judah L. Magnus felt that if the Jewish National Home cannot be established through "peace and understanding" "...it is better that the Eternal People that has outlived many a mighty empire should possess its soul in patience and wait" (*Dissenter in Zion*, ed. A. Goren [Cambridge: Harvard University, 1982], pp. 34-35).

97. *Midrash Lamentations Rabbah*, Introduction, section 14. Cf. II Kings 6:22 with I Kings 20:31.

98. Naḥmanides, *Commentary* ad Deuteronomy 23:10.

99. See above, n. 93.

100. See above, n. 92.

101. Ḥayyim Attar, *Or HaHayyim* ad Deuteronomy 13:18.

102. S.D. Luzzato, *Commentary to the Pentateuch* (Hebrew) reprint (Tel Aviv: Dvir, 1965), pp. 537-539.

103. Ḥaim Cohen, "Law and Reality in Israel Today," in *Violence and Defense in the Jewish Experience*, eds. S. Baron and G. Wise (Philadelphia: Jewish Publication Society, 1977), p. 372.

104. Josephus, *Contra Apion* II.212-213. For a more recent reflection of this view, see Naftali Zvi Berlin, *Ha'ameq Davar* ad Deuteronomy 17:3 (Professor Isadore Twersky drew my attention to this source).

105. Philo, *Moses* I.314.

106. So *Targum Yerushalmi* and *Or Hahayyim* ad Exodus 32:29. For Rabbi Abraham Kook's explanation of the apparent cruelty of biblical wars, see *Rav A. Kook Selected Letters*, translated and annotated by Tsvi Feldman (Ma'aleh Adumim, Israel: Ma'aliot Publications [Igrot 89]), p. 180.

107. Martin Buber, *Israel and the World* (New York: Schocken, 1963), pp. 246-247. A similar reluctance to attribute political evil, however necessary, to divine command apparently lies behind the refusal of *Seder Eliahu Rabbah* 4, ed. Friedmann, p. 17, to ascribe to God the Mosaic command to the Levites to slay their brethren.

108. See Ehud Luz, "The Moral Price of Sovereignty: The Dispute about the Use of Military Power within Zionism," *Modern Judaism* 7 (1987): 51-98, esp. p. 76. Luz's fine discussion cites many of the aforecited Zionist thinkers. It was Prime Minister David Ben-Gurion who made the purity of arms doctrine one of the dogmas of the Israel Defense Forces; see Cohen, above n. 103.

109. *The Seventh Day: Soldiers Talk About the Six Day War* (London 1970), p. 132.

110. Meir Pa'il, "The Dynamics of Power: Morality in Armed Conflict After the Six Day War," *Modern Jewish Ethics: Theory and Practice*, ed. Marvin Fox (Ohio State University Press, 1975), p. 215.

111. For Rashi and Naḥmanides, see Yehudah Girshuni, *Sefer Mishpat HaMelukhah* (Jerusalem 5744), pp. 130-134. For Maimonides, see *Hilkhot Melakhim* 6:1, 6:7, and 7:1 (following Gerald J. Blidstein, *Political Concepts in Maimonidean Halakhah* [Hebrew] [Ramat Gan: Bar-Ilan University, 1983], p. 221, n. 34 and Yosef Dov Soloveitchik, *Kovets Hidushei Torah* [Jerusalem 5743], pp. 128-131).

112. *Deuteronomy Rabbah* 5:13. See Maimonides, *Hilkhot Melakhim* 6:5; and Babad, above n. 52, for a *halakhic* context. This interpretation became widely accepted, see Nahmanides and R. Bahya ben Asher ad Deuteronomy 20:16, SeMaG positive mitsvah no. 118, *Sefer HaHinukh* 527, and possibly Saadyah Gaon, above n. 12, vol. 3, p. 251f.

113. *Deuteronomy Rabbah* 5:14, so *J. Shevi'it* 6:1, *Leviticus Rabbah* 17:6, ed. Margulies, p. 386; and Maimonides, above n. 110.

114. The expression and definition are found in Michael Walzer, *Just and Unjust Wars: A Moral Argument with Historical Illustrations* (New York: Basic Books, 1977), p. 246.

115. The sources are discussed by Blidstein above n. 66, pp. 225-227; and Samuel Morell, "The Constitutional Limits of Communal Government in Rabbinic Law," *Jewish Social Studies* 33 (1971): 87-119. The principle of representative government was articulated in a most influential manner by the thirteenth century rabbi, R. Solomon ben Aderet (Rashba) in his *Responsa*, vol. 1, no. 617, and vol. 3, no. 443. Both responsa are conveniently juxtaposed in Menachem Elon, *Jewish Law: History, Sources, Principles* (Hebrew) (Jerusalem: Magnes Press, 1973), vol. 2, pp. 588f.

116. Eliezer Waldenberg, *Sefer Hilkhot Medinah*, vol. 3 (Jerusalem 5712), pp. 90-97.

117. As noted by Blidstein, above n. 64, pp. 235-237, 252f; and Morrell, above n. 113, pp. 90-96. The decisive figure in articulating the principle of minority rights was the twelfth century rabbi, Rabbenu (Jacob) Tam; see Elon, above n. 113, pp. 580-587.

118. Maimonides, *Hilkhot Melakhim* 7:11. See Saul Lieberman, *Tosefta Kifshutah*, vol. 8 (New York 1973), p. 695, line 246.

119. *M. Sotah* 8:4.

120. Viewing the Levites as ideal types, Maimonides argued for their military exemption; see *Hilkhot Shemitah VeYovel* 13:12 along with *Midrash HaGadol Numbers* 1:48, ed. Rabinowitz, p. 10 and n. 8. (For the medieval discussion, see Girshuni, above n. 111, p. 425.) Whatever the case, it has been argued that even their exemption is rescinded in religiously motivated wars; see Rambam *Le'Am* (Mossad HaRav Kook) ad loc., p. 646, n. 54, and Menachem Schneersohn, *Chidushim UBiurim BeShas UBeDivrei HaRambam Z"L* (Brooklyn: Kehot, 1985), pp. 216-221. It has been difficult if not impossible to substantiate this position from classical rabbinic sources; see Shlomo Zevin, *Le'Or HaHalakha* (Tel Aviv: Abraham Zioni, n.d.), pp. 27f. Shmaryahu Arieli, *Mishpat HaMilhamah* (Jerusalem: Reuven Mass, 1971), pp. 37-42, concludes a survey of the evidence contending that if there

were such an exemption it applied only as long as the Levites served in the Temple.

121. On the religious dimension of the army, see Eliezer Waldenberg, "The Religious Dimension of the Army of Israel," (Hebrew) *HaTorah VeHaMedinah* 4 (5712): 197-216.

122. *Sifre Deuteronomy*, section 192, p. 233.

123. Shlomo Goren, *Torat HaShabbat, VeHaMoed* (Jerusalem 5742), p. 369.

124. See above n. 120; and S.H. Kook, *Iyyunim UMehkarim* I (Jerusalem: Mossad HaRav Kook, 5719), pp. 235-237.

125. Following David Halivni, *Mekorot U'Mesorot, Nashim* (Tel Aviv: Dvir 5719, *ad Sotah* 44a, pp. 473-474. Compare the contrasting glosses of Ibn Ezra and Hizkuni ad Deuteronomy 20:8.

126. Following Abraham Hen, *BeMalkhut HaYahadut* I (Jerusalem: Mossad HaRav Kook, 5719), pp. 36 and 101.

127. Naḥmanides, *Commentary* ad Deuteronomy 20:8.

128. Judges 7:2-3.

129. According to *Hazon Ish*, above n. 47, "Initially, there should be no embarking on a discretionary war if it is impossible to fight without the exemptees."

130. *B. Pesahim* 113a.

131. See Maimonides, *Hilkhot Terumot* 1:2, along with *Hilkhot Melakhim* 5:6, and the discussion of Samuel Atlas, *Pathways in Hebrew Law* (New York: American Academy for Jewish Research, 1978), pp. 66-75, esp. p. 79f. Cf. *Sifre Deuteronomy* 51, ed. L. Finkelstein, p. 116, esp. n. 16; and *Sheetat HaQadmonim al Massekhet Avodah Zarah*, ed. M. Blau (Brooklyn: Deutsch, 1969), p. 57f, esp. n. 93.

132. According to I Maccabees (3:56), draft exemptions are apparently operative in defensive wars in which the citizenry is not in imminent danger. See Yigal Yadin, *The Scroll of the War of the Sons of Light Against the Sons of Darkness* (Jerusalem: Bialik, 1957), p. 64f.

133. David Ben-Gurion, *BaMa'arekhah*, vol. 5 (Israel 5710), p. 292. For an American application of the "Clausewitzian trinity" of people, politicians and army, see Harry Summers, Jr., *On Strategy: A Critical Analysis of the Vietnam War* (Novato: Presido, 1982).

134. *T. Eruvin* 3:5; *B. Eruvin* 45a; *J. Eruvin* 4:3, 21d.

135. Following Ḥazon Ish, *Al HaRambam, ad Hilkhot Melakhim* 5:1, p. 841.

136. *Midrash Tanhuma* Tzav 3.1.

Chapter 11

ON POLITICAL REVOLUTION
IN THE JEWISH TRADITION

Gerald J. Blidstein

The following remarks are offered in full knowledge that they are both partial (indeed, one-sided) and preliminary. Materials are presented that view political revolution positively, whereas a balanced portrayal of the Jewish tradition's view of the matter would no doubt emphasize its conservative bent, crystallized in statements like: "Whoever rebels against the Davidic kingdom is to be killed." These materials are also presented in isolation from their possible historical connections and, especially, without considering possible influences of non-Jewish political thought and activity. But attempts to rescue minority opinions from oblivion necessarily demand suspension of a fixation on the dominant strain, if only temporarily. It is also hoped that the presentation of these materials will stimulate others to determine their connections with ideas current in the relevant times and places. One final point of clarification: this analysis is not concerned with revolution against alien rule, but rather with the more basic and problematic topic of revolution by Jews against a Jewish government.

I

It is natural to begin this survey with the Bible, both because of its commanding position with regard to most topics and especially because it in fact has been of major importance for both Jews and gentiles who have thought about this topic. At first glance, of course, the Bible would seem to legitimate political revolution, perhaps even to encourage it. Broadly put, political authority is desacralized by the Bible, which maintains that no human person or institution is fully holy; if this is so, then the king is as responsible before the bar of judgment as is any other person, nor is his office intrinsically, organically, and inalienably his. The apparent complement to this desacralizing of the kingly office is the biblical notion of covenant; in the covenantal framework, political loyalty and legitimacy derive (at least in part) from the consent of those they bind.

Seen in specifics, the Bible describes numerous successful and approved rebels — from David on. Yet the Book of Books has not really been an unambiguous ally of revolution. Christian rulers discovered that the status of "God's anointed" restored to the king much of the sacral power lost in a monotheistic system. For Jews, a different consideration held (and Jews, it must be recalled, did not have much opportunity to rebel against Jewish kings in the last 2,000 years). Jews typically examine specifics, and here they could not help but realize that all approved revolts were in fact either prophetically invited or blessed. The prophet Samuel anointed David in Saul's lifetime, and the prophet Ahiyya told Jeroboam that he, rather than the lawful heir Rehoboam, would rule most of Solomon's kingdom. For modern sensibilities, this fact merely testifies to the legitimacy of revolution, to its depth; for the tradition though, it meant that legitimate revolution could only be catalyzed by divine command, and that a thoroughly human revolution was unthinkable. This hermeneutic undermined the notion that revolution was a normal mode of social response to an intolerable situation, though it did not make revolution absolutely impossible. Other modes of reform were to be sought; "the prophets insisted that the only out was by moral reform on the part of the people, not resistance to the oppressor or tyrannicide."[1] A further point in this direction has been made by James Barr, who noted that after the period of the early prophets, who are politically active, God continued to work through political events, but these involved foreign countries that impinged on the fate of Israel: internal Jewish government did not occupy God or his messengers.[2]

II

Issues of governance and politics are hardly at the center of the talmudic enterprise, and the *halakhic* interest in these topics is even less than the *aggadic*. It is commonly held that the demise of Jewish political sovereignty in the first century C.E. was the fundamental cause of this cultural-intellectual retreat, but this claim, even if true, cannot be understood simplistically. The destruction of the Temple did not cause a corresponding disinterest in cultic law, for example, and Jewish political figures and institutions continued to function with great vigor despite the stateless character of Jewish social existence. Yet the fundamental fact remains, however, that talmudic *halakhah* does not devote much attention to matters political, that within this circumscribed concern the question of revolution is barely noted, and that such notice as does exist projects the assumption that rulers are not to be deposed, though they need not always be obeyed either.

The focus here lies with the exceptions to this general state of affairs. Both Talmuds tell the story of the deposition for ethical shortcomings of R. Gamliel from his post as either Patriarch or head of the yeshiva, a most significant difference, of course, as one post is political and the other primarily academic-religious.[3] A more general statement instructs the "people of the Lord" to remove notorious officials from office.[4] These instances produced only minimal ripples in the pond of Jewish political culture, however.[5] The one talmudic reference which does function with some (though limited) frequency takes off from biblical history — from the story of David and Absalom.

The Palestinian tradition makes two related points about the period of time during which David absented himself from Jerusalem, in flight from his son and usurper of his throne, Absalom. First, it is said, this six-month period is not counted by the biblical chronologist towards the forty years of David's kingly reign. This comment, actually, is more of a way out between two conflicting biblical texts; but the second point is a freely volunteered normative pronouncement. During this six-month period, we are informed, David would not have brought the special royal sacrifice but would have sacrificed rather as a commoner (Lev. 4:22).[6] It is quite true that these talmudic statements do not deal with the propriety of Absalom's revolt or, in a sense, with its legitimacy.[7] They do not reflect approval of the deposal of a king, but they do assert that the deposed king is in fact not a king, that he who does not reign in fact has lost his royal role. In brief, revolution is accorded de facto status. It should be recalled that Absalom's revolt was in large measure a popular revolt, that David was not deposed by an institutionalized organ of state, but by his son and men who had grievances against the king. Clearly, these two talmudic statements raise more queries than they answer, and were the Talmud a more systematic enterprise a discussion of these obvious problems could be expected. What, for example, is the nature of the deposed David's claim to be restored to his throne, and how does this relate to the status accorded the revolution? Here, however, later use of these comments will be reported and the career of these ideas will be traced in the thought of some medieval and modern commentators and scholars.

III

It is difficult to overlook Maimonides in a survey of this sort. Though he is not really a crucial figure for this topic, he is a commanding figure in the history of Jewish law, and he did produce the only systematic statement of the norms governing a Jewish polity.

In general, it may be said that Maimonides valued stability in government, and much of his law was shaped with that goal in mind. Anarchy is an evil greatly to be feared. He did stress, as did Islamic legists of his time, that the pious man ought not obey his king if directed to perform an act in violation of the higher, Divine law: political loyalty has its limits. But this assertion did not lead Maimonides or his Islamic contemporaries to consider the legitimacy of a king or state which made such demands of its subjects, or to discuss the nature of the citizen's relationship to such a state. Disobedience towards specific demands is not developed into a generalized denial of political legitimacy.

This author has discussed the specifically relevant Maimonidean texts elsewhere, and will merely summarize his conclusions here. Maimonides does not, it is true, herald the possibility of revolution loud and clear. On the contrary, he mutes the relevant talmudic norms and camouflages them whenever he can. He is nothing if not discrete, and the reasons for this discretion might be worthy of scrutiny in their own right. Moreover, the deposition of a king, he implies, lies in the domain of an institutionalized structure, the broadly representative Sanhedrin, and does not rest with the masses. Finally, such action must be generated by the ruler's objective wickedness (is this not always the case?) rather than by oppositionists' enmity. But all these qualifications and conditions accepted, it would seem that Maimonides allows for the deposition of the ruler, even if he be a king of the House of David.[8]

IV

It is in the twelfth and thirteenth centuries, in Provence and perhaps in Spain, that the most striking development of the motif of approved revolution may be noted. A major figure in this reevaluation is R. David Kimhi (1160?-1235?), the pioneering biblical exegete. R. Menahem HaMeiri, also of Provence (1249-1316), is similarly aware of this activist perspective. It is likely that R. Jonah (thirteenth century) and R. Nissim of Gerona (d. 1380) are also to be included in this roster.

Kimhi's remarks are to be found in his commentary to the Book of Kings. To begin with, there is his discussion of the incident in which Jezebel and Ahab have Naboth murdered in a staged accusation of blasphemy and *lese majeste* so as to be able to put their hands on his vineyard. Kimhi noted that the king and queen could not simply force the vineyard from its owner's hands, but had to act behind a mask of legality. He explained that: "Were they to murder and plunder in violation of the law, the people of Israel would have rebelled against them, for the people would not consent to be ruled by the king unless he stabilized the land with justice...."[9] Kimhi expected, then, that the people would revolt rather than be ruled by a monarch who trampled justice underfoot. But Kimhi's comments are not descriptive alone; they come quite close to being prescriptive, to announcing what would be the right thing to do in such circumstances. For by predicating the people's behavior on their desire to have justice reign,[10] he alluded to the basic goal and motive of government as described in the people's original request of the prophet Samuel: to establish justice in the land. Revolt against a monarch who himself is a fount of injustice is virtually a normative act; not merely expected, it is almost approved.

Kimhi makes this explicit in another instance. When it is noted that Joab participated in the revolt of Adonijah, but had not joined in the rebellion of Absalom, Kimhi explained that "since the entire people Israel wished to crown him (Absalom) king, this was not a rebellion punishable by death...."[11] It is possible to read this comment narrowly and legalistically, of course, noting that Kimhi only waived the threat of capital punishment but did not allow the revolt in toto. However, this is probably an overly formal approach, akin to excusing a man who drills a hole in the dike by saying that he only made a small hole after all. For once it is agreed that the desire of "the whole people" to depose one monarch and crown another has some normative force behind it, at least enough to derail the normal procedures attendant on revolution against the Davidic monarch, then a very major concession indeed has been made. It is hard not to recall at this point that Absalom's major charge against his father, and the charge that seemed to stimulate the most popular support, was that David did not provide justice for the people, a charge that tied in most neatly with Kimhi's comments on Jezebel, Ahab, and Naboth. The Palestinian traditions that recognized, in some fashion, the deposal of David should also be recalled. All in all, then, Kimhi apparently allowed revolution in certain circumstances, or at least agreed that the fabric of consent could be worn so thin as to make revolution a legitimate step. This is a major departure in traditional Jewish political thought, and one wonders whether it represents the impact of European intellectual and political history on the twelfth century Provencal figure.

R. Jonah's contribution, made also in the context of biblical commentary, has been preserved in R. Nissim's Eleventh Homily to the Torah: "The king rules in proportion to the honor and recognition given by the masses, so that if they deprive him of all that honor, they will also be completely free of their king."[12] True, this remark is tantalizing in its ambiguities: does it describe all kings, including Jewish monarchs? Is it a normative statement, or does it merely describe the political process as it functions in reality? Be all this as it may, R. Jonah is concerned with the fact of a king's being relieved of his powers and status, and the assumption is that the power to do this lies with the masses (*hahamon*) and not with the aristocratic classes.

Since R. Nissim embedded this remark in his treatment of Jewish kingship, it is apparent that he also considered it valid for the Jewish king described in Deuteronomy 17. It is still not fully clear whether R. Jonah's remark is seen here as normative or as descriptive, but since this citation is used to buttress R. Nissim's discussion of the fact that the king is to see himself as the people's servant and that kingship is an office and not a quality inherent in the king's person, it is likely that the removal of the king described by R. Johan is seen as a normative right of the people by R. Nissim (who did not discuss, though, *how* this was to be effected).

The remarks of the second Provencal rabbi, Menahem HaMeiri, can hardly be compared with those of Kimhi as to the substance of what each asserted. Yet at the same time, Meiri stressed notions that fit in well with those of Kimhi, notions that were not all that common in the writings of his contemporaries. First of all, Meiri was eager to accept the Palestinian traditions concerning David's truncated rule, generalizing that "a king who does not effectively rule does not have the status of a king."[13] Second, Meiri moralized that just as "the king is punished for the sins of his people because he is responsible to protest against their sins, so too are the people punished for the sins of their king because they must protest to him, and so the people were punished when David took a census."[14] Needless to say, the biblical-talmudic tradition of protest stands behind Meiri's last comment, but the Talmud does not usually see this duty in terms of the people standing over against its king (and even the prophetic ethic sees the unique individual as bearing the responsibility of protest, not the people as a whole). The stress in Meiri, then, also seems new and worthy of attention.

V

Though not directly touching on the issue of revolution, R. Judah Rosanes (Turkey, d. 1727) makes interesting, indeed curious, use of the David and Absalom materials. Rosanes understood these materials to mean that the unseated David completely lost his kingly status when driven from Jerusalem, and this fact became the basis for a generalization as to all monarchic status: what counts, Rosanes argued, was actual rule, not sacred anointment or the like. All this is discussed in *Al Parshat Derakhim*, Rosanes' recasting of biblical narrative and history as expressions of multi-layered scholastic concerns and concepts. In this case, Rosanes argued that the biblical incident involving David, Abigail, and her husband Nabal, an incident already expanded considerably beyond its biblical dimensions by the Talmud, was actually generated by a debate as to David's status at the time. David himself claimed, in Rosanes' version, that he deserved kingly regard, having been anointed by Samuel, while Abigail triumphantly retorted that inasmuch as he was not yet ruler of Israel (Saul was still alive), David had no kingly claim on her husband. This issue, Rosanes maintained, also seemed to explain other biblical events.[15]

A more far-reaching and explicit discussion of relevant talmudic materials is found in the work of R. Isaac of Karlin (d. 1910). Reverting to the David-Absalom narrative and its

301

implications, R. Isaac considered the possibility that "...it all depends on the people — for if they have consented to be ruled by someone they must be obedient to him. And it also depends on them to depose him from his office, as we read concerning David who would have brought a commoner's sacrifice, though he had originally been anointed king by Divine command."[16] R. Isaac did not, it is true, remain satisfied with this formulation of the power of popular consent and its withdrawal, yet the fact that this typical representative of rabbinic culture could consider the model described here to be a possible option is most revealing. It should be noted that this model speaks of kingly status in toto, not merely of the kingly sacrifice, and it speaks not only of the accession of a king, which is already a covenantal act in the Bible, but allows that the deposition of a kind is also in the hands of the people.

VI

Two additional figures will be mentioned briefly: R. Zvi Hirsch Chajes (1805-1855), and R. Abraham Isaac Kook (1865-1935). Neither raised the question of political revolution, yet they are relevant to this inquiry because each maintained a view of kingship (and, hence, of government) which was informed by broad consensual elements. Chajes, struck by the wide-ranging (indeed extraordinary) powers granted the king, concluded that these could be explained within the normal parameters of Jewish law as the result of a broad national consensus in the establishment of the office. It is difficult not to hear echoes of the social contract in his work.[17] Rabbi Kook propounded the thesis that monarchic power resided in essence in the people, whence it was derived. When a king in fact ruled, power and legitimacy flowed from the people; when there was no king, these same powers existed as the normative prerogatives of the nation.[18] In the early twentieth century context in which R. Kook wrote, this theory granted *halakhic* legitimacy to Jewish, Zionist nationalism, even in an age bereft of the normal political and social structures of classic Jewish existence. Neither Chajes nor Kook, then, raised the question of revolution or deposition, yet their work seems relevant to the issue within the broader topic of consent theory.

302

Notes

1. E.R. Goodenough, *The Politics of Philo Judaeus* (New Haven, 1938), p. 100.

2. J. Barr, "The Bible as a Political Document," in *The Scope...of the Bible* (Philadelphia, 1980), pp. 101-102.

3. *Berakhot* 4:1 (7c-d); b. *Berakhot* 27b.

4. *Horayyot* 3:1 (47a).

5. Actually, though, medieval authors do occasionally refer back to these incidents/sources as precedent for their activist inclinations; see Gerald J. Blidstein, *Political Concepts in Maimonidean Halakhah* (Hebrew) (Ramat Gan, 1983), p. 79, n. 62; pp. 80-81, nn. 69-70.

6. *Rosh HaShanah* 1:1 (56b) = *Midrash Ruth Rabba* 5.6. Interestingly, the Babylonian, Rav, explained the six-month discrepancy as due to David's leprosy (*Sanhedrin* 107a), and the Babylonian Talmud (*Horayyot* 10a; 12b) uses "leprosy" as a cause for a king's (temporary) deposition. Is "leprosy" code for revolution? Or is just the opposite true — that the Babylonian tradition offers "leprosy" as an alternative to revolution, an idea it wishes to evade?

7. One further caveat: "kingly status" may refer to the cultic provision alone, where the king's actual, effective rule may be the issue. See n. 11.

8. See Blidstein, *Political Concepts*, pp. 75-90, 190-196.

9. I Kings 21:10.

10. Note Kimhi's utilization of Proverbs 29:4, with its normative overtones: "By just government a king gives his country stability...," and see the completion of that verse.

11. I Kings 2:28. Compare II Samuel 20:21.

12. L. Feldman, ed., *Derashot HaRan* (Jerusalem, 1977), p. 202.

13. *Bet HaBehirah* to *Horayyot* 11a. Here, though, it is likely that Meiri refers to sacrificial law; cf. n. 7.

14. *Bet HaBehirah* to *Yevamot* 77a and *Shabbat* 54b. (The contrasting comment at *Shabbat* 11a may refer to the attitude proper towards foreign rulers, or to momentary excesses.) See also the detailed extrapolations made by Meiri from the story of R. Gamliel's deposition (at B.M. 27b).

15. *Al Parashat Perakhim*, sermons 11 (end) and 12.

16. *Keren 'Orah* at *Horayyot* 11b. For related discussion, see R. Abraham of Sochotchov, *Responsa Avnei Nezer, Yoreh Deah*, no. 312, especially paragraphs 1, 5, and 10-19.

17. Z.H. Chajes, "*Din Melekh Yisrael*," in his collected works, *Kol Kitvei Maharaz Hayyot*, I (Jerusalem, 1958).

18. A.I. Kook, *Responsa Mishpat Kohen*, no. 144-145.

Chapter 12

REFLECTIONS ON THE JEWISH POLITY AND JEWISH EDUCATION

Morton Weinfeld and Phyllis Zelkowitz

Introduction

This essay will explore several intersections between a system of Jewish education and a Jewish polity, at the local level. These reflections flow out of our recent involvement as directors of several studies of the Jewish education system in Montreal, focusing on systemic or communal characteristics rather than on evaluations of individual schools. Several of the dilemmas facing the Jewish education system of Montreal are illustrative of ambiguities of private responsibilities of Jewish citizenship and public responsibilities on the part of the community. Depending on the uniqueness of the Montreal situation, these dilemmas may have implications for other diaspora communities.

What follows is more a policy discussion paper than analytical social science. The discussion is geared at a framework or level which sociologists call, after Merton, "the middle range" — between abstract grand theory and excessively empirical micro-sociology.

As will be suggested below, based on enrollment figures, the emerging view in the Montreal Jewish community is that Jewish day schools are a kind of public school system of the Jewish community. They are not seen as elitist private schools selected by parents in an individualistic manner for their children. The principle of communal responsibility has been generally accepted, as it is elsewhere.

This means that Jewish education is seen more and more as a communal, rather than individualistic investment, and certainly not as a luxury, frill, or individual item of consumption. Most of the research literature on the consequences of Jewish education has been micro-sociological in nature and design, looking

305

at various levels of Jewishness for each institution, related to amounts of prior Jewish education. This approach deemphasizes the insight of human capital analysis in which the society as a whole benefits from investments in education. In other words, parents ought not be expected to bear the full brunt of the cost of their children's education; it seems in the interest of the polity to maximize the educational attainment of as many children as possible.

It is crucial to understand key differences between education in the general polity and Jewish education in the Jewish polity.

In both, the returns to education are both economic and non-economic. The former are measured in higher incomes for the more educated (including the paying of more taxes), as well as productivity gains which benefit everyone. The non-economic gains are harder to measure, but include dimensions of moral behavior, cultural development, tolerance, adherence to democratic norms, better health and consumer behavior, etc.

The Jewish day school is an investment which yields comparable returns. The economic return derives from the quality of the secular education which those schools provide. For most Jewish parents, particularly non-Orthodox, this education must be at least comparable to that available in the public sector, as it is a requisite for entry to college and the achieving of stable careers. This in turn will lead to graduates earning higher incomes which will afford them the means to contribute to the Appeals which sustain the Jewish polity. It is important to emphasize this point. The secular program of studies, therefore, becomes practically as meaningful as the Judaic program for the long-term survival of a local community. The two are not working at cross-purposes. In other words, educational, occupational and professional success will benefit the Jewish polity as well as the individual.

The non-economic benefits are of course crucial to Jewish schools. These benefits are the foundation for subsequent Jewish identification, and they consist equally of experiential dimensions which strengthen the bond with Judaism and the Jewish people, and cognitive dimensions which equip graduates with the requisite information to practice, appreciate and live out those commitments.

Yet there are several key differences between education in the general and Jewish polities. In the former, the state permits both a public and private school system to coexist. In general, the state funds public schools fully, while funding private schools either in part or not at all (depending on locale). School attendance is compulsory and universal up to the mid-teenage years. In the United States, over 85 percent of children attend the public school system.

Second, attendance at public school is free, paid from general tax-based revenues of one form or another. Indeed, in some polities such as the United States, where richer school districts may provide better quality education than poorer districts, legislative efforts attempt to equalize expenditures.

Third, public schools are under the direct control of central education bodies, whether of a local or state/provincial level. In Quebec, secular programs of study are determined rigorously by the provincial Ministry of Education, affecting curriculum, materials, evaluations, etc.

As a result, public schools, directly or indirectly, socialize students into the values and attitudes deemed appropriate in the general polity, or the local community. This is accomplished through a variety of classes in subjects like civics, citizenship, social studies, sex education, religion or moral reasoning, history, as well as all sorts of extra-curricular or special activities. Occasionally this leads to minor conflicts, as when a group of parents may object to a textbook, or to a book found in the school library. But the normative principle is that since the community — usually incarnated as elected school board officials or appointed superintendents — pays the bills, it must oversee what goes on in the schools.

Using as a primary focus the Montreal system, we note, by contrast, that there is a two-tiered "public" system: day schools and supplementary schools. Neither is, in theory, free. Attendance in either case is voluntary. And the principle of school autonomy dominates over any notion of centralized control or supervision, at least in the Judaic sector.

In light of these characteristics, two important issues facing the Jewish polity in the field of education are: 1) the feasibility of approaching universal, maximal Jewish education; 2) the degree and viability of communal (e.g., federation) laissez-faire regarding school curriculum or orientation.

The Montreal Context

By any relative or absolute standard, Montreal boasts a well developed, and diverse system of Jewish education. Unlike most American communities, the emphasis is on day school education.

As of 1984-85, there were over 6,600 children aged 5 to 17 (excluding nursery) enrolled in Jewish day schools, from kindergarten to grade 11, the end of high school. There are a total of ten day schools in the system, with several schools operating multi-branch facilities. The ideological spectrum of these day schools is broad, ranging from a large Yiddishist, semi-secular school descended from the populist *folkshule* model (and where Yiddish is indeed one of the four languages of instruction), to a traditional Hebraic, to Conservative, to neo- or modern Orthodox, to Hassidic schools and yeshivas. The overall budget of the day school system is about $26 million per year.

Using census and enrollment data, one can estimate that for 1981 the Jewish day schools enrolled about 66 percent of the eligible primary school-age Jewish population and about 28-30 percent of the Jewish secondary school-age population. These are extremely high proportions by any diaspora standard.

In addition, there is a supplementary Jewish education system, with nine schools which in 1984-85 involved about 1,800 students, almost exclusively of elementary school age. These included about 1,000 who attended afternoon supplementary schools, usually affiliated with synagogues, and 800 in supplementary classes offered in certain public schools to interested Jewish students. Over the past twenty years the day school system has seen sustained growth, while the supplementary school system has declined in size.

Day school growth in Montreal has been fueled by forces similar to those which have operated in the U.S.: perceived decline in the public schools, and fears of drugs or promiscuity. In addition, it has been relatively affordable. Not only has tuition been relatively low (see below), but these fees have been in large part tax deductible.

Historically, the Jewish day schools have long championed their autonomy and have resisted any perceived encroachment upon their independence. This autonomy has been sustained by the fact that, until recently, the schools have not had to rely on the local Jewish community for financial support. This was because the Province of Quebec, beginning in 1970, granted "Associate" status as public schools to those Jewish schools falling within certain guidelines (in practice these have had to do with teaching a required number of hours per week in French). Such schools have been eligible for per-pupil subsidies of more than 50 percent of the cost of education (at one point these percentages were higher).

Thus parental tuition fees must meet the costs of the Judaic curriculum alone, and fees have remained lower than comparable fees in the United States or other Canadian provinces.

In recent years, the Montreal federation, the Allied Jewish Community Services (AJCS), has become increasingly involved and sensitive to the importance of Jewish education. In the mid-1970s, a new agency, the Jewish Education Council (JEC), was created to serve as a coordinating umbrella agency serving the needs of all the schools (day and supplementary) in Montreal, and as a link between schools and the AJCS. The JEC consists of a lay board, with wide representation, and a professional staff of educators and educational advisors. In addition, the JEC administers the Educational Resource Center (ERC) which is active in curriculum development, in-service training and professional development, and has a library of audio-visual equipment and materials and a sound studio. The JEC and ERC are funded by AJCS.

The Jewish day schools felt the need for an organization devoted exclusively to their needs and as a liaison with education officials of the Province of Quebec. This organization, the Association of Jewish Day Schools (AJDS), is funded directly by day school subventions and has at times dealt directly with AJCS (bypassing the JEC) on relevant matters.

During the 1980s, several trends have posed new financial problems for the schools. The percentage of per pupil costs supported by the government grants to the day schools has declined steadily, while costs have increased. All individual Jewish schools have set aside scholarship assistance funds for Jewish parents who cannot meet full tuition fees (about $2,500 per year per child). In some schools, a day school education may be received gratis for those truly in need. Over the years, average tuition fees have been rising steadily to meet this developing shortfall on a cost-plus basis, with the surplus used for scholarship aid (i.e., with the wealthier parents paying full fee in effect subsidizing other parents). Yet the point has been reached where the day schools are becoming increasingly reluctant to raise tuition fees; nor will they turn away needy students. They are therefore now turning for the first time in any major sense to the AJCS for a larger measure of fiscal relief, whether as scholarship aid or via some other formula. The AJCS, on the other hand, is wary of embracing a large commitment to the schools without sufficient accountability.

The Non-Elitist Character of Jewish Day Schools

With almost 2/3 of maximal enrollment at the elementary level, the Jewish day school system of Montreal can no longer be considered a private school system, but has become, in effect, a public school system of the Jewish community. The Jewish day schools are no longer elite institutions in these senses:

1. They in no way cater to a financial elite. The tuition costs, while much higher than in public schools, are well below those of the other private day schools in Quebec, which receive no provincial subsidies and which as a result teach fewer hours of French. In addition, financial aid is available to needy parents. As a result, there is a heterogeneous student population within each school, measured by social class. However, it is also the case that schools vary in the relative degree to which they attract low income students, determined by their residential location, the amount of aid available, and their general image in the community.

2. They in no way cater to a Jewish elite, measured either by parental Jewish background or parental Jewish commitment. The student bodies of non-Orthodox day schools may well include large minorities, and in some cases majorities, of children whose homes are minimally Jewish. This poses both problems and opportunities for the day schools.

A major dilemma is that in many cases the Jewish child receives little support in the home environment for the Judaic objectives of the day school. Often the two work at cross-purposes, and in any event the conflict makes the realization of school objectives very difficult. On the other hand, a possible opportunity is that a process of reverse socialization is often found in which children socialize their parents Jewishly via school activities and influences, through peers, etc. Thus the school may become a major focus and source of Jewish identity for the marginal parent.

Another problem is that many of these marginal Jewish parents are least committed to Jewish education and most likely to leave the Jewish system for an alternative, either public or private. These parents set limits on how "Jewish" the school may be. Disgruntled parents have withdrawn children from day schools. The complaints have to do with perceived inadequacies in the secular program, or in English, or in lack of discipline. Some parents resent the "normalization" of the Jewish day schools; they prefer an authentically private school.

The concern with keeping enrollments up as a source of state funding and as a status/prestige symbol is a dominant one. Yet the focus on numbers may deflect from a concern with higher quality, effective Jewish education.

3. The Jewish schools are no longer elite institutions intellectually or socially. In earlier days the impression in Montreal was that students in the day school system were by definition above-average in cognitive ability, as they had to be able to follow a dual English-Hebrew curriculum. Thus a strong weeding out process took place through the grades. What has happened is that while high quality students remain in abundance in the Jewish day schools, substantial numbers of students whose abilities are average or less are now there. The prevailing thrust is not to weed these students out but to attempt to provide support and encouragement, where feasible, to enable them to remain in the system.

In addition, the Jewish day school population now includes numbers of children from homes which are economically disadvantaged, from single-parent families, etc., who have problems requiring the extensive use of social workers and other helping professionals. Both these trends add to school costs.

4. The Jewish day schools are not elitist in terms of their physical plant. They are, on the average, less attractive and spacious than the private schools and most public schools. Some of the schools are severely overcrowded and require renovation or replacement.

The Feasibility or Desirability of Universal Jewish Education

The importance of Jewish education to the future survival of diaspora Jewish communities has become an article of faith among Jewish communal leaders, often attaining motherhood status. Communities have monitored the numbers of enrolled Jewish students with a conviction of "the more the better." This conviction rests on research that Jewish education tends to have a positive effect on the Jewish identification of students in later life, independent of other factors such as family background. These

relationships may not be as strong as we might like, or as immediate or linear, but they are logical, though different types of education may have different impacts. More important for students
from minimally Jewish families, an intensive Jewish education
may be the only hope for future communal involvement or identification. This is said despite the fact that it has become fashion-
able to denigrate the education-identification relation because it is
too difficult to estimate precisely.

Yet even in a very Jewish community like Montreal, the vast
majority of the Jewish population is non-Orthodox and the majority of children in the day schools, specifically in the elementary
grades, are from non-Orthodox families. As indicated before,
many of these families have a lukewarm commitment to Jewish
education and feel that the Judaic studies are the least important
component of the curriculum.

If we assume that the community accepts a human capital approach to Jewish education, then there is an interest in maximizing the number of Jewish children receiving the most intensive
Jewish education. Yet schools will then include a large body of
parents uninterested in intensive Jewish education but who see it
as a necessary evil. Moreover, many Jewish parents might
waiver on the issue, requiring coaxing or incentives from the
community or the school to enroll their children.

Just as membership in the Jewish polity is voluntary, so is the
decision to opt for a Jewish day school. The decision is made by the
family of the child. To what extent can and must the Jewish community move to entice marginally committed parents to enroll
their children? On the one hand, the community is reluctant to
victimize a child, to deny them a Jewish education because some
parents — even among those who can afford it — do not think it is
worth the cost or the effort. On the other hand, it must be asked what
the presence of a large mass of such Jewish students does to the af-
fective and attitudinal Jewish education in a day school. Indeed,
this is precisely the type of problem which has long afflicted supplementary Jewish education in North America — a clientele of
relatively disinterested students from minimally committed
homes, where the Judaic goal for the parents is a bare minimum
rather than an enriching maximum.

Expansion of Jewish day school education into the non-Orthodox population in a community will introduce less committed students into the system. Schools may well become financially dependent on retaining these marginal students. Ideally one hopes

that such students, and perhaps even their families, may be transformed by the day school experience. But the other possibility is that such an eventuality might have a negative fallout potential. This has been a criticism levelled at some of the Jewish day schools in Montreal; the peer pressure and student cultures of the school tend to denigrate the importance of Judaic studies and Jewish commitments.

Just one example: A large (right-wing Conservative) day school has been trying without success to discourage parents from holding their young children's birthday parties in non-kosher venues and on Shabbat. Parties held at McDonalds on Saturday are commonplace. One party was held Saturday morning at a video arcade; another at noon on Shavuot in the parents' (non-kosher) home. The Board of this school has refused to insist that parents obey their guidelines on children's birthday parties for fear of antagonizing some parents. Some parents indicated they chose this school precisely because it was not Orthodox and therefore cannot understand the fuss.

Thus, in some of the Montreal day schools at present we find two conflicting sub-groups of parents; those wishing to deemphasize the Judaic program (i.e., reduction in hours) and a smaller minority who may want a more intensive program, in a more positively Jewish environment.

For too long the concern in the Montreal Jewish community has been the quantitative growth of day school enrollment. It may well be opportune to shift the emphasis to more qualitative concerns and to invest resources, both human and material, in maximizing the effectiveness of the Jewish instruction and in striving for excellence in teaching. It is clear that the dominant peer-group culture in the two largest Jewish high schools in Montreal (with a majority of non-Orthodox families) is perhaps negligibly different from that culture which can be found in non-Jewish public schools attended by Jewish teens. Patterns of comportment and of dress are comparable, as are tastes in music or life style. Patterns of sexual behavior and drug and alcohol use or abuse are also reportedly comparable to those prevailing in public high schools attended by Jews in Jewish areas. The traditional view was that those activities would be less prevalent in a Jewish day school. Summer trips to Israel held mid-way in the high school career (at a fee of $4,000 per student) are highly popular. While for many students these trips concretize the meaning of Israel and are positive Jewish experiences, for others they offer primarily an opportunity for experimentation and fun away from parental supervision.

The Jewish schools in Montreal and the communal bodies which support them have yet to come to grips with the implications of this intra-school diversity. It is not clear that every Jewish child can benefit equally from an intensive day school education. It may even be possible that substantial numbers of disinterested students may undermine the effectiveness for those who are more committed. At some point an equilibrium must be reached between potential positive and negative consequences of expansion into the perimeters of the community. That equilibrium may have been reached in Montreal — short of universal attendance.

If the past decade and a half was a period of expansion in Montreal day schools, it may be that what is required now is a period of consolidation and review. Are day schools truly Jewish schools, or just schools for Jewish children?

Ideological Diversity in Jewish Education: E Pluribus Unum?

As indicated above, the Jewish education system in Montreal contains a great deal of diversity both between and within schools. This is a trait which differentiates this system from public school systems in the polity. Those schools usually promote one form of citizenship, have a uniform curriculum, and attempt to promote comparable visions of the moral world. Indeed, these public schools scrupulously avoid any religious entanglements, at least in the United States, and in systems such as the Protestant School Board of Greater Montreal. Even the Montreal Catholic School Boards are not very Catholic, and the thrust in school reform in Quebec is to move completely away from religious to linguistic demarcations of school jurisdictions.

Jewish day schools are in an anomalous position. While the secular curriculum is under the rather rigid control of the provincial education authorities, the conditions with regard to the Jewish curriculum, despite Hebrew as a common denominator, are essentially anarchic. Schools fervently guard their own autonomy, and are supervised only by the lay school boards as to the content of the Judaic curriculum.

The policy of the JEC and the AJCS on this has been basically one of decentralization and laissez-faire. The JEC and the ERC provide service and modest funding to all affiliated day schools in a non-judgmental manner. Thus, within the JEC umbrella at present we find, for example, a Workman's Circle supplementary school (to the left of the mainstream Jewish People's School) and several hassidic day schools or yeshivas, at least one of which, along with the Bundist school, might be considered non-Zionist and where modern Hebrew or Israel are absent from the curriculum.

The question that arises is to what extent the Jewish polity would define within its public interest and fund Jewish schools which are anti-Zionist, non-Zionist, anti-Israel, anti-Hebraic, anti-religious, or quasi-racist (a la Meir Kahane).

In the Montreal Jewish community, the vocally anti-Zionist Satmar Hassidic day school is not included within the umbrella of the JEC and receives no funding. In part this is because they have not approached the JEC, but were they to do so it is likely they would not be accepted. The JEC monies, like those of all federation agencies, come from the funds collected annually by the Combined Jewish Appeal, which relies largely on Israel needs as a basis for the campaign. Using communal funds to support such a school might be too controversial.

The decentralized, relativistic and tolerant approach by most Jewish federations also may be problematic for achieving the goal of unity among the Jewish people. The divisions among the Jewish people in Israel and in the diaspora are becoming increasingly salient: religious vs. secular, Zionist vs. non-Zionist, Orthodox vs. non-Orthodox, Sephardi vs. Ashkenazi. In Montreal, the Jewish schools in what has been defined here as the public school system of the Jewish community certainly reflect and perpetuate these distinctions.

It is also likely that Jewish school systems may not be able to remain aloof from possible escalations in the conflict between Orthodox and non-Orthodox subgroups in the community on the "who is a Jew" question. Federations collect money from the entire Jewish community and may use portions of that money for Jewish education. It is probably the case throughout North America that Jewish schools, particularly day schools, are more religious or traditional in orientation (or more Orthodox) than the community at large. It is certainly the case that among big givers and lay leaders in most communities (as is the case in Montreal), the more religious or strictly Orthodox, while present, are underrepresented.

Federations, or the big givers who sustain them, may come to question the allocation of community funds (i.e., their own money) to Orthodox schools which refuse to recognize their status as Jews in cases involving divorce, intermarriage or conversion. Moreover, the Orthodox establishment in Israel might also taint Orthodox schools in the diaspora, in the eyes of federations and givers, because of the former's stance on "who is a Jew" and related controversies in Israel.

Since Jewish schools will increasingly play a role in Jewish socialization, and since patterns of socialization may shape future perceptions of legitimate status as a Jew, federations interested in promoting Jewish unity may need to involve themselves in the content of the schools which they fund. This may be needed to avoid future fragmentation of the polity, assuming that such fragmentation would be highly problematic. (This is an assumption. A reading of Jewish history reveals many cases of communal fragmentation, not all of which have been counterproductive. Nor is it clear that communal unity is desirable as an end in itself or as a measure for other objectives).

Can Jewish federations indeed remain agnostic about the ideological, cultural, or curriculum orientation of Jewish schools which approach them for financial and other assistance? The stance of neutrality implicitly assumes that all ways of being Jewish are equally valid. This may be true philosophically, but not communally. In addition, the diverse Jewish traditions and subcultures which are respected in some schools may be ultimately an impediment to achievement of effective Jewish communal unity.

Do central, communal organizations have a role to play in maintaining and even boosting enrollment in day schools? While each school in Montreal has jealously guarded its autonomy, it is difficult for an individual school to bear the costs of services which are increasingly demanded by parents: special programs for learning disabled or gifted children, computers, enrichment in the arts and sciences. Professional development, curricular innovation and program evaluation are other areas where a central body can serve to promote educational quality and thereby work to retain children within the day school system. However, it is essential that the constituent schools cease to view each other as competitors, but rather as partners in Jewish socialization.

In Montreal, school autonomy continues to make individual schools skeptical of the intentions of the JEC and reluctant to submit to community discipline or planning regarding the establishment of new schools or fundraising. Indeed, the traditions of autonomy are so strong that some schools have used them to reject the notion of a Jewish community high school which might result from some form of merger or federation between the two largest day school systems, saving resources.

Conclusion

One of the truisms in the sociology of education is that it is difficult, if not impossible, to isolate public school systems from the society and polity which reflect and fund those schools. This has often led to conflicts between educators who have favored educational autonomy, individualism, and training for independent thinking, and politicians concerned with the social consensus, political control and social stability.

When Jewish schools were truly private, divorced from the mainstream communal organizations, these problems did not arise. However, if the trend towards greater communal (centralized) funding and coordination of schools continues, they will become more and more public institutions, responsible to the community, not just to sub-groups of parents and educators. The requirement of financial accountability of schools by itself invites some measure of political involvement. Moreover, a Jewish polity concerned with future survival and communal cohesion may be unable to continue policies of relative detachment from the goals, orientations and content of Jewish schools.

GLOSSARY

alufim (singular, *aluf*) – leader of a thousand; military titles used to describe commander of tribal levies

am – people

amanot – compacts

amarkalim – treasury officials

aratzot – lands

auram coronarian – a Jewish poll-tax at one time paid to the Patriarchate

bat kol – heavenly voice

batei midrash – schools

batei va'ad – schools

bet av – households or extended family

bouletai – Greek: council-members

brit – covenant

Consistoires – the organizational system established by Napoleon assigning the conduct of the Jewish community to prominent members of the moderate bourgeoisie who were loyal to the central authority

dayanim – *halakhic* jurists

derash – scriptural analysis and exegesis

edah – congregation or assembled community

Eretz Israel – Land of Israel

Eved Adonai – God's Chief Minister, a title bestowed only on Moses and Joshua

foedus – covenant

gizbarim – treasury officials

goy – nation

hakhamim – sages

haskamah – public acquiescence

haskamot – articles of agreement

havurot – fraternities for religious study and observance

hazan – originally the governor of the synagogue, now the reader or cantor

herem – excommunication

herem ha-yishuv – ban on admission of new residents into existing Jewish communities

Hever ha-Yehudim – lit., "The Association or Community of Jews," i.e., the Jewish Commonwealth in its entirety

imperium – Latin: authority
ir – township
kehillah – community
ketarim – lit., crowns or investitures of authority
keter kehunah – the crown of priesthood
keter malkhut – literally, crown of kingship, understood more
    generally as the domain of civil rule
keter shem tov – the crown of a good name
keter torah – the crown of Torah
kohanim – priests
kohen gadol – High Priest
ma'arufia – an individual Jewish merchant's trade monopoly
    with a Christian client
malkhut shamayim – the Kingdom of Heaven
medinot – jurisdictions
melakhim – kings
meshihah – anointment
milhemet mitzva or *milhemet hovah* – biblically mandated war
milhemet reshut – discretionary war
minui – appointment
minyan – quorum of ten men
miqvah – an underground ritual bath
mishpahot – clans
mishpat hamelukhah – the law of the kingdom
mohelim – experts in performing circumcision
nagid – governor or high commissioner
Nasi – Patriarch
navi – prophet
nesi'im (singular, *nasi*) – erroneously translated as "prince" in
    many English versions of the Bible, and actually mean-
    ing "he who is raised up" or selected to represent; a rea-
    sonable English equivalent is magistrate
nesi'ei ha-am – magistrates
nesiei haedah – magistrates
nesiut – patriarchate
parnasim – officers of the community
Pirkei Avot – Sayings of the Fathers
posekim – *halakhic* jurists, rabbinic decisors
rabbanim – rabbis
rav – religious judge or head of the rabbinical court
ro'eh – seer

Rosh HaGolah – Exilarch; the chief magistrate and bearer of the
    keter malkhut in Babylonia
sarim (singular, *sar*) – officer; military titles used to describe
    commander of tribal levies
segan ha-kohanim – captain of the Temple
semikhah – rabbinical ordination; lit., a grant of authority
Shaarei Ha'ir – local councils; literally, the Gates of the City
shevatim – tribes
shofetim – judges
shohetim – ritual slaughterers
shotrim – officers
soferim – scribes
takkanot – ordinances
talmidei hakhamim – sages
torah she be'al peh – Oral Law
translatio imperii – transfer of authority
translatio studii – transfer of learning
yotzei ha-ir – the township assembly; lit., those who go out from the
    city
zekenim – tribal elders

ABOUT THE AUTHORS

Gerald J. Blidstein is Dean of Humanities and Social Sciences at Ben-Gurion University in Beersheva, where he is Hubert Professor of *Halakhic* Thought, and a Fellow of the Jerusalem Center for Public Affairs. He is the author of *Honor Thy Father and Mother* and *Political Concepts in Maimonidean Halakha*, as well as many essays treating the intersection of Jewish law and social thought.

David Cesarani is Director of Studies and Educational Activities at the Wiener Library and Institute of Contemporary History, London. He is editor of *The Making of Modern Anglo-Jewry* and has written extensively on Anglo-Jewish history and Zionism.

Stuart A. Cohen is Associate Professor of Political Studies at Bar-Ilan University and a Fellow of the Jerusalem Center for Public Affairs. He is the author of *British Policy in Mesapotamia, 1903-1914*; *English Zionists and British Jews*; *The Three Crowns: Structures of Politics in Early Rabbinic Jewry*; and, with Daniel J. Elazar, *The Jewish Polity*.

Daniel J. Elazar is President of the Jerusalem Center for Public Affairs, Senator N.M. Paterson Professor of Political Studies and Director of the Institute for Local Government at Bar-Ilan University, and Professor of Political Science and Director of the Center for the Study of Federalism at Temple University. He is the author or editor of over 50 books, the most recent of which is *People and Polity: The Organizational Dynamics of World Jewry*.

Ilan Grielsammer is Head of the Department of Political Studies at Bar-Ilan University and a Fellow of the Jerusalem Center for Public Affairs. He has written extensively on European Jewry and politics.

Reuven Kimelman is Associate Professor of Rabbinic Literature in the Department of Near Eastern and Judaic Studies of Brandeis University and Senior Scholar of CLAL, the National Jewish Center for Learning and Leadership.

Ivan G. Marcus is Professor of Jewish History at the Jewish Theological Seminary of America and an Associate of the Jerusalem Center for Public Affairs. He is the author of *Piety and Society: The Jewish Pietists of Medieval Germany* and writes on medieval European Jewish culture and society.

Chaim Milikowsky is a Senior Lecturer in the Talmud Department of Bar-Ilan University, and has served as Visiting Professor at the University of Maryland and at Yale University. His areas of specialty include rabbinic midrash and the intellectual history of Judaism in late antiquity.

Shmuel Trigano is Professor of Sociology at the University of Paris, and an Associate of the Jerusalem Center for Public Affairs. He is the founder of the Jewish studies review *Pardes* and the College of Jewish Studies at the Alliance Israelite Universelle, and has written extensively on Jewish identity, politics, philosophy and history.

Morton Weinfeld is Associate Professor and Chairman of the Sociology Department at McGill University in Montreal and an Associate of the Jerusalem Center for Public Affairs. Among his publications are *Old Wounds: Jews, Ukrainians and the Hunt for Nazi War Criminals in Canada* and *Trauma and Rebirth: Intergenerational Effects of the Holocaust.*

Jonathan S. Woocher is the Executive Vice President of the Jewish Education Service of North America (JESNA) and a Fellow of the Jerusalem Center for Public Affairs.

Phyllis Zelkowitz is Research Associate at the Institute of Community and Family Psychiatry of the Jewish General Hospital in Montreal and has specialized in the study of children's support networks.